AESTHETIC EXPERIENCE AND THE HUMANITIES

MODERN IDEAS OF AESTHETIC EXPERIENCE IN THE READING OF WORLD LITERATURE

FRANCIS SHOEMAKER

COLUMBIA UNIVERSITY PRESS

NEW YORK, 1943

Library of Congress Cataloging in Publication Data

Shoemaker, Francis, 1909–
   Aesthetic experience and the humanities.

   Originally presented as the author's thesis, Columbia.
   Bibliography: p.
   1. Humanities. 2. Aesthetics. 3. Literature--
Study and teaching. I. Title.
LC1011.S48 1972   001.3   70-176013
ISBN 0-404-05987-2

Copyright © 1943, Columbia University Press

From the edition of 1943, New York
First AMS edition published in 1972
Manufactured in the United States of America

AMS PRESS INC.
NEW YORK, N. Y.   10003

AESTHETIC EXPERIENCE
AND THE HUMANITIES

AMS PRESS
NEW YORK

FOREWORD

So far no one has ventured the phrase "global aesthetics." Teachers of the Humanities are generally too sensitive to the overworking of words (one of their chief quarrels with the professional educators) to expose themselves to such parodies as the "globaloney" of the clever congresswoman from Connecticut. Yet something very like global aesthetics has come to characterize our modern Humanities programs and other comprehensive literature and arts programs in the past two decades, as Dr. Shoemaker demonstrates in this book. And on this correspondence with other vigorous currents of thought today stands our chief hope for the future of the Humanities at a time when war has brought considerable fear for that future. Call it an increasing sense of "cosmic design" or what you will, it points to a revolutionary shift in our ideas about the significance of aesthetic impulses and aesthetic experience in our lives. In scope and emphasis it is very different from the green carnation aestheticism which has made aesthetics popularly suspect in America since the end of the nineteenth century.

Popular intuition of such ideas is evident in such current phrases and titles as "modern design," "Design for Living," "Design for Power," "The Shape of Things to Come," and for good and ill, "New World Order." In them the alert ear catches a common growing concern for a shaping and ordering of life that will be emotionally satisfying as well as technically efficient and socially significant. In short, they express an aesthetic impulse—the aesthetic impulse which we recognize in our quest for functional art, whether in automobiles or city planning maps, and which on a grander scale charges our new air-minded visions, world ideologies, great works of art, and vast designs of science, as Einstein has pointed out.

Dr. Shoemaker has set out in this book to explore this modern sense of the aesthetic impulse and aesthetic experience as it has run through modern Humanities and World Literature courses, and as it has been increasingly advanced by psychologists and anthropologists as well as by philosophers of literature and the arts. He has had particular reason for stressing psychologists and anthropologists. One of the major problems in the modern Humanities —and in aesthetics and in democracy—is the relation of the individual to the culture. When Dr. Shoemaker was commissioned by his college in Colorado several years ago to look into current developments in the teaching of World Literature and Humanities courses and to recommend lines of development for his own college, he started with the fact that students in the West characteristically approach literature and life in man-to-man fashion, more intent on individual values than on broad social patterns. A course in World Literature should give both, but should start where the students are. This suggested an initial study of ideas of the *self* and individual aesthetic experience (the psychological aspects) emphasized in some modern courses, and then a correlative study of society and social aesthetics (the anthropological aspects) conspicuous in others. These practical concerns are evident in the general patterning of Dr. Shoemaker's materials as well as in the particular consequences for his college course indicated in the last section.

Anyone who has attempted to deal with the key ideas of the evolving Humanities will recognize the problems Dr. Shoemaker has faced in shaping his materials. For sharpness of outline and conclusiveness, one would like a neat assembling of comparable ideas of psychologists, anthropologists, philosophers, and teachers of art and literature in successive chapters on "Design in Art and Life," "Confusion, Conflict, and Aesthetic Resolution," "Self-Expression and Self-Realization" and "The Harmonizing of Values." But this pattern would almost certainly give an impression of agreements, indebtednesses, and other connections where such inference would hardly be justified, and would discount contextual differences of considerable importance—as in the variable use of the recurrent expression "Great Books." A book so arranged should someday be written by an historian of ideas, when present developments in the Humanities have completed their cycle. Today it has seemed best not to try to pin them down too sharply, but to present the ideas of each spokesman in turn, suggest resemblances which the reader can check for himself, and summarize and exemplify in closing sections.

Similarly, ease of reading would have been increased in some sections if Dr. Shoemaker had simplified the thought and expression of the more complex thinkers and writers. Yet to have done so would hardly have given the pattern and texture of the originals. Where writers have been sharp and lucid themselves they tend to remain sharp and lucid in condensed accounts. Where they are complex and densely packed in the originals the effect of density is likely to remain or be increased in condensed analysis.

Another kind of problem has been presented by recurrent ideas from traditional philosophical aesthetics. Many ideas from modern psychological and anthropological aesthetics have their counterparts, cognates, and even sources in philosophical aesthetics. Yet many teachers of literature and the arts have lost touch with philosophical aesthetics. Some precautionary review therefore seems necessary. But obviously no adequate general introduction to philosophical aesthetics can be presented in a specialized book like this. What Dr. Shoemaker has provided is a highly condensed review of the related ideas on *aesthetic experience, self, expressive language,* and *values of art* in the writings of representative philosophers—the points most relevant to modern discussion—so annotated that the interested reader can go directly to texts of those philosophers. Unfortunately, most histories of aesthetics have not been so organized as to make for ready comparisons on these points with the ideas of modern psychologists and anthropologists. Here and in the section on college programs Dr. Shoemaker has had in mind the use of his book as a reference handbook, comparable to its predecessor *The Revival of the Humanities in American Education* by Patricia Beesley.

A final problem in a book largely concerned with a study of increasing agreement in ideas in the Humanities is the appropriate weighting of disagreements. Dr. Shoemaker has given considerable space to the views of Robert M. Hutchins, Mortimer J. Adler, and the so called Neo-Scholastic group at St. John's College. Unlike most teachers identified with the Humanities and World Literature programs in American colleges and high schools, they have turned back to the techniques of the Middle Ages for a comprehensive harmonization of the confusions of our time, giving little explicit attention to the large body of findings of modern psychology and anthropology. To avoid an effect of bias in the discussion of the views of this group is difficult if not impossible, since the group itself has started from a contentious position that most teachers of literature are on the wrong track, and as a result the group has been sharply attacked by various leaders in the modern Humanities whose views are presented here. Since the group thrives on argument, its purpose has probably been served more by opposition than by agreement. But with inherited Quaker conscience as well as scholarly conscience Dr. Shoemaker would warn against bias and the appearance of bias. Most teachers of the Humanities will pay tribute to the group for the service it has done in publicizing the Great Books, and for challenging other teachers of the Humanities to examine and define their own positions. Between the extremes of their position and that of the large number of modernists in the Humanities, there are, of course, all shades of conservatism and experimentalism, as the reader will be aware in comparing the various spokesmen and courses.

When Dr. Shoemaker returns from his service abroad as a field director of the American Red Cross, he proposes to publish the illustrative materials which he, his colleagues, and his students have worked out on the Greek, Medieval, Romantic and modern Naturalistic epochs, to accompany the selected materials on the Renaissance included here. They will be modified and extended by such notable new critical scholarship as Oscar James Campbell's "What

Is the Matter with Hamlet?" in the *Yale Review* for the winter 1943. Other teachers are at work on comparable materials. We have little doubt that this work will go on, along with our other essential work in meeting the challenges of war and of the peace to follow. Our modern Humanities courses grew out of the stocktaking of World War I, as Patricia Beesley makes clear in *The Revival of the Humanities in American Education* (1940). They gained force in the depression following the crash of 1929. They have gained further force and focus as we have had to arm ourselves against men and ideologies which threaten human freedom and the great designs of democratic life the world over.

To make plain these values and designs is the main concern of teachers of the modern Humanities, as books like Barzun's *Of Human Freedom,* Edman's *Fountainheads of Freedom,* Mumford's *Faith for Living* and, with some lingering questions about the modernity, Hutchins' *Education for Freedom,* emphatically show. The teaching of meteorology, mathematics and science by teachers of English, foreign languages, philosophy, history, and the arts is by no means a bad preparation for the broadened scientific humanism which our times appear to demand. And the broadened concept of human communication which should grow out of the comprehensive concern for observing, reading, writing, speaking, and listening in the Army and Navy college English courses—if we have imagination to see what they may lead to in the humanistic study of all media and all arts of communication in the making of world community—should hold hope for those who have feared the worst.

LENNOX GREY

Teachers College
Columbia University
February 25, 1943

ACKNOWLEDGMENTS

THE NATURE of this study, involving some acquaintance with many fields of inquiry—philosophy, literary criticism, psychology, anthropology, educational trends, and current scholarship—has made it in more senses than one a coöperative undertaking; first as one of a series of studies by the Coöperative Research Group in the Humanities at Teachers College, Columbia University, and second in the assistance from specialists in each of these fields involved.

To Lennox Grey I am chiefly indebted for the essential guidance in attitudes and scholarship which have made this research possible. Professor Grey recognized the related interests of a half dozen college teachers of English enrolled in Teachers College in 1938, and suggested the comprehensive outlines of coöperative studies in the humanities which began auspiciously with Patricia Beesley's *The Revival of the Humanities in American Education* in 1940. Through the four years of research, compilation, and exemplification of the ideas incorporated here in classes in World Literature at Colorado State College of Education, he has been stimulating, exacting, and patient.

In the same spirit, the Advanced School of Education of Teachers College, Columbia University paved the way for the early completion of this study through liberal financial aid in the form of an Advanced School Scholarship.

I am indebted to specialists from many fields, who have opened up profitable avenues without which this work could not have been completed—Irwin Edman, Columbia University; Ernest Hunter Wright, Columbia University; O. J. Campbell, Columbia University; Merle Curti, formerly of Teachers College, now of the University of Wisconsin, Robert S. Brumbaugh, Teachers College; Allan Abbott, Teachers College; Hoxie Neale Fairchild, Hunter College; Robert Herndon Fife, Columbia University; Arthur Christy, Columbia University; Ida A. Jewett, Teachers College; George Herzog, Columbia University; Ralph Linton, Columbia University; Gladys Reichard, Barnard College; Mark Van Doren, Columbia University; James Mursell, Teachers College; Ray Faulkner, Teachers College; Ralph Spence, Teachers College; and the score or more teachers of Humanities and World Literature who have written specifically of their courses.

So also my work could not have been carried through without the work of my colleagues at Colorado State College of Education: W. D. Armentrout, Vice-President of the College; Josephine Halverson, Librarian; Neal Cross, Leslie Lindou, and Evelyn Newman, fellow members of the Division of Literature and Languages; and the five hundred students and many parents whose concerns for human values have made the years of experiment thoroughly exciting. Finally, I am particularly appreciative of the innumerable helps of my most constant "colleague," Ruth Gunsaul Shoemaker, whose equal concerns with the problems and values of this study have made it in every way a joint enterprise.

Acknowledgment is due to the following individuals and publishing houses for permission to quote copyrighted material: to the American Catholic Philosophical Society for Mortimer J. Adler, *Tradition and Communication;* the American Psychological Association for Kate Hevner, "The Aesthetic Experience," in the *Psychological Review;* D. Appleton-Century Company for Louise Rosenblatt, *Literature as Exploration,* Norman R. F. Maier and H. Willard Reninger, *A Psychological Approach to Literary Criticism,* Ralph Linton, *The Study of Man,* Oscar James Campbell (editor), *The Teaching of College English,* W. Wilbur Hatfield (editor), *An Experience Curriculum in English,* and Ruth Mary Weeks (editor), *A Correlated Curriculum;* the *Atlantic Monthly* for I. A. Richards, *Science and Poetry;* the Columbia University Press for Robert S. Woodworth, *Dynamic Psychology;* Covici-Friede for Al-

ACKNOWLEDGMENTS

bert Einstein, *The World as I See It;* Crofts & Co. for Kimball Young, *Personality and Problems of Adjustment,* and Max Carl Otto, *The Human Enterprise;* Duke University Press for John W. Draper, *The Hamlet of Shakespeare's Audience; The Encyclopaedia Britannica* for the article by R. R. Marett on "Anthropology"; the *English Journal* for the reprint *Aims of the Teaching of Literature;* Harcourt, Brace and Company, for I. A. Richards, *Principles of Literary Criticism and Interpretation in Teaching,* Carl Jung, *Contributions to Analytical Psychology,* Kurt Koffka, *Principles of Gestalt Psychology,* Herbert S. Langfeld, *The Aesthetic Attitude,* Lewis Mumford, *The Culture of Cities, Men Must Act,* and *Faith for Living,* and Edward Sapir, *Language;* Harper & Brothers for Joseph K. Folsom, *Social Psychology;* the Hogarth Press for Sigmund Freud, *Collected Papers;* Henry Holt and Company for Melvin M. Rader, *A Modern Book of Aesthetic,* and Gordon W. Allport, *Personality;* Houghton Mifflin Company for Ruth Benedict, *Patterns of Culture,* and Hugo Münsterberg, *Psychology and Life;* the *Journal of Higher Education* for John F. Fitchen III, *A Challenge;* Alfred A. Knopf for Otto Rank, *Art and the Artist;* Little, Brown & Co. for Jacques Barzun, *Of Human Freedom* and *Darwin, Marx, Wagner;* the Liveright Publishing Corporation for Sigmund Freud, *A General Introduction to Psychoanalysis;* Longmans, Green and Co. for Mortimer J. Adler, *What Man Has Made of Man* and *Art and Prudence;* McGraw-Hill Book Company for H. D. Lasswell, *World Politics and Personal Insecurity,* and Louise Dudley and Austin Faricy, *The Humanities;* the Macmillan Company for Alfred North Whitehead, *Science and the Modern World,* Yrjo Hirn, *The Origins of Art,* Herbert Read, *Art and Society,* H. Munro Chadwick and N. Kershaw Chadwick, *The Growth of Literature,* and John Dover Wilson, *What Happens in Hamlet,* and also for articles in the *Encyclopaedia of the Social Sciences* by Max Lerner and Edwin Mims, Jr., Bronislav Malinowski, Edward Sapir, Franz Boas, and John Dewey; the Marquette University Press for Gerald B. Phelan, *Saint Thomas and Analogy,* and Mortimer J. Adler, *Saint Thomas and the Gentiles;* the Modern Language Association of America for Chauncey D. Leake, "Science Implies Freedom," in *Studies in the History of Culture;* the *Nation* for I. A. Richards, "What Is Belief?" Irwin Edman, "After a Mozard Quartet," and Mark Van Doren, "What Happens in Shakespeare"; W. W. Norton & Company for Irwin Edman, *Arts and the Man;* Oxford University Press for Sir Edmund Chambers, *The Elizabethan Stage,* and C. Wilson Knight, *The Shakespearean Tempest;* the Princeton University Press for Theodore Meyer Greene, *The Meaning of the Humanities* and *The Arts and the Art of Criticism,* and I. A. Richards, "The Interaction of Words," in *The Language of Poetry;* the Progressive Education Association, for *The Contribution of Education to Democracy* and *Democratic Education;* G. P. Putnam's Sons for John Dewey, *Freedom and Culture* and *Art as Experience;* Reynal and Hitchcock for Irwin Edman, *Fountainheads of Freedom;* the *Saturday Review of Literature* for Irwin Edman, "Man's Humanities to Man" and "Culture in a Democracy," and Jacques Barzun, "The American as Critic"; Science Press, for the article by Ralph Linton in *Science,* and the article by Frederick Osborn in the *Scientific Monthly;* Charles Scribner's Sons for Robert M. Ogden, *The Psychology of Art;* Simon and Schuster for Mortimer J. Adler, *How to Read a Book;* *Time* for Lewis Mumford, "Stanford Goes Humanist"; the University of Chicago for the syllabus *Introductory Course in the Humanities;* the University of Chicago Press for an article by Charles W. Morris in *The International Encyclopedia of Unified Science,* George Herbert Mead, *Mind, Self, and Society,* articles by Edward Sapir, W. I. Thomas, and Bronislav Malinowski in the *American Journal of Sociology;* Viking Press for John Steinbeck and Edward F. Ricketts, *The Sea of Cortez,* and John Steinbeck, *The Grapes of Wrath;* the Williams and Wilkins Company for Sidney Ratner, *Patterns of Culture in History,* Vol. VI; the H. W. Wilson Company for a review of John Dover Wilson's *What Happens in Hamlet;* the Yale University Press for John Dollard, *Frustration and*

Aggression, and Robert Maynard Hutchins, *The Higher Learning in America;* also to George Herzod for permission to quote from his *Jabo Proverbs from Liberia.*

For permission to quote from letters, I wish to thank Professors Elsie Brickett of Judson College; Dorothy S. Bucks of George Williams College; Robert Campbell of Hendrix College; Henry S. Cayley of New Jersey State Teachers College, Montclair; Norman F. Coleman of Macalester College; Claud L. Fichthorn of Missouri Valley College; Robert P. Griffing, Jr., of Johns Hopkins University; Ernest C. Hassold of the University of Louisville; Donald A. Keister of the University of Akron; Wilfred Payne of the University of Omaha; Lorraine Peter of Alabama College; Max Savelle of Stanford University; Melvin T. Solve of the University of Arizona; Raymond S. Stites of Antioch College; Robert W. Talley of the University of Houston; and Dorothy Weil of Woodrow Wilson Junior College.

F. S.

George Field
Laurenceville, Illinois
January, 1943

CONTENTS

Editor's Foreword, by Lennox Grey	v
Acknowledgments	xi
Introduction	3

Part I. Ideas of Aesthetic Experience underlying Modern World Literature and Humanities Courses

1. Ideas from Philosophical Aesthetics and the Tradition of Literary Criticism: a Brief Review	11
2. Ideas from Modern Psychology: Aesthetic Experience and the Individual	24
3. Ideas from Anthropology: Aesthetic Experience and the Culture	56

Part II. Enlarging Ideas of Aesthetic Experience among Spokesmen for the Humanities

1. The National Council of Teachers of English	74
2. Progressive Education Association	85
A. John Dewey: Social Philosopher	86
B. Louise Rosenblatt: Liberal Arts Progressive	92
3. Committee of Twenty-Four	98
4. Individual Writers on Various Aspects of the Humanities	104
A. Theodore Meyer Greene: Philosophical Spokesman for the Disciplines	104
B. Irwin Edman: Poet-Philosopher	116
C. Jacques Barzun: Humanistic Historian	123
D. I. A. Richards: International Psychologist-Semanticist	129

5. Advocates of a Return to the Medieval Liberal Arts	137
A. Robert Maynard Hutchins	139
B. Mortimer J. Adler	142
C. St. John's College	149

Part III. Converging Ideas and Practices in World Literature and Modern Humanities Courses

1. Formal Aesthetic Principles	156
2. Courses Emphasizing Chronology	161
3. Courses Emphasizing Types of Literature	166
4. Courses Based upon Relationships of Art and Society	171
5. Courses Based on Intellectual History	176
6. Courses Accenting Social Backgrounds and Culture Epochs	180

Part IV. Extensions and Exemplification of a Modern Aesthetic Approach to World Literature: *Hamlet* as Example	192
Conclusions	228
Notes	235
Bibliography	289
Index	319

AESTHETIC EXPERIENCE
AND THE HUMANITIES

INTRODUCTION

REASONS for greatly increased reading of world literature are obvious as America fights its second world war in twenty-five years. Spokesmen of all sorts, academic, artistic, scientific, and political, are urging it as a means of preparation for our world responsibilities. Reasons for approaching world literature with modern expanding ideas of aesthetic experience are less clear, perhaps, yet they too are being urged by many spokesmen who see a common aesthetic drive in the work of Einstein and a Steinbeck—and a devastating perversion of that drive in the "frustration and aggression" of an Austrian artist-paperhanger.

For certain men we know that the cosmic designs of science and the embracing patterns of the social studies have brought as profound an aesthetic response as that more commonly associated with any of the modes of expression in the arts and humanities. Sir James Jeans, English cosmologist, prefaces *The Stars in Their Courses* with reference to astronomy as "the most poetical of the sciences."[1] J. B. S. Haldane, English biologist, writes under the indicative title, "Science and Theology as Art Forms." Albert Einstein, in *The World as I See It,* writes of the significance to himself of his General Theory of Relativity:

Man tries to make for himself in the fashion that suits him best a simplified and intelligible picture of the world; he then tries to some extent to substitute this cosmos of his for the world of experience, and thus to overcome it. This is what the painter, the poet, the speculative philosopher and the natural scientist do, each in his own fashion. He makes this cosmos and its construction the pivot of his emotional life, in order to find in this way the peace and security which he cannot find in the narrow whirlpool of personal experience.[2]

John Steinbeck, American novelist, writes similarly in *The Sea of Cortez* that "the impulse which drives a man to poetry will send another man to tide pools and force him to try to report on what he finds there."[3] And the power of feeling that goes into modern political and social ideologies is one of the most moving facts of our day.

Such merging of scientific and humanistic concerns is a sign of the change which has come over our ideas of aesthetic experience, since the aestheticism of the 1890's brought aesthetics into bad repute. It presents a responsibility to modern educational scholarship which is met in some measure by the new programs of "Scientific Humanism" in the great technical schools, to find a pragmatic unity between the universal but impersonal knowledge of science and the imaginative, individualized values of art.[4] While the formative impulse is common to every human endeavor, for various reasons men continue to feel that it is in the fine arts and literature that the aesthetic experience is most appropriately studied.[5] But it must come under disciplined observation if the particular contribution of the arts to a man's conscious knowledge of human freedom is to be fully developed. To the extent that scientists concern themselves with aesthetic experience, and that teachers of literature and the arts concern themselves with science—to that extent we see a *rapprochement* among the arts and sciences for the world view we need.

Since 1928, as Patricia Beesley points out in *The Revival of the Humanities in American Education*,[6] approximately fifty American colleges and universities have introduced broad Humanities courses (in parallel with broad courses in the Natural Sciences and Social Sciences) where none existed before. This considerable number of courses bearing the name Humanities—wherein the Renaissance term *litterae humaniores* has been extended to include all the arts and the critical disciplines of history and philosophy—signifies a more than casual concern with man's quest for "more human values" through which the individual achieves and demonstrates the dignity of self. In varying patterns emphasis is placed now on literature, now on music or art, or on philosophy, history, and, in one or two instances besides those provided by Catholic schools, on religion. In most of these Humanities courses and programs, World Literature is the *constant*—in fact, in many instances the chief unifying factor.

To many young Americans of pre-war days, and probably to most teachers, "World Literature" has called up a picture of arm-filling anthologies of extracts from the poetry and prose of ancient Greece and Rome, medieval Italy, Renaissance England, and so down to the modern world of Whitman, Wolfe, and Mann. To many a student, we know, the binding of the book seemed the chief unifying factor in the collection and in the course where it was used, despite all the guidance the editor and teacher might give. In the past fifteen years, in many colleges and a few high schools, we have reached out ambitiously for the great books entire—thanks in part, no doubt, to our glimpses in previous anthologies. Yet whether our world literature is in one book, or in a hundred great books, the problem of the unifying factor remains, and the extent to which it provides for both breadth and unity, pattern and focus.

Questions of breadth and unity are relative, as we realize in comparing the concepts of "English" [7] and of "Comparative Literature" [8] and the later though more restricting moral-religious credos of the "New Humanist" movement led by More and Babbitt. In recent years in American colleges and high schools the scope of English has become increasingly American and increasingly international, so that with the declining challenge of differentiation from the classics the English concept has lost something of its original sharpness of focus. And with the growing consciousness of the contemporary social scene English has been variously concerned with social problems and the fringes of scientific knowledge, sometimes to the point of forgetfulness of its own distinctive purposes. To meet the critical demands of broadening subject matter, some of the disciplines of psychology, sociology, cultural anthropology, and human ecology have been added by individual teachers here and there to the biographical, historical, and comparative methods already in use. In *An Experience Curriculum* (1935) and *A Correlated Curriculum* (1936) the National Council of Teachers of English sought clearer patterns and methods, comparable to those emerging in the Humanities and the Great Books programs, to provide social and aesthetic experiences for students.

Teachers who have been following the development of "Great Books," "World Literature," and "Humanities" programs in recent years are broadly aware of various contending and complementary ideas for achieving both breadth and focus—among them the application of certain critical disciplines (for instance, the grammar-rhetoric-logic of St. Thomas Aquinas) to the great books generally, or the focusing on certain persistent principles in human art, or the tracing of evolving culture epochs. Each has its spokesmen. Each presumably has its merits and calls for study on the part of teachers of literature. Each must be subject today, and in days ahead, to certain conditions of time, social temper, and expert knowledge that may obstruct or favor it.

The present study is not bent on advocating any one of these three. It is concerned rather with certain modern ideas of aesthetic experience which appear to be running in some measure through all the courses, and which hold some promise of uniting the best features of a number of them as they mark out the symbols, values, and designs for living prized by various peoples. Roughly and with qualifications, we may say that the concepts of stages of cultural evolution are providing a broad *external frame* for the Humanities, while the expanding ideas of aesthetic experience are providing unifying *internal method*—even as the "Great Books" idea of John Erskine's Columbia Honors Course has provided external frame for the Hutchins-Adler-Barr-Buchanan program at St. John's College, while a revival of the grammar, rhetoric, and logic of St. Thomas has provided its internal discipline. Between the external frame of many modern Humanities courses and the St. John's Great Books course there is often no great difference; but between the modern analogical logic and feeling for design implied in modern ideas of aesthetic experience and the medieval syllogistic logic and dialectic of St. John's there is a profound difference. These similarities and differences indicate certain common interests and cleavages of interests within the loosely designated "Humanities" which must be kept constantly in mind, made the subject of constant reminders.

The modern ideas of aesthetic experience are very different from the "aestheticism" of the late nineteenth century; for chief among the sources of these ideas, apparently, are modern anthropology and psychology, which have been drawn on widely by workers in the fields of comparative literature, philosophical aesthetics, and others concerned with the criticism of arts and letters in broad context.[9] The several schools of psychology are dealing with the various modes of expression and development of self. Modern anthropology is concerned with language as the reservoir of human experience and with the arts generally as symbols of culture effecting the integration of self in the community through a patterned presentation of human values. From these sources have grown the expanding ideas of aesthetic experience in the arts as the creative-critical process originating in the artist's interaction with his environment and ending in the observer's reflective commitment upon the presentation of values in the work of art. It is with some of the main features of these broader anthropological and psychological interpretations and the alterations which they have brought about in traditional aesthetic approach to literature that we are concerned. We will deal chiefly with the direct bearing of these ideas of aesthetic experience on the study of world literature as expression of human values, and with the currency which these ideas have gained among modern teachers of various schools of thought.

Spokesmanship for the Modern Humanities

We find many writers in the field of literature who are contributing to the enlarged concept of aesthetic experience. That this study may be integral with the advances thus far made in bringing modern aesthetics to bear upon the study and teaching of literature, it is important that we establish points of reference with these spokesmen at the start. In so far as they may be expressive channels for ideas, it is important that we also trace their prime sources.

Spokesmanship includes the representative National Council of

Teachers of English, vitally concerned, as *A Correlated Curriculum* states, with the effective patterning of "the scientific, esthetic, philosophical, and ethical branches of the curriculum";[10] the Committee of Twenty-Four, whose "Aims of the Teaching of Literature" seeks to clarify the peculiar responsibility of literature in supporting "those values of individual enrichment without which the democratic state cannot long endure";[11] and the Progressive Education Association, whose point of view is that of John Dewey and whose aesthetic is made explicit in Dewey's *Art as Experience,* and Louise Rosenblatt's *Literature as Exploration,* in which Miss Rosenblatt explores the place of literature in helping each individual to achieve "some philosophy, some inner center from which to view in perspective the shifting society about him." [12]

In addition to these three liberal arts groups, numerous individuals have raised influential voices in concern for the nature and value of the aesthetic experience as it is exemplified in the modern Humanities. Professor Theodore Meyer Greene, of Princeton University, in *The Meaning of the Humanities* and in *The Arts and the Art of Criticism* shows the range of the modern idea of aesthetic experience from a philosopher's point of view. It is "both aesthetic creation and recreation—processes which resemble one another but which are clearly distinguishable." [13] Exploring the poetic qualities of philosophy and the points of convergence between the arts and philosophy, Professor Irwin Edman, of Columbia University, writes in *Arts and the Man* that "a world view, a metaphysics, a way of life, like a poem or painting, is an aesthetic response and, where it attains organic unity in principle or in mood, provokes an aesthetic response." [14] Professor Jacques Barzun, of Columbia University, emphasizing the historian's and anthropologist's concern for art in its social context, shows in *Of Human Freedom* that "culture must be free if men's bodies are to be free." [15] Professor I. A. Richards, of Harvard University, from the psychologist's and from the semanticist's points of view, emphasizes the harmonizing function of art and especially literature in orderly living for, as he states in his *Principles of Literary Criticism,* "No life can be excellent in which the elementary responses are disorganized and confused." [16]

A third phase of spokesmanship springs from the contemporary revival of "neo-scholasticism," with its emphasis upon the efficacy of the medieval liberal arts to meet "our political preoccupation . . . coupled with experimental science," as the Catalogue of St. John's College states.[17] This group-spokesmanship centers in President Robert Maynard Hutchins and Professor Mortimer J. Adler of the University of Chicago, and President Stringfellow Barr and Dean Scott Buchanan of St. John's College, Annapolis.

It is not our purpose in this study to make an eclectic patchwork of the ideas of these spokesmen, since their approach in some instances is fundamentally irreconcilable. The purpose is rather to discover: (1) what ideas these spokesmen hold in common; (2) the sources of these ideas; (3) what the chief roots of conflict among them are; (4) and by discovering further what other ideas have been gaining currency most rapidly in Humanities courses in operation to see and project the kind of design for studying literature that is emerging in recognizable form after the last half century of trial and error.

It is proposed in Part I of this study to consider first, and briefly, the relation of ideas of self, aesthetic experience, and values, in the history of philosophical aesthetics, as part of the background for the current literary aesthetics of teachers today; second, to consider outstanding contributions of psychology to our modern concepts of aesthetic experience, and to our concepts of values; and third, to consider major relevant contributions of anthropology. Part II will take up a systematic analysis of the proposals of the various spokesmen immediately concerned with the teaching of the humanities. Part III will give specific consideration to expressed aims and practices in Humanities and World Literature courses as they bear on aesthetic experience, and particularly to the evidence of common increasing and converging practices. Part IV will seek a systematic formulation of these practices and of trends in current scholarly criticism.

It will exemplify the resulting critique in an inspection of *Hamlet* as a representative symbol of Renaissance culture, one of the five most notable epochs in World Literature.

PART I

IDEAS OF AESTHETIC EXPERIENCE UNDERLYING MODERN WORLD LITERATURE AND HUMANITIES COURSES

---

1. IDEAS FROM PHILOSOPHICAL AESTHETICS AND THE TRADITION OF LITERARY CRITICISM: A BRIEF REVIEW

THE WIDESPREAD BREAK with classical education in America two generations ago meant for many teachers of literature a break also with the long tradition of philosophical criticism and philosophical aesthetics. This was true not only with the classical critics, including Plato and Aristotle, but with the long line of philosophers of literature who have followed in their train, whether in conformity, divergence, or protest—St. Thomas Aquinas, Spinoza, Kant, Hegel, Schopenhauer, Mill, Nietzsche, James, Croce, Santayana, even Dewey as aesthetician. Critical ideas have filtered through Sidney, Jonson, Dryden, Pope, Johnson, and the nineteenth century critics, to be sure, or more often through the handbooks where semi-anonymous ideas of "the unities," "purgation," "tragic flaw," "the sublime," "objective and subjective," "enduring literary types," "sublimation," provide a remarkable composite. But the old lines of communication were broken and tangled, and only partially restored by the introduction of courses in the History of Criticism in the colleges.

One important consequence has been the receptivity of teachers to ideas about aesthetics from other fields than philosophy to fill the void we intuitively recognize. Current concern with social pattern in literature, with the designs of psychoanalysis and Marxism, with the regional aesthetics of John Crowe Ransom, and with the studies in symbolic action by Kenneth Burke, suggest the range of fields to which teachers have turned.

Modern courses in World Literature and Humanities, or their counterparts under other names, are among the agents that have pointed the need for reordering and synthesizing our ideas on aesthetic matters. In these courses the revival of concern with traditional philosophical aesthetics has been attended by the introduction of ideas of aesthetic experience from other sources, chiefly psychology and anthropology, to illuminate the *individual* and *cultural* aspects of the humanities. Doubtless a feeling of the need for doing this has contributed to the introduction of Humanities programs in the first place—so that philosophy, history, literature and the arts may be reconsidered in their interrelationships. This reconsideration has led to greatly expanded conceptions of aesthetic experience from those prevailing two generations ago. It has led, on the one hand, to such formulations as Dewey's aesthetic presented in *Art as Experience,* and, on the other hand, to a "rediscovery" of the remarkable syntheses of Aristotle and St. Thomas Aquinas, which have engrossed the minds of Hutchins and Adler and their associates in their quest for certainty in the midst of current confusion.

In the present section it is not our purpose to undertake a technical review of the great tradition of aesthetic criticism. It is our purpose, rather, to mark in brief review for teachers of literature, and hence in relatively non-technical presentation, the key positions on ideas of self, aesthetic experience, and values of major "classical" philosophers and critics who have contributed to our ideas of aesthetics, aesthetic experience and human values—focusing on these chiefly—so that we may have some systematic pattern for estimating the changes introduced by psychological and anthropological aesthetics, and of appraising the various combinations of the old and the new in the ideas of current spokesmen for aesthetic experience. Attention will be directed first to philosophers, and second to some of the "classic" literary figures in English letters who have represented aesthetic criticism to modern teachers.

Philosophical Aesthetics

The philosophical designs of the twenty-five centuries since Plato lend themselves to the traditionally convenient "idealistic" and "empirical"[1] groupings, in which (since William James) inquiring college students have been schooled in introductory philosophy courses. While this bold statement of the main lines in these philosophical designs does violence to their qualifying technical detail, even as a line drawing of either painting or sculpture gives only a rough idea of the whole, it is to the main lines that we must cleave here.

Among the idealistic philosophers we find Plato, Kant, Schopenhauer, Santayana, Aristotle, and St. Thomas Aquinas. Among the influential empirical philosophers we find John Stuart Mill, and Nietzsche, Croce, James, and Dewey.

The designs of these philosophers are expressions of value—value placed upon life and specific aspects of life. All have treated the value of art and the values achievable in or through the aesthetic experience which it involves. Among them we see not only two great contrasted positions, but three main roads from which philosophers have approached values in aesthetic experience. One is *Rationalism,* conventionally identified with the idealistic philosophers, which places the highest human values in the portrayal of the ideal ultimate perfection. The second is *Hedonism,* associated of course with the name of Epicurus but entering more directly into English and American thought through John Stuart Mill, which finds value in the arts as they provide immediate sensations of pleasure. The third appears in the value theory variously identified with the names of William James and John Dewey—*Pragmatism, Radical Empiricism, Instrumentalism,* and *Cultural Naturalism*—which attributes the highest value to the development of the self through sympathetic and responsible interaction with society.[2] This last position, which draws most largely on modern science, places a premium upon the "more human" values of intellect, curiosity, imagination, sympathy, and intuition by which a man develops his *self* to include a large measure of the interests of others, and through which he works to fulfill his individual potentialities and recognize his own dignity and worth. These words, "individual potentialities," "dignity," and "worth" are being explored very insistently in discussions of contemporary education from all points of view, and especially in the modern humanities.

Idealistic philosophers.—"Back to Plato and Aristotle" is a familiar way of bracketing the two primary sources of much of Western criticism and aesthetics. It obscures a major difference between them —the broad cultural context, for instance, in which Plato considers works of art, and the sharply narrowed Aristotelian consideration of works in themselves or as species—but it is faithful to their kinship as idealistic philosophers.

For Plato (427-347 B.C.) Ideas alone are *real;* perfection rests in Ideas which are independent of man's mind or the limitations of observable matter. The perfection of the self rests in the clear, intellectual perception of each archetypal Idea, which produces the aesthetic experience.[3] Such perception is based on language, for it proceeds from acquaintance with the *name* of the given object and the *definition,* to the *image* and the *knowledge* of its function, and so to complete but incommunicable *understanding* in the soul.[4] The highest perception of beauty is the severely disciplined emotional experience of the philosopher[5] who, through Reason (in contrast to the poet's pleasurable but dangerously undisciplined emotional perception of imitations of the Ideal world)[6] comes to know in the symmetry and truth of the Ideal world the essential Form of Good.[7]

For Aristotle (384-32 B.C.) the most profound development of the self is the feeling of harmony which conduces to the supreme human good, happiness. The highest perception of beauty lies in the instinctive imitation of human action in art[8] which, as "a more philosophical and higher thing than history,"[9] presents in an ordered form[10] from the beginning through the middle to the end, a form of action which could or which ought to prevail.[11] This is most effectively accomplished through metaphorical language which, as the greatest attribute of poetic diction, is "a sign of genius, since a good metaphor implies an intuitive perception of the similarity in dissimilars."[12] In so far as the constricting emotions of pity and fear are in the work of art represented in their proper relationship to human existence,[13] the observer of the work of art experiences the essential feeling of harmony which accompanies action in accordance with the moral and intellectual virtues.[14]

Following the lead of Plato and Aristotle with their respective concern for perfection of Ideas and of species, idealistic philosophies of successive epochs have placed highest in their scale of values the purity of Reason and Imagination, for these are the values by which man establishes his goal, cuts through confusing imitations, and comes to Perfection.

St. Thomas Aquinas combined elements of classical idealism with Christian idealism in the *Summa Theologica* (1265) to form the medieval theocentric aesthetic.[15] Thomas Aquinas believed that all things, men, and angels, tend toward their Ideal Forms which started with the Word of God and exist in His mind.[16] The artist approaches the limits of his self in the perception of the beauty of each Ideal Form enveloped in its material object.[17] The only adequate critics for his representation of Forms are those in whom the highest value, the faculty of reason, nears the perfection of Divine Mind—philosophers, saints or angels.[18] Like Aristotle, the medieval linguist or grammarian distinguished between the functions and excellences of language when used in relation to different purposes.[19] The use of language by the poet stresses those qualities of language which are exemplified in poetic images, in his attempt to overcome what Maritain calls "the difficulties man experiences when he wants to tell himself and make himself really *see* the commonest things with the help of the imagery of language." [20]

For Spinoza, as the *Ethic* (1675) states, self-realization arises in the possession of "adequate ideas," [21] which raises man to the state "of human liberty"—as opposed to his state "of human bondage" when false or "inadequate ideas" conduce to action without deliberation as opposed to the rational consideration of alternatives prior to action. An individual experiences beauty, which marks the process of self-realization, whenever the imagination recognizes order where previously unrelated objects had presented a state of confusion.[22] In so far as words are "signs of things as existing in the imagination" rather than in the understanding, he tells us in *Improvement of the Understanding,* the aesthetic ordering of ideas depends upon strict uses of language.[23] Clearly related values amplifying and growing from the feeling of human freedom, and artistic teaching[24] which releases the imagination to move man toward responsible social action,[25] increase consciousness of self—the essence of man and the source of his religious experience.[26]

In *The Critique of Aesthetic Judgment* (1790) Kant holds that the full development of self rests in a man's recognizing his moral responsibility for self-improvement.[27] Two kinds of experience in the presence of the beauty of art created by genius conduce to this state: the aesthetic or the sublime. If aesthetic, the beautiful (as the symbol of the moral ideal of man) is recognized through subjective judgment of the degree to which the ideal is approximated;[28] if sublime, the observer recognizes the superiority over brute force which his human reason and spirituality provide. Because the highest form of aesthetic or sublime experience develops from the combination of *intuitions* and *concepts* involving respectively figurative and objective uses of language,[29] the cultivation of imagination, sympathy, and spirit as well as the cultivation of understanding is imperative.

Hegel's *The Philosophy of Fine Art* (1823) presents a hierarchy of three degrees of self-realization: man's urge to reshape the materials of his environment; man's ideas of love, law, and property which integrate human communities; man's idea of his individualized capacity to know God and Truth through the creation of beauty.[30] These phases of self-realization are symbolized in their respective art forms: symbolic,[31] characterized by architecture; classical,[32] characterized by sculpture; and romantic,[33] characterized by painting, music, and poetry, of which poetry is the highest form, for it alone can deal solely with ideas. Implicitly, these art forms provide symbols of scientific, social, and individual values.

To Schopenhauer in *The World as Will and Idea* (1819) selfhood is attained in a man's conscious knowledge of his own worth and ability.[34] The artist's achievement of this self-knowledge is his aesthetic experience arising from his will-less contemplation of the Ideal forms underlying the visible forms of nature, which he perceives through a superabundance of knowledge beyond the necessities of the "will to live." [35] When the artist records his experience in language, which alone is capable of representing all the objects and relationships in man's world, it is communicable to other members of human society who, in will-less contemplation of the work of art, come to understand more fully the values of love, law, science, and religion.[36]

For Santayana in *Reason in Art* (1924) the height of self-realization is achieved in the feeling of happiness which accompanies the conception of the rational conduct of life.[37] Beauty is "objectified happiness," created when the artist, granted leisure,[38] gives expressive form to his insight into the perfectability of the world and man.[39] Through an instinctual Sense of Beauty other individuals find self and happiness as they perceive in the form of the artist's work (in literature the sensuous harmony of words, the verse form, the grammar, and the plot)[40] a symbol of the genuine harmony of the aesthetic, moral, and philosophic values of Beauty, Goodness, and Truth.[41]

Empirical philosophers.—Empiricism to many Americans means the "tough-mindedness" by which William James characterized the individuals who did not "shrink from practical action to take refuge in an unshakable higher realm of fixed and antecedent Reality." [42] It is very old, however, and moderns like I. A. Richards have found stimulating precedents in philosophies as old as that of Mencius,[43] fourth-century B.C. Chinese sage, part of whose thought on the psychological aspects of language has entered the philosophic background of Richards' spokesmanship for the Humanities. Though science has prompted many of the modern developments in empiricism, there are numerous other currents.

Hume's *Treatise of Human Nature* (1739), one of the fountain-heads of modern empirical thought, states that "notions of personal identity" or self arise from knowledge of the unity and continuity of experience provided in language by the human qualities of memory, curiosity, imagination, and sympathy.[44] Contributing a major current of relativism, Hume affirms the interrelationship of individual and social values,[45] a theory which finds aesthetic application in Mill.

John Stuart Mill's *A System of Logic* (1843), building upon Hume, presents the highest development of the self as the application of intelligence to the rational conduct of society.[46] In both experiential and intuitional knowledge the core of thought is the feeling which engenders it, and language is "one of the principal instruments" by which it is carried on.[47] The aesthetic experience of the artist is the process by which he attains a unity of feeling as the overflow of emotion occasioned by intuition is harmonized in his work of art.[48] Re-experiencing through language the feeling of the artist contributes to the observer's intuitional[49] knowledge and makes for happiness through motivating coöperative social actions.[50]

For Nietzsche, as for Hume, the supreme development of the self is the understanding and acceptance of the totality of life; these, he tells us in *The Birth of Tragedy* (1872), call upon two art impulses, the Dionysian and the Apollonian, which together satisfy the human desire for form or balance.[51] Following the Dionysian impulse, man plunges exuberantly into the chaotic activities of living, loses his identity, and perceives that the essence of human life must always be misery and suffering.[52] So far, Nietzsche is like his fellow-German, Schopenhauer.[53] But rather than accept abnegation in the face of suffering, Nietzsche finds the formative Apollonian impulse entering to create Beauty through imagination most highly disciplined by the combined expressive media of music and language.[54] In this highest exemplification of the Will to Power the artist gains dominion over self and fellows through his creation of an individualized symbol of the universal. In this aesthetic experience he attains the highest degree of individual dignity,[55] in which the self is considered as a work of art, harmonizing and rising above, but not denying, the world's misery in a "tragic" perspective.[56] Central values are not moral but aesthetic.[57]

In *The Essence of Aesthetic* (1921), the introspective psychology of the Italian Croce holds that the self is achieved by the workings of the mind of genius when it perceives clear thoughts unified by "feeling," where there had been only indistinct intuitive images before.[58] Organic with this aesthetic experience is the impulse to expression, but the unifying "feeling" is the work of art more than the external expression. The aesthetic experience of the observer occurs when he re-experiences the feeling of the artist.[59]

While the American philosopher-scientist William James, like Hume before him, did not write extensively of art as such, his books and lectures from 1890 to 1910 helped to lay the philosophic base for modern ideas of aesthetic experience. Man's distinguishingly human attribute, his "deliberate intention to apply a sign to everything," [60] makes possible his "reflective knowledge of himself as a thinker." [61] Self-consciousness develops in the continuous physical and linguistic interaction with the environment.[62] The self grows as it becomes conscious of progressive degrees of unity in the designs of ethics, morals, science, and religion.[63] The extra-natural, absolute Ideal James supplanted with the concept of constantly expanding imaginative ideals which the self values.

For Dewey, whose aesthetic will be discussed later in detail, *any* experience is aesthetic when the self, seeking unity in its environment without forcing diversity into a single rational mold, achieves expressive form through a cumulative sequence of activities. The preservation and growth of the self through the aesthetic experience is the central value.

English Literary Criticism

For teachers who have been schooled in the English literary tradition rather than in that of the philosophers, aesthetic criticism means chiefly the ideas of Sidney, Ben Jonson, Dryden, Pope, Samuel Johnson, Coleridge, Carlyle, and Arnold. As we review the efforts of each of these critics to view aesthetic processes anew according to the new knowledge of his time, we may wonder that more teachers have not taken the clue from them to do likewise in systematic fashion.

Sidney's *An Apology for Poetry* (1583) both drew upon and departed from philosophical aesthetics. As a representative courtier of his day, Sidney knew the work of his Continental predecessors, Plato, Aristotle, Horace, and Aquinas. With his classical philosophic predecessors he recognized the emotional power of an art of imitation to move men to right action, and in Platonic spirit assumed a judicial tone with contemporaneous English drama. But as Renaissance humanist he moved beyond Plato and Aristotle in his concern for individual and communal values which literature affirms, and for the convergence of philosophy and literature in their treatment of human values. For Sidney as for Aristotle, poetry was superior to philosophy in its power to move men. The poet "yieldeth to the powers of the mind an image of that whereof the philosopher bestoweth but a wordish description; which doth neither strike, pierce, nor possess the sight of the soul, so much as that other doth."[64] Poetry shares also the intellectual content of the sciences and history, and with them aims at the highest human achievement, knowledge. But, like Bacon a little later, Sidney deprecates knowledge for itself, and lauds "the knowledge of a man's self, in the ethic and politic consideration, with the end of well-doing and not of well-knowing only."[65]

Ben Jonson, like Sidney, lies close to the Aristotelian concern for the wholeness of a work of art judged by the magnitude and coherence of the imitation which it is. Recognizing by 1635 the Renaissance diversity of literary forms, in "Timber; or Discoveries" he proposed Aristotelian standards for the evaluation of the fable, epic, and tragic or comic drama, for "they differ but in specie; either in the kind is absolute."[66] At the same time he extended Sidney's concern with the self to a concern with language also, which "most shows a man" for it "springs out of the most retired and inmost parts of us, and is the image of the parent of it, the mind."[67] In a similarly Renaissance vein he writes that,

Nothing is more ridiculous than to make an author a dictator, as the schools have done Aristotle. The damage is infinite knowledge receives by it. For to many things a man should owe but a temporary belief, and a suspension of his own judgment, not an absolute resignation of himself, or a perpetual captivity.⁶⁸

By 1668 Dryden in *An Essay of Dramatic Poesy* showed a growing consciousness of the cultural background of art and further restlessness about a dogmatic Aristotelianism.

Is it not evident, in these last hundred years . . . that almost a new nature has been revealed to us? that more errors of the school have been detected, more useful experiments in philosophy have been made, more noble secrets in optics, medicine, anatomy, astronomy, discovered, than in all those credulous and doting ages from Aristotle to us? ⁶⁹

This explicit recognition permitted Dryden to reëmphasize Jonson's break with scholastic authority. "The genius of every age is different," ⁷⁰ and, he implies, must be evaluated according to its own standards. In addition to emphasis upon this use of imagination, Dryden repeatedly draws attention to the place of imagination in the creative process—to "the design of the whole" and the "labyrinth of design" ⁷¹ by which choice of words and action produces verisimilitude.

Pope's *An Essay on Criticism* (1711) moves even farther than Dryden in the recognition of the cultural context—the "religion, country, genius of his age" ⁷²—in which each artist works, and of the necessity for each creator to "deviate from the common track" ⁷³ to reach his individually desired ends. In the same liberal spirit he demands that the critic identify himself with the author's intention and evaluate the work "with itself compared," for

> A perfect Judge will read each work of Wit
> With the same spirit that its author writ.⁷⁴

Despite these advances, Pope is thought of today as an arch classicist, for he was unable to move far from his French contemporary, Boileau, or the Latin and Greek critics to which they both adhere. He admonishes the prospective author to "Learn . . . for ancient rules a just esteem" ⁷⁵ and the critic to follow the precedents of "the mighty Stagyrite," "grave Quintillian," and "bold Longinus," for

> Those Rules of old discover'd, not devis'd,
> Are Nature still, but Nature methodiz'd.[76]

Early English literary critics, as we have noted, show less concern than do other world critics with the nature of the artistic process. But with Samuel Johnson we find a literary critic moving in parallel with his philosopher-contemporary, David Hume, and emphasizing the human quest for unity: "To proceed from one truth to another, and connect distant propositions by regular sequences, is the great prerogative of man . . . ."[77] Johnson further identifies himself with the stream of contemporaneous philosophic thought by placing the superior author under moral obligation to make his ideas intelligible and attractive to others by constant attention to meanings and connotations attaching to words in context.

As we have seen, the English tradition is not separable, really, from the development of other world criticism, though for many teachers of literature it has been separated. Periodically the connections have been strongly reaffirmed, as with Coleridge in *Biographia Literaria* in 1815-1817. In Chapter XIII, with the perspective of nineteenth century transcendental philosophy, Coleridge posits for man "a nature having two contrary forces, the one which tends to expand infinitely, while the other strives to apprehend or *find* itself in this infinity."[78] These two forces correspond to Coleridge's concept of Imagination (as opposed to Fancy) as primary and secondary.

> The primary Imagination I hold to be the living power and prime agent of all human perception, and as a repetition in the finite mind of the eternal act of creation in the infinite I AM. The secondary Imagination . . . co-existing with the conscious will . . . dissolves, diffuses, dissipates, in order to re-create.[79]

Both phases of the Imagination, and hence both contending forces in man, are drawn upon in the synthesizing role of the artist.

> The poet, described in ideal perfection, brings the whole soul of man into activity, with the subordination of its faculties to each other, according to their relative work and dignity. He diffuses a tone and spirit of

unity, that blends, and (as it were) fuses, each into each, by that synthetic and magical power to which we have exclusively appropriated the name of imagination.[80]

The consciousness of self which accompanies the aesthetic experience of the artist is the highest form of knowledge. And the aesthetic process is not limited to the creative author. The reader may have a similar cumulative experience.

The reader should be carried forward, not merely or chiefly by the mechanical impulse of curiosity, or by a restless desire to arrive at the final solution; but by the pleasurable activity of mind excited by the attraction of the journey itself.[81]

For author and reader alike "the high spiritual instinct of the human being impelling us to seek unity by harmonious adjustment" [82] leads to a balanced design of political, religious, and philosophical values.

Carlyle in *Heroes and Hero Worship* (1840) saw literature as the supreme aesthetic formulation of the dominant ideals of an epoch; he saw the author, with superior sincerity, imagination, sympathy, and "unconscious intellect," as creating in his individual struggle for expression a universal harmony for his contemporaries and successors. To him, seeing culture from the evolutionary view developing on the continent in Goethe and Herder, "Dante is the spokesman of the Middle Ages," [83] Shakespeare "the outcome and flowerage of all which had preceded," [84] Goethe "the prophecy and beginning of a New Time," [85] while in countries where no poet had yet risen (America? Russia?) through the power of literature, "Democracy virtually extant will insist on becoming palpably extant." [86]

These brief progressions through the aesthetic theories of English literary critics prepare us for Arnold's conception in "Literature and Science" (1885) of the aesthetic impulse as an "instinct for self-preservation in humanity," [87] carried forward by an individual interacting with his environment, for in "the creation of a master work of literature two powers must concur, the power of the man and the power of the moment, and the man is not enough without the moment . . . ," [88] Like Dewey, Arnold does not confine the aesthetic impulse to literary or other artistic creation; ". . . men may have the sense of exercising this free creativity in other ways than in producing great works of literature or art. . . . They may have it in well doing, they may have it in learning, they may have it even in criticising." [89] In general outline Arnold is notably modern in many respects. Anthropologists and psychologists have confirmed much that he thought, even while modifying it. The revival of the Humanities and the studies in World Literature in translation (to which he was a contributor) have prompted teachers of literature also to reëxamination and reappraisal of his "Victorian" ideas.

Highly abbreviated though these sketches are, they may serve as a rough measure of continuity and change in man's thinking about values in aesthetic experience as we move to a consideration of psychological and anthropological contributions. As we continue with a detailed study of modern spokesmen for World Literature and the Humanities, we may more readily recognize the varied sources from which modern teachers and writers have drawn. In the modern Humanities, as we shall see, aesthetic experience is not regarded as simply one of many human values, but one of the most important means for perceiving and revealing human values of many kinds, individual and social.

2. IDEAS FROM MODERN PSYCHOLOGY: AESTHETIC EXPERIENCE AND THE INDIVIDUAL

Among the many aspects of modern psychology that have affected the thinking and critical procedures of scholars and teachers of literature, psychoanalysis has undoubtedly been the most spectacular. Books like Krutch's *Edgar Allan Poe: A Study in Genius* (1926), Lewisohn's *Expression in America* (1932), and Van Wyck Brooks' *Ordeal of Mark Twain* (1933) give some hint of the extent to which ideas from modern clinical psychology have pervaded literary criticism in America. But this approach is by no means the only contribution from modern psychology, or necessarily the most significant. The effect of organismic or Gestalt psychology, which underlies much current teaching in our socially-minded schools today, has probably been quite as great, if less spectacular. And certain extensions of the work of American biologists like Herbert Jennings, moreover, may be more influential in the future, particularly as they point up the organic formative impulse basic to aesthetic experience.

All philosophies of life or aesthetics have certain psychological tenets, of course. Only a little more than a half century ago psychology was a branch of philosophy—before psychology, following Wundt's establishment of an experimental laboratory in 1879, became independent in response to a drive for scientific specialization. Modern psychologists have sought more and more to reach out from the restricted stimulus-response patterns of behaviorism which first engaged them and to recapture in their own right the breadth which they gave up when they broke from philosophy, until now the organismic psychologists seek to reckon with all aspects of the environment in studying the configuration of man's thoughts.

Informed philosophers have kept pace with psychologists; but too many teachers of literature have lost touch with philosophical aesthetics, as we have observed, and at best have had only partial views of the modern psychological approaches to aesthetics. We see various gestures to bring about a reconciliation of traditional philosophy and psychology with literary criticism, none more interesting than the efforts of Mortimer J. Adler to harmonize the faculty psychology of St. Thomas with the clinical psychology of Freud. All this is warning that we should not think of philosophy and psychology as following sharply divergent channels, or think of a philosophical aesthetic and a psychological aesthetic as different or incompatible.

What follows is the consideration of a number of major concepts, old and new, in various schools of psychology, which bear or promise to bear with some directness on ideas of "aesthetic experience" in the study of World Literature and the Humanities. The first for reasons of antiquity is the rather conspicuous if limited revival and modernization by Adler and others of the medieval "Faculty Psychology" of St. Thomas Aquinas. The second is Behaviorism with its "stimulus—response" formula. The third is Freudianism and related psychoanalytic groups. The fourth comprises a group of related theories which turn on the words "Einfühlung," "Distance," and "Empathy," involving degrees of identification with art or with perspectives from which to view art. The fifth is the "Dynamic" psychology of Woodward and others, with a treatment of art akin to that of Kant and Schopenhauer at various points, notably in its consideration of genius and the will-to-live. The sixth is Social Psychology. The seventh is organismic or Gestalt psychology, embracing in its study of psychological processes all physical, social, and ideological phenomena by which a being is affected. The eighth is a group of comprehensive syntheses by Lalo, Delacroix, Rusu, and Müller-Freienfels, which appear to spring from, or be cognate with,[1] the comprehensive biological syntheses of the American biologist, Jennings.

Modern Revival of Classical-Medieval Psychology

For various reasons it is appropriate to consider first the modern expressions of faculty psychology as a basis for art. Its historic significance is great. Its vocabulary is still with us despite the disproving of discrete psychological "faculties" by Thorndike in 1896. But "the faculties" of reason, imagination, will, and intellect is familiar idiom, and familiar idiom is important in popular presentations of ideas, as in *How to Read a Book*. Separated in spirit, interest, and method from modern scientific inquiry, faculty psychology nevertheless has a certain affinity with psychoanalysis, as has already been remarked. And in Aristotle, authoritative bridge between Plato and St. Thomas Aquinas, there was, of course, a scientific base of inquiry, adequate for many men for many centuries.

Modern exponents of classical-medieval psychology pay relatively little attention to current conceptions of biological evolution. Faculty psychology holds to an *a priori* duality of mind and body. The human mind has certain "faculties" by which to account for the activities of reasoning, willing, remembering, imagining, etc. These faculties are explained in isolation from the environment. Common sense tells man that these powers exist. Prudence or practical considerations have found them useful, whether as facts or generalizations.

Mortimer J. Adler, who has moved from psychology to philosophy, and thence to literature, is one of the chief contemporary spokesmen for the return to faculty psychology as an approach to art. He indicates his sources as Plato, Aristotle, Aquinas, and Freud. Franz Alexander, writing the introduction to Adler's published lectures before the Psychoanalytic Institute in Chicago, says:

As Mr. Adler himself very correctly put it, his lectures represent something which might have been the attitude of a contemporary pupil of Thomas Aquinas, or perhaps of Thomas himself if he could come to life again and be confronted with the new discoveries of Sigmund Freud.[2]

And Adler in *How to Read a Book* implies joint relationships between medieval and Freudian thought when, commenting on a group of his students, he says:

When I discovered that they had made no connection whatsoever between the physiology of emotion . . . and the passions as St. Thomas discussed them; when I found out they could not even see that St. Thomas was making the same basic point as Freud, I realized what I was up against.[3]

To understand Adler's concept of aesthetic experience, we need to consider in sequence his idea of the aesthetic experience of the artist, the nature of the work of art, the aesthetic experience of the observer and the critical approach to the values it presents. To do this we must look again at the Thomistic theory of art, which is integral with faculty psychology. St. Thomas indicates the natural tendency of each created thing to move toward perfection in its kind. Man, possessed of mind, seeks his perfection or full Being in Mind or God. His quest is for intellectual perfection, pure rationality unmoved by physical and emotional passion. "But no man is perfectly rational," says Adler, "which means that every man has disordered passions to a greater or less degree. Every man needs to learn the discipline of submitting passions to reason."[4] In so far as no man has perfected the "faculty" of reason, it is essential that his actions be guided by the virtue of prudence, the artist's no less than the observer's.

The artist approximates perfection of mind in his sudden insight into the absolute Form of created objects. This revelation, which could otherwise have come only through "reason" in contemplation, is his aesthetic experience. Given the insight, the artist invokes prudence to choose in the light of practical consequences whether to present his imitation of that Form for others to observe.[5] Because "the will is intellectual appetite," the observer wills to participate in the dramatic spectacle which the artist's imitation presents.[6] The artist's imitation "is responsible for the excitation which makes what is happening in some fashion happen to oneself. The difference in the imitation makes for impersonality; or, to put it another way, it allows one to contemplate oneself as an excited spectator of the exciting spectacle, and in this viewing of the soul by itself, understanding is achieved and the emotions are purged."[7] This cathartic action constitutes the aesthetic experience of the observer, and leaves the disordered soul rightly "submissive to the prudent will."[8]

In the revival of the classical-medieval psychology, art is paired with practical considerations, as in Adler's *Art and Prudence,* rather than with the higher more metaphysical *reason.* To the extent that art thus works the ends of prudence, it is itself subject to critical review in the light of the political preoccupations of prudence and is, as in Plato, inferior to pure wisdom.

Behaviorism

The chief contribution of Behaviorist psychology and of other schools of experimental psychology to the modernizing of ideas of aesthetic experience has been the denial of separate "human faculties" of imagination, will, and the like, and a stress on problem solving in all human activities, including art.

Behaviorist psychologists, as J. B. Watson pointed out in 1919 in *Psychology from the Standpoint of the Behaviorist,* recognize two characteristics as common to animals and men—the instincts of propagation and of preservation of the species. But because ability to form habits exists in inverse ratio to the number of instinctive behaviors, "man excels in his habit-forming capacities."[9] Behaviorists like Watson, therefore, see the goal of psychology as "the ascertaining of such data and laws that, given the stimulus, psychology can predict what the response will be; or, on the other hand, given the response, it can specify the nature of the effective stimulus."[10] Within this mechanical stimulus-response relationship there is still room for the development of new modes of behavior. Provided with a disturbing problem (S), the individual seeks the solution (R) in manual or language activity. In this process, "no matter what the human animal is doing he works as a whole."[11] In such mass action the person displays his individuality, which "seems in some way to depend upon man's unlearned behavior, not upon the presence of completed pattern types of responses."[12] The solution of the problem, Watson implies by reference to the individual's smiles, is accompanied by feelings of satisfaction which we may infer to be akin to aesthetic experience. Watson does not, however, stress any relationship between the solution of problems and the realization of the self. While the behaviorist started theoretically from a broad concept of the whole organism in the environment, in practice he concentrated on many minute details. The organismic psychologist, in reaction against this, as we shall see, reaffirms the larger setting.

Psychoanalysis

Sigmund Freud's *A General Introduction to Psychoanalysis* (1920), and later works of Freud and his exponents, presents the most arresting example of the clinical or case study method in psychology very explicitly concerned with aesthetic experience. The Freudian group of psychoanalysts see in various strata of the mind—conscious and unconscious—the causes of the individual's intellectual-emotional maladjustment to his environment and find in the designs of art both expression and cure. In clinical treatment, emphasis falls upon the unconscious, which has a kind of entity that brings it close to the medieval-classical faculties. This fact, as we have already noted, may offer reason for neo-scholastic interest in Freud as modern scientific substantiation of classical medieval theory. It may suggest, in part, why many people have responded to psychoanalysis, finding in it something that seems to coincide with old inherited ideas of faculties and even compartments of the mind.

The primary concern of the Freudian psychoanalyst is with the abnormal or disturbing tendencies in behavior. These, Freud states, arise from and are symptomatic of the repression of the fundamentally sexual drives of the libido, power and the love of women—values reminiscent of Nietzsche. Forced into the unconscious by the conscious censorship of the Ego, "the libido which lacks satisfaction is urged to seek other paths and other objects. . . . The circuitous paths are the ways of symptom-formation; the symptoms are the new or substitutive satisfactions necessitated by the fact of the privation." [13] For many people, day-dreams and phantasy provide this compensation.[14] The artist is no exception, for he is an individual seeking compensation in certain ways and certain media. His instinctual desires are stronger than those of the ordinary person, so that his condition constantly borders on that of the neurotic. But apparently his constitution is "strongly endowed with an ability to sublimize and to shift the suppression determining" [15] his conflict.

Through such shifting the "writer softens the egotistical character of the day-dream by changes and disguises, and he bribes us by the offer of a purely formal, that is, aesthetic, pleasure in the presentation of his phantasies." [16] This formal aesthetic pleasure is an "incitement premium" which lures the reader to release his own repressions through vicarious experience. By thus relieving the tension which accompanied hitherto inaccessible suppression, the artist brings solace and consolation to his readers. His own satisfaction lies in the sublimation of conflicts through the creative process, and in the fact that men find in his work valuable patterns of actual life.

Thus by a certain path he actually becomes the hero, king, creator, favourite he desired to be, without pursuing the circuitous path of creating real alterations in the outer world. But this he can only attain because other men feel the same dissatisfaction as he with the renunciation demanded by reality. . . .[17]

The artist "wins gratitude and admiration for himself and so, by means of his imagination, achieves the very things which had at first only an imaginary existence for him: honor, power, and the love of women."[18]

Freud explained not only the creative and appreciative processes in this manner. He also developed his theory of psychoanalysis as a critical method for evaluating literature. The tendency of psychoanalytic criticism as Freud demonstrated it in analysis of works of Shakespeare, Ibsen, and da Vinci,[19] is toward the development of symbols of kinds of maladjustment,[20] although, as Kenneth Burke indicates in *The Philosophy of Literary Form* (1941), Freud "had reservations against specific equations"[21] in the use of symbols. Carried to its logical extreme, psychoanalytic criticism, as Barzum indicates in *Of Human Freedom,* could become judgment based on inflexible standards of comparison.[22] This tendency toward "typing" of character judgments is apparent in Charles Baudouin's *Psychoanalysis and Aesthetics* (1924),[23] and in Ludwig Lewisohn's *Expression in America* (1932) which acknowledges the use of "the organon or method of knowledge associated with the venerated name of Sigmund Freud."[24] Kenneth Burke explicitly moves beyond other Freudians, stressing the values of clusters of symbolic actions to be interpreted in the context of imagery and ideas.[25]

Two of Freud's students, Otto Rank and Carl Jung, have launched independent psychoanalytical art theories differing considerably from Freud's. For Rank the "master emphasis," as Burke terms it, is upon the birth trauma as the prototype for all creative activity, whether in science, politics, religion, or art. According to Rank, the creative "process, though similar in principle to, is not a simple repetition of, the trauma of birth; it is, broadly, the attempt of the individual to gain freedom from dependence of any sort upon a state from which it has grown."[26] The artist, living in an established culture, has been nurtured by its ideas to the extent that the collective pattern has engulfed his individuality, and "in the course of his life . . . he must escape . . . from the ruling ideology of the present, which he has himself strengthened by his own growth and development, if his individuality is not to be wholly smothered by it."[27]

Looking at the successive art-styles symbolic of world views that have succeeded one another in Western culture, Rank holds that the individual artist is never alone in his tendency toward a new formulation of experiences. The artist is part of a movement which at first is "cultural and not individual, collective and not personal," [28] but "through his inner conflict, the artist gains the courage, the rigour, and the foresight to grasp the impending change of attitude before others do so, to feel it more intensely, and to shape it formally." [29] In the aesthetic process, he preserves his self from domination by the collective past by formulating the attitude toward life which will supersede that past.

Rank makes both an anthropological and a psychological approach to these ideas. From the point of view of anthropology, he is interested in the succession of world views which run through history. From that of psychology, he is concerned with the transformation of the self of the artist through the completion of the work of art. During the process of creation the work of art is the life of the artist, for "creation is itself an experience of the artist's, perhaps the most intense possible for him or for mankind in general." [30] While the work of art is emphatically not to be regarded simply as biographical fact, we infer that it is a symbol of the state of mind of the artist as he works to overcome "previous supporting egos and ideologies from which the individual has to free himself according to the measure and speed of his own growth, a separation which is so hard, not only because it involves persons and ideas that one reveres, but because the victory is always . . . won over a part of one's own ego." [31]

While the creative process is not always a self-conscious one for the artist, Rank points to an increasing tendency toward self-conscious artistry sensed by him first, as he tells us, in *Kunstler* (1905) and made explicit in *Art and Artist* (1932). In addition, in *Art and Artist,* he notes that artists who are conscious of their creative processes are moving increasingly toward exposition within their work of the methods of creation, which represent a "diversion of creation into knowledge, of shaping of art into science and, above all, psychology." [32]

The bases for Carl Jung's separation from the Freudian school in 1911 are nowhere more marked than in his concept of art set forth in *Contributions to Analytical Psychology* in 1928. Like Freud, Jung uses the term libido to denote the energizing force of human activity, but for him it is not a dominant sexual preoccupation, but the drive toward a progressive "satisfaction of the demands of environmental conditions." [33] It is the constant aesthetic impulse for achieving equilibrium among inharmonious forces which surround man.

Continuing his differences from Freud, Jung assumes three strata of mind. Every human psyche comes into the world with a complicated psychic precondition—the accumulation of ages of biological and cultural influences, which Jung calls the "collective unconscious." This deepest level of mind remains permanently beyond conscious control. It exists only in "inborn possibilities of ideas," primordial images and archetypes of human ideals, that may repeat themselves "in the course of history wherever creative phantasy is freely manifested." [34]

Through active participation in his environment the individual acquires the contents of the second level of mind, the "conscious," though these contents also are shaped and colored by the collective unconscious which pervades his environment. [35] The third level of mind is the "personal unconscious." This, Jung notes, is made up principally of the sense perceptions and ideas that are too weak to reach consciousness, but sufficiently strong to dissipate energies into other conscious functions in disturbing ways. [36] These different levels of mind need a cohesive force which is the property of the consciousness. Jung calls it the *ego*. [37]

When the energizing force of the libido is checked by environmental changes which temporarily it cannot harmonize, conflict arises in which the valuation of the opposing elements increases, emotional tension heightens, the conscious unity of the ego is threatened, and the stage is set for neurosis.[38] The preconditions of neurosis and artistic creation, according to Jung, are identical,[39] but the creative process of art is not a symptom of neurosis (as Freud would have it) but a balanced reorganization of the conflicting elements in the artist's personality.

Recoiling from the unsatisfying present the yearning of the artist reaches out to that primordial image in the unconscious which is best fitted to compensate the insufficiency and one-sidedness of the spirit of the age. The artist seizes this image, and in the work of raising it from deepest unconsciousness he brings it into relation with conscious values, thereby transforming the shape, until it can be accepted by his contemporaries according to their powers.[40]

The "reaching out" of the artist may take form in two types of creative processes. Both stem from the personal unconscious, which gives to the creative impulse such imperiousness that "it actually absorbs every human impulse, yoking everything to the service of the work, even at the cost of health and common human happiness."[41] The first type, according to Jung, seems to proceed wholly from the author's conscious efforts to mold his material to specific purposes—"he adds to it and subtracts from it, emphasizing one effect, modifying another, laying on this colour here, that there, with the most careful weighting of their possible effects, and with constant observance of the laws of beautiful form and style.[42] The exercise of his judgment in the selection and weighting of his material gives the artist a sense of complete freedom and self-regulation. This form of art is immediately clear to the reader. It appeals vividly to his "aesthetic sensibility, because it offers . . . an harmonious vision of fulfillment." [43]

The second type of art process subordinates the author to the artwork which flows "more or less spontaneous and perfect from the author's pen." Works of art so created, Jung continues,

positively impose themselves upon the author; his hand is, as it were, seized, and his pen writes things that his mind perceives with amazement. The work brings its own form; . . . his consciousness stands disconcerted and empty before the phenomenon, he is overwhelmed with a flood of thoughts and images which it was never his aim to beget and which his will would never have fashioned. Yet in spite of himself he is forced to recognize that in all this his self is speaking, that his inmost nature is revealing itself. . . .[44]

Because his inmost self is revealing its nature through the primordial image translated into the language of the present, it not only brings about the artist's self-regulation, but "makes it possible for every man to find again the deepest springs of life which would otherwise be closed to him."[45] This kind of art, Jung holds, need not be immediately clear to the reader. The symbols which it uses may even be "expressions of something as yet unknown," forecasts for humanity, whose meaning may remain hidden until "a renewal of the spirit of the time permits us to read and to understand,"[46] and to experience the feeling of harmony and fulfillment which constitutes the aesthetic satisfaction of the reader.

Psychological Theories of "Identification," "Detachment," and "Empathy"

The reaching out of teachers of literature for useful key ideas, not always in the whole context of a psychological system, is indicated in the popularity of the "empathy" of Vernon Lee, and other ideas developed in the past forty years.

The psychological doctrine of "identification" is the German theory of *Einfühlung* first expounded by Theodore Lipps in 1897. The aesthetic experience, according to Lipps, involves "feeling oneself into"—a projection of the self into—objects to the degree that the observer of a work of art, through an internal mimicry, may unconsciously make muscular adjustment to assume a position similar to that of the artistic object.[47] Other schools of psychology recognize this phenomenon, but they do not rest their idea of aesthetic experience in that alone. As Müller-Freienfels indicates, identifying one's self with literary characters in an objective way affords the highest aesthetic experience for the observer. But, he goes on to say, "With the catch-word 'Einfühlung' not much is gained. That is in many cases only one of the words which presents itself at the right time—to cover up the lack of clear factual observation."[48]

A representative spokesman for the theory of psychological "detachment" from the work of art was Hugo Münsterberg, of Harvard University. His concern is with response rather than creation. In 1899 his *Psychology and Life* implied many of the anthropological conclusions that have received explicit attention from literary critics since Taine. "We learn," he says, "to understand how climate and political conditions, technical, material, and social institutions, models and surrounding nature, brought it about that Egypt and China and India, or Greece and Italy and Germany, had just their own development of artistic production."[49] Notwithstanding this close relation between art and culture, the process of critical evaluation remained for Münsterberg one of detachment from the creative experience of the artist. In *The Principles of Art Education* (1905) Münsterberg writes that to evaluate a work of art

> . . . you must separate it from everything else, you must disconnect it from causes and effects, you must bring it before the mind so that nothing else but this one presentation fills the mind, so that there remains no room for anything besides it. If that ever can be reached, the result must be clear: for the object it means complete isolation; for the subject, it means complete repose in the object, and that is complete satisfaction with the object; and that is, finally, merely another name for the enjoyment of beauty.[50]

The extremes of isolationism suggested by Münsterberg are elaborated by Edward Bullough, whose "Psychical Distance" in the *British Journal of Psychology* in 1912 sets a "distance limit" for the subject matter of art, below or above which the experience of the observer is not aesthetic.

Allusions to social institutions of any degree of personal importance—in particular, allusions implying any doubt as to their validity—the questioning of some generally recognized ethical sanctions, references to topical subjects occupying public attention at the moment, . . . are all dangerously near the average limit and may at any time fall below it, arousing, instead of aesthetic appreciation, concrete hostility or mere amusement.[51]

The psychological theory developed by Vernon Lee in *The Beautiful* (1913) holds that one fundamental need is for "shapes" which supply balanced relationships congenial to our modes of motor imagery. The shape of a work of art (and it may have physical, verbal, or intellectual shape) [52] grows from the depths of the artist's "unreasoned, traditional and organized consciousness" as he seeks to express a feeling or elicit a specific emotion.[53] "Aesthetic Empathy" is the experience of the contemplative observer when he perceives the shape projected by the artist. The aesthetic experience is the intellectual-emotional activity of the observer as he takes in or grasps the dramatic relationships which make up the ultimate shape of the work of art.[54] The Statement of the Committee of Twenty-four in 1939, as we shall see (Part II, pages 98-104), speaks of empathy as an integral part of the imaginative experience with literature.

Dynamic Psychology

In Robert Session Woodworth's *Dynamic Psychology* (1918), the treatment of art suggests in various ways Schopenhauer's exposition of the "will-to-live" and Kant's emphasis upon "genius." As a modern "philosophical psychology" it differs from Gestalt in its primary insistence on the will in the individual rather than on the environmental "field" of the individual. The drives toward creative work are solely within the individual, who is interested in certain aspects of his environment because he has a response for them.[55] The genius is an

> . . . individual peculiarly adapted and responsive to certain aspects of reality. Contact with them arouses his responsive activity; he responds to them as naturally as a lion responds to the presence of prey. . . . The genius, having this capacity for dealing with some class of objects present in him to an unusual degree, is able to remain for an exceptionally long time curious about this class of objects and playful with them. The genius's activity, as has often been observed, though strenuous and painstaking, is rather play than work—which means that it is carried forward by its own inherent interest rather than by a drive from beyond itself.[56]

Social Psychology

The field of Social Psychology has contributed more than one approach to the question of aesthetic experience, especially on individual-social relationships, as we shall see in examining the work of McDougall, Folsom, Young, Allport, Dollard, and Lasswell. While the battery of instincts which McDougall listed in 1918 is less in vogue among younger psychologists in the field today than it was, his findings, like those of faculty psychology, tend to be perpetuated among laymen by loose phrasings about the instincts of curiosity, fear, pugnacity, abasement, display, parental care, reproduction, gregariousness, construction, and acquisitiveness, and their accompanying emotions of disgust, wonder, anger, elation, tenderness, etc.[57]

Modern exponents of social psychology who have moved beyond McDougall's theory of instincts nevertheless are still primarily interested in common tendencies of masses and types of individuals, and in "the discovery of general principles, of laws of human behavior."[58] Many show the influence of the Gestalt school (as we shall see in their attention to configurations of environment), and of cultural anthropology.[59] Many show the influence of the clinical methods of Freud and tend more and more to base their theory of art on Freudian aesthetics.[60] Joseph K. Folsom in *Social Psychology* holds that art assumes two major functions, both wish fulfilling. In its *ideal* form, typified by romantic fiction and Venus de Milo, art provides a substitute for more genuine objects with which the observer may identify himself. In its *realistic* form, art supplants normal curiosity, and through arousing latent emotions, acts as a cathartic for them. Folsom writes,

> Ideal art makes the imaginary world seem more real and hence more pleasant; realistic art makes the real world more pleasant. . . . Art provides response and adventure satisfaction to the appreciator, superiority and other kinds of adventure to the creator. . . . The Freudians claim that art is a sublimation of sex. In any case, the universality of art is due to the fact that it represents wish-satisfying social interaction between the appreciator and the creator.[61]

Kimball Young in *Personality and Problems of Adjustment* (1940), recognizes the previous work of Freud but explicitly seeks "to combine the standpoints and data of psychology, social psychology, and cultural anthropology." [62] With Kenneth Burke, Young holds that language is symbolic action through which the self develops in interaction with the culture.[63] Language symbols are "convenient devices by which to take hold of, or to control, the world of situations around us, both social and material." [64] The artist uses symbols to express philosophic interests or to depict his view of human suffering and happiness, or as compensatory "outlet for inhibited and blocked impulses." [65]

According to Young the value of art for the appreciator lies in a similar compensatory satisfaction "for wishful impulses and ideas." [66] Through the novel, motion picture, dance, or music "A person loses himself for an hour or so in the experiences of others or has aroused in him . . . a world of emotions and meanings that bring him intense pleasure or temporary forgetfulness of unsolved problems." [67]

The social consequences of imbalances in personality are brought home in John Dollard's *Frustration and Aggresssion* (1939) and H. D. Lasswell's *World Politics and Personal Insecurity* (1935). Dollard places the responsibility for neuroses upon the culture for failing to provide natural avenues of individual expression for integration with the group.[68] Although he does not treat aesthetic experience in detail, one theory is implied. Following the anthropologist R. S. Rattray, Dollard sees the aesthetic experience as the preception of the planned spectacle which restores balance by purging men of potentially anti-social emotions.

The expression of any form of aggression which is not dangerous to the society should have a cathartic effect and tend to reduce the strength of the instigation to other, more socially dangerous forms of aggression. It will be advantageous to any society, therefore, to permit the expression of certain forms of aggression.[69]

Lasswell shows a similar concern with repressions and aggressions and with the artful use of emotionalized symbols to maintain certain prescribed balances within current totalitarian political designs. "Indeed one of the principal functions of symbols of remote objects, like nations and classes, is to serve as a target for the relief of many of the tensions which might discharge disastrously in face to face relations." [70]

Gordon W. Allport, like Young, and like Muzafer Sherif in *The Psychology of Social Norms* (1936), is concerned with the development of the self in interaction with society. In *Personality, a Psychological Interpretation* (1937) he writes, "Personality is the dynamic organization within the individual of those psychophysical systems that determine his unique adjustments to his environment." [71] Allport is careful to deny the idea of determinism and to stress the responsibility of the individual in his relationships.

Above all, adjustments *must not be considered as merely reactive adaptations such as plants and animals are capable of.* The adjustments of men contain a great amount of spontaneous, creative behaviour toward the environment. Adjustment to the physical world as well as to the imagined and ideal world—both being factors in the "behavioral environment"—involves *mastery* as well as passive adaptation.[72]

The highest degree of self, according to Allport, is the mastery of experience to the point where the individual consciously develops a unifying philosophy "representing to himself his place in the scheme of things." [73] In so far as language is expressive action and linguistic style one of the most complex examples of the "style" of the personality, this is what the author achieves for himself in the delineation of character. "Goethe, too, found essential salvation for Faust in useful work that finally absorbed Faust's restless energies, and provided as nearly as possible the completeness that he sought. . . . Faust, as the prototype of man, found that striving for completeness was not merely an abstract matter. The only practicable condition of unity that he discovered was the seeking of specific objectives related to a life work." [74]

Allport leads us to infer a close relationship between the aesthetic experience of the author and the reader's experience. He notes that the student who reads a piece of literature and writes about his experience with it reveals his knowledge of the book, but that the style of his writing reveals "even more about his mind through which the pages have filtered." [75] Reading and critical evaluation of literature is one avenue to understanding the aesthetics of being one's self.

In these fields of psychological inquiry and in those to follow, we see the merging of various lines of modern and ancient inquiry that becomes most marked in the aesthetic theories of synthesists like Rusu.

Gestalt and Organismic Psychology

The Gestalt school of psychology enjoys at once a largeness, a certain unity, and aesthetic suggestion in its name alone. With its origins in pre-war German psychology, and beyond that in nineteenth century German philosophy, its German name carries overtones that the English terms "pattern" or "configuration" do not have. Gestalt is at once form and shape, mien and bearing, vision and design, all of which embody ideas of human significance, meaning, purpose, and art. As Koffka writes, attacking Watson and the Behaviorists, "A psychology which has no place for the concepts of meaning and value cannot be a complete psychology." [76] Gestalt psychology is a philosophical psychology, concerned at once with the physiological bases of experience and the psychological meaning of groups of experiences as these become contributory and related parts of individual will. In its regard for will, Gestalt psychology finds its roots in one of the main streams of German thought. The student experiences of Köhler, Wertheimer and Koffka reach back into the years of Wundt's influence on German thought through the establishment of the first psychological laboratory.

The Gestalt school brought to prominence three concepts, basic to its position, which demand attention before we turn to its specific implications for aesthetic experience. The first is Köhler's conception of "dynamic interaction" and Lewin's dynamic theory of personality, which indicated the importance of the unity of the organism, and in fact made the matter of configuration their basic tenet.[77] The second is the Law of Prägnanz, introduced by Wertheimer:

that "the psychological organization will always be as 'good' as prevailing conditions allow," [78] and that man always tends to perceive objects in the simplest and most intelligible shapes and patterns possible. This second phenomenon is the result of a still more fundamental drive toward organization in the perception of objects, events, or ideas.

The general aspects of the Law of Prägnanz, without the phraseology of configurationism, were demonstrated by Langfield in 1920 in *The Aesthetic Attitude.* Langfield's conclusions also grew largely from experiments in perception. He shows that a series of dots, equally spaced, tend to be seen in unified groups of five or six, which in turn tend to be perceived in higher orders or groupings, depending upon the experience and training of the individual. Generalizing from this, he writes:

> It has been shown that not only are such units combined into groups, but there is always a tendency to combine groups into higher groups so as to include more and more elements under a single heading until, as in the case of a picture, the parts can be grasped simultaneously—that is, until there is finally one total adjustment of the organism in the perception of the picture.

In extending the application of his theory of the Span of Perception to its functioning as an *economy of effort* for the organism, he continues:

> Generally a name or at least some sort of mental symbol is given both to small units and to those of a higher order, so that the mind may, in future reference, adjust itself instantly to the whole situation through the medium of the symbol instead of having to recall all the original process of adjustment, in order to have again the finished perception and the accompanying pleasure. In literary productions this mechanism is especially obvious. Here we find the letters grouped into words, and these into sentences, paragraphs, chapters, etc., until there is the finished unit of the whole book. To this final result one generally attaches some mental symbol of one's own individual choice, if the book has been successful as a work of art, and has as a finished product offered such total unity. This symbol then acts as a cue for the renewal of that final more or less complete adjustment which one has had at the

end of the book, and which underlies what we consider the general impression. . . . That such a process is economical is obvious. It is the principle that one finds not only in aesthetic reactions but in all intellectual processes; otherwise it would be impossible for the organism to develop beyond a certain stage, for its mass of past experience, which must be used for future progress, would become overwhelming. The aesthetic unity, therefore, becomes the model for our general activity.

From the foregoing it follows that the mind becomes more highly organized and action becomes more completely systemized the more fully our appreciation of beauty is developed. The aesthetic enjoyment, then, instead of being a mere indulgence, is seen to be the most broadly useful and far-reaching of all our activities.[79]

Neither Langfeld's Law of Economy of Effort nor the Law of Prägnanz is specifically invoked by spokesmen for the Humanities, but the process of symbolization which Langfeld sets forth is becoming more and more explicit—as for instance in Kenneth Burke's studies in Coleridge, briefly suggested in *The Philosophy of Literary Form*.[80] The closeness of Langfeld's theory to the psychology of language subsequently discussed under anthropology also is notable.

The third concept developed by Gestalt psychologists, which has significant implications for aesthetic experience, is that of the "field." Briefly, the "field" is the biographical as well as the geographical environment from which an individual observes a work of art at any given moment. The work itself may remain a constant,[81] but no individual approaches it in identical attitudes on successive occasions. The fund of knowledge and personal memories he musters, the imaginative sympathy with which he identifies himself with the artist or the work of art are highly individual matters, and the patterning of values perceived must be an individual process. The aesthetic experience of the observer must then be a singularly individual experience—although common funds of knowledge and experience accumulated in language may make it communicable.[82]

Some phases of the Gestalt concept of aesthetic experience have been carried into the field of literature by Norman R. F. Maier and H. Willard Reninger, in *A Psychological Approach to Literary Criticism* (1933). These psychologists point to the inception of a work of art as similar to creative thinking or problem solving in any field of inquiry. The author has a problem, perhaps only vaguely identifiable. Before the solution of his problem his mind is in a state of confusion. Suddenly the funded experience of the past is reorganized to meet the hitherto puzzling situation. "A new and different organization of elements replaces the former organizations. There is no conscious state between them. Thus the solution does not gradually develop from a nucleus, but appears as a complete unified organization." [83] This sudden reorganization is unpredictable. Frequently, because man thinks in symbols, the new configuration takes the form of a symbol. "The artist may suddenly see a storm as a struggle of the gods, or as movement and becoming, or as the chaos of life—all depending on the direction he has assumed, that is, the ways his feelings about things are running, or the mood he is in." [84]

The writer's new configuration is his response to a situation, and his language must convey in its direction and proportional emphasis something of the configuration itself. An important part of the aesthetic experience of the reader is his perceiving the values of the configuration.[85]

The concern for pattern in literature that Maier and Reninger demonstrate is evident also in R. M. Ogden's *The Psychology of Art* (1938). While Ogden states that "both biology and psychology lend support to the view that the aesthetic is a feeling for right adjustments as opposed to faulty . . . [and that] a work of art is a thing of beauty when it achieves a state of perfection that rewards the observer by its uniqueness, completeness, and finality," [86] he supports his ideas from the philosophic theory of Thomas Aquinas[87] and A. C. Bradley,[88] rather than by experimentation. Ogden also treats the aesthetic as a kind of problem-solving, indicating that the solution must not be so easy as to cloy on the reader. This aspect of his position finds a more positive presentation in "The Aesthetic Experience: A Psychological Description" by Kate Hevner in *The Psychological Review*. "The aesthetic moment is the realization of the felt want completely fulfilled. The deeper the want, the harder the struggle to fulfill it, the more mental and bodily activity involved, the greater the satisfaction." [89]

Other comparable experimental approaches to aesthetics have been carried on both here and abroad. The work of Viktor Löwenfeld[90] in Vienna is cognate with the work of Norman C. Meier in the Iowa State University laboratory where tests are carried on in the spirit of Fechner's earlier studies in the exact measurement of sensation. Case studies under Meier's direction of the creative paintings of children point to the relationship of age, intelligence, social background, and the complexity of art creations. They show that children even of pre-school age demonstrate a discrimination in compositional balance. The early appearance of a preference for bilateral balance as seen in the right-left symmetry of man's form, or the form of trees, radial balance as seen in flowers, starfish, and snow crystals, and the vertical balance of mountains or upright structures suggests a natural preference for balance over unbalance in tri-dimensional design.[91]

Further experimental studies under the direction of Meier show a relationship to anthropological inquiries. They indicate the degree to which subject matter in creative work lies within the previous experience of the creator whether through his home and community environment or travel, or through books, magazines, and pictures. Observation shows that the aesthetic tendency to draw numerous aspects of experience into one artistic composition varies among individuals. Gifted individuals tend to be more keenly aware of their surroundings, and more frequently to reach a higher compositional level than that achieved by less gifted individuals.[92]

Related investigation in the nature of *Aesthetic Measure*[93] is also being forwarded in research laboratories at Harvard University under George D. Birkhoff. Postulating that the quality of aesthetic perception is related to the individual's ability to establish valid connections, Birkhoff has sought to measure this quality by experimentation with the relationship of order to complexity in configurational observation. Aesthetic measure, M, is to be found in the formula $\frac{O}{C}$, where O is order of presentation of constituent parts, and C is the complexity of the finally perceived configuration.[94]

Newer Syntheses

As we have indicated earlier, numerous laymen and professional psychologists have been moving toward points of convergence in these schools of psychology, finding in their common elements valuable matters for inquiry in many fields. One fundamental point of convergence which is pertinent to modern ideas of aesthetic experience is recognition of the human *self*.

The second point of convergence among schools of psychology is upon the subconscious. The functioning of subconscious mental activity is differently ascribed, to be sure, but the phenomenon is recognized as an element of personality or self.

The third respect in which psychologies are in accord with each other and also with anthropology, is in recognizing the biological impulse toward perpetuation of the race through reproduction, and toward the preservation or conservation of the individual of the species.

A sense of this unity, apparently, provides a basis for the various efforts toward synthesis of biological, anthropological, and psychological research in the interest of a coherent idea of aesthetic experience. Such an effort among psychologically minded critics of literature is apparent in Louise Rosenblatt's *Literature as Exploration,* and in comments on literature by Lewis Mumford and others. The work of the American biologist, Jennings, points toward it, particularly in *Prometheus* (1925) and *The Biological Basis of Human Nature* (1930)—both of which are part of the context from which John Frederick Dashiell writes of "Some Rapprochements in Contemporary Psychology."[95] The most striking expressions of such synthesis have come from Europeans who have derived their basic ideas from Americans. Müller-Freienfels in Germany, basing his early work on the biological data laid by William James, is one notable early example. M. Charles Lalo, Henri Delacroix, and Liviu

Rusu in France stem from Jennings. Among their syntheses, that of Rusu is most striking—*Essai sur la création artistique comme révélation du sense de l'existence*, (1935). The aesthetic theory which we present in the following pages under topical headings is a summation of Rusu's *Essai*, with pertinent extensions from and comparisons with the other workers in this field.

Natural bases of artistic creation.—Rusu denies any philosophical a priori assumptions or conclusions. He bases his fundamental concepts of artistic activity on the definitive researches of Jennings. As summarized by Rusu these indicate: (1) The movement of any part of an animal is accompanied by a corresponding readjustment of every other part—no change takes place which is not related to the entire organism; (2) Every exterior movement of an animal is the *expression* of inner tensions aroused by hunger or discomfort; release of both of these tensions is essential for conservation of the individual; (3) Every such expression is *not* reaction *against* factors threatening existence—it is an action directed *toward* establishment of a new equilibrium; (4) The newly achieved equilibrium is never the same as the previous one, for the readjustment has added to the animal's fund of experience. The more complex the organism, the more complex is the expression toward equilibrium. The highest degree of biological complexity is present in man, where it is matched by the most complex form of expression, language.[96]

Artistic expression, peculiar to man, arises from the disequilibrium of self, man's singular possession, as it struggles to maintain or re-establish its individuality by willfully constraining otherwise dominant animal tendencies.[97] Anticipating this, Müller-Freienfels had indicated in 1912 that the constraint may be so marked that even the usually dominant tendency toward self-preservation in the biological sense is subordinated:

Our total "I" which includes everything which we love, hope, and believe is much more inclusive than the physical existence. It embraces elements which in importance for the consciousness of the individual far outweigh the physical life, and it follows from these elements that we often do things which directly endanger our physical life. A scholar unhesitatingly endangers his life just to fill in a gap in his and the universal wisdom.[98]

Creative expression, according to Rusu, does not represent a specialized extension of any instinctive tendency (play, sex, construction, etc.) but a dynamic activity, in which the whole organism engages in the conflict of the spirit [99]—a conflict which could be resolved only in the creative effort [100] through which the personality affirms its self.[101]

The creative process.—The creative process involves four stages: (1) the phase of the unconscious, the preparatory phase in which the subconscious mind is sowed deep with certain tendencies; (2) the phase of inspiration; (3) the phase of elaboration; (4) the phase of execution.[102]

(1) The phase of the unconscious: The unconscious may be divided into the *innate* and the *acquired*. The innate is the source of psychic tendencies. It comprises the impressions made upon an individual which are never actually subject to conscious control. The greater their range and depth, the more individual the person becomes. Innate qualities like intellectual capacity, imagination, sympathy, and intuition determine the extent to which the personality can identify itself with other aspects of life. The "acquired" is made up of the knowledge gleaned from conscious participation in the culture.[103] "Acquired" knowledge, as soon as it loses its immediacy, sinks into the unconscious to form the fund of experience from which the artist must necessarily draw much of his material. By some this might be called intuition or "apperceptive mass."

Interaction of innate and acquired experience is the spur to creation. From his own imaginative sympathy the artist sees in his culture the yet unrealized potentialities for human advancement.[104] The artist is disturbed as he compares his vision of the possible with what he sees about him. To preserve his self from dissipation in the face of the chaos he experiences, he seeks support in concrete external form. He does not find such support already prepared. Two courses of action are open to him. He may follow the path of least resistance

—an ever-present egocentric tendency to draw the self into a protective shell. This is the way of inertia; it is the renunciation of spiritual life.[105] An alternate course is to create the form which will exteriorize his values. While he creates a design in which the chaotic oppositions are reconciled, the expressive, centrifugal tendency must wage unequal war with the egocentric one. This internal conflict is severe. It involves profound emotional tension, physical and spiritual suffering, and hard intellectual effort. It involves the whole organism. The self is not really born until the expression is complete. Not to complete it is ruinous. The difficulty and pain involved in disciplining the self which is maturing during the process of creation gives value to the work of art. For the artist, it affirms the presence of self. But this self is not a static entity. The self is a continuous creative synthesis. When the unity of self is menaced and then affirmed through exteriorizing its values in a work of art, the new unity is superior to the old. The creative process has consolidated the experienced world, and the semblance of a higher spirituality is seen in the artist. This ever more inclusive, singularly human drive for synthesis appears to Rusu to be dominant in modern research in form, wholes, structures, and configurations.[106]

There are implications for human liberty. In each phase of the creative process, as the envisioned order takes increasingly clear form under the impulsion of human will, the artist feels an increasing sense of freedom for self-direction.[107] The gradual process of affirmation of self constitutes the aesthetic experience of the artist.

(2) *The phase of inspiration:* The individual is not always certain of the cause of his emotional disturbance. The internal conflict between the centrifugal and egocentric tendencies can be resolved only as the hitherto nebulous reason for the felt disturbance is brought into sharp focus, or, as Rusu suggests, rises to consciousness.[108] The rise to consciousness is the dynamic result of intense inner agitation. It occurs when an image or series of images appears to clarify the source of disturbance. "This clarification, this rise to consciousness of a conflict with the aid of an image, or a series of images, is what is generally called inspiration." [109] Inspiration impels the individual,

with heightened inner tension, toward the continued search for order.

Inspiration does not appear always in the same guise. Individual differences among artists reveal at least two general types of inspiration. One is "intuitive," the other "reflective." Intuitive inspiration is the more spectacular, for in it the multitude of inner experiences of the artist are elaborated without his consciousness or will.[110] Reflective inspiration, on the other hand, is the result of intense studious effort. Müller-Freienfels on the same point offers illustrative example from the correspondence of Goethe and Schiller. Schiller: "How much we are after all, despite our boasted independence, bound to the forces of nature! On this I have already brooded fruitlessly for five weeks. That was released within me in three days as though by a sunbeam. To be sure, my previous steadfastness may have prepared me. . . ." Goethe: "We can do nothing but build the woodpile, and dry it out properly; it bursts into flame at its own time, and we are astonished by it ourselves."[111]

In either type of inspiration, as Rusu sees it, the image which clarifies the conflict is an "incarnation of the specific atmosphere which torments the soul of the artist and it is in the quality (role) of a symbol of that atmosphere . . ."[112] that it has meaning. Comparably, interrupting Rusu momentarily, it is instructive to find Stefan Zweig, modern self-conscious author, commenting on his experience in creating the drama, *Jeremiah,* as his personal response to the chaos of Europe in 1917:

In such moments, when the external course of fate is beyond one's control, the writer's only salvation will always lie in giving form to his experience. I therefore sought for a symbol to express these problems: of solitude in the midst of hypnotized masses, of tragic forebodings and painful presentiments.[113]

At the moment of inspiration, according to Rusu, "a meaning conceived in the most intimate recesses of the soul rises to consciousness. Through this moment, the internal life of the artist begins to assume a more distinct form, his *chaos* tends to become a *cosmos* and he will henceforth oppose himself more vigorously to the exterior world."[114] He aspires toward a life determined by himself rather than to conformity with the outside world.[115]

The initial image which appears to the artist, the "idée mère" which becomes the focal point for the organization of his expression, is not different for the several arts. The distinction among the arts lies only in the medium used. The essential factor for all creative work is the mental attitude, the feeling within the symbol around which the orderly pattern is established. The same emotion may prompt a symphony, a poem, or a pictorial composition. This mental attitude, called inspiration, searches for harmonious expression charged with meaning. The great majority of artists find only one medium of expression, but to some artists symbols suggest themselves in several media.[116]

(3) The phase of elaboration: The dynamism of inspiration erases any real distinction between the phase of inspiration and that of elaboration, for the tension created is a continuous impulsion toward clarity and a sense of mastery. In addition to the form which the image assumes, it embodies also a *sens* or meaning which may be attached to it at any time because of its context.[117] "*When one speaks of the creative imagination, it must not be attached only to the fact that, in the consciousness of the artist appears these images, but above all to the fact that these images are the symbol of a meaning.*"[118]

The meaning of any image depends on the new synthesis of experience which the artist achieves as his imagination delves into the fund of the "unconscious acquired" to elaborate and fill out the designs of the image. The work of art is therefore distinctly not new; it is a fresh design of acquired experience.[119] At this stage, more particularly than at any other in the creative process, the thinking of genius is to be distinguished from the thinking of the average individual. On this point Müller-Freienfels draws attention to a fact subsequently accented by Gestalt psychologists that we all experience moments when previously unassociated ideas or events suddenly assume a new significance through a new relationship in our minds.

For genius, the relationships of ideas and events are farther reaching, more unusual, broader in their deviation from conventional ones. More alert senses and a more retentive memory lead to the more complex syntheses of genius,[120] for the scientist and original religious thinker no less than for the artist.[121]

(4) The phase of execution: The "symbol of meaning," or the artistic idea, imaginatively elaborated from the artist's background, is not yet a work of art until it is objectified in material form—a significant difference from the earlier ideas of St. Thomas and Croce, for instance, which make the execution only incidental. The execution, as both Rusu and Müller-Freienfels agree, is a prolongation of the original conception.[122] The generative idea assumes ultimate aesthetic value only through the artist's struggle to wrest from his particular medium a form which realizes the values of his artistic idea.[123]

The process which started with a threat to the integrity of the artist's self, ends with affirmation of that self. We must remember, however, that at any stage of the tedious creation, amid intense physical and spiritual agony, the artist might have abandoned his quest for spiritual security. The creative process is a perpetual state of inner conflict. Its completion is possible only by the stern invocation of will. Without conflict and will,

> ... the keenest desire may never lead to a realization of a work of art. ... He [the artist] wills a crystallization, indifferent to the nature of the excitation which has provoked the interior chaos. The work of art is then the work of the *will*. By the creative act the artist affirms his will to surmount the primitive aspects of his nature. The greater the effort, the more profoundly the self feels consolidated and lifted up.[124]

By the same token, the more intense his creative effort, the more aware he is of his ability to determine the course of his own action. The more intense his effort, the more intense the sense of liberty that is born then.[125]

The artist who thus affirms the integrity of self is able to do so only through exercising judgment in the use of materials and tools of human experience accumulated through countless similar efforts.

There must take place, as Müller-Freienfels indicates, "a testing, discarding, and selecting, which means a quite definite organization of the image-material and moreover, an organization achieved from a definite point of view."[126] The fact that the self-preserving selection and organization of materials must be made from the collective elements in the artist's society gives the work of art a vital cultural significance, says Rusu. Because the creative process arises from confusion in the most profound recesses of the soul it is evident that "the more profoundly the artist penetrates his interior life, the more he approaches the depth where his individuality is allied with other individualities."[127] The symbol with an originally private meaning now establishes a common base for artist and audience. And where the new work of art represents the highest degree of individuality, it also expresses the common—and the culture has its clearest example of "unity in diversity" fundamental to democratic life.[128]

Rusu does not extend his idea of the aesthetic experience beyond the creative process. He does say, however, that the study of the creative process is valuable only in so far as it aids in the understanding of a work of art. It is purely psychological and not aesthetic unless it contributes to the establishment of aesthetic criteria.[129]

The critical process.—Müller-Freienfels had taken up the question of the critical process in this same spirit in 1912. He implies in frequent mention of the artist's conscious striving for aesthetic effect[130] that the aesthetic experience is not complete until a reader has been carried through a somewhat similar process. The individual who achieves the perspective of the artist, and sees how the artist has designed an imaginative synthesis of irreconcilable opposites is the reader to whom the work reveals its highest qualities—and the one who achieves the highest degree of affirmation of self.[131]

The intercommunication between artist and reader on any of these levels of interpretation, according to Müller-Freienfels, has a biological base in the sensory experiences which are communicable through language. Through the sound-qualities alone of certain letters of the alphabet, thought, feeling, and meaning are created—an idea receiving attention from thoughtful critics like Kenneth Burke in

The Philosophy of Literary Form.[132] Thus the lower vowels "o" and "u" have a feeling value opposite to "e" and "i," just as, analogically, musical tones of lower register with a broader, thicker value have a darker, thicker color which is intensified through outer associations but which can not be made explicit.[133] The uses of these vowels, as well as the consciously planned spacing of certain consonants like "r" and "l" are closely related to rhythm and to the architecture of literary form. Sensory images stimulating imaginative re-creation of sight, sound, smell, taste, or touch, may also enliven the inner experience of the reader. This places a premium on concrete imagery, especially for our time, for the majority of people seem "unable to think abstractly and a thought rarely becomes a reality."[134]

Sensory impressions have literary value as they help the reader interpret the ideas and values of human characters created by the artist's design. The design, consciously shaped by the author who knows the means for producing desired effects, is achieved through rhythm, repetition, emphasis, and direction which stimulate the imagination of the reader.[135]

Müller-Freienfels goes beyond this concern with technical qualities of language, and emphasizes the "values" with which Gestalt psychologists, as we have seen, are also concerned. Value, he says, must be measured pragmatically on standards relative to the heightening and intensification of the singularly human aspects of life—the spiritualizing, "life-furthering" effects upon the individual self, and with regard to the reconciliation of "inner-individual" and "over-individual" conflicts contributing the largest sum of "goods" to human life.[136] Phrased differently, value is relative to the balance achieved between individual privilege and social responsibility, an increasingly pertinent concern in modern world society, where, as we shall hear from anthropologists and philosophers, individuality must be developed through increasingly communal activities.

To make this kind of evaluation of values the critic must distinguish the literary genres—epic, lyric, dramatic—by their characteristic "feeling tones." He must see these forms as symbols of phases of cultural advance and the development of individuality. In ancient Hellenic and Germanic cultures. Müller-Freienfels shows that "we must not place the great epics with which our literary histories begin at the beginning of the development. They are not at all an early art in the sense of primitiveness, but stand at the end of long developments that have disappeared in the darkness of sunken centuries. They are peaks, not roots." [137] They are peaks of synthesis for multitudes of primitive balladesque lyrics whose central feeling tone is a passionately concise "we-ness" of the tribal group.[138] The heroic epic which follows this personalized group loyalty is itself an evolutionary type crystallized into its present shape when social conditions made written form more appropriate than oral presentation. The feeling tone peculiar to epic statement is breadth of group values narrated with a "comfortable tarrying," a leisurely reminiscence. Epic statement is not confined to the specific form we know in Homer and the Nibelungenlied. As soon as changing sociological conditions detracted from the aesthetic effect of the older heroic epic—"as soon as the narrative became an offering expanded for individual readers in print, it sought for itself at once another circle of material and another form without being for that reason unepic. If we do not look upon the concept of epic as a one-sided abstraction, if we understand the concept of epic as a form of narrative which has proved itself impressive on the grounds of its psychological effect, then the modern prose novel is just as epic as the old heroic epic." [139]

The third significant literary form is drama, where the configuration of composition, stage technique, and acting produces the most forceful aesthetic effect through the intensified conflict of human values. Like the other literary forms, the drama is also evolutionary with roots paralleling in time and spirit the epic form, but coming to full flower within a specific culture under conditions favorable to the gathering of large groups of people in specific places.[140]

There are implications in this psychological-anthropological aesthetic for the demarcation of cycles of culture. Müller-Freienfels' copious exemplification from primitive and modern literary forms tends to organize Western Culture into two broad cycles, Hellenic and Modern. Although this idea does not become explicit, analogical thinking so characteristic of both Rusu and Müller-Freienfels may subsequently provide explicit extensions applicable in our study of World Literature as one of the Humanities.

The tendency of both of these psychologists, Rusu and Müller-Freienfels, to rely upon a logic of close analogy rather than of syllogism is also pertinent to our study of spokesmenship for the Humanities. It is in harmony with I. A. Richards' studies of the constantly metaphorical character of language (and presumably of thought), and with an increasingly current use of symbolic reasoning that may have much to do with the advance of ideas of aesthetic formulation.

From this chapter and the next we shall readily see how the largeness of new ideas of aesthetic experience matches the largeness of the new Humanities and World Literature programs—and how their union is bringing the aesthetic resolution of human values more and more to the fore as the unifying factor in such programs.

3. IDEAS FROM ANTHROPOLOGY: AESTHETIC EXPERIENCE AND THE CULTURE

While anthropologists have not taken the study of aesthetic experience as one of their chief concerns,[1] they have been very influential, directly and indirectly, in modern thinking on the subject, particularly through their emphasis on symbols of culture, culture patterns, and culture epochs—all important in the aesthetic syntheses of World Literature and Humanities courses. As Max Lerner states in one of several articles in *The Encyclopaedia of Social Sciences* dealing in teachers' terms with the individual-social relationships, "The functionalist standpoint as developed in anthropology is illuminating when applied to the setting of literature in a culture." [2] What Edward Sapir, in the May, 1937, *American Journal of Sociology*, terms "the symbolic role of words in the development of personality and the continuation of mutually beneficial 'interpersonal' relations"[3] is a primary concern of anthropologists and philosophers alike. Ideas of symbols of culture have assumed more and more prominence through the work of such historians, sociologists, and critics as Beard, Toynbee, Sorokin, and Mumford. Ideas of "types of literature" as symbols of culture and culture epochs have come with increasing sharpness through such works as R. R. Marett's *Anthropology and the Classics* (1908) and "Anthropology" in *The Encyclopaedia Britannica* (1929), Franz Boas' *Primitive Art* (1927) and *Race, Language, and Culture* (1940), and H. M. and N. K. Chadwick's *The Growth of Literature* (1932-1940). These anthropological ways of thinking are becoming more and more explicit for teachers of literature generally as we see in the orienting "story" which precedes selections from various literary periods in E. A. Cross's *World Literature,* and in Louise Rosenblatt's extended discussion of anthropological concepts for teachers of literature in *Literature as Exploration.* And the symbol of culture is becoming a more and more important factor in the *aesthetic-values equation* in modern Humanities courses. The anthropologist, synthesizing many arts and sciences, serves as a kind of mediator among the historical, philosophical, and artistic concerns. All can meet on *language, symbols,* and *values.* As Charles W. Morris, considering a linguistic base for science, notes in "Foundations of the Theory of Signs," "The concept of sign may prove to be of importance in the unification of the social, psychological, and humanistic sciences in so far as these are distinguished from the physical and biological sciences."[4]

In our consideration of the relation of anthropology to modern ideas of aesthetic experience and the formulation of Humanities and World Literature courses, we shall look first at the findings of physical anthropologists upon biological characteristics giving rise to creative abilities, and second, at the contributions of cultural anthropologists to our understanding of the integral relationship of *language, symbols of culture,* and *values.*

Physical Anthropology.—Ralph Linton writes in "The Present Status of Anthropology" in *Science* for March, 1938, that "the main contribution of physical anthropology to date has been to establish man firmly in his place among other mammals, indicate the probable line of his evolution, and, through classification, to bring some order into the confused field of his variations."[5] In this essentially aesthetic quest for order, physical anthropologists have considered the nature of the aesthetic impulse itself. They have sought the base of creative activity in some specific physical impulse.

Nineteenth century evolutionary scientists, notably Darwin and Spencer, attributed art origins to a kind of animal display on the part of the male to attract a mate. Commenting on these early speculations in *The Origins of Art* (1900), Yrjo Hirn says: "But even where there is no competition between rivals, sexual emotions may still find an artistic expression. In short, sexual selection is a cause of erotic art, but it is not the only cause."[6]

A kindred theory still widely held finds the origin of art in a separate instinct of play. As early as 1795 Friedrich Schiller propounded this theory of the art impulse. As Melvin Rader notes in *A Modern Book of Aesthetics*,[7] Schiller saw in the universality of play, and in the disinterested participation by which it is characterized, qualities analogous to the universality of art and the impersonal character of artistic creation and enjoyment. Art for him was the spontaneous though controlled play of the imagination; this subjection of the imaginative "overflowing life" to intellectual restraint enlisted the energies of the whole organism.

In 1901, Konrad Lange and Karl Groos had elaborated upon this general theory.[8] Art and play alike were seen to spring from the need for fuller exercise of impulses and instincts. Both were escapes from the oppressions of reality and boredom into an ideal world. More recently, Ralph Linton has written in *The Study of Man* (1936) of the "inner drive" through which man enjoys playing with both his mind and his muscles.

He takes delight in setting and solving for himself new problems of creation. The thinker derives pleasure from speculating about all sorts of things which are of no practical importance, while the individuals who lack the ability to create with either hand or mind are alert to learn new

IDEAS FROM ANTHROPOLOGY 59

things. It seems probable that the human capacity for being bored, rather than man's social or natural needs, lies at the root of man's cultural advance.[9]

From a psychological-anthropological point of view, Herbert Read in *Art and Society* (1937) considers a fundamental impulse which makes itself evident in what he calls *hedonistic, purposive,* and *expressive* action.

These three aspects of art, which we can already discern as the primitive stage of man's development, remain the general types throughout the history of human society. Man emerges from the chaotic darkness of prehistory; his consciousness evolves out of fear and loneliness and desire; he forms tribes and societies and adopts various modes of economic production, and in the process his soul is swept by those alternations of superstition and joy, of love and hate, of intellectual confidence and humble faith, which transform his life, making and unmaking dynasties and nations and civilizations. But throughout all this welter of forces and contradiction of aims the aesthetic impulse, like the sexual impulse, is essentially constant.[10]

This constant impulse, W. I. Thomas states in "The Comparative Study of Cultures" in *The American Journal of Sociology* for September, 1936, is—like intellectual abilities, powers of will and logical thought, and capacities for emotional reaction—not inherently different for different peoples.[11] Frederick Osborn pursues the same point in *Scientific Monthly* for November, 1939.

Many of the qualities commonly spoken of as 'racial characteristics' are now known to be matters of social rather than genetic inheritance.[12]

Since races possess generally equivalent capacities, intellectual ability must be gauged in terms of reactions which a given group is normally called upon to make in its own culture pattern. And capacities for emotional reaction must be viewed in the light of the stimuli to which persons are susceptible as individual members of a particular cultural background.[13] Within each culture pattern, Read points out, art stems from an insistent quest for form and meaning achieved through the

Capacity to create a synthetic and self-consistent world: a world which is neither the world of practical needs and desires, nor the world of dreams and fantasy, but a world compounded of these contradictions: a convincing representation of the totality of experience.[14]

Cultural Anthropology

Cultural anthropology, according to Malinowski in *The Encyclopaedia of Social Sciences* (1937) concerns itself with the totality of culture—its material artifacts, its funds of knowledge and custom by which systems of moral, spiritual, and economic values coordinate human communities, and its language, the reservoir of these symbols and values which provides a continuity to human experience and permits the single personality to integrate himself with the larger groups of individuals who comprise his culture.[15]

Anthropology has dealt with its findings in two different methods in the past half century, *evolutionary* and *diffusionist,* and is now perfecting a third, the *functional* approach. "The *evolutionary* school," Malinowski states, "has regarded the growth of culture as a series of spontaneous metamorphoses proceeding according to definite laws and producing a fixed sequence of successive stages."[16] Contemporaneous with Darwinian natural science, "the method of evolutionary anthropology was based primarily on the concept of survival,"[17] and attempted to reduce the major lines of cultural development to laws everywhere applicable.[18]

The method of the historical or *diffusionist* approach to anthropology "consists in a careful mapping out of cultural similarities over large portions of the globe and in speculative reconstructions as to how the similar units of culture have wandered from one place to another."[19] The diffusionists hold that if two groups of people in widely separated parts of the globe are found to possess an identity of development, this similarity "must always be due to migration and diffusion."[20] This point of view stresses cultural inventions by specific persons and peoples.[21]

The *functionalist* approach to anthropology, says Malinowski, looks upon culture as "the body of commodities and instruments as well as of customs and bodily or mental habits which work directly or indirectly for the satisfaction of human needs. . . . The primary concern of functional anthropology is with the function of institutions, customs, implements, and ideas" according to "laws [that] are to be found in the function of the real elements of culture."[22] This relativistic point of view brings the anthropologist to psychological consideration of the individual as the medium of all society, the innovator of new materials, and the originator of new values and customs. It directs attention to language and literary symbols of culture as aesthetic harmonizations of individual-social relationships, for it is only in language and literature that these become clear. Language is the central nervous system of human communities.

Anthropology and language.—Consideration of language, symbols, and values cannot be carried on in tight compartments, as we see in George Herzog's exemplification of anthropological method in evaluating symbols of culture within literary patterns in his study, *Jabo Proverbs from Liberia* (1936).[23] Herzog describes his entering a community with no predisposition toward finding certain elements or characteristics of language present. In the rapid acquisition of a working knowledge of the language of the Jabo people, he found one characteristic of their language, the use of proverbs, significant. During the first few days, as this became apparent, he made a systematic effort to record as many as possible of these pithy sayings, together with the situation in which they occurred. During the remaining part of nine months' participation in community activities and study of interrelationships of various aspects of the community life, this list of proverbs and contexts was added to as occasion arose. One hundred and thirty proverbs were recorded in all, as well as masses of pertinent data.

Subsequent sorting of all the materials accumulated gave Herzog a basis for generalization on the significance of the proverb as a form of expression in Jabo life. He found that the proverb is the primary medium for legal proceedings; it is the accepted means of social participation, either as "advice, instruction, or as a warning—always to prevent or lessen friction."[24]

Herzog discovered that the Jabo proverbs are couched in language possessing a distinct symmetry and rhythmical structure. Forms of the proverbs vary in accordance with the use to which they are put. They are frequently grouped into new patterns or used cumulatively for emphasis. The informality of the use of some proverbs reveals a close parallel with the flexibility of the social and legal organization of the community; it reveals also that proverbs are the means by which social solidarity is insured, and the prerogatives of the home and the rights of seniority enforced. The use of "we" for approved behavior and "one" for inacceptable conduct, and the fact that the negative preposition, *nē,* covers both "does not" and "cannot" suggests the moral and ethical codes expressed in the proverbs. Finally, the use of proverbs is the means by which the individual integrates himself in the society, for the Jabo people are conscious of a distinction between ordinary statements of fact and proverb analogy.[25] Ability to use proverbs provides the scale on which the individual is rated socially, intellectually, and personally. Respect for seniority, upheld by proverbs and proverb-quoting ability, tends to restrict wide diffusion of values from foreign influences.

Instead, then, of saying merely that proverbs are used symbolically in Jabo language, Herzog asserts:

> Proverbs and related forms function very powerfully in Africa in describing, characterizing, evaluating persons, events, phenomena, situations. The proverbs more than any of the other categories of formalized expression serve to transform particular experience into terms of previous, controlled experience, or, in law and ethics, of traditional observance. They are almost the exclusive, certainly the most important, verbal instrument for minimizing friction and effecting adjustment, legal, social, or intellectual. Far from being the dead cliches which proverbs are for us, they form a vital and potent element of the culture they interpret.[26]

Questions of language and personality, which are important in ideas of aesthetic experience, have been variously treated from the philosophical-anthropological standpoint by Sapir, Mead, Richards, and others. We find explicit concern for the function of language in the development of individuality in Sapir's "Language" in *The Encyclopaedia of Social Sciences*:

In spite of the fact that language acts as a socializing and uniformizing force it is at the same time the most potent single known factor for the growth of individuality. The fundamental quality of one's voice, the phonetic patterns of speech, the speed and relative smoothness of articulation, the length and build of the sentences, the character and range of the vocabulary, the stylistic consistency of the words used, the readiness with which words respond to the requirement of the social environment, in particular the suitability of one's language habits to the language habits of the person addressed—all these are so many indicators of personality.[27]

Previously in *Language* (1921) Sapir had written that he was "strongly of the opinion that the feeling entertained by so many that they can think, or even reason, without language, is an illusion."[28]

Also questioning the idea that people build up arguments in their minds and then put them into words for communication to others, George Herbert Mead, from the philosopher's standpoint, writes in *Mind, Self, and Society*, "Actually, our thinking always takes place by means of some sort of symbols."[29] And the process of thought is a process of self-communication, for

Thinking always implies a symbol which will call out the same response in another that it calls out in the thinker. . . . A person who is saying something is saying to himself what he says to others; otherwise he does not know what he is talking about.[30]

Similarly, according to I. A. Richards, psychologist-semanticist, language is the primary means by which individuals solve problems confronting them. "Every problem is new to the mind which first meets it and it is baffling until he can recognize in it something which he has met and dealt with already."[31] For Richards, facility with language rather than dependence upon ready-made formulae for choosing one's values provides the essential "difference between the mind which can clear itself by thought and the mind which remains bewildered. . . ."[32] Further, according to Mead, through the language symbol the most intricate value of all develops—recognition and understanding of the self.[33]

Anthropology and symbols of culture.—Among functional anthropologists the belief is fairly general, paralleling Langfield's application of the Law of Prägnanz, that language is the fundamental manifestation of man's aesthetic impulse to achieve form and design in experience. Sapir holds language to be the most pervasive evidence of the aesthetic impulse. Language is "the slowly evolved product of a peculiar technique or tendency which may be called the symbolic one, and to see the relatively meaningless or incomplete part as a sign for the whole."[34]

Ralph Linton recognizes this function of language when he writes that language does not express the totality of a given sensory experience, but selects certain parts which become symbolic of the whole.[35] So fundamental to human living is this symbolic process that it has been studied in other fields of knowledge concerned with individual-social relationships. E. E. Eubank, sociologist, describes the development of human understanding from the formulation of progressively wider generalizations or *concepts* arising out of the association and interpretation of separate sensory impressions called *percepts*.[36] As James has put it for the philosopher-psychologist, through the symbolic process the mass of *"particular material things present to sense"*[37] is enormously simplified. "Only so," writes Sapir in *Language,* "is communication possible, for the single experience lodges in an individual consciousness and is, strictly speaking, incommunicable. To be communicated it needs to be referred to a class which is tacitly accepted by the community as an identity."[38] According to Sapir in "Time Perspective in Aboriginal American Culture, a Study in Method" (and as we have already seen in Herzog's study), "language is not a disconnected complex apart from culture but . . . an important part of the culture of a particular people living at a definite time and place."[39]

The psychological aesthetic of Rusu, as we have seen, indicates that an emotional-intellectual attitude toward some phase of culture lies at the base of the creative process, and that the emotional tension is released only when the artist has clarified for himself the pattern of values he holds. Selection and elaboration of an image embodying his emotion eventuates in a symbol of some phase of the culture in which he lives. The anthropologist recognizes the symbol of culture in many uses of language symbols, from the "psychological-tone" of individual words[40] to phrases, proverbs, and major works of literary art. Hence Linton sees in the Marquesas' practice of calling all trade "gift exchange" [41] a symbol of their valuation of generosity. Boas points likewise to phrasings as symbols of prevailing modes of thought in different cultures. An Indian's saying, "the son was the reason for the father's housebuilding," indicates his culture's emphasis upon causality, whereas the American phrasing of "the father built a house for his son" symbolizes our preoccupation with purpose.[42] More recently, under "Anthropology" in *The Encyclopaedia of Social Sciences,* Boas treats the narrative form as a symbol of primitive culture. "Since the tale is an artistic unfolding of the happenings in human society, it must reflect the habits and conflicts of the society in which the narrator lives." [43] Symbols used in the narratives may be chosen from the immediate society "to reflect intimately the cultural life of the people," or may be drawn from historical data to reflect "the cultural life of a passing or past period." [44] In every instance "the forms vary according to local style and occasion," [45] and are therefore symbols of phases of their culture.

We see this also in C. G. Seligman's article "Anthropological Perspective and Psychological Theory," in the publication of the Royal Anthropological Institute of Great Britain and Ireland,[46] where from an explicitly psychoanalytical point of view the social ritual in Bali communities is classed as drama through which the purgation of antisocial emotion is effected. From a similarly psychoanalytical point of view Rattray interprets the dramatically-rendered tales and legends of the Ashanti as symbols of a culture which provide release for the natives to indulge their periodic tendencies toward license and cruelty.[47]

Form is directly influenced by the types of action and motivations for conduct peculiar to a given culture, but form is not dictated by the culture. As Boas writes in "Stylistic Aspects of Primitive Literature"[48] and in *Primitive Art*,[49] and as Gladys A. Reichard also stresses in "Form and Interpretation in American Art,"[50] form is influenced by the cultural outlook on historical happenings. This point had been developed in Posnett's *Comparative Literature* (1886), an early approach to literature from the anthropological point of view. In his comparative study of Greek literature and culture, Posnett showed that the lyric or personal clan poetry gave way to epic forms when the head men assumed privileges of hereditary chiefs and the mass of clansmen sank to simple freemen or serfs. In later urban society the drama paralleled the rise of individuality. Posnett concluded that literary form accompanies and reveals growth in the most fundamental characteristic of human society—the "comprehension" and "extension" of individualized personality.[51]

More recently, H. M. Chadwick and N. K. Chadwick have developed a similar theme in *The Growth of Literature* (1932-1940).[52] Investigating comparatively the milieus from which heroic poetry and saga emerged in Hellenic and Teutonic literatures—and in Hebrew, Russian, Jugoslavian, Dyak, among others—they show the similarities in form and content of sagas arising from each culture at corresponding periods of development. In Hellenic and Teutonic literature, where diffusion from more advanced cultures was not prominent, there was a long, slow development from the idealized tribal "personnel of the *Iliad* [which] consists almost wholly of princes and their military followers," and the members of "courts or military retinues of princes" in *Beowulf*,[53] to the "poems and passages which . . . show a further development . . . in so far as the subject of the picture is no longer a purely hypothetical person or a representative of some class of humanity, but has a definite individuality of his own, though the timeless nameless character remains."[54] In contemporary cultures the process is materially accelerated through diffusion. Hence, in Jugoslavian literature "the close of the Heroic Age may be equated with the end of Turkish rule and the introduction of modern civilization." [55]

Lerner and Mims emphasize the selective process by which the individual author projects "certain dynamic and significant issues into the consciousness of the time . . . weaving them into a pattern which is compatible with his standards of art and his view of human life." [56] As literary technician he "arranges his language in word patterns of sound and thought which are emotionally evocative." [57] The resulting "forms and genres of literature respond to the social compulsion of a period." [58] In Greek literature and culture the emotional tone of 7th and 6th century culture expressed itself in lyric poetry. In the 5th century this gave way to the sharper emotional conflicts of urban Athens, where the choral ode was finally supplanted by the drama.

Because Greek civilization provides an example of a completed cycle of culture, such an archeologist and folklorist as R. R. Marett, for instance, and such comparative literature scholars as Werner Jaeger in *Paideia, The Ideals of Greek Culture* (1939), and H. D. F. Kitto in *Greek Tragedy* (1939), and such a psychologist as Müller-Freienfels, have reached common ground in their recognition of literary types as symbols of phases of Greek culture. Increasingly we see scholarly attempts to extend this idea into Western culture and literature by philologist-critics, Karl Vossler for one. In *The Spirit of Language in Civilization* (1929) he holds that "the lyric is the outpouring of the lonely heart; for the epic a hearer is needed; and the drama presupposes at least three persons or situations: protagonist, antagonist, and spectator, all of which, it is true, the poet can represent himself, just as in a song a hundred minds and voices can flow together into a choir." [59] This growing emphasis upon types of literature as symbols of culture is related to the persistent emphasis upon "types" within World Literature courses, despite opposition to such emphasis in many quarters.

Comparative literature, comparative studies in the arts, comparative religion and philosophy, and the study of the history of science in relation to other aspects of human life all have given rise to the idea of contemporaneous expressions of value in many media and many kinds of symbols. The parallels have prompted J. B. S. Haldane's[60] perception of theology and science as art forms, and W. P. Montague's[61] and Irwin Edman's[62] vision of philosophy and art as similar, though not identical, syntheses of human values in any age. Hence, too, the social generalization of Lewis Mumford[63] upon the parallels of technics and civilization, and George Sarton's[64] definitive history of science in its relation to man's social and spiritual values.

When the comparative studies of which these are representative are synthesized, there emerge the philosophies of history, the theories of cultural evolution,[65] set forth by such men as Taine, Adams, Friedel, Spengler, and Toynbee. Pointing in detail to the anthropological bases for the idea of the *culture epoch,* and to the fact that "the synthetic method is needed to complement the analytic method,"[66] Sidney Ratner in "Patterns of Culture in History" in *Philosophy of Science,* concludes: "Each civilization has its own cultural configuration, its dominant trends or emphases, its distinctive hierarchy of values."[67] And while the configuration "is sometimes complicated by several complex sub-patterns appearing within the framework of a civilization,"[68] which "have to be studied both in their geographic setting and their socio-economic stratification,"[69] the significant symbols of each way of life will be found in literary art.[70]

Anthropology and values.—Functional anthropologists, as we have noted, are concerned with the relationships of every process and value and medium in society—with language as "the most massive and inclusive art we know,"[71] the greatest instrument for "human survival,"[72] the "prototype of symbolism by which values and rules are transmitted."[73] Through language symbols man is freed of the necessity of learning everything by direct experience, coöperative action is possible and, as Mead notes, reflective conduct refines the quality of social intercourse through the "presence of the future in terms of ideas."[74]

All of these concerns lead ultimately to the individual, his integration with the established institutions, customs, and ideas of his culture, and his participation in their evolution. As Ruth Benedict writes in *Patterns of Culture* (1934):

Society in its full sense . . . is never an entity separable from the individuals who compose it. No individual can arrive even at the threshold of his potentialities without a culture in which he participates. Conversely, no civilization has in it any element which in the last analysis is not the contribution of an individual.[75]

Anthropologists agree upon the need for social organization in which the moral force of personal attachments and human loyalties is not constrained from without. In "The Group and the Individual in Functional Analysis," Malinowski holds that "the individual, both in social theory and in the reality of cultural life, is the starting point and the end. . . . Culture remains sound and capable of further development only in so far as a definite balance between individual interest and social control can be maintained. If this balance be upset or wrongly poised, we have at one end anarchy, and at the other brutal dictatorship."[76] The necessary balance is sought in syntheses of new facts, ideas, and attitudes. To perform its functions successfully, writes Linton, "a culture need only be integrated to the point where it has eliminated paralyzing conflicts in emotional responses and overt behavior."[77]

From anthropological findings we sense that the democratic way of life has its distinctive aesthetic. Teachers are seeing certain aesthetic implications of the "genetics of society"[78] in our time. Among others: (1) The basis of value is the "life-furthering" effect upon the human self; (2) The aesthetic experience through art is the process of self-realization for both creator and observer; (3) Art has its base in the imaginative conception of human values more fully realized than in the immediate environment; (4) The aesthetic experience may come through channels other than art as the individual perceives a balanced and harmonious synthesis of ideas and values previously in flux or conflict. The challenge of dictatorships is sharpening certain anthropological ideas with practical consequences—as we suspect when Nazi Germany must legislate its own anthropology. We recognize that in a society so rigidly organized through authoritarian control or intense pressures of social tabu and custom as to eliminate disturbing emotional drives by stultifying the imagination, art in its highest sense is non-existent, because self for any appreciable number of people remains indistinguishable. As Max Carl Otto warns in *The Human Enterprise* (1940), our present social organization must make increasing allowance for creative, coöperative living:

> This change may take more creativeness and courage than we possess. If we are wise and courageous enough, have time enough, and are favored by good luck, we may be able to institute a communal life [one in which individualities realize themselves along with, rather than over against, community effort of others] in which the many will find new opportunity to enjoy novelty of experience in their personal tastes, in their relaxation, and in the work they do to make a living. If this coöperative form of individuality is out of the question, individuality for the many will vanish. It will be reserved for the few who prove to be powerful enough to seize and hold the privilege until their game too is up. The masses of us will take orders from those few. Individuality will either become communal, or in any liberal sense it will disappear, and with it will go the supreme quality of human nature.[79]

If at the other extreme we postulate a social organization so loosely integrated as to approach anarchy, there occurs either paralyzing conflict, as Linton suggests, or a concern for trivial values such as Athens experienced in the days of late comedy—and eventual subjugation. "The theoretical discussion of the relation between the individual and the group," says Malinowski, "has thus in our present world not merely an academic but also a deep philosophical and ethic significance." [80]

In a society like ours, alteration of values demands ever-new designs of ideas and values reconciling inevitable conflicts that arise as one value after another enters the fluid zone. We see this idea explicitly in Dewey's *Art as Experience*[81] and though not in aesthetic terms, in his *Freedom and Culture*.[82] It is present in Jacques Barzun,[83] Louise Rosenblatt,[84] and Lewis Mumford—particularly in his *Men Must Act*[85] and *Faith for Living*.[86] In all of these statements are implications for the aesthetics of democratic government, embodying as it does the methods for perpetuating through balances the rhythmic harmony-disharmony-harmony of human advance.

The place of art in our society is important from both the standpoint of the artist and that of the observer. The artist must accept the soul-searching challenge of the most profound problems of society, as Robert Sherwood consciously did in *There Shall Be No Night*,[87] and as Norman Corwin did in the radio drama "We Hold These Truths."[88] The citizen must put aside the traditional combative approach to interpretation, according to I. A. Richards, and "look before he leaps to any conclusion as to what it *must* mean—to look rather lingeringly for what it *may* mean, and to consider the very important differences between these possible meanings."[89] These anthropological "ways of thinking and feeling, choosing and judging"[90] would provide the citizen with methods of sorting and manipulating intellectual and emotional discriminations which keep their order only through words.[91] Through language, according to E. E. Eubank, we are "heirs to all the ages,"[92] though, as R. R. Marett warns us, we have not always claimed our heritage. "Culture is communicable intelligence. . . . Communication is a two-sided process, taking in being just as important as giving out; so much so, indeed, that the tragedy of history may be said to consist in the fact that the nations have so often failed to interpret what their men of genius sought to express."[93] Today men of genius like Thomas Mann and Lewis Mumford are calling for a militant democracy to preserve the integrity of the individual spirit, never forgetting the tortuous process by which the *human self* has emerged to consciousness through symbolic objectification of its values. This process, as we shall see later, is the central concern of modern humanists and modern courses in the Humanities and World Literature.

CONCLUSIONS OF PART I

As we draw together the varied concerns for the nature of aesthetic experience revealed in philosophy, psychology, and anthropology, we find divergences that may suggest that any attempt at unification would be futile. Yet there are certain broad convergences apparently gaining in currency, which require recapitulation at this point. Primary among these is the recognized value of self, achieving and perpetuating its identity through the aesthetic impulse toward proportioned and ever-more-inclusive formulations of things, ideas, and values. Language symbols exemplify this impulse and extend human environment through time and space. Language and culture are mutually dependent; they develop simultaneously, for they are at once the methods and materials of human adjustment to increasingly complex modes of living. Language is the primary method-material by which men and women pursue individual thought processes and coöperative activity. Language is therefore the fundamental social cohesive. Loss of adequate use of a common language by any large proportion of a social group, or restriction of otherwise freely undertaken artistic formulations in literature, leads logically either to chaos or authoritarianism in which individuality in any generous sense is unrealized.

Literature, employing as its medium this greatest of human inventions, as Mumford calls language, is the most revealing symbol of the culture from which it grows. The symbols which it incorporates may most adequately represent the depth and breadth of human values entertained within definable culture epochs. Through the use of the methods of anthropology and the specific disciplines of language, Sidney Ratner tells us in "Patterns of Culture in History," the reader may recognize those symbols of culture and come into rapport with his own cultural heritage and with the culture in which he is a contributing member.[94]

Practically all of the ideas from philosophy, psychology, and anthropology traced here have been translated by various writers or spokesmen into argument for the revival of the Humanities and the great books. Between 1935 and 1942 at least ten major figures in education, representing their own or group points of view, have spoken explicitly for the aesthetic experience as an approach to the larger "human values" of the Humanities. In those seven years more than thirty Humanities programs have been instituted in American colleges and universities,[95] in addition to the courses and programs under way before 1935.

We come now to the central part of our inquiry: to see how such modern ideas of aesthetic experience as we have traced here have come into the writing and speaking of leading teachers, and how these newer ideas have tended toward a more and more unified approach to the "more human values" of the modern Humanities.

PART II

ENLARGING IDEAS OF AESTHETIC EXPERIENCE
AMONG SPOKESMEN FOR THE HUMANITIES

To WHAT EXTENT, in this period of synthesis, have teachers of literature generally been moving in harmony with interests current in psychology and anthropology as well as in the longer established aesthetic? Have they drawn ideas from psychology and anthropology to the extent that psychologists and anthropologists have drawn ideas from literature? The spokesmen examined here are evidence of the current interests of literary scholars in psychology and anthropology, and they provide us with measures of the degree of synthesis being achieved. They have been selected for examination here because of their representativeness or their conspicuousness, starting with collective and representative spokesmanship in The National Council of Teachers of English, the Progressive Education Association, and the Committee of Twenty-Four, and proceeding to representative philosophers, historians, and teachers of literature.

1. THE NATIONAL COUNCIL OF TEACHERS OF ENGLISH

In seeking to answer questions of the degree to which the newer ideas of aesthetic experience have spread or are spreading, we must consider representativeness with some care, and also the relative part which ideas of aesthetic experience play in the whole context—keeping in mind related ideas of "self," "creative formulation," "symbolization in language," and "values," as they converge toward an idea of aesthetic experience.

In 1930 the Executive Committee of the National Council of Teachers of English established a Curriculum Commission. Many teachers had asked for help in redefining aims and in reorganizing or planning new courses of study. Not wishing to legislate, the Commission set out to assemble and publish records of successful experimental courses of study that might be used as points of departure for other teachers who were interested in pursuing the same values.

The Curriculum Commission had more than one hundred members—representatives from the National Education Association, the American Association of Teachers Colleges, the National Association of Teachers of Speech, the National Association of Journalism Advisers, the North Central Association of Colleges and Secondary Schools, and the Southern Association of Colleges and Secondary Schools.[1] The Commission did its work through three major Committees, each of which published its own monograph. The first to appear was *The Teaching of College English* (1934), edited by O. J. Campbell, then Professor of English and Comparative Literature at the University of Michigan,[2] now at Columbia University; the second was *An Experience Curriculum* (1935), edited by W. Wilbur Hatfield, Secretary of the National Council of Teachers of English and Chairman of the Curriculum Commission and Professor of English at the Chicago Teachers College; the third was *A Correlated Curriculum* (1936), edited by Ruth Mary Weeks, of the Experimental Junior College, Kansas City, Missouri, and Chairman of the Committee on Correlation.

The attempt to establish a broad "frame of reference" was noteworthy both in the representativeness of the commission, and in the breadth of idea in the reports; various effects will be seen in the statements of values attainable in or through literature and the arts as set up by these committees. *The Teaching of College English* is primarily concerned with the values of language. *An Experience Curriculum* seems in various ways to be moving toward an aesthetic experience concept. *A Correlated Curriculum* in its major design seems to imply the evolving culture concept which interweaves with a psychological-anthropological aesthetic.

A. The Teaching of College English

The Teaching of College English is a composite of reports of committee members on the problems of articulation between school and college, freshman English, first courses in Literature, programs for English majors, honors courses, and the preparation for graduate degrees, with an interpreting introduction by Professor O. J. Campbell. The introduction to the monograph shows a fundamental concern with language, through which students of the modern Humanities and World Literature carry on their own thought processes and through which they become acquainted with their cultural heritage, aesthetic and otherwise. The monograph explicitly recognizes the psychological-anthropological concept of language noted in the preceding chapters: language is the primary social cohesive which makes possible coöperative undertakings and the projection of future group efforts.[3]

Equally explicit is concern for English language as more than a skill to be used for handling the materials of other areas of inquiry. English enjoys its own disciplines, as exacting as those of history or of the sciences.[4] English, moreover, is the means by which the individual moves toward his highest intellectual-emotional potentialities, for "language is an essential part of the process of thinking. It is not the medium but the means of thought . . . ," and the person who uses inaccurate, hazy, ambiguous language is guilty of like-calibre thought.[5] Such an individual, to repeat, is losing the primary value of English which might become the development of an "independent philosophy of life."[6] Because language is the reservoir of cultural achievement, literature is the repository of human values translated into intellectual-emotional experience for future generations.[7] It is this reservoir of values which facilitates man's existence on a singularly human level, for "literature made vital experience teaches the individual to substitute civilized values for purely animal ones."[8] There is more than a passive substitution implied; the substitution becomes a passionate drive, an "ethical stimulus" toward an individually-idealized circumstance. It is this "objectification of our ideal selves," we gather, that is the aesthetic experience for the reader, the cumulative process through which "we behold a fuller, more capacious individual than we ever are—one who becomes our wish." [9]

Within this context "wish" should not be construed from a Freudian point of view. Instead, there is the idea of the reader's finding a harmonious resolution of previously conflicting values which contribute to his sense of order and consequent well-being. According to Professor Campbell, "This experience gives to the superficially disjointed incidents of living a continuity and sense of controlled progress which transforms them into integrated human life. Literature should thus not be regarded primarily as an escape from reality, not as a pleasant employment for vacant hours, but as one of the formative experiences of civilized life." [10]

Another aspect of aesthetic experience through literature is its "service as an emotional prophylactic." [11] Through tragedy particularly the reader finds a "safe release to socially dangerous primitive emotions lying imperfectly caged within us. . . ." "Safe release" by itself might suggest phases of Freudian or Aristotelian catharsis, or that noted by Rattray in anthropological investigation. But it is used in context with "purge," which here has a specific meaning. "In identifying ourselves with such passions expressed in literary form, we purge our minds of them and conserve the energy which would drive them into active expression, for socially healthful impulses." [12] This therapeutic quality of aesthetic experience lies close to that implied in the objectification of an ideal self, for "release" and "purge" as here used do not so much imply removal as diverting, redirecting, or conserving emotional energies that can be harmonized for constructive expression. This similarity is borne out in a later reference to "the state of mind . . . which permits a harmonious organization of the greatest number of different impulses," [13] and which (acknowledging the influence of I. A. Richards) "requires the frustration and starvation of the fewest impulses and so organizes the personality most comprehensively for freedom and happiness." [14] The endorsement given to these ideas in the Statement of the Committee of Twenty-four, to which Professor Campbell was a contributor, will be considered later.

B. *An Experience Curriculum*

Implicit in the title of this monograph is the concern of the editors for the whole experience of the individual, patterned to give order and meaning to its parts. This is the concern of Dewey in *Art as Experience.*

The seven parts of the monograph are devoted to an Introduction, which establishes the commission's "conception of the curriculum as a body of *guided experiences paralleling present and future out-of-school experiences,*"[15] and six subsequent parts laying out representative programs for grades 6-12 in Literature, Reading, Creative Expression, Communication, Corrective Teaching, and electives in Speech and Journalism. From the Introduction and from the activity programs exemplifying the concepts of the Introduction we learn something of the three phases of the creative process: "observation, imagination, and reflection,"[16] and something of the values to be attained in discussion upon "main events and impressions, upon the larger aspects of character, and upon the theme if there is any."[17] Sensory observation fills the storehouse of memory, and "with sleepy ease the imagination associates one object with another into a long chain of impressions. When we are half asleep, or ill with fever, when the will falters, our imagination thus holds full sway," and from the welter of associative imaginings, reflection achieves an "order, logic, meaning, significance, and so forth."[18] We find that "the author's sensory and social experiences, his imaginings, and his feelings are what he has tried to put into his writing" either because they "seemed worth sharing" with an audience or because they "seemed to him to have intrinsic value."[19] In this there is an obvious awareness that the cultural background figures largely in creative expression, though we are led also to believe that such expression is quite as much a factual record of contemporaneous events or personal imagination as an imaginative synthesis incorporating in symbols the values of the culture—perhaps more. We learn, for instance, that there was "interaction between Dickens and the London of his day," [20] but we also find topical attention to "some typical problems of social controversy and appropriate literary works in which they are discussed." [21]

The primary value projected in the Introduction of this second monograph applies to the whole curricular offering—the development of "the flexibility and power of self-direction requisite for successful living in our age of swift industrial, social, and economic change." [22] But to achieve this within the patterned curriculum, each department "participates when and as it can." English, specifically, is used to "provide the communication . . . necessary to the conduct of social activities, and to provide indirect (vicarious) experiences where direct experiences are impossible or undesirable." [23] Although the social-cohesive value of language is accented here, there is no indication that language is the primary process of self-realization. We do learn, however, that "the principal objective of creative expression in school" is "the individual pupil's joyous realization of the values of his own experiences," [24] or sharing "some outward or inner experience that is too good to keep." [25] This considerable attention to the pleasure of intense and heterogeneous experience is borne out in suggested activities for exciting "interest in one's own sense-reactions to nature," and awareness of *"moments of heightened susceptibility."* [26] In the study of literature, a similar breadth of experience is projected, for "since the value of literature, beyond the immediate one of pleasure, is in the enlargement of the individual by means of indirect experience, the more directions the enlargement takes the more valuable the literature will prove." [27]

All this suggests the comprehensiveness of the aesthetic experience as conceived by many modern thinkers. We find concern for exploration of the physical world;[28] exploration of the social world;[29] enjoyment of various kinds of characters;[30] sharing lyric emotion through delight in physical nature, enjoyment of the merely ludicrous, enjoyment of rhythm, sharing expressions of friendship and tenderness for pets, friends, or family;[31] giving fancy rein in the enjoyment of fantasy, allegory, and myth,[32] and in solving puzzles presented through mystery stories.[33] Contributory to all of these enjoyment values are the aesthetic concerns for form, rhythm, color, line, symmetry, balance, proportion, etc.—hardly new in themselves, but embodied in a changing context. Awareness of literary types characterized by pervasive emotional tone suggests a movement toward modern psychological-anthropological concepts of literary genres. Further evidence of the emergent quality of thought expressed in the monograph appears in sections on radio and movies as art, and in the concern for critical standards of a non-hedonistic nature to "distinguish excellence from trash."[34] Primary attention is placed on the social values of critical standards, rather than upon the fulfillment of the self through the manipulation of language. To repeat then, the monograph focuses attention on the curriculum as an orderly program of experiences which "will develop the flexibility and power of self-direction requisite for successful living in our age of swift industrial, social, and economic change."[35]

C. *A Correlated Curriculum*

A Correlated Curriculum is a mosaic of curricular programs in operation in schools and colleges—introduced by committee comment in Chapters I and II on the Theory of Correlation, and interwoven with editorial statement. The editors are simultaneously concerned with the largeness of curricular patterns embracing "scientific, esthetic, philosophical and ethical"[36] knowledge and attitudes, and with the aesthetic unity these achieve in "the psychological growth pattern of the individual."[37] This editorial concern for breadth and focus is supported in a subsequent statement by Robert Spiller, of Swarthmore College: "Correlation means a development of relationships and should lead to a more closely knit rather than a more enriched curriculum."[38] The monograph is particularly concerned with the place of literature and language in a well-organized curriculum in which the individual achieves "a feeling of certainty and satisfaction, a realization of meaning in what he is studying, and the ability to use what he learns in life situations. . . ."[39]

In Chapters I and II on the Theory of Correlation the editors discuss the basic principles in essential areas of inquiry—the physical, biological, and social sciences, and philosophy, religion, and the arts. Subsequent Chapters III to VII exemplify five patterns of curricular organization which bring together those subjects having a marked degree of interdependence.

   III. Correlation of English with Other Fields Through Incidental References and Isolated Projects
   IV. An English Course Based on Correlation with Other Subjects but Not Implying the Modification of Courses in Any Other Field
   V. The Fusion of English with One Other Subject
   VI. The Fusion of Groups of Subjects (of similar origin or emphasis, as the arts and Humanities)
   VII. A Curriculum Based on the Integration of All Educational Subjects or Transcending Subject-Matter Divisions

Section VIII provides an overview of "The Administrative Organization of the School as a Whole on a Correlative Basis."

While Chapters III, IV, V show explicit concern for "self-discovery," it is Chapter VI, "The Fusion of Groups of Subjects," that bears out our earlier inferences about the unifying force of ideas of aesthetic experience—the larger the pattern, the greater the need. The chapter deals with the fusion of groups of "subjects which are based on common principles, . . . which are mutually interdependent since one cannot be understood without the rest, or . . . which are similar in their content." [40] Such groups *A Correlated Curriculum* outlines as (a) World Literature, (b) the Fine Arts, (c) the Humanities, and (d) English and Foreign Languages. We shall be concerned with the principles of the first three, giving special attention to the ideas of aesthetic experience which provide their unity, values, and critical and teaching methods. A comment on the newer survey courses is suggestive: "The final force operating to produce such survey courses has been the awakening realization that disjointed information is not wisdom, that things have meaning only when seen in their relation to other things. . . ." [41]

   (a) World Literature: As presented, the chief purposes of World Literature are to give the student "a truer historical and social perspective" and "offset the narrowing tendencies of an exclusively nationalistic cultural education, promote world friendship and world peace, develop an international viewpoint, reveal the traits, interests problems, thoughts, and feelings common to all peoples of all times." [42] These aims represent a synthesis of contributions from history, comparative literature, folklore studies, and philosophical concerns with the history of ideas. A representative course showing these unifying aims is that described by Hanna E. Kirk in the Swarthmore High School, which reveals a now familiar composite attention to all of these orientations[43] as it moves in large rhythms over the literature of the East, Near East, and Greece, and over the literary periods of the Renaissance, the Reformation, the Age of Democracy, Imperialism, and Aftermath: Criticism and Depression.

(b) The Fine Arts: The fused courses listed under "Fine Arts" have their base more explicitly in a psychological-anthropological concept of aesthetic experience. "The fine arts—music, poetry, design, painting, sculpture, the dance, and architecture—all express a similar attitude toward life and employ a similar method of mastering experience." [44] The artist's aesthetic experience grows from his representation of what he contemplates and enjoys. One of the values sought in such a fused course is the understanding of the creative impulse. "To trace through all the arts this attitude of contemplative enjoyment, this delight in the concrete and the particular, and this effort to master experience by creative expression will reveal to the student more clearly the meaning of art and the nature of the artistic impulse." [45] As the observer submits to artistic disciplines and traces "through all the arts the fundamental principles of expressiveness, truth, rhythm, balance, and proportion" [46] his life assumes a more singularly human character—one above "the animal level of mere physical activity and creature comfort." [47] If large numbers of individuals grow in this direction, the prospect for the nation is comparatively good: "ripe civilizations" sooner or later move out of the ethical to the aesthetic basis of conduct, "and the subsequent strength or decadence of a nation hinges upon the soundness and fineness of its esthetic discrimination." [48]

According to the editors of *A Correlated Curriculum,* fusion courses in the Fine Arts have four general organization patterns: period by period, art by art, theme by theme, or basic principle by basic principle. The course in the history of the arts, offered by Mary Graves at the University of North Carolina, is cited as an example of the first pattern. The Humanities course offered by Louise Dudley at Stephens College is cited as an example of the second pattern. The course organized around themes or moods, taught by Merrill Bishop in the Junior High School of San Antonio, Texas, is an example of the third type. The organization which proceeds basic principle by basic principle receives most attention in the monograph and is exemplified in the course formerly taught by Ruth Mary Weeks, editor of *A Correlated Curriculum,* and Thelma Winnberg, in the Experimental Junior College, Kansas City, Missouri.[49] In a five-part organization the course takes up the symbolic expressiveness, truthfulness, rhythm, and symmetry, balance, and proportion of the various arts, including the moving picture and radio, and holds that beauty is the "combined effect" of these six principles.

(c) The Humanities: The Humanities concept, exemplified in the monograph by the Humanities General Course at the University of Chicago, offers a somewhat more specific focus upon the human values common to the Humanities than does either of the concepts and courses just described. Implicit is the idea that the name *Humanities* itself offers clear unity. While the Humanities course, like the World Literature course at Swarthmore High School, is oriented toward types of thought in the heritage of Western civilization, it is specifically concerned with "the *growth* of European culture," thus pointing up the organic quality of culture rather than merely chronological succession of events and literary epochs. Moreover, the expressed focus is upon the human values which emerge through this growth—upon "all the attempts of men to arrive at the meaning of life." This all-inclusive synthesis indicates a concern for symbolism that reaches far beyond the arts. It indicates an idea of aesthetic experience pervading every phase of life in which man at a given time and a given place seeks form and significance for his life. History, religion, philosophy, scientific speculation, painting, sculpture, architecture, music, and the literary forms are synthesized in the theme of the origin and nature of modern thought and art. This aesthetic emphasis has become increasingly marked in successive revisions of the Humanities syllabus, as we shall see in consideration of the University of Chicago program in Part III.

Chapter VII, "A Curriculum Based on the Integration of All Educational Subjects or Transcending Subject-Matter Divisions," moves beyond the fusion of the Humanities, which find their unity in various ideas of aesthetic experience, toward a fusion of "all subjects either around some central thesis or around the growth needs of the student, so that each subject will relate to every other subject as a supporting pillar in this educational structure."[50] In quest of meaningful design, themes and core problems dealing with modern living become the organizing centers for all school activity. This core organization has found wide acceptance in high schools and junior colleges, where the centralizing theme in many instances has been the composite picture of American history, its sociology, economics, literature, philosophy, art, and science.[51]

As we review this analysis of *A Correlated Curriculum* from the standpoint of the nature of the aesthetic experience, we find no one clearly consistent idea of aesthetic experience as an approach to human values in World Literature. But we find significant trends toward the study of what Ales Hrdlicka in the appendix on anthropology calls the "progressive 'humanization', physical and above all intellectual"[52] by which man is able to achieve the ideal set up by Robert Millikan in the appendix on physical sciences—"a more rational, a more objective, a more scientific attitude toward life and all its problems."[53]

2. PROGRESSIVE EDUCATION ASSOCIATION

In the monographs of the National Council of Teachers of English there is constant emphasis on the interplay of all aspects of education and life, with English in the center drawing into itself increasingly wider ranges of materials and methods. A somewhat different design, in which subject matter is important though not primary, comes from the spokesmen for Progressive Education.

At the time of its organization in November, 1918, the Progressive Education Association emphasized psychological needs. More recently, it has stressed the social. Both points of view contribute to the Association's conscious role as one of many active agencies working in our democracy to extend faith in the worth of human individuals.[1] In this faith each individual is never a "means merely but each one always an end in himself, worthy of respect for what he is and for what he may become."[2] Democracy from this standpoint is more than political organization, more than participation and decision by majority vote, more than freedom to claim certain privileges before the law. As the Board of Directors of the Progressive Education Association state in the pamphlet "Democratic Education,"

It [democracy] survives as a superior type of life only if it develops the will and the machinery to discover and accept expert knowledge, and forceful, disinterested leadership. More than its opposite, totalitarianism, it releases and encourages the free play of thought, criticism and the patient, untrammeled labors of science. Thus, by intellectual freedom, it promotes the vital means to its continued growth. But it requires intensive, prolonged study and experience through years of education to develop the critical judgment and insight among its citizens which will result in making popular decisions wise decisions.[3]

Drawing upon Dewey for substantiation of a similar point,[4] William H. Kilpatrick states that there must be "a responsible share on the part of each person, in proportion to capacity, in shaping the aims and policies of the social groups to which he belongs."[5] These values are not peculiar to the Progressive Education Association, of course, but they are indications of emphasis.

Contributing to this large individual-cultural pattern, various individuals and appointed commissions have spoken for one or another phase of education in the whole design. No one has been more influential in shaping this educational philosophy than John Dewey.[6] And probably no book comes nearer to defining our emerging concepts of aesthetic experience than his *Art as Experience,* holding that aesthetic experience is central in any philosophical study of experience generally.[7] Yet its idiom is so unlike that of the teacher of literature that its influence has been diffused through other critics rather than direct. Louise Rosenblatt's *Literature as Exploration,* written for the Commission on Human Relations of the Progressive Education Association, explicitly brings many of its ideas into play —anthropological, psychological, and so on, and has been directly influential.[8] Together these books give a useful picture of the progressive position.

A. John Dewey: Social Philosopher

The two factors, "art" and "experience," in Dewey's title call for examination at the outset. Always, in Dewey's philosophy, a work of art, or an experience, is valued for what it does or has done.[9] An individual becomes aware of a "plus moment," when a sequence of related activities takes on expressive form. This cumulative process leaves the individual most intensely conscious of his power for self-direction and self-criticism. The experience is the cumulative process which leaves the human self with a feeling of amplitude and harmony. No single terminal moment, however much more poignant it may seem than its predecessors, is the experience any more than a drama or a novel is its final statement. "The end, the terminus, is significant not by itself but as the integration of the parts."[10] Aesthetic experience so conceived is implicit in all human experience; it becomes explicit through art.[11] And the *"idea* of art as a conscious idea [represents] the greatest intellectual achievement in the history of humanity."[12] In his ideas of the origins of art, the nature of the work of art itself and the values attainable in or through specific critical methods, Dewey has synthesized the results of inquiry in many fields—biological, physical, social, artistic. From the findings of biological sciences, Dewey (like Rusu and Müller-Freienfels) points out that the live creature, whether simple in organization as the hydra or complex as man, has a tendency toward conservation of energy. The simple organism acts only when a "need" vital to its existence institutes "impulsions" toward a new equilibrium within its experience world.[13] If the creature is not able to reëstablish harmonious relationship with its environment, it dies.[14] If it makes a successful readaptation but learns no new ways for retaining or regaining equilibrium in the future, it merely subsists. The live creature grows when a temporary imbalance with its environment leads to the organism's development of new ways of meeting future problems. When, after its interaction with its environment, the organism reëstablishes its feeling of harmony and order, "it bears within itself the germs of a consummation akin to the esthetic."[15] In this Dewey works from scientific concepts, or in terms at least of a scientific analogy.

In man organic life reaches its greatest complexity.[16] Man has in common with other animals the same body parts, the same fundamental drives for perpetuation of the species and conservation of the individual of the species. But man's humanness lies in potentialities for the development of self-conscious knowledge of self.[17] The distinctly human attribute which makes the realization of self a possibility is mind. "Mind is primarily a verb. It denotes all the ways in which we deal consciously and expressly with the situations in which we find ourselves."[18] Mind is an active reservoir of funded experience, either as conscious memory or as a subconscious (though not less active) background[19] of meanings and attitudes which are retained as a kind of symbolic quality of the things done and undergone.[20] "Mind . . . is formed out of modifications of the self that have occurred in prior interactions with environment. Its animus [intention] is toward further interaction."[21] Mind is the formative impulse that emotionally and intellectually seeks ever more inclusive syntheses of human values.[22]

In the process of readjustment from which new syntheses grow, the individual attains consciousness. The more acute the degree of readjustment, the more intense is consciousness. Only in purposeful surmounting of obstacles through consciously chosen methods can "the self become aware of itself."[23] "It is in the purposes he entertains and acts upon that an individual most completely exhibits and realizes his intimate selfhood."[24]

Here we turn to the stages of the creative process in which the "more human values" of curiosity, imagination, sympathy, and memory come into play. The artist tends to possess more than average sensitiveness to his environment.[25] Through observation and imagination he becomes aware of inharmonious values and of unrealized possibilities inherent in the context of his society.[26] The imaginative perception of discrepancy between the actual and the possible is itself emotionally charged. The emotion arouses the entire organism to activity, and "stirs up a store of attitudes and meanings derived from prior experience,"[27] which have sunk in the subconscious. Emotion prompts interest; interest acts as "the dynamic force in selection and assemblage of materials"[28] and culls from the conscious memory meanings which are pertinent to the prevailing emotion. Deep within the subconscious, interest sets up a process of "compression" of meanings which gives rise to conscious emotionalized images.[29] This rise to consciousness of a symbolic image with its accompanying feeling of excitement and impulsion from within is *inspiration*.[30] Because of the nature of the emotion, a constant mood pervades the whole process.[31] The appearance of the image is marked by "a total seizure, an inclusive qualitative whole not yet articulated, not distinguished into members."[32]

The appearance of an image suffused with a characteristic emotion is the beginning of the experience leading to the work of art. In the "period of gestation"[33] lies one great difference between ordinarily perceptive (and often technically skillful) individuals and the artist. More than other individuals, the artist possesses "capacity to work a vague idea and emotion over into terms of some definite medium."[34] In some instances this involves little effort, for the symbolic emotionalized image appears to him replete with elaborative details from the content of their culture. This effortless synthesis of prior meanings and new experience is intuition.[35] But "oftentimes the union of old and new, of foreground and background, is accomplished only by effort, prolonged perhaps to the point of pain."[36] In either instance the ordering of emotionally felt meanings and their actual expression through a definite medium involves intense self-discipline. Because the artist could abandon his task and does not, even in the face of intense organic distress, the product which he completes assumes value for him as objective evidence of his mastery of self.

Each medium involves its own disciplines. The symbolic nature of language and its unique value as the cumulative content of human culture demands that the author organize his materials with a critical eye toward his readers' clear understanding. In his role of creator-critic the artist does not act in a judicial capacity. He is not concerned with an absolute good or bad, right or wrong, but with the balanced form which his concept of human values is assuming under his conscious design. "What might be or might have been stands always in contrast with what is or has been in a way only words are capable of conveying."[37]

At the same time that any groups of words are current in a given culture there are also prevailing rhythms of activity which mark the "ordered variation of changes"[38] which is the basic pattern of the relations of the individual to his environment.[39] These rhythms enter intimately and of necessity into the work of art.[40] Rhythm is not imposed by man as an external form for art. Rhythm is inevitable;[41] it is the cumulative process "toward a consummating close."[42] Dewey's idea of literary form also falls in with a psychological-anthropological conception of types of literature recognizable through their internal moods of lyric spontaneity (as in Keats, Wordsworth, or Housman), epic solidarity (as in Mann's *Magic Mountain*), and dramatic conflict (as in *Hamlet*).[43] *"Form may then be defined as the operation of forces that carry the experience of an event, object, scene, and situation to its own integral fulfillment."*[44]

For Dewey the aesthetic experience of the author in the achievement of form extends through the reader's experience also, for "the work of art is complete only as it works in the experience of others than the one who created it."[45]

Working "in the experience of others" has a specific significance for Dewey as it must have for the teacher. Dewey recognizes the psychological fact that each reader approaches a work of art from a different background and consequently observes a different work of art from that seen by anyone else.[46] He indicates, in addition, four levels of appreciation on which reading may proceed: a mere vicarious experience shared with the characters of the selection; a mere attention to form and techniques; a concern wholly for meanings incorporated in the work of art; and identification of oneself with the author's creative experience.[47] Within the first three levels, "criticism" may be either "a process of acquittal or condemnation on the basis of merits and demerits"[48] or its opposite extreme of "impressionistic" statement growing from a mere "it seems to me."[49] On the fourth level of appreciation we find a three-fold concern for form in relation to matter, for the disciplines of the medium of language,[50] and for the act of creation—in short, perception of *"what* it is because of *how* it is done."[51]

This high level of critical evaluation is grounded in the enlarged idea of aesthetic experience which extends through both creative and recreative-critical processes. The finest type of criticism, "explication of the content of an object as to subject and form"[52] necessitates *rapport* with the artist, for we can "lay hold of the full import of a work of art only as we go through in our own vital processes the processes the artist went through in producing the work."[53] This demands of the critic "a philosophy of experience that is keenly sensitive to the unnumbered interactions that are the material of experience [for such] is the philosophy from which a critic may most safely and surely draw his inspiration."[54]

The literary critic or the teacher of literature reveals to less highly perceptive readers the unity of a work of art when he can "seize upon some strain or strand that is actually there, and bring it forth with such clearness that the reader has a new clue and guide in his own experience."[55] What this strain or strand may be is indicated as we look into several parts of Dewey's statement.

One mode of unification on the part of the critic is as legitimate as another—provided two conditions are fulfilled. One of them is that the theme and design which interest selects be really present in the work, and the other is the concrete exhibition of this supreme condition: the leading thesis must be shown to be consistently maintained throughout the parts of the work.[56]

Just as the artist's aesthetic experience is the affirmation of self in the cumulative process of giving form to his attitude toward life, so the re-creation of the creative experience of the artist through the manipulation of materials[57] is the critic's aesthetic experience and affirmation of self. These are both expressions of life-attitudes. Hence, the "unifying strand" for criticism (using the analogical logic implicit in *Art as Experience* and later explicit in *Logic, A Theory of Inquiry*) is the manner in which a *self* is shown clarifying its life-attitudes.

In this idea of aesthetic experience with its broadening and deepening of imaginative conception through which the individual enjoys the quality of being a whole and of belonging to the larger whole which is the universe[58] we find explanation for the religious feeling which accompanies aesthetic perception. In our introduction into "a world beyond this world which is nevertheless the deeper reality of the world in which we live our ordinary experiences" [59] there is an intensifying of the human values which make religious insight possible and, although Dewey does not say as much, presumably an increased readiness to believe.

The primary values pursued by science have been the revelation of man's relationships with the rest of nature through specific methods of observation, experimentation, and maintenance of perspective.[60] A sense of these values is inherent in Dewey's idea of aesthetic experience. But even as art and aesthetic criticism tend to acclimatize scientific values in a common culture, "the disclosure by science of the resistance that environment offers to man will furnish new materials for fine arts." [61]

As with profound religious insight, cosmic scientific schemes, and artistic formulations of human values, so with philosophic designs. Dewey holds that the concept of art must be the core of a great philosophy of experience.[62] Philosophy seeks a harmonious and proportioned design for the meaning of all areas of human inquiry, but art, which incorporates experience for objective scrutiny, "provides a unique control for the imaginative ventures of philosophy."[63]

In Dewey's analysis art embodies certain instrumental functions which bring it into harmony with his world philosophy. Through appreciation of a work of art, he writes: "We are carried to a refreshed attitude toward the circumstances and exigencies of ordinary experience." With nice discrimination he continues: "The work, in the sense of working, of an object of art does not cease when the direct act of perception stops. It continues to operate in indirect channels—"[64] channels which lead to the heightening of individual and social consciousness and the drive to effect ideal goals. This end is aided by art, for "Tangled scenes of life are made more intelligible in esthetic experience"[65] and clear knowledge increases the freedom of the individual to pursue optional courses of action, and to carry any one of these to its conclusion.

B. *Louise Rosenblatt: Liberal Arts Progressive*

Louise Rosenblatt's *Literature as Exploration* is an extension of Dewey's philosophy with specific reference to teaching literature.

Professor Rosenblatt opens her discussion by pointing up the supreme value of "some philosophy, some inner center from which [the student may] view in perspective the shifting society about him."[1] This idea is reiterated in varying terms throughout the book, in connection with the dignity and worth of the individual,[2] the necessity for a student's setting up more rational personal and social goals,[3] or the teacher's responsibility for "the development of individuals who will function less as automatic bundles of habits and more as flexible discriminating personalities."[4] The whole corps of teachers with whom a student comes in contact should stress the human meaning of the facts and concepts encountered in their fields, and the teacher of literature, while he may not be expert "with subjects and problems usually thought of as the province of the sociologist, the psychologist, the philosopher, or historian," [5] should have a working knowledge of the basic concepts involved "in the development of human personality and in the patterning of human society" [6] which the sciences of human behavior are building up. When methods and materials of these fields, particularly of biology, psychology, anthropology, and sociology, become familiar to the student, education will have partially fulfilled its obligation "to supply him with the tools, the knowledge, the mental habits, and the emotional impetus that will make possible a successful solution of his future problems." [7] While the factual materials of these sciences may not be permanently applicable to the student's life in an evolving culture, the development of "faith in the scientific method itself" [8] is an enduring value.

Literature as Exploration, as its title indicates, is less concerned with the creative process than with the appreciative critical function of the reader. But we find sufficient discussion of the cultural origin of art to round out a fairly complete idea of aesthetic experience. In keeping with a general emphasis upon the modern, Professor Rosenblatt deals primarily with the artist in interaction with the forces and movements of contemporaneous society. Following the findings of psychology and anthropology, and writing in the same vein as Alice Keliher in *Life and Growth,*[9] she shows that the individual from the moment of his birth is under the influence of the general culture which surrounds him, and of the subculture with which he is in most intimate contact.[10] The influence is not entirely of the culture upon the child. The life and growth of the individual depend upon some degree of interaction between self and environment.[11] Interaction on the level of constructive thinking, as Professor Rosenblatt states on Dewey's authority, "usually starts as a result of some conflict or discomfort, or when habitual behavior is impeded and a choice of new paths of behavior must be made." [12] The artist is more sensitive than many individuals to inharmonious values and relationships and "to new tendencies at work in the society about him." [13] Imaginatively, he projects the consequences of these tendencies, and in the "questing spirit" similar to the scientist's[14] gives form in some medium to these imaginative "images of new goals."[15]

The imaginative perception of potentially realizable human values does not lead to an effortless outpouring of a work of art. Imaginative perception is merely a challenge to open "new paths of behavior." It grows from and continues in "some sort of tension, some emotional impulse . . . [which] contributes the impetus toward seeking some solution . . ."[16] The artist's solution lies in organizing in some medium everything of value from his literary heritage without letting it screen from him the special qualities of the new way of life about him."[17] The resulting work of art is then a synthesis of pertinent factors in the cultural heritage of his time and of contemporaneous scientific, political, and philosophical thought.[18] The synthesis in literature is achieved through the disciplines of language,[19]—grammar-logic-rhetoric, as I. A. Richards conceives them. In so far as the work of art is "nourished by the intellectual climate"[20] of the author's times and represents human values through the synthesis of accumulated cultural materials, we may consider it a symbol of some phase of the author's culture. By inference the depth and breadth of values incorporated in the symbol determine the value of the work of art.

There are certain values attained in the completion of the symbol of culture. In the artist's intellectual-emotional experience of creation he achieves "fulfillment of those culturally valued satisfactions of which he is potentially capable."[21] Opportunities for such fulfillment are basic to a philosophy which recognizes the "fundamental dignity and worth of the human being."[22] The artistic synthesis is a "kind of critical activity,"[23] as it is for Dewey in *Art as Experience:* "A sense of possibilities that are unrealized and that might be realized are, when they are put in contrast with actual conditions, the most penetrating 'criticism' of the latter that can be made."[24]

Like authors, readers also move toward maturity within the intellectual climate of their culture.[25] No two individuals, Professor Rosenblatt points out, can have grown with precisely the same funded meanings and ideas, but they possess sufficient common elements of experience for a measure of communication to be possible.[26] Through imagination and sympathy it is possible for the reader to enter vicariously into the range of events, emotions, and values represented in the form of the work of art. If he is untrained in critical analysis he may be unconscious of the effect of formal and stylistic elements, and of the disciplines of language which he uses to grasp the artist's design. These disciplines are those of I. A. Richards, with specific reference to the "inner logic"[27] of a work of art.

These disciplines call for awareness of a word's sensuous values, intellectual values, or symbolic meanings when used in specific contexts.[28] "Context" includes all the formal relationships within the literary work—verse form, rhyme, sentence structure, imagery, and the emotional overtones and subtly varied rhythms—which one encounters as he moves through a work of art. The reader's sense of orderliness, balance, and completeness arises from the fact that the particular series of images, emotions, and ideas and no others "are experienced in particular relations to one another"[29]—although he may not think of them as "form."

As the reader experiences the emotional-intellectual identification with literary action, he may be unconscious of these many values as values, for it is a peculiarity of art that it concentrates attention upon "the patterns of sensations, feelings, concepts, it evokes."[30] But the reader should seek the fullest possible apprehension of these ideas, feelings, and concepts in their patterned relation to one another. This interactive process leading to the "sense of an organized structure of perceptions and feelings . . . constitutes for us the esthetic experience."[31] Awareness of the aesthetic experience as such sharpens the experience.

According to Professor Rosenblatt, the values inherent in the aesthetic experience are integral with the growth of personality. They include the value of "escape" in the sense of refreshing rhythms of modern life,[32] and the compensatory value of the reader's "identification" with characters who exemplify qualities that he has never achieved. In addition to this form of compensation, the individual has "many latent capacities for modes of life and action that he would not particularly desire, but whose exercise through literature will nevertheless give him satisfaction."[33] Related to this is the objective presentation of problems and conflicts[34] where, through identification with some literary characters, the reader finds that he is not alone in his quandaries. He achieves a certain detachment, a more objective understanding of his own situation.[35]

These values all seem intimately related to the value particularly stressed—stressed also in *The Teaching of College English*—the therapeutic. It has two aspects. The first concerns the redirection of antisocial emotions. Professor Rosenblatt avoids corroboration of or disagreement with the schools of thought concerned with "literature as a means of 'sublimation' of socially disapproved impulses."[36] Recording the claims of these schools and indicating their possible alignment with Aristotelian philosophy, she writes:

The desire for violence and cruelty; the need to dominate others; the need for sex expression when, as in the case of the adolescent, society prevents it; the wish to strike back at those who place restrictions upon us—these are tendencies for which literature is said to provide an outlet. In some ways this theory seems to restate the function of literature foreshadowed in Aristotle's much debated remarks concerning the catharsis or purgation of the emotions of fear and pity that results from the experience of tragedy.[37]

When Professor Rosenblatt opens the next paragraph with: "Literature may perform an even more constructive service for the individual," we are still uncertain of her position on the question of "sublimation," but we are given a lead in the second interpretation of therapeutic—the concept of redirection of impulses. The therapeutic function of literature is explicitly analogous to the work of the psychiatrist who aids his patient "to bring into consciousness various experiences, attitudes, or impulses which, because of some feeling of guilt about them, he has submerged or 'censored.'"[38] Through vicarious experience the reader may participate in attitudes and emotions which tend to bring into consciousness similar elements of which he was aware. "This may provide the basis for a release from unconscious fears and obsessions of guilt."[39]

A further value inherent in the aesthetic experience is the reader's heightened consciousness of his environment and an emotional-intellectual appreciation of the meanings of various aspects of his culture. The aesthetic experience is a means of enhancing the effectiveness of social science concepts in the individual's life, but, Professor Rosenblatt is careful to tell us, this should not reduce the teaching of imaginative literature to a text on social conditions.

Critical evaluation begins where the reader reflects upon his reaction to the work of art, "when he attempts to understand what in the work and in himself produced that reaction, and when he goes on thoughtfully to modify, reject, or accept it." [40] This involves vicarious projection into the attitudes and values of the author during his creative undertaking through analysis of the relationship of form and content.[41] In so doing, says Professor Rosenblatt, the critic may become aware of wider implications of the work of art than the author had been conscious of.[42] While there is no clear indication that a critic should submit his valuation to writing, we infer from several references that written comment may aid the reader to clarify the reasons for his particular reaction to the work of art.[43]

Finally, as spokesman for aesthetic experience addressing herself particularly to teachers of English, Professor Rosenblatt is concerned with materials to be used in the study of literature. Consistent with the idea that a reader finds readiest identification with the familiar, *Literature as Exploration* emphasizes the teacher's use of "literary materials that will have relevance to the general emotional and intellectual level of his students and to the possible points of stress in their particular home and community background." [44] Still, "to cut off the child from the literature of the past would be absurd." [45] In achieving a nice balance between contemporary literature and literature of past epochs, "The teacher should be eager to find those books of the past and present that will have a living meaning for his students." [46] In Professor Rosenblatt's explicit concern for literature of successive historical epochs and for values in representative literature of Greek, Medieval, Renaissance, 18th century, and modern times,[47] we have some indication of the breadth of experiences she would provide for students of literature, even as in her concept of aesthetic experience we see the necessity for sharp focus upon values recognized in critical analysis.

3. COMMITTEE OF TWENTY-FOUR

In December, 1938, Oscar James Campbell, Louise Rosenblatt, and Howard Mumford Jones submitted a statement on "The Aims of the Teaching of Literature" to a group of twenty-four teachers of literature then in attendance at the Fifty-fifth Annual Meeting of the Modern Language Association.[1]

At the meeting where the statement was adopted there was some questioning of the emphasis on differences between the Humanities and the Social Studies,[2] but none on the ideas of aesthetic experience which run through the several parts. The idea of aesthetic experience is not the only unifying idea stressed, of course, or necessarily the most important one.

All the members of the committee agreed on the need for stressing "enduring values" in our democracy. All were agreed on the need for stressing individual as well as social values. These were the major explicit ideas. But these depended tacitly on the idea of aesthetic, or emotional-intellectual formulation, through which the individual in a democracy achieves integrity and health. The tacit agreement of the three writers, who informally represent the National Council of Teachers of English, the Progressive Education Association, and the Modern Language Association, and of the score of signers who represent a considerable range of colleges and universities—undergraduate and graduate liberal arts—and departments of literature in professional schools of education, is of considerable importance for our inquiry here.

The first of four sections of "The Aims of the Teaching of Literature" is devoted to a differentiation of the values peculiar to the Humanities from those pursued by the Social Studies. The study of the values pursued by "men in the mass,"[3] is implicit in the name Social Studies; the arts and Humanities are primarily concerned with the development "of richly endowed and self-reliant individuals, sensitive to the individual lives of their fellow men and to their own potentialities."[4] There is thus a divergence of interests between the Humanities and Social Studies, but also a convergence at that point where the self-reliant individual sees himself in the social context of which he is a part. Literature is first of all important in the development of the individual. In literature, he finds the most comprehensive patterns of human values and conduct. It is through the individually experienced values of imagination and sympathy that the reader experiences the emotional-intellectual identification with these values and patterns. As an individual he enters into them vicariously and "learns through his evaluation of different images of life to build and to refine his own system of values."[5]

The remaining three sections of the statement, *Literature as Delight, Literature as Imaginative Experience,* and *Literature as Document* discuss the contributions of the teaching of literature to the development of individual potentialities within the culture. With considerable attention focused upon effective teaching method, no one of these sections attempts extended discussion of the nature of the creative process or the nature of a work of literary art; but underlying *Literature as Document* are familiar modern ideas of the cultural roots of art. The creation of art is dependent upon exceptional talent, but it should not be considered "as though it were solely the expression of some gifted individual."[6] Even gifted individuals are an integral part of their own milieu; and in their expression of values they use the symbols and reflect the values of their own societies. Literature, therefore, is "part of the living tissue of its society,"[7] and as such is intimately related to the expression of human values through other symbols and other media.

The figure, "living tissue of society," is made more explicit in other parts of the Committee statement. Literature is "undeniably one phase of social history."[8] A work of literary art is "a document in the history of civilization."[9] This implies that it is simultaneously contributory to and indicative of the organic growth of human culture. Literature is a "succession of historic documents uttered at particular times and places by particular men." [10] "Succession" by itself might indicate the unselected chronological sequence of the world's literature; but in the context of "particular times and places by particular men," it suggests human perspectives embodying the "enduring record of the intellectual and spiritual achievements and aspirations of mankind." [11] Even in the shaded meanings of "achievements and aspirations" there is the implication of simultaneous synthesis of past human efforts and projection of their meanings and consequences for human growth.

The idea of mountain peaks in human culture combined with that of "living tissue of society" implies some concept of cultural evolution. While no specific idea of cycles of culture is indicated, the implied existence of such cycles is borne out in further phrases showing that literature "cannot be understood by a person innocent of any philosophical conception of history or devoid of knowledge of alternative theories of what the factors are which determine the character of society." [12]

Section two, *Literature as Delight,* holds that one "important end of literary study is the heightened enjoyment of art and life," [13] but that this is not to be loosely construed to mean simply the "worthy use of leisure time," since that is necessarily relative to other possible choices of time-consuming activity.[14] But granted that reading is the activity in which an individual is engaged, there is a distinction to be made among the levels of appreciation on which he finds his enjoyment. Some individuals find their immediate satisfaction more readily in following the sequence of exciting events in detective stories than in "first acquaintance with a literary classic." [15]

Heightened values will be attained through an understanding of the subtleties of expressive form, "the perception of the artistic excellence of more difficult material." [16] "More difficult material" is that which requires strengthened, disciplined intelligence if the reader is to enter into a sympathetic analysis of the "harmonious intellectual order, often subtly revealed." [17] *Literature as Delight* concludes by explicit reference to the "sound aesthetic insight" [18] which follows disciplined inquiry into the intellectual order of a work of art.

"The Aims of the Teaching of Literature" does not make the attainment of sound aesthetic insight an end in itself. Section three, *Literature as Imaginative Experience,* goes on to say that the aesthetic experience entails two broad complementary consequences: (1) It makes possible the social value of sympathetic understanding of other people, essential to the continuance of democracy. (2) It also has potentially two specific (though not mutually exclusive) effects upon the individual reader. One is therapeutic; the other is character forming. These are old ideas but they have modern connotations.

Through the aesthetic experience literary study therefore stimulates imaginative identification of the reader with all sorts and conditions of men, notably with persons totally different from those he knows in actual life. We have already noted the importance of this wide, sympathetic understanding in a democracy. But besides the social value of this imaginative identification, it renders important services to the individual. His feelings are purged and disciplined by an application of the familiar psychological doctrine of empathy. He feels his impulses toward unruly and subversive emotions to be at once released and controlled by adopting for the moment the careers of fictional characters swayed by the same emotions. In this way his brute instincts are transmuted into civilized values.[19]

One immediate implication of this statement is the fundamental similarity and difference between man and other animals. The implied responsibility of man to conduct himself on a distinctly human level re-accents the idea already noted in *The Teaching of College English.*

"Purged," "empathy," and "disciplined" require further clarification before we can understand the transmutation of brute instincts. "Purged," if we bear in mind Professor Rosenblatt's earlier statement in *Literature as Exploration,* explicitly goes beyond the Aristotelian idea of *catharsis* of *pity* and *fear* in tragedy.[20] The suggested sublimation of desires for cruelty and violence, in addition to that of sex, implies but also goes beyond a Freudian interpretation. Some similarity with the psychological-anthropological findings set forth in one instance by R. S. Rattray in *Religion and Art in Ashanti* might also be inferred. It is in the ampler context of *Literature as Exploration* that we find valuable leads for interpreting the Committee of Twenty-four's use of "purged." It is used in Professor Rosenblatt's book in the psychoanalytical sense of bringing into "consciousness various experiences, attitudes, or impulses which, because of some feeling of guilt about them, he has submerged or 'censored.'"[21] Just as a patient who is led to see his impulses as scientifically explicable and humanly governable is freed of fears and obsessions, so in literature the adolescent reader "becomes aware of the fact that his present experiences and anxieties are not unique and that others have had the same impulses and conflicts." In consequence, "he may be better able to handle them."[22] By virtue of the objectivity provided by experience through literature, the disturbing impulses may be seen in proportioned relationships and a piece of literature "may provide *liberation* from blind fears and guilt."[23]

The theories of empathy expounded by Lipps and Lee—in which the observer unconsciously feels himself into the physical and spiritual attitude and atmosphere seen in the work of art—are here expanded to include the imaginative identification of the reader with the emotions and impulses of literary characters. Taken by itself "empathy" conveys the idea of a phenomenon which automatically disciplines the subversive emotions of individuals who have them. In context with "purged" and "disciplined," we may think of it as a phenomenon within the province of human control. Without this interpretation, the doctrine of empathy raises a significant problem that we cannot escape. Through empathy the individual is purged of anti-social impulses; but what insures the continuance of socially desirable ones?

From this therapeutic value, the discussion turns to the creative: "But literature as an art serves the individual in an even more important way. The delight he feels when ideals charged with life and passion are thrust into his inmost consciousness becomes in a mysterious way the objectification of his ideal self." [24] Once more the question arises of the ideal self's being an undesirable citizen in a democracy. It is possible for the reader to "behold a fuller, more capacious individual than he ever is—one who becomes his wish" [25] —in a literary figure portraying anti-social qualities. And a further question centers in the fact that while imaginative identification may lead to emotional stability and be formative of rounded personality, it may also, when carried to a logical extreme, lead to injurious escape from reality and indulgence in wishful thinking. Presumably it is the teacher's role to provide guidance for each student to "realize for himself an ever widening range of values" [26] which he may enlist "in the service of a firmly integrated personality." [27]

The harmonizing of such modern ideas of aesthetic experience as we have been concerned with is definitely sought in this section of the article. As we have noted, it places primary value upon literature in its aiding the enlargement and realization of self which comes when "superficially disjointed incidents of living . . . [attain] a continuity and a sense of progress which transmutes them into integrated human life." [28]

What is the relationship, finally, among aesthetic values, critical methods, and teaching methods?

In so far as a work of art grows from the matrix of society and is one symbol of a given cultural period, it is essential that the work of art be seen in the context of contemporaneous historical forces. It provides enduring record of their meaning to human individuals— the "record of intellectual and spiritual achievement and aspiration." [29]

These meanings, however, must be drawn from valuable literature through intellectual discipline. The intellectual disciplines associated with literature we may supply as logic, grammar, rhetoric, and history, although these words do not appear in the statement. The logic to be employed in critical appreciation we infer to be analogical. The committee report calls attention to its own metaphor in comparing gradations of musical appreciation and levels of value gained from the reading of literature. The report explicitly attributes to intellectual discipline the perception of expressive form. Hence the aesthetic experience must be a cumulative process, and the teaching method must involve coöperative guidance, not "exhortation or apostrophe" or " 'spectator sport,' in which students observe their professor performing . . . feats of appreciation or criticism." [30]

The "aesthetic insight" that is involved in disciplined emotional-intellectual analysis of masterpieces is presumably keyed to the "aesthetic experience" that facilitates both the empathetic spending of subversive emotions and the "mysterious" objectification of ideal self. If it were assumed that the disciplined inquiry into the orderly form of literature gives confidence for similar inquiry into analogous life-situations, the statement would have implied a humanly measurable process for the control of emotions. If, on the other hand, this is not to be inferred, then other critical methods seem essential for bringing each individual reader, with his individual psychological problem, into contact with precisely the right book to treat his case. This assumes that teachers are more or less informed on modern psychological thinking. It leaves open various questions, of course, about the hazards of amateur psychiatry which Barzum raises in *Of Human Freedom;* but teachers of literature have always faced such questions. We may conclude that the Committee statement definitely reflects and depends on the acceptance of modern broad concepts of aesthetic experience by many representative college teachers.

4. INDIVIDUAL WRITERS ON VARIOUS ASPECTS OF THE HUMANITIES

A. Theodore Meyer Greene: Philosophical Spokesman for the Disciplines

Thus far, except for John Dewey, philosopher and pioneer educator, we have chiefly considered teachers of English and Comparative Literature. Among important spokesmen also are other philosophers, historians, and semanticists. Many teachers emphasizing literature in the modern Humanities expect their broad field to deal emphatically with philosophy and the history of ideas. Philosophers like Theodore Meyer Greene and Irwin Edman put much emphasis on ideas of aesthetic experience in literature.

In Greene we see an increasing emphasis on this idea since his editing of *The Meaning of the Humanities* (1938), with its statements from five distinguished scholars in the Spencer Trask Series at Princeton University in 1938.[1] This book does not present a detailed statement of Greene's ideas about aesthetic experience, but it points clearly toward such a statement in his *Arts and the Art of Criticism* (1940). In his prefatory essay in *The Meaning of the Humanities,* he is more concerned with synthesizing the wide-ranging lectures with specialized scholarship, both in art and science. He discusses "the nature of the humanities and their worth for man"[2] in a world where "the contemporary threat to human values lies in the deliberate activities of certain individuals and groups whose ideologies are monopolistic and totalitarian and who, in one way or another, have acquired autocratic power in our society."[3] But the humanistic endeavor is not merely a means to combating totalitarian denial of human freedom; it is an end in itself, the coöperative attainment of whose highest form, the historico-philosophical synthesis of cultural achievement, should be the moral imperative of every humanist. Aesthetic concerns are always present.

Greene defines the historico-philosophical synthesis by investigating the nature of the human spirit in its quest for enduring values. In doing so he takes account of recent biological, psychological, and anthropological findings. Yet, rather than start with biological similarities to other animals, Greene has us imagine human individuals existing on five experience levels, beginning with that of "atomistic awareness," and extending to the humanistic ideal of historico-philosophical synthesis through graduated stages of interaction with environment.[4] He would show how far man has advanced beyond other animals.

On the lowest level of atomistic awareness (analogous to the hydra which Dewey mentions?) we find a merely sentient being, one capable of sensation, emotion, and feelings of pleasure and pain.[5] This purely imaginary level of human existence is more easily defined in its limitations than in positive qualities. The merely sentient being lacks memory, reason, and imagination. With no accumulated learnings, its present exists without interpretative understanding from a remembered past. With neither memory nor imagination, it possesses no conception of futurity and hence lacks purposive thought or conduct, the ultimate expression of the self. Furthermore, it lacks the means of acquiring a sense of comparative values, the pertinence of which to human development is implicit in Greene's comparative presentation of five levels of being.

On the second level is the conscious being to whose mere sentience are added the human faculties or operations of mind called memory, reason, and imagination, but who, from the moment of birth, has been denied all contact with human society.[6] This imaginary creature possesses a sense of temporal and spatial order. Memory enables human beings to fund their experience and to sharpen their consciousness of the meaning of the present through comparison with the past; imagination makes possible a conception of the "not-yet-present" and the meaning of the present in terms of this future. With funded meanings drawn from quantitative and qualitative comparisons and discriminations of physical and mental states, this second imaginary being is capable of modifying its behavior for increasing purposiveness.[7] With the achievement of some measure of security and leisure through its purposive, single-handed mastery of physical environment, it might engage in speculative concern about its own nature, might feel the sense of strangeness and mystery that is "the raw material of man's developed consciousness of the divine,"[8] and might express aesthetic response to its environment through "simple patterns of color and sound for its own amusement."[9] All of these responses we see as elementary evidences of the formative impulse, for this being, through its own resources, is transforming its solitary "world" from "a mere chaos of particulars . . . [to] the primitive beginning of an orderly cosmos."[10]

The limitations of this creature—the necessity of its acquiring directly all the techniques of mastery of environment, the lack of language to record and accumulate its rudimentary discriminations, and by implication the lack of incentive for these things—all force our imaginations to a conception of the third level of experience, a social existence which human life normally affords.[11]

On the third level of "social convention" the distinguishing characteristics are *language, tradition,* and *institution*. Greene defines language as "any vehicle, adopted by convention, which is suitable to the purpose of organizing, recording and communicating human thought and experience." [12] Within this range, come verbal language, certain gestures and bodily movements, and works of art in each of the artistic media. Written language and permanent art works make possible the preservation and accumulation of cultural achievements. The usefulness of language is augmented by social institutions such as the family, state, school, and church. The cumulative social influences constitute the "culture pattern" in which human individuals grow. "We are not only *what* we are because of the cultural heritage into which we have been born; our lives are as *rich* or as *impoverished* as they are largely because of the cultural value, or lack of value, of the particular culture pattern in which we find ourselves." [13]

This attention to cultural influences implies no elements of determinism, however, for "even the most submissive and unimaginative of mortals has some capacity for original creation and criticism" of the social conventions within whose context he lives.[14] Individuals vary in their capacities for curiosity and imagination, in their concern with more adequate resolutions of problems, and in their imaginative projection of such harmonizing of values. As each individual works to achieve his measure of critical reorganization of social convention, society becomes dynamic. It undergoes continual transformation, and the individuals interacting with it through criticism retain their sense of sufficiency, their spirituality.[15]

We have seen that every individual has some capacity for critical-creative reorganization of his environment. The diversity of human interests and capacities leads to a diversity of special areas in which contributions are continuously being made to society.

This gives rise to Greene's fourth level of experience, that of "creative and critical specialization," [16] in which the more original individuals make unusually extensive contributions in the fields of art, science, and religion, and of politics, history, and philosophy.[17] No marked differences are distinguishable among the creative and critical thought-processes in these areas of specialization, but each area demands a nice balance between creative and critical thought, for "creation wholly undisciplined by critical analysis and evaluation runs riot and issues in mere ebullient novelty, while criticism which is not vitalized by the creative imagination and which is not concerned with man's creative products feeds on itself and ends in sterility." [18] The greatest contributions have been made by individuals through "disciplined imagination, that is, by original invention and constructive criticism functioning as aspects of a single organic process." [19] This union of creative-critical activity in one individual does not eliminate the more highly specialized contribution which comes from individuals who are either primarily creative or primarily critical thinkers.

Inherent in specialization is the tendency for the specialist to become removed from broad acquaintance with his social context. The more extreme this specialization becomes, as for instance in the progressive subdivision of universities into schools, schools into departments, departments into specialized courses, "the more urgent the need for effective coöperation between specialists of every type." [20] In so far as specialists have demonstrated in many instances the parochial limitations of perspective on their work and that of others, some comprehensive synthesizing agent must seek the human meanings of the aggregate of specialized findings and bring into focus a "comprehension of the parts in their relation to the larger whole." [21] Only through "an effective re-definition of man's true end and the enlightened re-discovery of our larger cultural heritage" can the accomplishment of contemporary specialists be given "a frame of reference within which all partial insights can have their place and contribute to a cultural perspective."[22]

This brings us to the fifth and highest level of experience, "the humanistic ideal as an historico-philosophical synthesis."[23] Here we find a *rationale* for linking the work of the scholar specialist with that of the synthesizing teacher of the Humanities. While Greene includes history and philosophy in the level of creative-critical specialization, the inclusive nature of their subject-matter gives these subjects peculiar responsibility for synthesis of meanings, "because they constitute the only possible ways in which the particular experiences of the race and of the individual can be interpreted in their relation to one another and to reality as a whole."[24] Re-emphasizing the same point, Greene writes: "There are two, and only two, basic modes of interpretation, the historical, in terms of temporal sequence, and the systematic, in terms of more enduring quality and structure."[25]

When Greene emphasizes two modes of interpretation, he implies that the final historico-philosophical synthesis can be made only after the disciplines of history and philosophy have been invoked for critical evaluation within each of the areas of specialization, for workers in each area should be aware of its historical emergence and systematically concerned with its basic concepts, materials, and methods. "Thus the social sciences, literary and artistic criticism, and the study of religion are all, in essence, both historical and systematic inquiries, and even the natural sciences, though primarily concerned with enduring structure, cannot ignore their own historical development or the temporal character of their subject-matter."[26]

The arts converge at this point with history and philosophy, for these disciplines are themselves interdependent; as they draw upon all the materials of culture, history makes its interpretations in the light of certain philosophic values, and philosophy makes its evaluation of temporal and purposive experiences of mankind. At the same time philosophy must be aware of its own historical growth, of its nature as "an historical phenomenon to be understood adequately only in its historical context."[27] It appears, like art in any culture, as a high order of man's formative impulse. Like philosophy, art is interpretable only in its historical context as a symbol of culture, but it differs from philosophy in the expressive form through which it bodies forth its system of values.

Thus far in Greene we have seen briefly the larger *formative* aspect of the aesthetic experience, its integral relationship with the culture in which it expresses itself, and the organic relationship between creative and critical effort. We have seen little of the values of aesthetic experience to the individual creator or critic, and little of the disciplines involved in the organic process itself. We find many extensions of these ideas in the essays on Philosophy, History, Art, Religion, and Literature[28] which follow Greene's editorial introduction to *The Meaning of the Humanities,* but much more explicit revelation in his *Arts and the Art of Criticism*.

Two statements, already noted, in *The Meaning of the Humanities* provide a close link with Greene's increased concern with aesthetic experience in *The Arts and the Art of Criticism*. He refers to the formation of "simple patterns of color and sound" for the amusement of primitive man, and to creation and criticism "as aspects of a single organic process." In *The Arts and the Art of Criticism,* he furthers the idea of organic process by using aesthetic "to signify the distinctive common quality of *any* object of awareness which is capable of evoking a *re*-creative response in an aesthetically sensitive spectator."[29] He extends the idea of pattern by showing that the form or design which makes an object recognizable is "not autonomous or independent of the medium, it is merely the manner in which the medial elements are related to one another."[30] These statements provide us with the range of Greene's idea of aesthetic experience. This relativistic organic creative-critical process we should examine further in certain particulars.

Greene recognizes "that human consciousness is not a mere aggregate of unrelated mental states."[31] Save in extreme pathological cases, "consciousness is at each instant a function of a more enduring self ... persisting in time as a relatively enduring pattern of memories, habits, impulsions, etc."[32] It is from this enduring background that the individual interacts with his environment and maintains a sense of "identity amid the flux of inner and outer change." [33]

As we observed in *The Meaning of the Humanities,* the "more human values" of imagination, memory and reason, which make for conscious selfhood, are not limited to a few men. The artist is a "specialist" who, within the matrix of his culture, indulges his aptitude for perceiving with imaginative sympathy the unique quality of many situations, the tones and colors of objects, and the moods and aspirations of men. He projects himself in imaginative sympathy into the lives of other men.[34] "He selects from among his own experiences and those of his fellow-men the experiences which seem to him to possess universal meaning and significance." [35] The artist gives form to these ideas and experiences not as duplications of what he has perceived but as "interpretations of his subject-matter which he believes to be both true *and* significant." [36] Greene is here drawing upon art history as it has been built up from art historians, anthropologists, sociologists, and psychologists whose findings present "overwhelming evidence that art in the various media has arisen from the artist's desire to express and communicate to his fellows some pervasive human emotion, some insight felt by him to have a wider relevancy, some interpretation of reality other than the work of art itself in all its specificity." [37]

The work of art has its inception in the artist's interaction with his environment—in his perception of the values it holds and his imaginative projection of more fundamental values underlying the situations he is immediately aware of. The apprehension (or intuition, as Croce calls it) of this basic reality involves expression in some appropriate medium. Acknowledging Croce's insight into the creative process, Greene writes: "Thought and its expression are aspects of a single organic process. We do not first apprehend a situation and *then* express our apprehension of it in some medium; we apprehend it from the very outset only in and through some cognitive and expressive medium...." [38]

For the literary artist the expressive medium is language, whose three types of verbal meaning, "conceptual," "imagistic," and "emotive-conative," lend themselves to the elaboration of artistic device.[39] The first is the naming of particulars and universals. The second, through the imagistic associations of words, makes possible the revival and communication of sensory perceptions of tangible objects. The third, the emotive-conative quality of words, carries the emotional charge and the overtones of value that arouse in certain contexts more or less specific emotionalized attitudes.[40] In addition to these qualities (as Müller-Freienfels and many others point out), language possesses certain physical properties of sound in which word symbols are couched—timbre, pitch, intensity, and rhythm. All these are the "raw materials" of the literary artist. As a specialist in their manipulation, he exploits the emotive-conative properties of language and utilizes the sensuous qualities of sound and rhythm for the expression of values within a specific context. Moreover, he uses the "metaphorical dimension" as a means of clarifying meanings by particularizing the abstract and universalizing the particular.[41] Here Greene reaches out toward I. A. Richards' insistence on the relative metaphorical values of language, in opposition to the Hutchins-Adler insistence on words as absolutes to be used syllogistically in pursuit of truth.

The expression which the author achieves, because it represents his self's continuous efforts to maintain its identity in a changing environment, is at once an expression of that self and of some aspect of the artist's culture. Greene holds, as does Dewey, and as does Ralph Barton Perry in "A Definition of the Humanities," that

the doctrine of art as self-expression implies that the subject-matter of art is, in any concrete instance, not merely the enduring self of the creative artist but as much of the objective world as the artist has assimilated in the development of his own personality.[42]

It is not only in subject-matter that the work of art is symbolic of its author's culture. Greene states more explicitly than Dewey or Professor Rosenblatt that its form is integral with the predominant emotional tone of contemporaneous culture. Such tones may be lyrical, reflective, dramatic, and descriptive. These pervasive emotional atmospheres of literature are comparable to literary *genres* or types as Posnett uses the term. They subsume the externally recognizable kinds of literature,—prose, poetry, etc. A work is *lyrical* in proportion to its treatment of feelings and emotions of individuals or a group of individuals sharing certain sentiments and ideals. The lyrical, moreover, stresses these emotions rather than their causes.[43] A work is *reflective* in proportion to its inclusion of "man's thoughts or reflections about himself and the larger reality of which he is a part"—its achievement of "a sense of perspective and a realization of the significance of intellectual inquiry and its discoveries. . . ."[44] *Dramatic* treatment, as for Aristotle and for modern comparative literature scholars like Bovet, is typified by the degree to which the human will is presented in dynamic conflict as it attempts to "translate ideals into actualities by volitional effort."[45] It is the supreme indication of man's "effort to adapt himself to his physical and social environment and to mould this environment to his own needs and desires."[46] The *descriptive* treatment is pervaded by man's concern with the thoughts and feelings which nature inspires in him, and his conception of his place within the world of nature.[47]

Greene does not explicitly attach significance to the order in which these types predominate within any cultural period. By inference the *lyrical* springs from an awakening society in which individuals are exploring their self-consciousness, the *reflective* originates in a culture seeking perspective on its development; the *dramatic* rises within a maturing society where, in urban organization, human conflicts become more pressing. In the exemplification which Greene offers from Tennyson, Lucretius, Wordsworth, the *descriptive* grows in a society which has achieved a wide passiveness after major rhythmic conflicts have been resolved.

With the completion of the work of art as Greene sees it, one phase of the organic process is concluded—the aesthetic experience of the artist. In so far as his creative activities were carried on with the reader consciously in mind, there follows a comparable kind of activity on the reader's part, but less active. As Nietzsche has also stated, Greene indicates that the reading process is "essentially docile and assimilative ... motivated by a desire not to create something new, not to impose upon some medium a beautiful and meaningful form, but rather to discover and enjoy what has already been aesthetically ordered."[48] On a critical level, reading involves "establishing artistic *rapport* with the work of art."[49]

Achieving *rapport* involves a process of "aesthetic re-creation"[50] for which certain disciplines and attitudes are indispensable. According to Erwin Panofsky in "The History of Art as a Humanistic Discipline," the observer must "re-enact the actions and re-create the creations" of the author.[51] Just as the author is a specialist, with particular imaginative sympathy for values in human experience and for the expressive qualities of his chosen medium, so should the critic be a specialist with similar awareness to environment, with expert knowledge of the disciplines of language, and with sufficient control to maintain "psychical distance" as he views the work of art. "The greater his capacity for imaginative sympathy, the more catholic his outlook, the clearer his historical perspective—in short, the greater his awareness of *pervasive* human attitudes and *recurrent* patterns of belief, the more objective will be his appraisals of artistic greatness."[52] These qualities demand knowledge both of the subject-matter and disciplines of anthropology, sociology, archeology and psychology which, while maintaining scientific objectivity, "treat art as a *human* product and seek to relate it to its social context...."[53]

By invoking all these abilities and disciplines in the evaluation of a work of art, the critic can orient a work of art in one of the major epochs of Western civilization, Greek, Roman, Medieval, Renaissance, or modern, and within that orientation use the disciplines of language to evaluate the quality of the work. He will necessarily "refrain from transforming *any one* specific pattern of beliefs, factual or normative, into an absolute criterion of objective greatness."[54] He will refrain from making "invidious comparisons between masterpieces" and, we infer, from setting up any rigid list of "best books" for all people.

Critical re-creation will tend—as the appendix to *The Arts and* the *Art of Criticism* shows in a supplementary essay on Beethoven's Third Symphony by Roy Dickinson Welch[55]—toward a running comment on the work of art as it is experienced in its own order by the reader or listener—a method we also see exemplified in Mark Van Doren's *Shakespeare*. Critical appraisal will tend toward one of five levels, from the purely formal to the philosophic. The first level concerns "style" or the artist's distinctive manner of organizing his media. The second level builds from the first and has to do with "artistic quality or perfection"—the extent to which the medium has been exploited for expression of a specific idea.[56] The third level is dependent upon levels one and two and concerns "artistic integrity," or the felicitous presentation of a coherent interpretation of a given subject-matter.[57] The fourth level, "artistic truth," is a product of the previous three levels, for the "truth" of an artistic expression is dependent upon the correctness and felicity of artistic perfection, the coherence of artistic integrity, and the satisfaction of all artistically available, relevant, and reliable empirical evidence which is "artistic correspondence."[58] The fifth level is that of "artistic greatness"—the depth and breadth of *insight*. To apprehend artistic greatness, the critic must have "the ability to share imaginatively in many different types of experience and to comprehend diverse interpretations and evaluations of these experiences."[59] Furthermore, from a philosophic angle he must have "the ability to evaluate the profundity or triviality of these experiences and their normative interpretations."[60] The achievement of an imaginative-sympathetic understanding of the philosophy of life presented is the aesthetic experience of the critic.[61]

Beyond the aesthetic experience of the specialist critic, the advancement of society demands the historico-philosophical synthesis of "art in general." Greene sees this as an undertaking for "the philosopher of art who possesses the requisite philosophical training and who is scientifically, critically, and historically oriented."[62] The challenge which Greene implicitly leaves to education is the pragmatic one of translating the historico-philosophical synthesis into daily practice in Humanities class rooms.

B. Irwin Edman: Poet-Philosopher

Irwin Edman, like Greene, speaks from a philosopher's point of view. As staff member for both the advanced "Colloquium" and the Humanities course in Columbia College, as poet in his own right, and as musician and student of music, he represents a balanced resolution of numerous modern currents of thought.

Like Dewey, Rosenblatt, and Greene, Edman is concerned about the complexities of modern society in which the supreme value of human individuality is threatened with suppression for large numbers of people. "It is well," he says in *Fountainheads of Freedom* (1941), "to look back on the history of the democratic idea, and to see that, where courage and intelligence and united good will were brought to bear, such perils of internal diseases and outside enemies have been surmounted before."[1] In *The Saturday Review of Literature,* under "Man's Humanities to Man," he realistically faces the educational phase of the problem, knowing that whatever cultural heritage we transmit to the present school generation "must have its career in the midst of chaos."[2] With this realization, he writes that we must attempt "to make education an equipment for understanding the present and facing the future with courage, serenity, and understanding. . . ."[3] Here he emphasizes individual values, individually experienced and individually expressed. They are both the product and producer of democracy, for "democracy taken seriously involves the assumption that genuinely free institutions nourish, liberate, and cultivate personality."[4]

To find a basis for constructive work in the face of fanaticism, inhumanity, and the resignation fostered by prophets of doom, Edman points, in "Culture in a Democracy" in *The Saturday Review of Literature,* to the imbalance of curricular offerings in American schools and colleges in the immediate past. He notes the exhaustive and necessary concern with science and scientific discipline, the pervasive concern with social problems through too vaguely defined disciplines and objectives, and an amorphous mass of study about literature and literary influences. In all three he finds little provision for a deeper understanding of the meaning of life and the value of human dignity. To rectify this breach in the transmission of our heritage, Edman noted in 1935 that there "has dawned upon educators," [5] and again in 1939 that educators had "hit upon," the value of the great books.[6] These phrases do not indicate a casualness about the revival of the Humanities. Edman shows, rather, that the revival of the Humanities has sprung at once from a philosophic recognition of the worth of the human individual [7] as the base for a free society, and from a modern psychological-anthropological concept of aesthetic experience as man's quest for design in life, whether this be through historical perspective, a world view, metaphysics, or a work of art. Both the impulse to achieve this design and the response to it are aesthetic.

Like Greene, Edman achieves a resolution of many scientific, religious, and philosophic values now current. He has, however, emphasized poetic resolution where Greene is concerned more with harmonizing the roles of the specializing scholar and the synthesizing philosopher. In consequence, Edman's poetic resolution reveals harmonies in aspects of philosophies as different as Plato's and Dewey's. In this idea of aesthetic experience we see that while Ideas are essences of the One, the Absolute, each Idea, as Schopenhauer indicates, has many manifestations[8] of which individual men are aware. These awarenesses are each man's world; the degree of his awareness determines his system of values and, hence, the nature of his purposive participation in society.[9] At this point Edman draws close to the philosophy of his teacher and colleague, Dewey.

It is significant that, with his sustained emphasis upon Plato as a philosopher who presents his philosophic synthesis in poetic fashion, and in his attention to the integral unity of form and content, Edman himself exemplifies the poetic presentation of his idea of aesthetic experience in the six sections of *Arts and the Man* (1939). Titles of the sections indicate an internal logic that is borne out in critical reading. We move from (I) "Art and Experience" with its attention to consummatory action which constitutes for Dewey "an experience" and for Edman "a moment crowded with vitality and order," [10] to the nature of a work of art as a symbol of its culture in (II) "Art and Civilization." The physical center of the book, (III) "The World, the Word, and the Poet," indicates Edman's concern with the microcosmic designs of great literature—designs nowhere so panoramic in the other arts. In (IV) "The Thing, the Eye, and the Plastic Arts" he treats of the values of painting and sculpture, and in (V) "Sounds, Ears, and the Musician" of the musical presentation "of such rationality as no society has as yet exemplified." [11] In the final section (VI) "Art and Philosophy" we reach the synthesis of Art and that "finer kind of music" which, for Edman, philosophy represents.

But despite the differences and the enmities between the two enterprises, art and philosophy both resemble and involve each other. The artist when he ceases to be merely a gifted and trifling craftsman turns out to be, in his very choice of themes, in his selection of materials, in his total and residual effect, a commentator on life and existence; in his immediate and imaginative way he is a philosopher. The philosopher, constructing through the apparatus of definition and demonstration, or of discovery and synthesis, a complete vision of life and existence, is making a canvas of the whole of experience, composing an intellectual symphony, and fabricating a poem, however much his language be prose. "Philosophy," Socrates is made to say by Plato, "is a finer kind of music," and like serious music, however unmoved the mind that went to its making, it is moving.[12]

Edman's idea of aesthetic experience clearly draws on modern psychological and anthropological inquiry. There is intrinsic value in experience itself, for it is the irreducible base of human life. "The realm of art is identical with the realm of man's deliberate control of that world of materials and movements among which he must make his home, of that inner world of random impulses and automatic processes which constitute his inner being." [13] But between the extremes of James' "blooming, buzzing confusion" and the inchoate vegetation of insensitive men there is the possibility of an existence in which acuity of perception and intellect makes life lucid and intense.[14] "Experience, apart from art and intelligence, is wild and orderless. It is formless matter, aimless movement." [15]

Those moments in which art and intelligence impress form or "pure spirit" upon "poor matter"[16] are those which achieve the vitality and unity, harmony and proportion, that the human mind treasures. Art, then, "is the name for the whole process of intelligence by which life, understanding its own conditions, turns them to the most interesting or exquisite account."[17]

What is the process by which art achieves this deliberate control, particularly in the medium of language? One pervasive impulse in man is the formative, in which animal senses, instincts, and varying degrees of intelligence combine to clarify the succession of impressions "through some deliberate and explicit pattern."[18] In primitive cultures, granted the necessary leisure, sheer delight in color and line challenge imagination to beautify even those utensils in common use.[19] In the more complex processes of doing and undergoing which make up modern experience[20] there are numerous emotional overtones from contacts with events and individual people in which unity, integrity, harmony, and clarity are lacking.[21] These the artist deliberately cultivates, "for what starts that ferment of images and music, which is the beginning of poetic creation, is some intensity of living, some depth of passionate feeling which the poet wishes to utter, and, though he may not realize it, to share."[22] This incitement is the unifying mood which fuses into a single living organism pertinent images, insights, and ideas from the artist's memory and subconscious.[23] These funded meanings have necessarily come from the artist's own interpretations of experience; he "selects his facts and materials and gives them their particular order by impulse, reflectively disciplined,"[24] with regard to his chosen medium. Any great work of art is therefore an expression, a symbol, of its contemporaneous civilization, for it is the stabilization of the flux of experience.[25]

Working in language, the author is forced by the nature of his medium, which is at once practical and musical, logical and melodic,[26] to write in either prose or poetry. Whichever style he chooses, he works with words which in their tonality and their cumulative associative content carry overtones of feeling.[27] In addition to the psychological connotation of words,[28] the cadence in which they are arranged determines their reception.[29] Metaphor is a further expressive device which the author consciously uses in "rebellion against routine impressions," [30] and through which he vivifies certain aspects of experience. Of all technical devices, rhythm, with its biological-physiological bases, is the most important single element. In poetry it aids the communication of the "impression of something Platonic and eternal and living . . . ," [31] or in the novel it helps to body forth a world of living characters.[32]

In *Arts and the Man* Edman is more concerned with poetry than with prose, though not exclusively. Among the arts, "poetry is more specifically an art where the medium of language is itself in the foreground, and where not the poet nor his hearer ever quite forgets the language in what is being said." [33] So important is the sensuous surface of the work of poetry, that poetry might be "an abstract architecture of exquisitely chosen vowel and consonant sounds as meaningless and absorbing as the colors in an oriental tapestry." [34] The lyric in poetry, as in music, is usually a presentation of a personal emotion.[35]

The expansive depth of the novel stands in contrast to the lyric. Edman sees the novel as the most forceful literary art form in our time. In the creation of the novel the author ranges through all of the cultural heritage of his time, selects events and circumstances, and constructs a rationally ordered world simultaneously with the critical appraisal of his own.[36] The characters who people this world are more fully individualized than characters whom we meet in normal life, or at least the simplicity of pattern reveals their maturity with greater clarity. And in showing them in clear form, the artist has actually achieved the end toward which his formative impulse moved him, the harmonious patterning of human values in clarity and brilliance. The process by which he attains these ends is a painful, arduous one of submitting to the disciplines of his medium, language. If means are integral with ends, and the end is a self-revealing formulation of values in language, then the mastery of the disciplines of language becomes the artist's means of realizing "what his artistic self is." The culmination of this rhythmic process in "a moment crowded with vitality and filled with order"[37] is the artist's aesthetic experience.

While Edman frequently refers to the arts as escapes for both artist and observer from the grossness and awkwardness of things and events, we are reminded that no animal simply reacts against a phase of his environment; his expressive movements are always toward a state of harmony. This helps us to clarify Edman's idea that "the arts have been escapes . . . to a section of light and color, of sound, of imaginative reverie, which was not only bearable but beautiful."[38] To this we must add his frequent emphasis that it is the artist's own mastery of certain disciplines which creates the desirable state—his own intelligence functioning "freely over tractable materials"[39] that changes the feverish Dionysian quality of experience into Apollonian repose. "Escape," so considered, is a self-preserving and self-realizing activity in which the individual artist, through his medium, asserts mastery over the anarchy of events as he witnesses them.[40] In that mastery are revealed explicit patterns of the potentialities in nature and society.

Such harmonious arrangements are . . . not simply solaces and escapes. They are symptoms and premonitions. They intimate, they are anticipations of what order in society might be. The discipline, self-imposed and controlled by means and materials, is an indication of the vital discipline which avoids the chaos of barbarism or hysteria on the one hand, and on the other the factitious order of the regiment or the drill sergeant or the dictator. In the arts, individuality comes to measured realization. It is something that life has not yet found, either in democracies or tyrannies.[41]

We have already noted Edman's belief that the artist, consciously or unconsciously, desires to share the formulation of values which he achieves. This makes the aesthetic experience continuous from creator to critic. Edman shows that the artist's meanings are seldom achieved in equal measure by all his audience. The aesthetic experience comes only with critical evaluation, which Edman interprets in a manner similar to that of Dewey, Louise Rosenblatt, and Greene.

Criticism is not "legislation" or "vague appreciation," Edman states; it is "the application of standards to perception, like those the artist, the scientist, and the practical man use for estimating the effectiveness of their techniques."[42] Criticism is a reflective examination of the use of the disciplines through which the artist communicates his sense of values. It involves a vicarious creative process through expertness in the medium which the artist has used; it is enlightened and exact perception of the artist's discrimination. The ingredients of such perception are intelligence, imagination, and sympathy, where, in the final analysis, intelligence is "directive and disciplined imagination"[43] seeking order and harmony for human life. Critical evaluation of a work of art reveals the order and harmony, the extent of rationality achieved in the microcosmic structure of the work of art. We may infer that this harmony is seen in the growth toward self-realization of the character or characters portrayed. Perception of the manner in which self-realization is revealed gives the critic insight like that of the author, and the sense of "something far more deeply interfused," which is his aesthetic experience.[44]

Edman, like Dewey, considers finally the relationship of aesthetic experience to the values of philosophy, science, and religion, and a rational civilization. At the level of aesthetic experience art approaches the imaginative realm of religion, and may in fact "render the reality of God as no theologian or philosopher would be able to do."[45] Also, in the necessity for disciplined control, self-imposed, creation and criticism of art approximate one of the values of scientific speculation and research.[46] And the moving designs of both philosophy and art are concerned with the nature of the good life, a program for the future, the projection in imagination of realizable human potentialities.

Philosophy, the intellectual synthesis of human meanings, is cognizant of the values presented in art,[47] which Edman exemplifies in the poetic resolution of his sonnet, "After a Mozart Quartet":

> Only another music could translate
> This music, and that melody were this;

As well seek language that could utter fate,
As well find metaphors for speaking bliss.
Rather be silent that the themes may flow,
Rivers of liquid and insouciant joy,
Here rushing into rapids, here a slow
Lyric without refining or alloy.
Rather at once be one with perfect things,
All earth's poor infelicities forgotten,
Fly in this laughing heaven with borrowed wings,
Immortal once before your body's rotten
While briefly yet the living mind can hear
This paradise so gay, abstract, and clear.[48]

Because philosophy is criticism of criticism, a harmonizing of values already harmonized within smaller areas of experience, "the arts have attracted the professional attention of philosophers from the fact that the order they would demonstrate is perhaps exemplified or achieved only in the organization of a masterpiece where all the parts interpenetrate and constitute living rationality such as the universe may, but only possibly may, be."[49] For contemporary man, rational direction of future society resides in the arts, where "that richness of sensuous material . . . , that intensity of feeling, are an intimation of what intelligent contrivance might make of all life, if the whole of life and society should be made the materials of a comprehensive and major art."[50]

C. Jacques Barzun: Humanistic Historian

Jacques Barzun has been, like Edman and Adler, a member of the Columbia College Colloquium. As historian, he lays a somewhat different emphasis from that of philosopher or dialectician on the values of literature.

Barzun's *Of Human Freedom* begins thus:

When our children ask us, twenty years from now, "What did you accomplish in those days?" we shall perhaps be glad to answer, like the French revolutionist after the Terror, "I survived."[1]

Throughout, basing his belief on the pragmatism of William James, he stresses the significance of the Humanities for human survival and ends with this naturalistic point of view:

... in the name of peace and pragmatism, let us face with open eyes a pluralistic world in which there are no universal churches, no single remedy for all disease, no one way to teach or write or sing, no magic diet that will make everyone healthy and happy, no world poets and no chosen races cut to one pattern or virtue, but only the wretched and wonderfully diversified human race which can live and build and leave cultural traces of its passage in a world that was apparently not fashioned for the purpose.[2]

Like the others, however, Barzun is concerned with the relation of the arts to democratic culture—a question "of human freedom" opposed to questions "of human bondage." So significant is that relationship, and so important is its dissemination through education, that "if it could be grasped by any generation of teachers and critics, they would be enabled to leap over the cultural lag of twenty-five years and understand their own artists. . . ."[3] He accents the fact that democracy is more than a form of political organization. Democratic governmental form is merely the external symbol of a way of living; it is a culture which recognizes man's natural diversity and his desire to maintain that diversity through free physical and spiritual activity.[4] From this follow his basic tenets: "Culture must be free if men's bodies are to be free, and culture perishes if we think and act like absolutists."[5] Because art is a kind of criticism of life, mirroring democratic diversity,[6] appraisal of art by each individual to the extent of his critical ability[7] is as vital to the evolution of human culture as the creation of art itself. The intellectual freedom essential to the continuation of human diversity includes the many human values which seem to be essentially attitudes that make for intelligent critical participation in society. These are attitudes which hold one to precise thinking,[8] to pertinent comparison, to "concentration and curiosity, [and to] the repression of intellectual fear and intellectual egotism. . . ."[9] Barzun places primary emphasis, as do James and Dewey, upon seeing life as many-sided, and upon evaluating its situations from the pragmatic base of appropriateness and relative worth.[10]

Though Barzun uses the term "aesthetic" only twice in *Of Human Freedom,* and then in context which does not define it, he recognizes here and in several articles in the *Saturday Review of Literature,* the *Nation,* and the *English Journal,* the pervasiveness of the arts, and artistic experience as a satisfying organization of materials or ideas. He suggests that there may be varieties of artistic experience[11] to replace the pernicious confinement of art appreciation to matters of form devoid of human meanings, or to make us more aware of the individual values which individual diversity will find in many and varied works of art.[12]

Drawing explicitly upon the sciences of anthropology and psychology, Barzun pictures the artist living in a given society, influenced by its changing social pressures and conventions, by its increased scientific knowledge which extends man's control over nature, and by the cultural heritage which education and previous art have provided. The artist, more acute and imaginative than other individuals, as Greene and other spokesmen hold,[13] perceives certain aspects of life which are unobserved by others.[14] When these acquired impressions and ideas become fragmentary, and for lack of organization chaotic and emotionally disturbing, the artist is impelled to set them down in orderly form; in so doing he exercises his responsibility as cultural agent.[15] "Art is always organization, modern art most of all precisely because it has to do with a harsh, noisy, crowded, superposed kind of life."[16] As we have already noted, "the artist, if he is creative at all, is with his own time, even when he works against it. He is organizing (pro or con) the perceptions that he acquires from the process of living and not from the contemplation of past art."[17]

Barzun holds that the artist's deep desire for organization and order causes him to create pictures of the world in which he lives.[18] "He seeks to mold materials to his will by taking advantage of their nature."[19] The shaping process is not an easy one, for his materials and his medium are refractory. "He works with an unwavering eye for the only durable kind of success, and therefore works at what he is after and not upon some easier task next door."[20] The aesthetic experience of the artist, the feeling of satisfaction in achieving equilibrium in his presentation of values, arises from the cumulative emotional-intellectual experience of overcoming the resistance of matter[21] in creating a communicable aspect of reality. The finished work of art is then one individual's participation in society and, because of the nature of the participation, a symbol of the culture in which the artist lives.

Each reader or observer of a work of art comes to it from a different cultural background and with an individual system of values.[22] For communication to take place between artist and reader, some active participation must be offered by the reader. An understanding of words as referents to things,[23] a recognition of them as pragmatic devices for communication,[24] must precede any mutual understanding between author and reader. But if words are to carry the author's intent, the reader must surrender himself to his book; he must discard all irrelevant emotions, giving himself over to the immediate "pleasure" of the experience.[25] Pleasure here should be interpreted as something akin to, yet deeper than, vicarious experience; it is projection of one's self in imaginative sympathy into the point of view of the period from which the art came, as though in "conversation with the dead or distant, free from ulterior motives and from pride of knowledge." [26]

Close identification necessitates a familiarity with the historical epoch in which the author lived, and historical knowledge of the significance of the material organized into the work of art. Barzun recognizes that the data of any phase of a culture epoch may be organized to different degrees of comprehensiveness in different works of art. He uses the work of Thomas Mann and Temple Bailey as exemplifications of the "amount" of literature incorporated in a given page.[27] But there are readers for whom Temple Bailey satisfies a need, for whom Temple Bailey's organization of values resolves the emotional-intellectual problems of which the individual is aware. This is the aesthetic experience for such readers[28] and a more valuable experience for them than that possible through their attempting to reach the level of comprehension demanded for Mann. A work of art is not an absolute good in itself;

its value is relative to the comprehension of the reader to whom it communicates or does not communicate a pattern of values.[29]

On more complex levels of comprehension, the aesthetic experience of the reader is also more complex. An imaginative projection into the spirit of the historical epoch remains basic, but a critical evaluation beyond one of approval or disapproval is necessary. Approval or disapproval is not commonly evaluative criticism; it is legislative and savors of moralistic absolutes.[30] Critical evaluation inspects what is offered and makes a comparative statement of the relative cultural value of the book.[31] This is not to say that standards have been abolished, for as Barzun states in his favorable critical review of Greene's *The Arts and the Art of Criticism*, ". . . a thing related is a thing fastened. . . ."[32]

The artistic organization of the materials, as Barzun sees it, grows from a central mood or idea which the author injects into it. Constructive critical evaluation should proceed from a working hypothesis to clarify that central idea.[33] Barzun does not explicitly state what that central value might be, for in his concept of aesthetic experience it must necessarily differ from book to book and reader to reader. He does, however, indicate the self-fulfilling values of the creative process. Mature critical evaluation, he says, might presumably make critics "feel surer and happier. . . ."[34] If, then, the artist achieved a secure individuality through the creation of a symbol of his culture and the critic's personality is also amplified through his evaluation, we see "the true, the only relation between art and society which dictators, critics, and prophets are fumbling for."[35] Presumably the critic's main concern lies with the way the author reveals the growth of individuality in his work of art.[36]

As we have seen, Barzun is concerned with the transmission of cultural ideas through critics and critical teachers in education. He says explicitly in his review of Launcelot Hogben's *Scientific Humanism* that education is a means of social reform.[37] In *Of Human Freedom* he discusses two "inchoate but growing" movements in American education, each presenting methods and materials aimed at social reform. One of these movements Barzun identifies as Progressive Education, the other as the revival of the Humanities.

Barzun's general tone toward Progressive Education is one of suspended judgment. His attitude is too judicial to condemn or laud all of any movement without evaluating separately its various parts. "Progressive Education is not a whole. It is the name for a series of practices, some of which are absurd, and some admirable." [38] It falls short, he states, in its absence of discipline, its shallowness of subject-matter, its loss of distinguishing disciplines in correlation, and its tendency toward amateur psychoanalytic interference with students' personal problems.[39] "At the same time," he notes, "progressive education would remould society by altering the individual's response to it, making him more coöperative, more tolerant, more diversified in his interests. Progressive Education is working for a self-governing egalitarian democracy." [40]

These aspects of Progressive Education seem to be problems of methods and materials which can be adjusted within individual courses and by individual teachers, for we find both Barzun and Louise Rosenblatt starting from the same pragmatic base, and with the same preoccupation with the preparation of self-directive members of society.[41]

Barzun's discussion of the revival of the Humanities also suspends judgment. In *Of Human Freedom,* he questions the return-to-the-classics-via-the-trivium as advocated by Hutchins and Adler and exemplified in the curriculum at St. John's College, Annapolis.[42] On the other hand, in the Columbia College Humanities Course, with its modern spirit, he sees great promise. His position here is especially interesting because of Adler's previous connection with Columbia, and his repeated references to the similarity of materials used in Columbia and St. John's. Hutchins' way, Barzun intimates, would use the classics as a panacea,[43] an established permanent order founded in the classification of Aristotle and the hierarchy of St. Thomas. But such a return is not "order" for a modern interdependent world, Barzun insists. "Disputation and excommunication are its devices; but disputation is not discussion and excommunication is, on the face of it, lack of communication. Orthodoxy is the antithesis of a living and variegated culture; it is undemocratic at the very root of democracy, which is the individual mind." [44]

There are many potential values in a revival of the Humanities as Barzun sees it. The first of these is their diversity. At the same time, among all the many forms that art and literature have assumed, there remains a core of human unity in their attention to timeless world values whose realization is integral with the realization of self-control and self-respect.[45] These constitute "the only durable kind of success," [46] for they are acquired through a mastery of matter which enforces a recognition of "the need for patient application, and the indefinable worth that intelligence confers on mechanical skill." [47] When the classics are used with regard for the variety of facts and feelings which they communicate,[48] they awaken imagination and sympathy and a sense of perspective for coping with the problems of modern society.[49] The Humanities (and perhaps we should infer from Barzun's "The Humanities—Proper Study of Mankind" that they include any books properly taught) fill historical background with meanings and references which are part of daily figurative language.[50] The Humanities aid in finding meanings of words within their contexts, a necessity in a relativistic approach to human values.[51] All of these values converge in the emotional-intellectual balance and harmony of previously disorganized particulars which is an aesthetic experience for the individual. The "largeness" of this "unifying" concept is exemplified in Barzun's *Darwin, Marx, Wagner,* where, seeing these men as "representatives of the dominant tradition we live by," he seeks a pragmatic unity for the "three great relations that cause us the deepest concern— science and religion; science and society; society and art. . . ." [52]

D. *I. A. Richards: International Psychologist-Semanticist*

Thus far we have been concerned with teachers of literature, history, and philosophy who are intimately connected with the teaching of Humanities courses in American colleges and universities. In the work of I. A. Richards, British semanticist, we face something more complicated; yet a certain magic has come to be connected with Richards' name, and teachers show a disposition to try to grasp his meaning and method, attracted often by reports of other teachers who have encountered his ideas in educational workshops or progressive courses.[1] His attention to metaphor and analogy and to relative values seems to come close to modern ways of thinking and feeling in America—ways perhaps more common in America than in England, and accounting in part, perhaps, for Richards' coming to this country. This is speculative hypothesis, of course, but we need such hypothesis to grasp Richards' popularity despite his complexities.

In *Interpretation in Teaching,* Richards states that the province of education is facilitating the use of language "To orientate, to equip, to prepare, to encourage, to provoke, a mental traveller to advance by his own energies in whatever region may be his to explore; to make him think for himself *and* make him able to do so sanely and successfully. . . ."[2] This is a blanket statement which does not differentiate Richards from other responsible leaders in education. But his distinctive focus is apparent when he states: "To live reasonably is not to live by reason alone—the mistake is easy and, if carried far, disastrous—but to live in a way of which reason, a clear full sense of the whole situation, would approve."[3] His emphasis upon the wholeness of a situation reflects his psychologist's concern for ways of thinking "which recent experimental and theoretical investigations of the 'Gestalt' School are indicating," as he says in *Principles of Literary Criticism.*[4] It prepares us for his contention that in any expression through language, creative or critical, there is a simultaneous employment of the arts of rhetoric, logic, and grammar.

In Richards' concept of relativistic disciplines we may find one common base among the spokesmen previously examined, and the central difference between their position and that assumed by Hutchins and Adler. In Richards' modern reinterpretation of the modes of the trivium, and Hutchins' seeming revival of the ancient and medieval meanings of the three arts, we may find the fundamental difference between the Humanities courses with which men like Barzun and Edman identify themselves, and the one which Barzun terms medieval, at Saint John's College. These hypotheses will be examined later in our study.

As we examine Richards' idea of aesthetic experience, we note the increasing comprehensiveness which it shows from the publication of *Foundations of Aesthetics* (1922) through *Practical Criticism* (1929) to *Interpretation in Teaching* (1938). In this fact we see exemplification of Richards' "clear full sense of the whole situation" —in this instance his awareness of growth in the inquiries of modern psychology and anthropology.

Foundations of Aesthetics offers a "sorting" (to use Richards' word) of the various "senses" of Beauty, arguing for the concept of synaesthesia, or the approximate identification of the reader with the state of mind of the author during the creative process.[5] In 1923 *The Meaning of Meaning* explored more fully the uses of language which conduce to synaesthesis. In 1925 Richards' "Science and Poetry" in the *Atlantic Monthly*, held that ". . . the time has come to attempt some practical applications"[6] of the science of mind, psychology, to the interpretation of values in literature.[7] For this, he declared that "both a passionate knowledge of poetry and a dispassionate capacity for psychological analysis are required. . . ."[8]

In 1934 Richards explored these two streams essential to a values approach to literature. The "passionate knowledge of poetry" he explored in *Coleridge on Imagination*, accenting semasiology or the science of the development of meanings as the "most central incipient science of the future."[9] In 1925 "Psychological analysis" meant for Richards a concern with the battery of instincts, emotions, and impulses which social psychologists like McDougall were then attributing to the human organism.[10] In 1934, his *Principles of Literary Criticism* mentions behavioristic and psychoanalytical schools but, as we have noted earlier, finds most value in the concepts and methods of the Gestalt position.[11]

Richards sees man very much as Dewey does—as a complex physical structure possessing capacity for sensory awareness, and embodying mind—a nervous system capable of recording and coördinating aspects of experience gained in interaction with environment.[12] Mind possesses the attributes of "knowing, willing, and feeling, three irreducible modes of being aware of or concerned with objects."[13] The most pervasive activity of mind is its coördinative one, its "tendency toward increased order,"[14] which is carried forward consciously and unconsciously. So central to his well-being is the organization of his impulses that in a state of disorganization he will "not live ten minutes without disaster."[15] Other human qualities to which Richards devotes explicit attention are memory, imagination, intelligence, and "good will" or sympathy.

Individual men show varying degrees of acuteness in each of these attributes and qualities, but every man (as Dewey and Greene have indicated) uses all of them to some extent in interaction with his environment.[16] The extent of self-realization is dependent upon a man's susceptibility to sensory impressions, his memory, his facility in perceiving relationships, and his consciousness that these are essential to his development.[17]

The "tendency toward increased order" seems similar to the formative impulse noted in the aesthetics of each of the spokesmen examined. One of the primary functions which it serves is the conservation of energy through a process similar to that stated in the Law of Prägnanz, although Richards does not use that term. Man is aware of many particular items in his experience, but these tend to be organized into related groups through conscious effort or unconscious impulse. These relationships flash upon him with a luminous quality which intensifies his consciousness and gives to the related particulars the "wholeness" of an experience which is simultaneously physical-emotional-intellectual.[18] Human energy is conserved when one aspect of the experience, an image pervaded by a particular feeling or attitude, remains as a symbol of the whole. When a new configuration of impressions characterized by a similar feeling tone arises, the symbol may be recalled. The recollection of the symbol is accompanied by varying amounts of detail from the original experience.[19] In his awareness of particulars, in his acuteness in perceiving relationships, in his consciousness of symbolic images, the artist is superior to many men and is artist for that very reason. This idea is common to most if not all the spokesmen for a modern aesthetic.

In "Science and Poetry" Richards shows that the artist is challenged to his creative task by an inharmonious situation and its accompanying emotional tension. As his only means of escape from chaos, of release from tension, he is forced to some kind of organization or "self-conquest," [20] a conscious process for increasing numbers of individuals with scientific knowledge of psychology. The work of art is the record of the harmonizing process which, depending upon the individual, involves varying amounts of self-denial and self-discipline.[21] More specifically, it is a self-imposed discipline to express himself through the disciplines of his chosen medium. The rigor of his discipline, the extent to which it involves denial of other values, determines the value which he places upon his final expression.[22]

Language has several functions and qualities of which the literary artist may or may not be consciously aware, although he must demonstrate their use with some facility.[23] The functions of language are two, *symbolic,* in the sense of naming specific objects or recording facts, and *emotive,* or "the use of words to express or excite feelings or attitudes."[24] In symbolic statement, we may make theoretically verifiable reference to the color of a cat's eyes, but the factual truth or falsity of that color makes little difference in emotive language such as Richards quotes in the *Nation:*[25]

> Sir, say no more:
> Within me 'tis as if
> The green and climbing eyesight of a cat
> Crawls near my mind's poor birds.

The literary artist is dependent upon both functions of language, but in so far as his business is not primarily factual but interpretive writing, "any symbolic function that the words may have is instrumental only and subsidiary to the evocative function." [26]

In the functioning of language on either symbolic or emotive levels, certain qualities of language are discernible through the psychophysical reaction which they set up in human beings.[27]

There are no sounds which are always evocative of gloom or gladness.[28] But in their contexts, says Richards, vowel and consonant sounds, accumulated meanings, and rhythmic and metrical arrangements of words combine to evoke distinguishable attitudes. We commonly recognize these qualities in our description of rhythm as "swinging," "rolling," "heavy," and our designation of emotions controlled through meter as "lulling," "stirring," "solemn," "gay."[29] These physical qualities of language are integral with the artist's use of the interdependent disciplines, rhetoric, logic, grammar, through which he achieves communicable form for his ideas and attitudes. Rhetoric is the discipline of "sorting" the modes of expression appropriate to his need.[30] To large extent the mode of his creation is determined by the mood which pervades his agitation.[31] In this concept of rhetoric, there seems to be little preoccupation with it as the instrument of political persuasion which characterizes it in the medieval trivium.

Logic is the "discipline of managing our sortings,"[32] of arranging and organizing them to a specific end. In metaphorical expression the sorting of meanings reaches its greatest complexity. Within any context, meanings chosen through comparative sorting must be so ordered as to communicate the sequence of the author's ideas. Quoting C. S. Peirce, Richards notes that "logic is the ethics of thinking in the sense that ethics is the bringing to bear of self-control for the purpose of realizing our desires."[33]

Grammar, the third of the liberal arts in Richards' modern reinterpretation, is *"the co-operation of words with one another in their contexts,"* that is, an ordering which pervades both rhetoric and logic, to create recognizable form. Expression involving interactive rhetoric-logic-grammar uses form and matter as relative ideas, not absolutes. Matter, for Richards, is "that activity of self-discovering thought," which gives rise to the form or arrangement of language through which the artist expresses his sense of values.[34] As he states in "The Interactions of Words" in *The Language of Poetry* (1942) "the poetic problem is precisely the maintenance of stability *within* minds and correspondence *between* them. It is *not* how to get the flux into molds supposed somehow to be fixed already."[35] "Correspondence *between*" demands the reader's use of rhetoric, logic, grammar, as we shall see.

In formulating his *self*-expression the artist draws upon his own funded images and symbols of previous experience. The imaginative range of his new projection of values is governed by the extent and availability of those images—by the artist's "vigilance," which distinguishes him from more ordinary men.[36] As we have noted, in the psychological aesthetic of Langfield, conservation of energy makes it possible to revive an experience without necessarily reviving the details of when and where or how it occurred. It is sufficient that the image carries with it "that peculiar state of mind" unique to the experience.[37] But the image, no less than the experience for which it stands, is part of the artist's own culture or cultural heritage. Hence, the configuration of images which makes up his work of art is a symbol of some phase of his culture. The depth and breadth of his symbol is the measure of self-realization achieved in the creative process, for "the most valuable states of mind are those which involve the widest and most comprehensive co-ordination of activities and the least curtailment, conflict, starvation and restriction."[38] In achieving this new world view, Richards says the artist "is the point at which the growth of the mind shows itself."[39]

What comprises the aesthetic experience of the reader for Richards? It too has a psychophysical base. The cumulative process begins with a need which the reader feels and hopes to satisfy through reading. Then follows the agitation of the retina, and, when he reads aloud, the emotional reaction which accompanies the rhythmic succession of sounds and syllables.[40] When he reads silently, he is similarly stimulated by "the sound of the words in the mind's ear."[41] It is the psychophysical effects of sound which "get to work first, and the sense in which the words are taken is subtly influenced by this fact."[42]

Through the disciplines of language the reader, like the author, feels the reconciliation of discordant values. Through their patterned formulation he experiences a catharsis of his emotional tensions,[43]—a "correction and refinement" which can come only through such artistic design.[44] With catharsis comes a sense of fullness and composure—an "organization for freedom," a disinterestedness and objectivity which opens for rational consideration the values which have been presented. The emotional-intellectual experience reveals to the reader many new ways of acting, demonstrated by the literary characters. But these ways of acting do not become matters of choice or alternatives for him until he has completed the final phase of the aesthetic experience—his evaluation of the state of mind which synaesthesis has produced in him.[45] Only in this critical act, in the explicit self-evaluation, does the reader achieve a state of selfhood similar to that of the author when he finished his creation.[46] In his critical evaluation the reader may scale higher than the author, for he may be able to reach a more significant resolution of values than the author.[47] In this whole creative-critical process no single phase is isolable as the aesthetic experience. For Richards, as we have already seen for Coleridge, whose ideas underlie many of Richards' poetic theories, it is an integral, cumulative process in which "the reader should be carried forward, not merely or chiefly by the mechanical impulse of curiosity, or by a restless desire to arrive at the final solution; but by the pleasurable activity of mind excited by the attractions of the journey itself." [48]

For Richards, as for Dewey, art has an instrumental value in raising the level of conscious response to environment [49] and hence fitting the individual to assume greater responsibility in his society. Pragmatically considered, a work of art is valuable to the extent that "readiness for this or that kind of behavior" [50] is established by the reader. The value of any one type of behavior is relative to its logical effects in "the largest, most completely ordered, system of ideas we can attain to." [51]

Surveying the range of the world's literature, Richards points to the "unassailables," the literary artists who have achieved compre-

A RETURN TO THE MEDIEVAL LIBERAL ARTS 137

hensive systems of ideas and values in successive historical periods—"Dante, Shakespeare, Goethe."[52] Richards sees the aesthetic experience of each of these artists as the farthest emotional-intellectual grasp of the contemporaneous human mind.

The artist is concerned with the record and perpetuation of the experiences which seem to him most worth having . . . he is also the man who is most likely to have experiences of value to record. He is the point at which the growth of the mind shows itself. His experiences, those at least which give value to his work, represent conciliations of impulses which in most minds are still confused, intertrammelled and conflicting. His work is the ordering of what in most minds is disordered.[53]

Richards writes therefore of the "biological calamity of the first order"[54] which would follow a dulling of imaginative sympathy and a lowering of the level of response to artistic formulations of human values.

Neatly opposed to Richards and most of the teachers of world literature and the humanities we have considered are the so-called "neo-scholastics," commonly regarded as reactionary. Some of their uses of psychoanalysis have been observed. Other relations to modern thought must be considered.

5. ADVOCATES OF A RETURN TO THE MEDIEVAL LIBERAL ARTS

The so-called neo-scholastic group offers a study in marked contrast to the other persons and more loosely organized groups we have considered, and by this contrast serves to point up the prevailing temper. Although the group emphasizes the "Great Books," its concern has not been largely with aesthetics or aesthetic experience, but rather, as the St. John's Catalogue suggests, with certain "political" considerations—in which art is subordinate to, or a means toward, the "profitable communication" of more effective academic and religious statesmanship. This suggests Plato, of course, and the medieval emphasis upon the persuasion arts as they served practical ends. It suggests also the potential appeal, in our present world "confusion," of certain moral-religious values architecturally balanced. As Gerald B. Phelan notes in *St. Thomas and Analogy,* The Aquinas Lecture for 1941: "The philosophy of St. Thomas purports to provide the rational explanation (complete in principle and capable of indefinite development in demonstrative detail and application) of the universe as a whole and of its relation to God, the Creator and Ruler of the world, in so far as such explanation can be afforded by the light of reason unaided by Faith."[1] It seems to be in this philosophy that so diverse a group, comprising a professor of law, a psychologist, a philosopher, a scientist, and a teacher of European History, finds its unity. The synthesizing forces at work to bring them together call for an introductory note.

Before he became president of the University of Chicago, President Hutchins was dean of the Law School and professor of law at Yale University. This legalistic background suggests the legalistic mind which Hutchins demonstrates in the administrative economy of the University of Chicago Plan, in *The Higher Learning in America* (1936), and *No Friendly Voice* (1936), and in his appeal to the authority of the "Great Books."

Mortimer J. Adler writes from a mixed literary-philosophical legal-theological background—an associate professorship in the philosophy of law at the University of Chicago, and some twenty years of study of the philosophy of St. Thomas Aquinas. Adler's early educational experience came in Columbia University, where he moved from studies in the psychology of music, through the study of the Great Books in John Erskine's Honors Course, to participation in the People's Institute of New York City, to the writing of a book on dialectic, thence to work evaluating the teaching of law at Columbia, and so into company with Hutchins at the University of Chicago. In this remarkable and many-sided quest, he has come to find increasing satisfaction in the reconciliation of Aristotelian and Christian values worked out by St. Thomas Aquinas. When Adler was an instructor in the People's Institute, Scott Buchanan was assistant director, and Richard McKeon a fellow instructor.

With the passing of the People's Institute in 1929, Adler went to

Chicago with Hutchins, Richard McKeon followed a little later and became Dean of the Humanities Division, and Scott Buchanan went to the University of Virginia "to teach philosophy and do some metaphysics myself," as he states.[2] At the University of Virginia Scott Buchanan, and Stringfellow Barr, then professor of Modern European History, found common enterprise in research in the liberal arts. At Chicago Hutchins and Adler collaborated in 1931 in a course "Classics of the Western World." A similar list of books, with the addition of the scientific classics, was taught by Barr and Buchanan at the University of Virginia from 1930-1934.

At the invitation of Hutchins, Barr and Buchanan and Charles Wallis, then a student at the University of Virginia, joined the Committee on the Liberal Arts at the University of Chicago in 1936, a committee at first loosely attached to the Humanities Division under Dean McKeon, but subsequently designated a President's committee. From the Committee they went in 1937 to St. John's College as president and dean and tutor respectively. With them were associated two other members of the Committee, Adler and his assistant in a special prelegal course in the University of Chicago, Catesby Taliaferro. Hutchins became chairman of the Board of Visitors and Governors of the resuscitated college. By so doing, states Buchanan, he "can at least vicariously pursue an educational policy to which he is devoted. . . ."[3]

A. Robert Maynard Hutchins

Like other spokesmen for aesthetic experience and human values, Hutchins starts from observations of modern society and its system of education. But unlike most other spokesmen, he dates the "confusion" of modern times from the Renaissance, when the theocentric unity of the Middle Ages disintegrated. By implication, Hutchins suggests that return to the unity which the theology of the Middle Ages afforded would be the ideal organization for our time. As substitute or supplement for this ideal he would call upon Greek metaphysics as the unifying science which would provide for the study of first principles, of the fine arts and literature, of social sciences and of natural sciences.⁴ In this division of fields of inquiry, we see how Hutchins can approve the administrative economy of the Chicago Plan with its Divisions of Natural Sciences, Biological Sciences, Social Sciences, and the Humanities, without approving the manner in which their courses are conducted.

Hutchins, in company with many other spokesmen, urges "general education" to offset the disintegrating tendency of specialization. "General education" as we see it in his concept would fulfill two functions. It would provide a common denominator for all intellectually superior specialists entering upon "the higher learning." In one sense this implies a common fund of information and knowledge gleaned from the "best books." "Everybody cannot be a specialist in every field. He must therefore be cut off from every field but his own unless he has the same basic education that other specialists have. This means more than having the same language and the same general interest in advancing knowledge. It means having a common stock of fundamental ideas." ⁵ In another sense, it implies that with the liberal arts, rhetoric, grammar, and logic, Hutchins would have his specialists able to communicate freely on the subjects of their inquiry. If this were the case, we could see a similarity to the ever more inclusive syntheses for which the *rationale* of Greene, for instance, provides.⁶

The second function of general education would be to provide training for the great mass of people for whom it was terminal education, in the formal sense of education. In fulfilling either function, Hutchins is "interested in drawing out the elements of our common human nature . . . in the attributes of the race, not the accidents of individuals." ⁷

An understanding of Hutchins' use of "common human nature" is basic to further inquiry into his idea of aesthetic experience. We might interpret it, along with "attributes of the race" as emphasis on the "typical" qualities of undifferentiated personalities—a possibility in the slightly derogatory context of "accidents of individuals." We might interpret it to mean the "more human values" by which other spokesmen differentiate men from other animals. We might think of "common human nature" as the singularly human attribute of intellect through which the faculties may apprehend absolute truth.[8] Hutchins' meaning seems to lie nearest this idea, for even cultural variations do not affect this entity. In *The Higher Learning in America,* citing St. Thomas, he writes: "Education implies teaching. Teaching implies knowledge. Knowledge is truth. The truth is everywhere the same. Hence education should be everywhere the same."[9] The meaning he attaches to "common human nature" is partially clarified when, on the authority of Aristotle's *Politics* he states that "the cultivation of the intellect is the same good for all men in all societies."[10]

Hutchins advocates mathematics and the liberal arts in conjunction with ancient and medieval classics[11] as the disciplines through which the human intellect is schooled to reach its end. The question arises of the extent to which the rhetoric, grammar, and logic which he advocates represents the medieval trivium of the time of St. Thomas, or the classical disciplines of Aristotle, or some modern reinterpretation of the ancient terms. *The Higher Learning in America* does not answer our question entirely. "Grammar disciplines the mind and develops the logical faculty."[12] Rhetoric constitutes the rules of effective speaking and writing. "Logic is a statement in technical form of the conditions under which reasoning is vigorously demonstrated."[13] In its most precise form in mathematics, this logic to which every person should aspire "is not affected by differences in taste, disposition, or prejudice."[14] Failing to find a satisfactory modernization of the ancient disciplines, Hutchins would revive the functions of rhetoric, grammar, and logic, using St. Thomas as his guide. Presumably, the modernization of I. A. Richards would not be satisfactory because of its relativistic emphasis, at odds with absolute ideas and faculties.

Hutchins touches twice upon the problem of aesthetics in *The Higher Learning in America.* He uses the word aesthetics only once, and then in a context indicative of the classical-medieval tradition. He comments upon the inadequacy of one critical method he observed in a class discussing *Faust.* With some training in metaphysics, he suggests, the class would have known "the first principles of aesthetics" which would have enabled them to consider "the artistic merits of the play." [15] His meaning of "first principles" is clarified later: "In metaphysics we are seeking the causes of the things that are. It is the highest science, the first science, and as first, universal. It considers being as being, both what it is and the attributes which belong to it as being." [16]

With this metaphysical aesthetic in mind, we look at a second statement of Hutchins implying a correspondingly medieval-classical idea of aesthetic experience. Listing the intellectual virtues, he bases the following statement on St. Thomas:

The ancients distinguish five intellectual virtues: the three speculative virtues of intuitive knowledge, which is the habit of induction; of scientific knowledge, which is the habit of demonstration; and of philosophical wisdom, which is scientific knowledge, combined with intuitive reason, of things highest by nature, first principles and first causes. To these they add the two virtues of the practical intellect: art, the capacity to make according to a true course of reasoning, and prudence, which is right reason with respect to action.[17]

In his concern for the medieval practical virtues of art and prudence, which are of necessity concerned with "the first principles and first causes," Hutchins takes us back to a metaphysical aesthetic but does not elaborate it.

B. Mortimer J. Adler

Adler also turns to St. Thomas as his chief authority. His uses of the older "faculty" psychology have been noted. We have now to observe the way in which his ideas of aesthetics (and Hutchins' presumably) become part of a design for philosophical and religious statesmanship, rather than a concern with aesthetic experience as a resolution of values.[18]

Adler's chief professional statement on aesthetics is *Art and Prudence* (1937); his popular statement is *How to Read a Book* (1940). The central problem for Adler, as for Hutchins in his search for a stable educational pattern, is one of control of what seem to him tendencies toward chaos in society. The issue lies between the centrifugal force of art in its diversity and freedom and the centripetal pressure of convention and morals, represented by the prudent man or statesman whose concern is the maintenance of a stable social order.[19] Adler presents the conflict with its implications for censorship[20] in this fashion:

In one respect, by reason of its speculative character, art is independent of prudence; but in another respect, in which art is viewed not in itself, but in relation to man, prudence must govern art. The prudent man, who judges all things from the angles of morality and politics, judges the work of art only in terms of its consequences and not in terms of itself. Aesthetic and political criticism are independent of each other; but art is nevertheless properly subject to the extrinsic considerations of morality and politics and religion. These considerations require prudence.[21]

For the philosophic base of this conflict, Adler leads us back to "Aristotle and St. Thomas as sources of wisdom"—via Jacques Maritain's *Art and Scholasticism* (1930), which Adler terms "the best analysis of all the problems of fine art."[22] This is a helpful lead to the reader who may find *Art and Prudence* difficult in its dialectic.

Maritain's aesthetic is wholly Thomist, but Adler supplements it with Aristotle and Freud. From Maritain we learn that God—as Pure Form, Pure Mind, or Intelligibility—was the First Cause. Inherent in every object of nature is its intrinsic Idea which is the Idea of God. In keeping with this, Adler states the creative artist is "a remote image of the divine,"[23] who intuitively sees behind the natural form of objects to their divine Idea. In this Idea (to return to Maritain) the artist perceives true proportion and integrity with a clarity, brilliance, or luminosity which is the Form of God shining upon the surface of the work of art. The work of art which he produces is made to "imitate nature by making objects which are like natural things either in form or in function."[24]

In the art of imaginative literature, continues Adler, the author uses sensuous and symbolic language, subjected to the disciplines of rhetoric, grammar, and logic, to represent his imitation of human action.[25] In *The Proceedings of the American Catholic Philosophical Association* for 1937, we find Adler's explicit statement about the nature of the liberal arts. Under the title "Tradition and Communication" he writes: "Grammar has to do with operations involving the physical, not the mental, word."[26] An individual may carry on thought with concepts or mental words, without the aid of grammar; grammar is brought into play when an individual attempts to communicate the thought in speaking or writing.

Rhetoric is of two kinds, practical (persuasive) and speculative (convincing). "Practical rhetoric is addressed to the practical intellect, the will and the passions, and is concerned with *persuading* for the sake of action or the moral virtues."[27] Hutchins and Adler both state that the practical intellect includes art and prudence. Rhetoric, therefore, in the use of language for art "is primary because it is most intimately concerned with the end for which the arts are used —knowledge as communicable—and here grammar and logic are ordered to it as means."[28]

"Speculative rhetoric is addressed to the theoretic intellect and is concerned with *convincing* for the sake of knowledge or the intellectual virtues."[29] Logic is similar in its function to speculative rhetoric. Logic, whether called a science or an art, is "an instrument for causing knowledge."[30] As we have seen, men by nature have the creative power of reason, but "they need the art of syllogizing in words to convince others or to be critical of what is proposed to them."[31] Adler emphasizes the primary importance of rhetoric, both in a footnote lauding the speculative rhetoric of Euclid, Plato, and St. Thomas,[32] and in this statement from "Tradition and Communication":

There is neither time nor need to expound the arts of grammar and logic. I shall confine myself to a few ultimate principles of speculative rhetoric which bear on the problem of profitable communication. The subordinate logical and grammatical aspects of these principles will then become apparent.[33]

Both practical rhetoric and speculative rhetoric, with their respective emphasis upon *persuading* and *convincing,* take precedence over

A RETURN TO THE MEDIEVAL LIBERAL ARTS

grammar and logic. This is consistent with a summary statement in "Tradition and Communication," that "the liberal arts of the trivium are primarily and essentially the arts of teaching and being taught.... Strictly they are not arts of thinking, of conception, judgment and reasoning, in so far as these are natural intellectual processes by which a man is able to learn by himself." [34] Granted words of absolute meaning (as in this grammar), with logic subordinated to the "profitable communication" of rhetoric, we find a means of buttressing "the truth [which] is everywhere the same," as Hutchins holds. This is consistent also with the "political preoccupations" explicit in the St. John's program. It helps us to understand Hutchins' call in *The Higher Learning in America* for an "evangelistic movement" [35] to introduce the study of the "liberal arts." It helps us likewise to understand Adler's discussion of political censorship of art in *Art and Prudence,* and repeated references in *How To Read a Book* to attitudes of teaching and being taught,[36] which he epitomizes in *St. Thomas and the Gentiles.*[37]

What values accrue to author and observer from a work of art? In *Art and Prudence,* Adler draws upon the Freudian idea of sublimation to support the classical-medieval idea of catharsis:

Freud discovered the indispensable role which sublimation of the emotions plays in the healthy ordering of the soul. In sublimation, he rediscovered the medieval value of catharsis. Man living in society cannot express all his emotions in their natural directions; he is not able to control them rationally; he must not for his health's sake, repress them irrationally.[38]

Suggesting that the Freudian process of sublimation is a conscious one, Adler states that "the sublimation of them [emotions] is the prudent alternative." [39]

Adler continues his demonstration of the similarity of the Freudian psychoanalytic point of view and his interpretation of Aristotle with the somewhat startling statement that "Freud first saw the presence of sublimation in the activity of the artist, as Aristotle saw purgation as an effect of art." [40]

For rhetorical reasons, apparently, Adler stresses this Aristotelian-Freudian concept rather than the Thomistic (although he does call it "the medieval value of catharsis"), and perhaps for the same reason devotes attention to the spectator role. "Purgation is the effect of any art, of any imitation; similarly, not only the artist achieves the sublimation of his emotions, but the spectator succeeds in this as well."[41] Adler, referring to the "great insight and sensitivity" of M. Alain,[42] "sees the marks of imitation and the spectacle in many corners of our social life, and not only in its obvious place among the arts and its even more obvious locus in the theatre."[43] While this gives some intimations of a pervasive aesthetic experience, the use of "spectacle" and "corners" does not suggest the basic formative impulse which underlies the aesthetic of other spokesmen. We find this description of spectacle as aesthetic experience:

Such natural events as public executions, murder trials, fires, mob demonstrations, as well as such events as parades and pageants which have artistic direction, are spectacles, and as spectacles are imitations for their audiences, and effect purgation of the emotions they excite. Thus, in the public execution, what functions psychologically for the difference which every imitation must have, is the victim's disconnection from one's self. He is not felt as a human being to whom something is really happening; one doesn't know him; one doesn't care much about the consequences of his feelings and actions. Because he is *like* a human being, we suffer pity and terror; because he is *different* from a human being—a human being is somebody we know and love—we enjoy those feelings contemplatively and are, at that terribly low and ghastly level, purged of them. The murderer on trial or being hanged is no more a human being than the bull-fighter; and only slightly more so than the actor in the melodrama. . . . The Greek tragedy at its best is the best sort of spectacle, achieving its perfection by means of a chorus which offers itself as a sort of model for the spectator. The emotions of the chorus are aroused and purged, and the spectacle thus includes the image of a spectator already purified.[44]

Before proceeding further with analysis of the critical method implicit in this idea of aesthetic experience, we should note, as we did repeatedly in the careful redefinition of catharsis by O. J. Campbell and Louise Rosenblatt, that modern aesthetics looks on emotion not as something to be purged but as something to be made a part of our understanding, both intellectual and physiological; Richards, for instance, stresses it as a part of the human mosaic, part of the "designing" influence, in our whole intention of human life.

Like other spokesmen, however, Adler holds that each individual approaches the work of art from a different experience background. The reaction which each one has to a given work of art is therefore different. At the same time properly disciplined reactions to a work of art are alike, for the work of art itself is the absolute model for the experience of each observer. Writing of the artist-reader relationship, Adler apparently draws on his early experiences with the psychology of music: "We are like so many instruments for him to play upon, each with its special overtones and resonances, but the music he plays so differently on each of us follows one and the same score. That score is written into the novel or poem." [45] For the translation of that score in a book Adler's "diabolical plan" [46] includes specific rules interestingly legalistic in statement:

The right maxim [for critical approach to art] is like the one which regulates the trial of criminals. We should assume that the author is intelligible until shown otherwise, not that he is guilty of nonsense and must prove his innocence. And the only way you can determine an author's guilt is to make the very best effort you can to understand him. Not until you have made such an effort with every available turn of skill have you a right to sit in final judgment on him. If you were an author yourself, you would realize why this is the golden rule of communication among men.[47]

Reading proceeds, according to *How to Read a Book*, on three levels, *structural, interpretative,* and *critical*.[48] Adler emphasizes the first and third. On the *structural* level, he shows a marked concern with kinds of literature, their differences and similarities—familiar ground for many who teach literature by "types." In a representative paragraph in *Art and Prudence,* we find that "epic narrative is more like history than the drama is." [49] This might lead us to see an emotional tone pervading the two kinds, but we are led on to other considerations of plot which characterize Aristotelian criticism:

The difference and similarity between epic and historical narration is best illustrated by the *Iliad* and by *War and Peace*. In neither case is the whole war the subject of the poem, even though the war had a beginning, a middle, and an end. But the *Iliad* is much better as a novel because it describes a single action, projected against the background of the war, and the incidents of the war are selected or rejected for the sake of illuminating this action. *War and Peace* is more like a fragmentary history. It lacks plot and character development.[50]

The ideal singleness of action of the novel implied in *Art and Prudence* is modified in Adler's comparison of novel, play, and lyric in *How to Read a Book*.

A lyric tells its story primarily in terms of a single emotional experience, whereas novels and plays have much more complicated plots, involving many characters, their actions and reactions upon one another, as well as the emotions they suffer in the process.[51]

The extent to which these structural distinctions tend to become primary is implicit in his statement concerning the novel, drama, and motion picture.

. . . the motion picture differs from the drama in being like the novel; but it also differs from the novel in being like the produced drama, in making imagination unnecessary by presenting to the senses the actions as well as the speeches of the characters.[52]

While this may obviously refer to imagination only on the level of supplying background and speech inflections, etc., "unnecessary" is here unqualified, and leads us to Adler's primary concern with technique and structure rather than· with the human significance of the actions portrayed.

On the second level, *interpretation,* Adler is implicitly concerned with art as a symbol of culture when he says that *"The Divine Comedy* reflects the *Summa Theologica* of St. Thomas, Aristotle's *Ethics* and Ptolemy's astronomy."[53] He tells us too of the chronological sequences by which the formulations of later artists draw upon their predecessors. In his attention to types of literature, however, we find predominant concern with the chronological sequences within a given type, rather than with the genre as symbols of stages of cultural development. Hence his grouping of modern novels and their prototypes, modern plays and their Greek backgrounds, and the pairing of long epics, as Adler terms Goethe's *Faust* and Dante's *Divine Comedy,* with the *Iliad* and *Odyssey.*[54] One of his major contributions to criticism on the level of interpretation—however great his preoccupation with censorship—is his accent upon the moving picture as an art form.

On the third level, *critical judgment,* the reader imposes either logical or aesthetic criticism.[55] In either instance, following the "right maxim," he "judges the author, and decides whether he agrees or disagrees."[56] In logical criticism he imposes four specific criteria to show wherein the author's work is: (1) uninformed, (2) misinformed, (3) illogical, (4) incomplete. In aesthetic criticism there are five leading questions which may aid in objectifying taste:

(1) To what degree does the work have unity? (2) How great is the complexity of parts and elements which that unity embraces and organizes? (3) Is it a likely story, that is, does it have the inherent plausibility of poetic truth? (4) Does it elevate you from the ordinary semi-consciousness of daily life to the clarity of intense wakefulness, by stirring your emotions and filling your imagination? (5) Does it create a new world into which you are drawn and wherein you seem to live with the illusion that you are seeing life steadily and whole?[57]

If we "learn to read,"[58] then these Aristotelian-Thomistic criteria, wherein art is looked on as *illusion* rather than as *experience,* will aid us in formulating "the ultimate critical judgment which concerns the objective merits of the work."[59]

C. St. John's College

How to Read a Book, as noted, makes frequent reference to the unity of ideas shared by Hutchins and Adler, and to their unity of effort through "The Classics of the Western World" both at Chicago and at St. John's College, to teach the classics and the seven liberal arts.

Since 1937 St. John's College catalogues have devoted from 17 to 25 pages to interpretation of the St. John's program. Regarded historically, these official statements reveal several things to us. We see an attempt to reconcile an American historical emphasis (Barr, we recall, was an historian from the University of Virginia) and the classical-medieval emphasis of Adler, Hutchins, and Buchanan. This attempt at reconciliation seems to have been constant, though with some changes in emphasis. Throughout, catalogue statements maintain emphasis on the Great Books and the revived liberal arts. But from mention, in 1937, of American historical backgrounds and explicit reference to St. Thomas, in 1940 they expand their historical detail, and delete the explicit mention of St. Thomas.

In the catalogue for 1937-38, we find that "St. John's College is deeply rooted in the American tradition" which recognizes that "the liberal arts are the three R's, reading, writing, and reckoning . . . [and that] it is their integrity and power that still lure us back to the little red school houses where our fathers and grandfathers studied and practiced them." [60] The catalogue goes on to say then that "the clearest historic pattern of the liberal arts for the modern mind is . . . to be found in the thirteenth century. At the time of Dante's *The Divine Comedy* and St. Thomas' *Summa Theologica,* they were listed as follows:

Trivium	*Quadrivium*
Grammar	Arithmetic
Rhetoric	Geometry
Logic	Music
	Astronomy" [61]

To say "at the time of . . . St. Thomas' *Summa Theologica,*" of course, neither asserts nor denies the authority on which the trivium should be invoked.

In 1938-39 St. John's Catalogue—the 1937-38 edition had been subject to a good deal of critical questioning—reference to St. Thomas was not included. For the trivium of grammar, rhetoric, and logic, *grammar, rhetoric,* and *dialectic* were substituted. Dialectic, Adler defines in his *Dialectic,* as the art of disputation, and in *How To Read a Book,* as the "etiquette of controversy," the latter exemplified with "the four ways in which a book can be adversely criticized." [62]

The catalogue for 1939-40, as we observed, likewise makes no mention of St. Thomas, although six pages of school history stress the affiliation of the nation's Founding Fathers with the school, and the 1937 intention to restore a "traditional program of Classics and Liberal Arts unique in American Colleges of today." [63] In addition, under the division heading of The Liberal Arts, the catalogue interprets the college insignia on the covers of the catalogue:

The figures on the seal represent the seven liberal arts as they were traditionally conceived for about two thousand years, up to the beginning of the nineteenth century. In ancient style they are grammar, rhetoric, dialectic, which form the trivium; and arithmetic, geometry, music, and astronomy making the quadrivium.

Subsequently, this statement appears: "The last term in each year is devoted to the writing of grammatical, rhetorical, and logical commentaries on the texts with a final emphasis on original writing on the topics suggested by the texts." [64] And elsewhere: "The first criterion is that a classic must be a masterpiece in the liberal arts. It must have that clarity and beauty on its surface which provides an immediate intelligibility and leads the mind of the reader to its interior depths of illumination and understanding." [65] The vocabulary here, (clarity, intelligibility, illumination) as well as the logic of the appreciative process is similar to that of the *Summa Theologica*.

The subject-matter of the St. John's curriculum is based on 118 classics which are read over a period of four years. The first year is devoted to the Greek classics, which, according to the catalogue distribution, include nine fictional authors, three authors dealing with the liberal arts of the trivium, and five with the liberal arts of the quadrivium. The second year moves chronologically through the medieval period, which is spanned by ten fictional authors from Dante to Cervantes, eight authors dealing with the trivium and eight (including Descartes) with the quadrivium. The third year has its unity mainly in the fact that many of the books were written in the Romance Languages, sixteen authors of fiction, ten authors dealing with the trivium, and eight authors dealing with the quadrivium. The fourth year concentrates on the writings of the nineteenth and twentieth centuries, with fifteen, ten, and sixteen authors in respective groups.

Teaching method and critical method in the study of great books converge in five specific teaching techniques which are uniform through the college, the Language Tutorial, the Mathematics Tutorial, the Seminar, the Lecture, the Laboratory.

(1) In the Language Tutorial the "aim . . . is to use some external device that will induce the strengthening and disciplining of the imagination." In so far as "the imagination is the place where intellect touches human experience"—and in so far as "liberal artists" know that imagination is polished and adjusted to receive intellectual light by the foreign languages—Greek, Latin, French, and German are studied in successive years. Attention in these language studies is upon formal grammar, and passages of prose or poetry "are committed to memory by rote." [66]

(2) The Mathematics Tutorial likewise focuses upon the use of models. Euclid's *Elements* is studied exhaustively. "This is the book that made European mathematics possible, and it can still be used to remedy our deficiencies." [67]

(3) The Seminar is an exemplification of the art of conversation, for which Plato's *Dialogues* "set the models." [68] Critical analysis is taught in the seminars, both literary and scientific. Dialectic is the discipline here acquired. With the subject matters of the language and mathematical studies, dialectic "reaches the fundamentals and ultimates, and in the process the book under discussion may be torn to pieces." [69] It is only at later meetings of the seminar "that the text delivers up its meaning." [70]

(4) In the Formal Lecture, delivered before the whole school, "students learn to listen to good talk, to talk that is often over their heads, but talk that is remembered and absorbed long after the immediate hearing." [71]

(5) In the Laboratory, students work at mathematical construc-

tion, learn instruments and techniques of measurement, repeat crucial experiments and combine their findings in solving problems.[72]

The emphasis through all of these techniques seems largely upon the mastery of previous exemplary uses of the liberal arts so that knowledge so acquired may be used elsewhere. Mastery appears to be essentially a matter of following models. This is consistent with Adler's statement that grammar, logic, and rhetoric, "in Thomistic terms, . . . are the arts of instruction, not discovery." [73]

CONCLUSIONS OF PART II

In Part I we noted trends toward unity among the fields of philosophy, psychology, and anthropology, on the place of language in the aesthetic formulations from which conscious selfhood arises. In Part II we have examined the statements of ten representative groups and individuals speaking for the values of the modern humanities. Here again we noted common tendencies, particularly to redefine aesthetic experience in the light of philosophic belief and the findings of modern psychology and anthropology. In our detailed analysis of spokesmanship for the humanities two streams of influence in contemporary education have become apparent. In the main current of the stream of empiricism and modern psychology and anthropology are such groups as the National Council of Teachers of English, the Committee of Twenty-four, the Progressive Education Association represented by Louise Rosenblatt and John Dewey, and individual scholars, Irwin Edman, Theodore Meyer Greene, Jacques Barzun, and I. A. Richards. In the other stream are spokesmen for a return to medieval-classical idealism with the addition of Freudian psychology.

Among the spokesmen for the modern humanities we find that there is both explicit and implicit recognition of the arts as symbols of the culture from which they grow. There is considerable stress upon literature as the art which, based on language, most comprehensively deals with the values held by men in successive epochs of Western civilization, and upon the need for making this heritage of values clear. There is universal concern among the spokesmen with the development of the self of the artist through his creative process, which both implicitly and explicitly is considered to be his aesthetic experience. There is considerable stress on the consciousness of the creative process, and general agreement upon the realization of self which takes place in the critical reader as he attempts to re-experience the aesthetic process of the author. There is also a growing concern with the relationship of critical method and teaching method as they combine to foster self realization of students.

A counter current has been set up by some teachers who would recapture the medieval unity, with some additions from Freudian psychology. This group is also concerned with teaching method to exemplify and disseminate its ideas. We have reviewed that exemplification in the St. John's College program, noting the tendency throughout this spokesmanship toward authoritarian attitudes and rules, in contrast with the relativistic attitudes and practices of the spokesmen for a modern idea of aesthetic experience.

With this orientation, we may review and extend the evidence of aesthetic emphasis in the range of courses in Humanities and World Literature listed by Patricia Beesley in *The Revival of the Humanities in American Education*.

PART III

CONVERGING IDEAS AND PRACTICES IN WORLD LITERATURE AND MODERN HUMANITIES COURSES

Between 1928 and 1942 fifty-seven colleges have instituted courses or programs in which, in varying designs and combinations, literature, music, art, religion, philosophy, and history have been brought together as "separate condensed surveys" or more inclusive Humanities programs. It is appropriate, now, to turn to those courses to understand the latitude of the broad concept of aesthetic experience within which many of them work, examining those similarities and differences which will afford a working picture of most recent developments and which distinguish these courses from the nearly one hundred and fifty additional courses concerned solely with the literature of the world.

Information concerning degrees of emphasis on aesthetic experience in these Humanities and World Literature courses has been assembled from several sources. The primary source has been letters from professors offering or coöperating in these courses. Printed articles, syllabi, and college catalogues have been used as other major sources.

Few course syllabi or explanatory articles published by instructors of Humanities courses undertake very explicit statements of an idea of aesthetic experience. There is a generally implied recognition, however, that aesthetic experience involves to some degree a creative-critical process which is important in the study of literature in any culture, and that this is one of the unifying principles. Six patterns, at first sight suggesting as many different unifying principles, are found in such courses:

1. Formal aesthetic principles
2. Chronology

3. Types
4. Relationships of art and society
5. History of ideas
6. Social backgrounds and cultural epochs

1. FORMAL AESTHETIC PRINCIPLES

Courses at Stephens Junior College, New Jersey State Teachers College at Montclair, Colgate University, Antioch College, the University of Florida, and Boston University emphasize basic aesthetic principles underlying the several arts. Examined severally, they show many differences, but more similarities.

A. Stephens Junior College

"The Humanities" at Stephens Junior College was instituted in 1928 with the expressed purpose of studying art for its own sake and, by showing relationships among the arts, of finding "how the same principles apply in more than one art." [1] The humanities, as Louise Dudley and Austin Faricy's detailed text *The Humanities* (1940) explains, are "all the subjects of learning except the sciences," [2] and are to be distinguished from the sciences primarily through differences in "the way of knowing;" [3] i.e., "The sciences belong to the class of logical knowledge, whereas the humanities belong to the class of intuitive knowledge." [4] Intuitive knowledge is "so different as hardly to deserve the name *knowledge;* it is usually called *appreciation;* a better word is *experience.*" [5] The humanities in which this kind of experience is available are the "five arts: literature, music, architecture, painting, and sculpture." [6] Because of the quality peculiar to them, "the end and aim of all the humanities is experience, appreciation." [7]

In acquiring "experience and appreciation," the several arts are considered in detail from five angles: (1) background, (2) medium, (3) elements, (4) organization, (5) style and judgment.

The attention paid to the artist's choice of subject and to critical judgment in terms of the fitness of the subject implies the idea of aesthetic experience as a continuous creative-critical process.[8] The major concern of the text is with the critic's reaction to each work of art—to his "judgment" of the values that art "experience" or "appreciation" produces. Judgment in each art consists of a detailed analysis of the medium, the elements, and their organization. In literature the medium is language, whose elements include many kinds of words and word orders, tone color, characteristics of free verse and the various meters. Organization deals with the lyric kinds of verse forms, types of narratives, drama, and history. With the increased sensitiveness which this analysis affords, the critic can, in Aristotelian language, demand that the work be "serious, complete, and of a certain magnitude." [9] These classifying criteria are further subdivided into sincerity, sentimentality, and mechanical work, "sense of completeness," [10] and gradations "in the kind and degree of the emotions involved," [11] reaching their height in the sublime. In *The Humanities,* Miss Dudley and Mr. Faricy present their ideas of aesthetic experience with quotation from Aristotle, Schopenhauer, and Bradley. But the final value judgment on a work of art is apparently individual. "The only value of art to any individual is the experience he gets from it. Moreover, almost any reason for liking art is a good reason, and any liking of art is for something good in it." [12]

B. *New Jersey State Teachers College at Montclair*

The courses in "Music and Art Appreciation" and "World Literature" were introduced in 1928. The World Literature course has undergone some changes in the past few years, under the direction of Professor H. S. Cayley, formerly a member of the Humanities staff at Stephens. As he describes the present organization of the course, the

> ... aim in each field has been to get at the basic problems of appreciation ... [on the assumption] that until the student has become responsive to each medium of expression—of visual forms, of words, of sounds, or of words and sounds—and to the various ways which have been employed in handling these, he is in no position to talk about art in general.[13]

The "ways of handling" are identifiable in the schools of classicism, romanticism, realism, and abstractionism.

The course gives evidence of a greater flexibility in attitude and critical methods than this may suggest. As Cayley writes, the

> ... usual apparatus of source study, and the influence-of-the-influence of somebody on somebody has been largely supplanted by the direct attempt to examine one's reaction in the presence of the work itself, and with this as a basis, to improve.

This in turn has led to the substitution of "methods of comparison and other methods which look first at the effect of the whole, and from this move to consideration of the parts." World Literature is not studied from an omnibus volume of short excerpts. The instructor chooses, rather, to concentrate over longer periods of time upon his own selection of parts from single volumes.

C. Colgate University

"The Fine Arts and Literature" was introduced at Colgate in 1930. In 1934, according to Professor John F. Fitchen III, the course was reorganized and renamed "Survey in Fine Arts." The course has stressed the arts as the aesthetic formulation of the cultural concerns of a period. Major emphasis, as at Stephens, is upon basic aesthetic principles. In "A Challenge" in the *Journal of Higher Education* (April, 1937) Fitchen describes how

> ... each aesthetic concept is made part of the student's mental equipment at the start; he learns to comprehend the significance of line, mass, pattern, and the various qualities of color.[14]

Beyond these principles common to all the arts, the student

> ... should learn to know their possibilities and the interpretation of subject matter of which each is capable. He should be aware of their limitation and of the characteristics which differentiate one form of artistic expression from another.[15]

These underlying principles afford the basis for a seriatum consideration of the various arts, starting with literature. Again, the course proceeds from the general to the specific. Consideration is given to an overview of "the various forms of literary expression, the rhythms of prose and poetry, and the connotation and sound of words."[16] In the study of literature, attention centers in the drama, ". . . because it embraces as many avenues of study as any other major literary form. . . ." An examination question is further illustration of the emphasis upon form:

The task of every artist is to reduce the raw substance of nature to articulate, meaningful form. The dramatist constructs a pattern of events by the use of variety, unity, contrast, emphasis, simplification, symbolism. Select a play of Ibsen and show specifically how each is employed.[17]

As the result of his experiences with all the arts, the student acquires "the power to mold and transform his individual environment, and the means to realize what philosophers call the Good Life."[18]

D. Antioch College

"Creative Aesthetics" was started in 1930. Professor Raymond S. Stites, who has developed the course, sets up four objectives for it in his text, *The Arts and Man* (1940):[19]

1. To bring the student into close contact with a few great works of art so that he may see how they arose from their pertinent culture patterns. This we shall call "understanding the classics of art."
2. To acquaint the student with the formal principles of composition in the arts illustrated. This we call "recognition of the formal principles."
3. To demonstrate that intelligent criticism has enhanced rather than destroyed the creation and enjoyment of fine works of art. This we call the "critical use of art principle."
4. To encourage the student to take an active part in the creation of the art of our times. This we shall call "enjoyment of art through re-creation."

The course aims "toward a universal aesthetic" in which all art may be classified as Primitive, Classical, Gothic, Oriental. "These systems do not coincide with historic periods in sequential progression, but to states of being." [20] They are really aesthetic types corresponding to the Dionysian plunge into experience,[21] and the philosophies of life which Spengler designated the Apollonian, Faustian, and Magian.[22] These have combined to form our contemporary culture pattern.

Lacking acquaintance with all these styles, modern man cannot hope to form an intelligent judgment of the worth of present-day artistic creations.[23]

This idea finds expression in the examination standards for the course stated in the Syllabus:

> . . . any student unable to give evidence in the final examination that he has been able to progress from the views of art held by primitive man, i.e., that he is still in the primitive mental state as regards the arts, will not be given a passing grade. . . .[24]

The criteria by which these systems are judged are different in each case. Hence a premium is put upon what the syllabus terms "the intellectual aesthetic detachment necessary for an unbiased objective judgment." While no one of these sets of criteria is "applicable to all media at all times," the significance of "toward a universal aesthetic" is explained in "there should grow in the student a faith that some unity may underlie the diversity of man's spiritual needs as shown in his art." The objectivity that this attitude demands is a test of "mastery of self" [25] which is the end-value of the course. The intellectual emphasis is supplemented by a workshop in which a student gains appreciation of the difficulties overcome by the creative artist.

E. *The University of Florida*

"The Humanities" was started in 1936. The Humanities course opens with a survey of aesthetic principles common to all the arts —dominance, unity, repetition—and in literature, specialized considerations of diction and imagery. This is followed by a chronological survey of the philosophic expressions of classicism, romanticism, realism, and idealism. The values aimed at are (1) an increased understanding and enjoyment of the arts, (2) methods of systematic thought, (3) understanding of the world, and (4) the development of a serviceable philosophy of life.[26] Recent trends in the course, as Professor James D. Glunt reveals in his letter of March, 1942, place "emphasis upon the teachability of materials," with increased concern for the contemporary.

F. Boston University

"The Appreciation of Art" was first offered in 1940. The catalogue description points explicitly to aesthetic values as the unifying factor in the arts: "Aesthetic experience, its characteristics and significance; the nature and occurrence of aesthetic values; the principles of art; the criteria of aesthetic judgment . . . the work of art, its structural elements and formal organization."[27]

2. *COURSES EMPHASIZING CHRONOLOGY*

Numerous Humanities courses follow a chronological organization of materials. Within the chronology, however, varying emphasis appears, as we shall note in looking at the courses offered at Reed College, Johns Hopkins University, Missouri Valley College, Bucknell University, Talladega College, Northwest Missouri State Teachers College, Alabama College for Women, Eureka College, College of St. Scholastica, Dominican College of San Rafael, and Duchesne College.

A. Reed College

The Reed College course, "General Literature," was started in 1921. Up to 1937 the syllabus described it as a two-semester course paralleling a similar course in "History of Civilization." The first semester was devoted to Egyptian, Greek, Chinese, Indian, Roman, and Hebrew cultures. The second semester emphasized the literature of Renaissance Italy, and of England and France. There seemed to be relatively slight attention to modern literature.[28]

The Bulletin for 1941 reveals considerable shift in emphasis in the parallel "General Literature" and "History of Civilization" courses. Both courses are two-year sequences. Emphasis in "History of Civilization" is not upon "information primarily but a thoughtful acquaintance with what civilization has been, how it has changed, and what our inheritance has been." In "General Literature" the first year is devoted to "selected works of poets, dramatists, and philosophers of West and East from Homer to the middle of the eighteenth century, illustrating the achievements of different ages and peoples in thought and expression." [29] In the second year "prose and verse of modern literature are studied, both as examples of changing literary art and as significant expressions of thought arising out of the background of revolutionary idealism in the midst of which they were written." In both instances there seems to be concern for written critical statements.

An indication of further shift in emphasis is an alternate second-year course, "Introduction to American Literature," dealing with "the varying aspects of a national development, idealistic and material, as recorded in our literature." [30]

B. Johns Hopkins University

At Johns Hopkins University "History of Occidental Civilization," begun in 1930, is a two-year sequence in which conventionally recognized periods of historic development are investigated separately in chronological order. This continuity is essential, for, as Frederic C. Lane writes in "Why Begin at the Beginning," man invents myths to satisfy his curiosity about his origins if historical data cannot present the truth. "So insatiable is man's interest in his distant past that imagination assists the weakness of memory." [31] This explains the origin of the Romulus myth and presumably of much modern literature, for, if the historians,

. . . the professional dealers in second-hand memories, do not respond, the answers of such soothsayers as the politicians, the novelists, and the Sunday supplements will be accepted.[32]

This has been predominantly a history course, but in 1940-41 it was for the first time combined with a new course entitled "Art in the Occident."

"Art in the Occident," as Robert P. Griffing, Jr., describes it in his letter of June 1940, emphasizes

> ... religion and philosophy, as the recorded corpus of human thought ... with historical facts supplying the necessary documentary framework.[33]

The course is apparently presented with a feeling for the values of individually-perceived design. Mr. Griffing writes:

> I think I am right in believing that the freshman and sophomore, generally speaking, should not be exposed to esthetics in the pure state. It is more important for him to get at them from an analysis of various works of art in different media to the extent that he will ultimately realize, without anyone telling him so, that there are certain principles which underlie all art forms. This fact will hit him sooner or later, depending on the individual, and he will certainly realize its implications much more vividly if he makes the discovery for himself.

C. Missouri Valley College

The "Masterpieces of World Literature" was first offered in 1931 as part of a Humanities program including "History and Appreciation of Art" and "Appreciation of Music." According to catalogue statement, "Masterpieces of World Literature" was designed

> ... for the purpose of enabling each student to acquire a comprehensive and integrated view of world literature. Following a brief survey of mythology as a foundation for the understanding of literature, the work consists of a comparative study of the masterpieces of literature by periods from the ancient to the contemporary. . . . These courses are essential in assisting the student to prepare for the comprehensive examination in literature.[34]

The appreciative and critical process moves, Dean Claude L. Fichthorn states, "from the whole to its parts, and using the comparative approach rather than the purely analytical. . . ."[35]

D. Bucknell University

A group of courses was introduced at Bucknell in 1932, including the "History of Art," "World Literature," "Musical Culture," "Philosophy of Life and the World," and "History of Western Civilization." Of "History of Western Civilization" the catalogue states:

> A chronological survey of the civilization of the Western world from early Egyptian times to the present day. The development of government, social life, religion, art, music, philosophy, industry and commerce.[36]

"World Literature" is divided into two semesters, the first treating "world literature to the middle of the eighteenth century,"[37] the second moving into literature of modern times. "Philosophy of Life and the World" considers "how the individual fits into the scheme of things. The nature, value, method, and history of philosophy. A synthesis of the sciences and other knowledge and experience. The meaning and tests of value, particularly of the humorous, the beautiful, the true, the good. The relation of body and mind, of matter and spirit. The nature and destiny of life and personality."[38] The course is not open to freshman students. The aim is to draw together, on an upper class level, the "realm of values" with which other courses are necessarily concerned.

E. Talladega College

The two-year "Humanities Survey" at Talladega College was introduced in 1933. The first year, as we learn from the catalogue, provides,

> ... a course designed to acquaint the student with man's great contributions in literature, philosophy and religion, and art from ancient times to the present day, to introduce him to standards for judging the quality of such work, and to develop in him an appreciation for the best in these fields. The historical approach will be used.[39]

The second year seems to place less emphasis upon chronology and more upon the students' adjustment to contemporary life.

This course includes a study of literature, its techniques and types, intended to develop literary appreciation on the part of the student; of the major problems of philosophy with emphasis upon current trends of thought; of the fine arts and the application of artistic principles to everyday life so that the student's enjoyment of the beautiful, and his taste in fine arts may be developed.

F. Northwest Missouri State Teachers College

"Humanities" was introduced here in 1934, as one of several general courses, which, while providing a base for further education, are considered valuable experience for students seeking terminal education at the sophomore level.

The purpose of this course is to acquaint the student with the best in literature, fine arts, and music produced since the Middle Ages, and to develop an appreciation of the religious, philosophical, and cultural aspects of our civilization in Modern Times.[40]

G. Alabama College for Women

"The History of Civilization" was introduced at Montevallo in 1934. There is recognition of the effect of the emotional-intellectual aspect of aesthetic experience, but it is apparently relied upon principally to vivify historical material, and to establish a relationship between the remote and contemporary aspects of our culture, and more recently, as Professor Lorraine Peter writes, March, 1942, "to tie it up with the present world situation."[41] The main current of the course is established by materials from history and literature. Unity of the arts is demonstrated in the fact that at different times and places similar symbols have been exploited in different arts. Hence the study of Greek mythology is paralleled with the playing of Gluck's Aria from *Orpheus and Euridice,* or of the Ballet *Dance of the Blessed Spirits.* Similarly, Euripides' *Alcestis* is supplemented by Gluck's March from *Alceste,* and the *Nibelungenlied* by Wagner's *Ride of the Valkyrie.*

Course examinations indicate a strong demand for recognition of technical aesthetic terms, particularly in architecture and music, and in literature for factual knowledge of plot and setting.[42]

H. *Eureka College*

"Humanities 107" was started in 1935. The course is specifically designed to

> ... give a sense of the continuous development of man's effort to find civilization and thus help the student gain a historical perspective and a sense of human values.[43]

"The continuous development of man's effort" is apparently given a rhythm through accenting "the great periods of history." At the same time, there is a significant aesthetic pattern suggested:

> It [the course] should give the student a sense of the relations between the social, economic, and political pattern of any particular period of human development and its science, its religion and its philosophy, and the relationship of all these to its art and literature.

I. *College of St. Scholastica*

In Catholic colleges and universities the term Humanities has long been used for courses in the classics. It has been applied to chronological surveys of literature, art, history, philosophy, and religion. Such a course was introduced at the College of St. Scholastica in 1937.[44] Also in 1937 the Dominican College of San Raphael and Duchesne College introduced "humanities" courses "to integrate subject matter,"[45] and to provide "integrated cultural background."[46] In 1939 the American University in Washington, D. C., started "Human Living: the Humanities," but in 1940, according to Dean George B. Woods in his letter of March 11, 1941, the idea of the broad survey course was abandoned because of its difficulty for freshman students.

3. COURSES EMPHASIZING TYPES OF LITERATURE

Almost all Humanities courses involve attention to types of literature, reflecting a contribution of Comparative Literature that has now become widespread in colleges and high schools. In Allegheny College, Omaha Municipal University, St. Cloud Teachers College in Minnesota, the Florida State College for Women, and Queens College, the emphasis upon types seems to provide central logic for the courses.

A. Allegheny College

"Introduction to Literature" was first offered in 1929. Companion courses in music and art were introduced in 1932 and 1937 respectively. The course in literature is "not a survey in the historical sense," as Professor Julian Ross notes in describing the course in *The English Journal*.[47] Its expressed purpose is to show the student "the maximum number of separable elements contained in literature." Artistic technique is first demonstrated through an *explication de texte,* of several poems, pointing up "images, emotions, stories, ideas, character, patterns, and rhythmical devices." These elements are then applied to literature to show "that every type and every age of literature involve the same essential elements that have already been found in the poems." Two primary results are seen from this approach. "The student discovers that a Greek play, a medieval epic, and an eighteenth century novel all appeal to the reader's senses and emotions, tell a story about human characters, imply a general idea, and are arranged in a definite pattern." In this respect, as also in providing critical method for future reading, the course resembles somewhat that at Stephens. The course aims at general abilities suitable for terminal education and for advanced study. "The student who studies no more English . . . has laid foundation for future leisure-time activity. The student who goes on to work in advanced courses has mastered a method of analysis which can be applied to all further literary study."

B. Municipal University of Omaha

"Introduction to the Humanities" was first offered in 1933. The orientation in the first semester is through historical epochs, with special emphasis, as Professor Wilfred Payne writes, upon "views of life" [48] as revealed in the arts. In the second semester attention is directed to clearly defined types. According to the syllabus, the first semester is devoted to surveying "a number of periods, now past, during which, for a brief time, at a restricted locality, life came to a sharp focus...." [49] "Brief time," "restricted locality," and "sharp focus," suggest the desire for clarity which permeates the whole course. The student writes papers, e.g., "The Greek View of Life," "The Hebrew View of Life," or "The Age of Reason View of Life," etc., to develop his "capacity to master a single unit of life." [50] It is the "views of life" and "not the transitions between them" which are the most important aspects of the course. Art and philosophy appear in supplemental, not complementary, roles; ". . . since formal philosophy is often merely a species of wishful thinking, we shall be driven to reliance on literature and art, as well as philosophy, to attain a clear picture of the ideals functioning in each period." [51] Despite the connotations of "driven," there is the implication that philosophy and art at their best are syntheses of human values, not literal reconstructions of historical happenings.

The second semester is devoted to formulating a "synthetic perspective" which will reveal the "view of life which functions in the present." There seems to be a tacit recognition that no one view functions today, for the assigned papers concern topics like Contemporary Novel and Contemporary Drama. Again, these topics are designed to show the "student's ability to master a single unit." In the seriatum consideration of types of the novel, types of music, types of poetry and poetic themes, types of biography, types of drama, as well as architecture, dance, painting, essay, short story, and philosophy, there is indication that emphasis is less on philosophic values than upon the kinds of art and the identifiable types within them.

C. St. Cloud State Teachers College

The Humanities Program at St. Cloud State Teachers College includes a course in "Appreciation of Art," begun in 1934, "to create an interest in art by giving contact with its various phases, such as painting, sculpture, commercial advertising, etc."[52] The approach is essentially chronological, as it is in the "World Literature" course introduced in 1935. Chronology in "World Literature" is only a framework, however, within which the central focus is types of literature.[53]

D. *Florida State College for Women*

"The Humanities" was introduced in 1936. The course deals with the "forms of human energy" that comprise the Humanities—philosophy, literature, and art. While the course in the Humanities involves a chronological consideration of classical, Hebrew, and Christian philosophies which provide the basis for divisions in literature and the arts, a marked emphasis on types warrants its inclusion in this group rather than in the chronological. The Christian era is presented in detail under the subheads of Early, Medieval, Renaissance, and Modern. Tendencies in the Modern period are suggested under the major head of Neo-Classicism, Romanticism, and Realism. It is within these schools that illustrative literature is considered from the standpoint of "type." Poetry, to judge from the comparative space provided in the syllabus, receives preponderant attention, with a tripartite classification into (1) epic, dramatic, lyric (and all their sub-divisions); (2) subjects, i.e., love, religion, patriotism, etc.; (3) unclassified, i.e., didactic, satiric, pastoral. The course also turns attention to uses of language, the formal elements appearing to be most important. Rhetorical devices, for instance, are any "used to enhance expressive speech."[54] Some shift in emphasis is suggested by Professor Anna Liddell in her letter of May, 1942, stating that the staff has recently worked toward simplification through more intensive study of fewer literary selections.

E. *Queens College*

One of the clearest examples of the types approach is the "Introduction to Literature," begun in 1937. It is one of three courses in the Queens College Humanities Program. The other two are "History and Appreciation of Art," organized around art principles and history, and "History and Appreciation of Music," which centers in analysis of musical forms, movements, and schools.

"Introduction to Literature" is directed toward the cultivation of "an appreciation of the significance of form in art." [55] Underlying the consideration of all the arts is the basic assumption that the creative process involves three activities: selecting, harmonizing, and focusing experience. The study of types of literature is divided into four sections concerned respectively with short story and novel, drama, poetry, and non-fiction. In each of these divisions a significant limitation or potentiality of an art form is stressed. The instructors have great freedom in the selection of material for any of the sections. One of the most significant aspects of the course is a conscious and extensive use of the facilities which metropolitan New York offers in museums and theaters.

"The History and Appreciation of Music" is similarly concerned with the nature of the creative process. Frequent mention of the artists who "have something to say, and a burning need to say it," [56] indicates a further emphasis upon the selecting, harmonizing, and focusing experience. It suggests a strong emphasis also upon interaction of the individual artist with his culture. The musician's "message may be a bit more elusive than that of the poet and painter, because he is using a more fluid language; but like them, he seeks to capture and recreate the essence of human experience in terms of his own medium." [57]

The unity of art and philosophy as symbols of culture is suggested in the fact that the *Zeitgeist* finds expression in the arts and contemporaneous philosophy. The subject matter of this course centers in Classical and Romantic music (with incidental reference to the other arts and philosophy). In considering this particular transitional period, art is seen both as a positive expression of ideas and implicitly a negation of outworn values of the artist's society. "Only by acknowledging this [social background] can we explain the fact that at a certain time a number of artists scattered in different countries, unknown to each other, begin as though at a signal to grope their way in the same direction." [58]

4. COURSES BASED UPON RELATIONSHIPS OF ART AND SOCIETY

Humanities courses are all implicitly or explicitly concerned with the integral relationship of art and society. Some show marked emphasis upon a social aesthetic in which contemporary art is revealed as a part of modern life; for instance, those at Pasadena Junior College and the University of Minnesota General College. Other courses give additional consideration to philosophic concerns; for instance, those at the University of Louisville, George Williams College, the University of Georgia, Menlo Park Junior College, Columbia College, Columbia University, Macalester College and the University of Houston.

A. Pasadena Junior College

"Humanities Survey" was offered first in 1934 to lead the student to a keener appreciation of the expressions of "inner emotions" which through the ages man has made "in public buildings, in theaters, in concert, in church and church ritual, in practically everything he sees and hears." [59] We learn from the syllabus that recordings of music, pictures and illustrative literary selections accentuate "standards of artistic appreciation, common to music, art, and literature." From broad acquaintance with the evidences of art in daily living the course moves to a consideration of the cultural heritage and the knowledge "that only those things that have had real worth have survived." Knowing these things should "help students as individuals to experience, enjoy, and appreciate the best things in their personal everyday living." [60]

B. University of Minnesota General College

The series of courses in "Art Laboratory," "Art Appreciation," and "Art and Science" were instituted in the General College in 1932, and have since been continued in the College of Education. They are expressly concerned "with the study of all art *forms as they relate to society*," [61] and with fulfilling

> ... a universal need for and satisfaction from sensitivity to and understanding of fundamental life situations that arise directly from art, whether ... in the form of materials and objects surrounding one in home and everyday activities, the illustrious products of the artists of the past, music, direct or by radio, the stage, and motion pictures, or literature which is being produced and distributed in increasing quantity very cheaply and very beautifully.[62]

The emphasis is placed first, as at Antioch College, upon creativity in workshops in each of the arts, "to give a better understanding of art creation" rather than "technical dexterity."[63] Attention then turns to the individual's reaction to works of art, and to a conscious recognition of the similarity of response called forth by the various art forms.

C. *University of Louisville*

The course designated as "The Survey of the Humanities," introduced in 1932, is explicitly concerned with the "values approach." According to Professor Ernest Hassold, there is a consciousness of values distinct from those pursued in the fields of science and the social studies: "... the humanities course [gives] some sense of the *experience* of living in the modern world."[64] The course is based on the "common functions of the arts of expression in interpreting human experience."[65]

The primary concern throughout the sections of the course devoted to philosophy, literature, and art is the development of the individual student. This viewpoint is apparent in the foreword to the philosophy section of the syllabus, " 'Not *philosophy, but to philosophize*' is our motto."[66] Hassold continues, "In literature the emphasis is on ideas, in philosophy on ethics, in art and music more on forms. But the main point of the course is to give the student adequate reading techniques in literature, art, music, and philosophy, so that he can continue to pick his way about."[67] According to the prospectus for the course for 1942, the literature covers nineteenth and twentieth century European and American fiction and drama, since these lie "nearer to the reading capacity and interest of the general student than poetry." Some emphasis has been placed upon schools and techniques, like Naturalism and Regionalism, "but at all times, the endeavor has been to stimulate more thoughtful, as well as more extensive reading by pointing out the various ways in which literature still performs its function of exploring and interpreting human experience."[68] Critical method, according to Professor Hassold, writing in March, 1942, involves "analysis of the structure of the organized work of art and the function of it, as a means of re-experiencing the work in a synthesis of these two aspects."[69]

D. George Williams College

"Introductory General Course in the Humanities" was begun in 1935. From the College Bulletin we learn that it is

A co-ordinated survey to bring before the student a wide variety of representative experiences of mankind in some of the areas generally classed as cultural—literature, religion, philosophy, and the fine arts—with the aim of securing an appreciative evaluation of the achievements of man in the art of living, and with the further aim of enriching the student's life through his increased understanding and appreciation of the intellectual, emotional and artistic values in life.[70]

According to Professor Dorothy Bucks, the course stresses "art as a product of a particular culture pattern," and is making increasingly wide use of the drama available in the city of Chicago.[71]

E. University of Georgia

The "Humanities Survey" was introduced in 1935 into the fifteen schools which make up the University of Georgia system. From the Bulletin of the University of Georgia[72] at Athens, we note that

This course will include material from English literature, ancient and modern foreign literatures, and the fine arts, such as music, painting, sculpture, and architecture. It is designed to develop in the student some knowledge and an appreciation of these vital factors in life.

According to the 1942 Bulletin of the Georgia School of Technology, the Humanities Survey is still a "uniform part of the curriculum of all units of the University System of Georgia."[73] Recently, however, the various participating schools have followed individual practices in the presentation of the course. At the Georgia School of Technology, Professor A. J. Walker states, the trend is away from the arts in general and toward "an acceptance of literature as the expression of the great philosophies of the ages as they have reached the majority of men." The course uses an anthology.[74]

F. Menlo Junior College

The "World Literature" course at Menlo was opened in 1936. The logic of this course is the sequence of events in contemporary society.

This course draws upon the best literature of all countries and all times as illustrative material on the themes which are of vital concern to the world in general and college students in particular.[75]

With a similar flexibility the course in "Masterpieces of Literature" centers in the literature which each student taking the course might find advantageous to his own personal growth.[76]

G. Columbia College, Columbia University

The two-year "Humanities" course was begun in 1937 in order, as Professor Barzun states,

> ... to get young minds acquainted with great ones; to break down barriers of distaste and diffidence in order to establish communication; and in effect not so much to educate as to start self-education.[77]

The College Catalogue states that the first year of the plan is devoted to heightening

> ... literary taste and judgment, as well as habits of philosophical analysis. It is based upon reading, in more or less chronological order, out-

standing masterpieces in the literature and philosophy of the European tradition.[78]

Professor Barzun extends this statement:

> To be sure, the chronological sequence in which the Columbia freshmen read the books provides ample opportunity to bring out the historical relations of the men to one another, to compare their attitude, and to note secular changes in style and spirit. But these things are incidental to the process of getting the first view, of measuring the scope, of assimilating by analogy or contrast the human experiences embodied in the play or epic, the philosophical prose or satirical verse.[79]

The course procedure calls for short factual tests each week before the Great Book under consideration has been discussed in class. From three to six class periods are devoted to discussion of the book.

Four times during the year essay examinations are given in order to test the student's power of organization and discrimination on a cumulative list of works.[80]

Through this sequence of experiences the student achieves

> ... a mental life which makes him at will independent of his surroundings and circumstances, and enlarged powers of communication with his fellows.[81]

These are the "social as well as individual consequences" with which the Humanities course is ultimately concerned.

"Humanities B," the second year of the Columbia College plan, takes up the other arts. The organization includes explicitly many of the principles we have noted in other courses, and provides for a rhythm of culture epochs within the chronological frame. It is arranged, Professor Moore states,

> ... to include preliminary lectures which seek to establish principles and methods of approach. From this point on, the chronological study begins—a consideration of the various great epochs of art from the time of the Greeks to the present day, not regarded as a history of art or of music, but in the light of the great masterpieces themselves as reflecting the culture and thought of the period.[82]

H. Macalester College

"Introduction to the Humanities," begun in 1939, emphasizes somewhat similarly the use of discussions, literary selections, and written statements which, according to the text developed from the course, *Earning Our Heritage,* have "intrinsic value as personal and cultural orientation." [83] Specifically, this value is seen in learning *"by practice* to speak, read, and write intelligently—to learn those language arts which instructors in all courses expect them to know and use.[84] Considerations of art, history, literature, music, philosophy, and religion form the "intellectual and social motivation of the language arts." [85] According to Professor Norman F. Coleman, writing in March, 1942, "There has been increasing emphasis upon Art, Music, and Religion, as the development of these is coördinated with the development of Literature." [86]

I. University of Houston

"Survey of the History of Art" was introduced in 1941. According to Professor Robert W. Talley, writing in March, 1942, this course emphasizes "the unity of all the arts: literature, music, the dance, and plastic arts." This is not "a technical course in art history" but one emphasizing "the historical influence on aesthetic formulations of the various cultural periods." [87]

5. COURSES BASED ON INTELLECTUAL HISTORY

Most Humanities courses are concerned in some measure with intellectual history, but at the University of Arizona, the University of Akron, Princeton University, Rollins College, the University of Pittsburg, the University of Wisconsin, and Adelphi College, we find a more explicit concern for this approach than elsewhere.

A. University of Arizona

The "General Course in the Humanities" was introduced in 1933. The students are told in the syllabus to "reach out for meaning in life"—because "we shall understand ourselves better if we know something about our ancestors."[88] There is a different emphasis here, however, from that of pure chronology, the distinct cultural epoch, or the theories of cultural transition.

In the three thousand years which we trace, we observe not only changes in man's attitude and his changing notions of beauty and morality, but also the basic ideas and attitudes which give unity and continuity to the story.[89]

This is achieved, according to Professor Melvin T. Solve, writing in March, 1942, by having students "read complete works or long selections from about fifty authors" and by correlating "developments in philosophy, art, and architecture with the development of literature in the cultural periods from Homer to the present in America."[90]

B. University of Akron

"Introduction to the Humanities" was started in 1935. It follows a chronological sequence of human history from primitive man to modern times. The sequence embraces art, music, literature, philosophy, and history—approached primarily through lectures and collateral reading. According to Professor Don A. Keister, writing in March, 1942, "There has been a slow drift in the direction of the history of ideas (as practiced by Lovejoy, Boas, *et al.*)," and an increased concern for the arts as formulations of the cultural concerns of a period.[91]

C. Princeton University

The philosophical synthesis also characterizes the comprehensive and balanced four year Divisional Program in the Humanities at Princeton, begun in 1936. The departments of Philosophy, History, English, Classics, Art and Archeology, and Modern Languages cooperate over a four year period to

introduce the student to the civilization of his own day through a many-sided understanding of the major movements of Western culture which have formed it, and to train him to judge ideas for himself clearly and coherently, relating his own thinking to an understanding of its historical background."[92]

Throughout his curriculum, the student's supervisor directs his "study towards a mature integration of the several aspects of his humanistic studies in preparation for his divisional examination," which is taken at the end of the senior year and may cover such areas of specialization as "the Renaissance or eighteenth century ... an aspect of the Drama ... the Romantic Movement, or American Civilization and its European background; or ... a critical and philosophical problem." [93]

Within this program Theodore Meyer Greene offers his course in "Philosophy of Art," described as "a philosophical analysis and appraisal of the aesthetic experience in its relation to other types of experience. Consideration will be given to distinctive problems relating to literature as well as to the fine arts." [94]

D. Rollins College

The "Humanities Basic Course," begun in 1939, is an optional four-year curriculum for students at Rollins. In the catalogue description we find concerns for the relationship of the artist and society which was accented at Queens College, and to individual and cultural development also stressed at Columbia. The course includes:

> ... fields of knowledge which present man as an individual, expressing his life experiences in literature, in works of art, and music, and explaining their meaning in terms of religion and philosophy. This course aims to provide an understanding of the cultural forces that have shaped present-day intellectual, artistic, and spiritual life. The historical approach is employed in tracing the intellectual and cultural life of the western world from the ancient civilizations of the Near East through the civilization of contemporary America.[95]

Part of the four-year sequence is devoted to a "philosophical synthesis" in which the student is led to see the interrelationships of the fields of inquiry, and their contribution to the planning of his life.

E. University of Pittsburgh

The "Humanities" was begun in 1939. According to the Bulletin for 1940-41, this four year program represents "a balanced curriculum in cultural subjects, centering above all around those great men and women, leaders in thought, action, letters, and the arts, whose personalities and achievements have moulded the world's culture." In a series of parallel courses, the student examines in successive years the history of civilization and the principles of art; literature from Homer to Boethius, and contemporaneous history, philosophy, and art; literature from Dante to Goethe and contemporaneous culture; and contemporary literature, music, art, and American society.[96]

F. University of Wisconsin

The *Course in The Humanities* was introduced in 1940. It is a four-year program providing a "substantial introduction to the four great fields of learning: language and literature; history and its correlated branches; science; philosophy and mathematics." The "masters of English Literature" are given heavy emphasis; in addition, students come into "vital contact with one of the great foreign civilizations of the ancient world." Through the methods of approach to past cultures they "acquire the power to acquaint themselves with at least one of the great foreign civilizations of the modern world." [97]

G. Adelphi College

The philosophical synthesis of four years of work which is common to many of these schools is significant of the feeling for pattern that characterizes modern aesthetics. Focused more specifically upon the arts, the "Philosophy of Art" course at Adelphi College, opened in 1940,[98] attempts a somewhat similar synthesis to that at Rollins and Princeton. From the independent courses in the several arts which students take at Adelphi, this course seeks to find a common "denominator of various courses in art in the college" and to show the similarity of response to the several arts. In this respect it closely resembles the "Arts Today" begun in Minnesota General College, and like that course may represent a pattern which will become increasingly important in Humanities programs on the general college level.

6. COURSES ACCENTING SOCIAL BACKGROUNDS AND CULTURE EPOCHS

A representative group of courses are organized chronologically, but with an explicit concern for the historical periods and culture epochs distinguishable through man's expressions of his attitudes toward life—very much as we have already seen in "Humanities B" at Columbia College. Such courses we find at Scripps College, University of Chicago, Colorado State College of Education, Illinois Wesleyan University, Chicago City Junior Colleges, Hendrix College, Stanford University, Oklahoma Agricultural and Mechanical College, University of West Virginia, Judson College, and the University of Minnesota College of Science, Literature, and the Arts.

A. *Scripps College*

The most extensive development of the culture-epoch pattern is presented in the three-year Humanities sequence at Scripps College, introduced in 1928. During the first year, a study is made of the cultures of the ancient world. In subsequent years three divisions (fifth century A. D. to 1750, medieval Europe to early eighteenth century, the Modern Age) are bound together by two assumptions:

(1) that the life of the Western world subsequent to the fifth century A. D., has a common "stream of tendency" and therefore that it has a chronological unity; (2) that the changing pattern of its social life is the foundation on which an understanding of its political, intellectual, and artistic achievement should rest.[99]

This sequence is aimed at a *"cultural self-understanding* for better direction of our lives," an "understanding of the civilized, the *humane life,* that is the Western heritage." [100]

B. University of Chicago

"Introductory General Course in the Humanities" opened as a survey of literature and art in the history of civilization in 1931, and shows an interesting development toward clearly defined epochs. In 1937, the Syllabus showed concern with rhythms of culture-patterns:

... our main purpose is to bring the student into immediate contact with as many as possible of the masterpieces of thought and art of the long line of our cultural ancestors.[101]

A familiarity "with the political, social, and economic forces of each succeeding epoch," necessitates a mastery of "the historical and institutional setting out of which a given body of art and literature came." [102]

Works of literary art selected for this course were included on the basis of their intrinsic interest, their significance in the Western tradition, and their value for illumination of the periods which produced them.[103] A changed tone enters the Syllabus for 1939, with stress on critical evaluation: "forming judgment as to *how good each book is of its kind, and why.*" [104] In the critical annotation of many of the materials of the course, aesthetic considerations are given extended attention. These considerations, however, are predominantly in terms of "constant sharpening and clarification of definitions for such terms as literature and such subdivisions as epic, drama, tragedy, comedy, lyric, novel. It is also important to distinguish as clearly as facts permit between poetry, history, rhetoric, and philosophy." [105]

Commentary on the *Iliad* runs:

Though the *Iliad* is a mine of information about the customs and beliefs of the earlier Greeks, though it is invaluable in a study of the development of Greek grammar, though it may legitimately and profitably be studied from these and various other angles, we nevertheless invite you to study it as an example of epic poetry. In the limited time available we concentrate on the organization of the incidents of the action which makes the *plot,* on the characters as revealed by their speeches and actions, and . . . on the style or diction.[106]

This implicit disposition toward Aristotelian criticism becomes more nearly explicit in subsequent commentary upon the *Poetics:*

Aristotle's *Poetics* . . . is not the Bible of our course and you may dissent from any of its conclusions without penalty of excommunication. You are however expected to know what Aristotle's positions are and to be prepared to explain your reasons for dissent.[107]

This statement reflects the conflict between the relativistic point of view of the members of the Humanities course staff at the University of Chicago, and the Hutchins-Adler position which would emphasize the Aristotelian-Thomistic methods primarily.

C. Colorado State College of Education

"World Literature" was introduced as a freshman course at Greeley in 1931 under the direction of Professor E. A. Cross. His pioneer anthology, *World Literature,* grew from the experiences of the course. Since 1935, according to Professor E. E. Mohr, writing in Lamar Johnson's *What about Survey Courses?* (1937), courses involving creative and appreciative experiences in the other arts[108] have been part of the freshman program, and in 1940-42 "World Literature" was moved to the sophomore year. In 1942-43 it became a junior-senior course.

Like most other courses in the Humanities these have undergone appreciable revision year by year. Sections of the music courses under Professor Mohr are reaching out for cultural backgrounds and common denominators with the other arts. The World Literature course since 1940 has stressed chronological sequence of culture epochs as these reveal individually-expressed values and contemporaneous attitudes toward life. We find in the staff report to the Committee on Evaluation of the College (spring, 1941) this description of "organization, materials, methods and values in World Literature." The report notes the values of the Sciences and Social Studies, and the focus peculiar to the Humanities

... upon the "more human" values of curiosity, imagination, sympathy, human dignity, by which alone each individual recognizes his own identity.[109]

In the College Catalogue for 1942-43 we find this reference to materials, values, and organization:

60a,b-160a,b—Landmarks in World Literature: Five culture epochs in Western Civilization, with particular attention to the changing concept of "self" revealed in the outstanding literary symbol for each period. Symbols of culture studied include a group of Greek plays, Dante's *Divine Comedy,* Shakespeare's *Hamlet,* Goethe's *Faust,* and Melville's *Moby Dick* (60a), and a selection of contemporary literature with world perspectives (60b).[110]

Aesthetic criticism is sought through a "clarifying" critical paper following the reading of each work of art. In 1942-43 consideration of these world views occupied two quarters' work. The third quarter is planned as an introduction to the concept of regionalism as seen in contemporary literature of the United States.

D. Illinois Wesleyan University

The "Survey of the Humanities" was begun in 1932. The course as organized pays considerable attention to types of literature, using as it does an anthology emphasizing types of world literature. The catalogue description of the course, however, stresses progression of culture patterns, "with attention given to all the various avenues through which the great minds of each period have sought to interpret the dominant cultural ideas of their own time. Through such an approach the student is enabled to trace the dramatic story of man's constant quest for beauty, truth and goodness, gaining a synthetic and organic view, not a fragmentary and disjointed one." [111] And Professor Ralph E. Browns also emphasizes the staff concern with dominant ideas of successive cultures, and a present trend toward "reading more whole works, instead of excerpts." [112]

E. Chicago City Junior Colleges (Herzl, Wright, Woodrow Wilson)

The "Humanities Survey" was introduced in 1934. Originally it examined chronologically history, art, music, literature, philosophy, and religion, which "grow out of the times, the interests, and the conditions which are dominant during any given period." [113] The aim was "to assist the student to orient himself in the world in which he lives by helping him to understand the complex foundation upon which our present civilization is built." [114]

The Syllabus for the course

. . . is intended merely to afford the student a framework of facts upon which to hang the study of the actual cultural materials which are the primary consideration of the course.[115]

Critical methods and values are evident in the elaborate comprehensive examinations in which technical aspects of literature and the arts and of types of literature are heavily weighted.[116] Annotations in the Syllabus for many of the works of art indicate additional critical methods in use. These seem predominantly biographical, psychological, philosophical, and historical.[117] In the discussion of Whitman, however, reference is made to the "stirringly effective interrelation between subject matter and technique . . ." [118]

In a letter of March, 1942 Professor Dorothy Weil notes two major shifts from this predominantly historical approach to the Humanities. The first involves a new introductory unit considering "the nature of art, music, and philosophy; important problems in the careful reading of literary work; the significance of the Humanities in the world today." The second change has to do with "greater consideration of actual creative materials instead of mere talk about them." [119]

F. Hendrix College

The four Humanities courses introduced at Hendrix in 1934 deal with as many culture epochs: "The Ancient World"; "The Medieval

World and Renaissance"; "Classicism and Romanticism"; "The Modern World." These courses are offered in sequence and "attempt to awaken and develop a genuine appreciation in such cultural areas as music, art, literature, philosophy, and religion." [120] According to Professor Robert Campbell, in 1941, another course using Dudley and Faricy's *Humanities* was introduced "to acquaint the student with the fundamental principles that underlie all aesthetic experiences so that he may better understand and appreciate a particular artistic form." [121]

G. Stanford University

"The History of Western Civilization" was introduced at Stanford in 1935. It emphasizes culture epochs with a significant attention to the gradual transitions by which they have evolved. There is recognition of the significance which certain arts have assumed in expressing the particular values of a given period.

The life of medieval man found its highest satisfactions in the symbols and art forms of the church. At first the austere dignity of the Gregorian chants sounding among the massive columns of a Romanesque abbey, later the new contrapuntal music rising like clouds of incense toward the soul-shattering beauty in the painted windows of the white Gothic cathedral; these gave the ordinary mortal man a taste of the forecourts of heaven.[122]

In placing emphasis upon a single isolable tendency of a past epoch, the Syllabus stresses the heterogeneity of values in diversified modern culture.[123]

This aspect of the course is increasingly marked in subsequent editions of the Syllabus. The tenets of pragmatism set forth by James and Dewey are compared with those of the intuitionism of Bergson, and of neo-scholasticism as set forth by its exponents, Etienne Gilson, Jacques Maritain, and Mortimer J. Adler. There is a recognition of the near-anarchy to which the canons of aesthetics have been carried in literature and art, which probably accounts for the "slight increase in the emphasis placed upon aesthetics and aesthetic experiences" reported by Professor Max Savelle in April, 1942.[124]

In the spring of 1942 the School of Humanities was created, bringing into administrative unity literature, arts, history, languages, music, and philosophy. But the name Humanities also provides a significant unity here, for the basic course offered by Lewis Mumford is devoted as he says, to the "production of complete human beings, harmoniously disciplined to create within themselves and within their society the order that will banish the barbarous mechanisms and the mechanized barbarisms that now threaten us." [125]

The School of the Humanities provides a four-year program, the first year of which emphasizes "the History of Western Civilization, a study of the development of, and the relations between, the religion, art, thought, and economic and social forms of our Occidental tradition." [126] The second year involves a "similar, but even more intensive, course in the History of American Civilization." [127] With this foundation in subject matter and ways of thinking, speaking, and writing, the student enters in his third year a basic course in Humanities, which involves "a fundamental study of man conceived as a being trying to understand, and adapt himself to, the natural environment in which he is placed, the social environment created by the fact of fellowship, and the realm of 'value' which he discovers both within and outside himself." [128] In the fourth year appropriate specialized course work is paralleled with a seminar in the area of major interest, which terminates in a special research study planned to "assist the student to correlate all his humanistic studies." [129]

H. Oklahoma Agricultural and Mechanical College

"Humanities 214, Western Culture" was first offered in 1937. This course is offered in much the same spirit as that of "The History of Western Civilization" at Stanford. It emphasizes philosophical-aesthetic concern with "the worth and responsibility of the individual," and "the Greek taste for balance, unity, and completeness as reflected in art." [126] It also emphasizes strongly the influence of the cultural pattern upon the arts. A final examination question reads: "Write a unified and well-written essay illustrating *precisely and in detail* effects that the rise of the middle and lower classes has had on Government and the arts (including literature) since the Renaissance." [127]

In addition to the survey of Western culture a second course entitled "Interrelation of the Arts" shows further feeling for a modern aesthetic. This is an evening course devoted to reading aloud several plays, listening to recordings of opera, analyzing in detail shorter musical selections, and scanning poetry. The latter part of the course is devoted to showing the interrelationship of poetry and music through the joint consideration of lyrics as poems, songs, and as salon compositions.[128]

I. University of West Virginia

The "Humanities General Course" was introduced in 1937. Attention to social background is prominent, but greater emphasis seems to be placed upon artistic qualities than upon cultural origins of the arts. Art is not only a positive expression of human values; it may represent a "rebellion" against the vapid forms of a preceding period.[129] The several arts are considered from the standpoint of the effectiveness with which each medium expresses the social values of a period. No hierarchy is established, though considerable attention is given to the potentialities of the expressionistic drama as a synthesis of all the arts. According to Professor Claude C. Spiker, the Syllabus for the course is revised yearly, and serious consideration is being given to organization based on a sequence of historical periods.[130]

J. Judson College

"Survey Course in the Humanities" was introduced in 1938. The college catalogue describes it as "a study of selected world literature which aims to provide the student with a knowledge of representative cultures." [131] Originally the study of cultures was carried on under four heads: Greek-Roman, Hebrew, French-German-Italian-Spanish, and English-American. Within the past year curtailment of staff has led to the use of a comprehensive anthology of world literature, with a judicious elimination of "lesser writers, and expanded material for some of the major figures." [132]

K. *University of Minnesota: College of Science, Literature, and the Arts*

In 1940 a comprehensive "Course in The Humanities" was introduced in the College of Science, Literature, and the Arts. Through "a systematic coördination" of history, philosophy, the fine arts, and music of four great periods—Ancient, Medieval, Renaissance, modern—the student acquires "a well-ordered knowledge of our cultural development." The course provides for specialization in one of the four great epochs, so that the student "may study critically in historical sequence the great monuments of creative energy and may thus acquire a precision of method and thought no less exact or useful than that of the natural and physical sciences." [133]

In addition to these Humanities programs there are a number of similarly titled programs further representative of the variety and originality of organization that typifies "the revival of the humanities." The two-year sequence offered by the Division of Humanities at the University of Newark is one. Here there is concern for the language arts, for "readings, chosen to increase skills and develop interest," for "various literary types and critical theories," and "a consideration of the general principles of aesthetics"—all augmented by opportunities for creative work and acquaintance with great art through field trips.[138] So with other schools of technology.

The Humanities Department of The Cooper Union for the Advancement of Science and Art offers a varied program of courses including "Western Civilization," "American Civilization," and "Approach to the Arts," employing texts which represent a wide range of aesthetic concerns for formal art principles, types of literature, and culture epochs.[139]

Another pattern comes from Knox College, where the Department of English offers a "Regional Survey in Humanities" dealing with the "Literary and artistic, religious and philosophical expressions of the Mid-west mind" [140]—a variant on courses in American Civilization that in increasing numbers are being introduced in Humanities programs.

In addition to these Humanities programs and the numerous World Literature courses which form a base for them, there are, as we have noted, approximately one hundred and fifty courses in World Literature in other colleges and universities, which have no formal connection with courses in the other humanities. Like the Humanities programs, these courses have been introduced in the past fifteen years as partial answer to our quest for breadth and unity in the study of literature. In many instances they may be considered as initial steps in the formation of additional Humanities programs drawing into an economical aesthetic pattern the related concerns of history, philosophy, and the other arts.

CONCLUSIONS OF PART III

Values

The revival of the Humanities in American education is marked in actual practice by numerous tendencies which may be considered indicative of growing unity despite great initial and persisting diversity. For the teaching of World Literature as one phase of the Humanities, these indicate trends toward sharper focus in an approach to values. In a variety of phrasings the Humanities courses emphasize as "more human" values: (1) sympathetic understanding of other people; (2) imagination to project oneself into unfamiliar situations or states of mind; (3) intellectual capacity essential to such projections; (4) dignity of self and its attainment through self-direction.

Unifying Concepts

In organizational pattern there is observable convergence upon six broad types. Most reflect a modern psychological-anthropological concept of aesthetic experience. These patterns of orientation—basic aesthetic principles or classifications; art in society; chronological sequences of subject matter; social and cultural epoch approaches; classification by types; history of ideas—are not mutually exclusive. A significant feature of many courses is the inclusion of two or more patterns of which one remains dominant. In many instances the form of organization is varied at certain phases of the course to meet the exigencies of subject matter. Through many courses, as at Columbia, Chicago, Colorado State College of Education, Stanford, there seems to be a growing prevalence of the "cultural evolution" external frame, and a growing intimation of an emotional-intellectual "aesthetic" resolution of design in such phrases as "forms of human energy," "life coming to sharp focus," and "world view."

Subject Matter

There is a heavily weighted deference to those works of literary art that have been important through the years. In many schools there is increasing concern for the whole pattern of fewer works of art in preference to many shorter selections. There is little indication, however, that any book is a "best" book, or that any list of significant titles comprises the key to any liberal education. This is consistent with the exploratory, relativistic nature of the courses which marks them off as distinct from the authoritative St. John's pattern. Modern literature is used widely as incorporating contemporary world views; the geographic-world pattern is significantly represented in increasingly numerous works of art in translation that have achieved a world-perspective. There is also increasing concern for the American scene considered from the standpoint of history and regionalism.

A further check is to be made. How far are scholar-specialists in literature putting their research in a larger frame, and at the same time gaining unity? Are they reëxamining our great books in such ways that teachers may draw directly on their work for a modern aesthetic approach to "human values" in world literature? Ideally, our final chapter should consider this question in connection with an outstanding work in each of the great culture epochs. Practical considerations must limit us largely to one work—Shakespeare's *Hamlet.*

PART IV

EXTENSIONS AND EXEMPLIFICATION OF A MODERN AESTHETIC APPROACH TO WORLD LITERATURE: *HAMLET* AS EXAMPLE

THE TENDENCY to select a few complete works that presumably speak for major epochs in Western culture, and to examine them as aesthetic formulations of the great issues and experience of their time, has been observed in several schools—such as Columbia, Chicago, Colorado State College of Education, and Stanford. If the assumption is sound that these works do represent their times—or, put another way, if the inquiries of scholars bear out the inclination of teachers to focus on five or six great books as representative of epochs—then the teacher of World Literature finds a hopeful economical way between the one-volume anthology and the hundred great books. He has, in addition, a clear unified progression for his reading and discussion that may be hard to achieve in either the anthology or the hundred great books.

Modern scholarship lends its authority to such choice. It has also been turning attention increasingly to aesthetic formulations of epochs. The extent to which this is true has been made the subject of extensive investigation in introducing the new course in World Literature at Colorado State College of Education in 1940. The course represents a conscious extension of trends traced through these several chapters, with substantiation in accepted modern scholarship.

"Landmarks in World Literature" stresses the world views in great books of five epochs—seeking at once economy of time and worldwide range. Following in more detail the World Literature staff's Report to the Committee on Evaluation of the College, we find these summary statements revealing the logic of the course:

(1) The Greek view of life we present in a series of Greek dramas in which Aeschylus, Sophocles and Euripides in three successive generations used the same symbol, Electra, to present their attitudes toward life. In the sequence we see the emergence of self from tribal loyalties to individual values.

(2) The medieval view of life we present through Dante's poetic formulation in the *Divine Comedy* of the philosophy of Thomas Aquinas—man achieving selfhood through absorption into the Mind of God—a philosophy still current, sympathetic understanding of which is essential for harmonious human relationships.

(3) The Renaissance world view we present in Shakespeare's *Hamlet,* where "self" emerges to consciousness in a highly individualistic pattern of action.

(4) A fourth world view emerges in Goethe's *Faust* during the transitional half-century which spans the last quarter of the eighteenth and the first quarter of the nineteenth centuries. Here the individual is seen to grow from irresponsibility to selfhood in the conscious pursuit of a valued cultural design.

(5) In Melville's *Moby Dick* (chosen to give one American work of current interest) an individual-social self emerges with consciousness of scientific method and responsibility in a world where human design can work destructive or constructive ends—ideas we are now re-discovering in the purposed design of dictatorship and the need for conscious planning to extend "human" culture.

(6) Extensions of Melville's symbol of culture are found in a wide range of twentieth century literature, starting with *Anna, Karenina* (1876) and including works like *The Forsyte Saga, The Great Hunger, Jean Christophe, The Magic Mountain, Of Human Bondage, The Grapes of Wrath, The Nazarene, You Can't Go Home Again, Storm,* etc.[1]

Because of its familiarity, *Hamlet* should make a good test case.[2] Here the theme is the "emergence of conscious-selfhood," emphasized in most modern conceptions of aesthetic experience, and basic presumably to both Renaissance humanism and to the modern humanities.

Conservatively enough, the study begins with Elizabethan cultural backgrounds and the play itself. Our concern is with the process of formulation before we gauge the perfected product. Scholars have been ahead of us on many points.

Recent Trends in Hamlet Scholarship

Modern scholarly criticism of the past fifteen years has stressed many different aspects of *Hamlet*. Critical attention has been turned to dramaturgy, to linguistics, to psychological studies of character, to discussion of philosophical values, and to the many relationships between the play and its cultural background. Some critics have been preoccupied with only one of these phases of *Hamlet* scholarship. Other critics, concerned with a patterning of several phases, see a rounded aesthetic experience in the progression of the play, based on some understanding of Elizabethan culture. It is with these more comprehensive designs that we are concerned—aesthetic designs which clearly take into account the social concerns predominant in our schools today, and which also recognize the ultimately individual character of art and aesthetic experience. Three scholars, one Canadian, one English, and one American, suggest trends in this direction: G. Wilson Knight, John Dover Wilson, and John W. Draper. To the highly conservative scholar comprehensive aesthetic designs are sometimes questionable; but no Shakespeare scholar today fails to reckon with them, and most modern scholars, like O. J. Campbell, Mark Van Doren, E. E. Stoll, Caroline Spurgeon, David Hardman, M. R. Ridley, share many views with them.

Knight's critical approach to Shakespeare provides an extreme case of individual resolution of values. *The Shakespearean Tempest* (1932), reveals his search for "clear aesthetic philosophy"[3] which will provide the "unity" which intelligence demands and yet take into account "an especial intuition which transcends all reasoning."[4] His aesthetic philosophy holds that "a man may be divinely inspired when writing poetry,"[5] and while he may be influenced by contemporary events or striking ideas of previous writers, his work of art is not to be explained by these "sources." "We cannot say about any one symbol that it means anything more or less than it must mean in its particular context."[6]

The symbol that pervades Shakespeare and gives unity to all his work as well as to individual plays is the *tempest* set off against the harmonious atmosphere suggested by music. "Therefore, in the Shakespearean system, we shall be forced to regard either the sea in all its variations or the tempest-music opposition (these being equivalent since the sea, variably rough and calm, tends to include the modes suggested by the other terms) as fixed; and we shall say that plots are built round tempests—or, to be more exact, round the tempest-music opposition—rather than that tempests are inserted into plots."[7] The tempest symbol is then "Shakespeare's intuition of tempestuousness at the heart of existence,"[8] and the critic's aesthetic concern must be with the resolution of the conflict of human values symbolized in a work of art. They are philosophical values, as he tells us in *The Imperial Theme* (1931), like "conflict and concord; evil and love; death and life."[9] These symbols are not symbols of Elizabethan culture, but symbols of universal human values.

Knight's criticism displays an increasingly pointed search for the unity of each play in a philosophical core, some phase of which is metaphorically represented by one character. In *The Wheel of Fire* (1930) Knight says, "Now the theme of Hamlet is death."[10] In *The Imperial Theme* he noted that the core of the play was the Ghost as the symbol of Death,[11] and Hamlet as the instrument of Death suffers the death of his own soul[12]—as opposed to Laertes whose exuberance in Life symbolizes the opposition to the Ghost's forces. The conflicting interaction of these forces is symbolized by "tempest" scenes and allusions, and the resolution of their opposition is symbolized in "music." In *The Imperial Theme,* he continues:

"Music" and "tempests" are of all our most important symbols. Their interplay is the axis of the Shakespearean world, style of verse, types of play, imaginative themes, "character," veins of imagery—all pass in turn, altering, changing, blending, as the great planet swings over: but all revolve on the "tempest" "music" opposition. These two correspond to the most fundamental of ideas necessary to natural, human, or divine realities.[13]

This trend in Knight's critical approach to Shakespeare, and particularly to *Hamlet,* reaches a focus upon the musical harmonization of tempests within a single character in *The Shakespearean Tempest.*

In the first act Hamlet's tempest is suggested in Horatio's warnings of danger of the raging sea to which the Ghost may lead him:[14]

> What if it tempt you toward the flood, my lord,
> Or to the dreadful summit of the cliff
> That beetles o'er his base into the sea . . . (1.4.69).

"And Hamlet lives a life of death henceforth," writes Knight, although there is one supreme moment of "music" in his life midway through the play. "It is significant that in a moment of exultation, when he has recaptured his sense of purpose directly after the play, and makes harmonious though hostile contact with the reality of his world, Hamlet first sings and then calls for music:[15]

> Ah, ha! Come, some music! come, the recorders! (3.2.291)

Ultimately Hamlet's conflicts are resolved in music. "All must be related to the death atmosphere of this play. This death theme attains a solemn beauty of its own in the dead march played at the end. In death there is no disharmony. So the 'soldiers' music' speaks for Hamlet at the last." [16]

John Dover Wilson's approach to *Hamlet* also emphasizes aesthetic resolution but makes *Hamlet* a moving symbol of Elizabethan culture, in which conflicts of specific human values are harmonized.

Stress on the unfolding aesthetic experience is evident in Wilson's editing of *Hamlet*. Through copious interpretative notes he attempts to make the reading version of the play a guide to imagining how the play looked to an Elizabethan audience. In the extended commentary of *What Happens in Hamlet* this emphasis upon *rapport* with Elizabethan attitudes is even more explicit.

Hamlet was "written by an Elizabethan for Elizabethans." [17] The Danish setting of the play is only a "mirage" for the Elizabethan court. Historical accuracy in Danish customs, or strict analogy between Danish and Elizabethan customs, is of little critical consequence. "Verisimilitude and not consistency or historical accuracy is the business of the drama." [18] *Hamlet* is therefore comprehensible to us only in so far as we project ourselves in imaginative sympathy into the Elizabethan's values and attitudes, and live through them vicariously with Hamlet.

Exemplifying his feeling of the importance of Elizabethan culture for an adequate interpretation of *Hamlet,* Wilson opens his commentary with a chapter on The Tragic Burden which faces Hamlet, an Elizabethan individual trying to retain and express his individuality in opposition to other individual and social pressures. Within this chapter a section on The State of Denmark makes clear the Elizabethan attitude toward the throne. A second section on Gertrude's Sin sets for us the atmosphere in which Elizabethans generally and Hamlet particularly must receive a queen's and mother's incestuous relationship with a usurper to the throne. This is followed by a third section on The Task which faces Hamlet, of regaining his individual dignity after his "great and noble spirit [has been] subjected to a moral shock so overwhelming that it shatters all zest for life and all belief in it." [19] The task also faces us as a twentieth century audience to sympathize with Hamlet, to "think ourselves into the position of this hero. . . ." [20]

The second chapter, Ghost or Devil?, makes more possible our identification with Hamlet, for it builds into our conscious background the Elizabethan attitude toward the supernatural which is essential before we witness the first scene of the play. Explicitly, Wilson draws attention to the necessity for this basic Elizabethan outlook. The richer the background of understandings with which we start the play, the more far-reaching are the implications of the sequence of events which follow.

From backgrounds Wilson moves into the opening lines of the play, and for the rest of the book treats the action in the order in which it unfolds upon the stage. Carefully he avoids isolating elements of the play and discussing them out of the context of the events as they are presented. Where extended comment on qualities of one character seems essential, he includes an appendix so that the continuity of the play is not violated. His critical method recognizes that each scene of *Hamlet* is what it is only because of its predecessors and our imaginative anticipation of its consequences in future scenes. Because of this, Wilson's commentary is a re-creation of the creation, for his readers are growing in their understanding of the play as its design unfolded in the mind of the author himself.

Wilson draws attention to his own method of running comment through comparison with the "vicious habit of taking stock of the whole play at once, instead of treating it as a serial work of art in which incidents and events are arranged in a certain order and intended to be apprehended in a certain order." [21] The significance of his attention to the form of the play has been recognized both here and abroad. The Literary Supplement of the London *Times* noted that Dover Wilson "has been twitted before now with his imagination and his enthusiasm; but imagination is no bad quality in the interpreter of high tragedy, especially when his eye is so firmly held to the object as in this book." [22] In a similar vein Mark Van Doren wrote in *The Nation,*

> The test of a Shakespearean critic is not so much his truth as his tact, taking that word in its noblest sense and letting it mean almost as much as wisdom. . . . Mr. Wilson . . . seems to me one of the two or three best critics of Shakespeare today quite as much because he tends to be a poet as because he certainly is a scholar. And his latest book on "Hamlet" . . . seems to me one of the best of all books on the subject because it adds life to a masterpiece which is already unspeakably alive. . . . It is as if an incomparably beautiful animal had been placed on exhibition and the man exhibiting it had turned out to possess, in addition to the finest knowledge of those points which all experts are trained to recognize, the finest understanding of the creature as a whole, so that its beauty came suddenly to seem something quite near to us, and, without losing its mystery, natural.[23]

While both of these comments on *What Happens in Hamlet* laud Wilson's attention to the aesthetics of cultural origins and expressive form, they do not attach an underlying significance to Wilson's moving through the events of the play sequentially, though Van Doren follows the same sequential procedure in his *Shakespeare* (1939). Wilson himself leaves us to infer from one early mention of the burden of self-preservation which faces Hamlet, and a final reference to "the tremendous self that death has recovered for him," [24] that all that lies between is exposition of the process of one individual's growth.

John W. Draper, like Dover Wilson, points the need for understanding Elizabethan culture if we are to establish *rapport* with the *Hamlet* of Shakespeare. "Of supreme importance in studying his work is the surging and pulsating society of the Elizabethan age, the only society that he and his audience really knew, and, therefore, the only social idiom by which he could hope for verisimilitude." [24] Draper, therefore, turns critical attention upon uses of language by specific characters under specific circumstances, for "the style of the play, indeed, is not alone great poetry, but great poetry subtly modulated to the occasion, to the speaker's immediate feelings and purposes, and to the surroundings in which he speaks: in the Renaissance, with its stringent laws of etiquette, conversation, to be real, could not be otherwise." [26]

As to its symbolic value, "*Hamlet* is a microcosm of the Renaissance state and of Renaissance society. It is a national tragedy—quite as much as the *Iliad* is a national epic—centered, as everything must be centered in the Renaissance, at court." [26]

Draper's critical approach varies somewhat from the running comment of Dover Wilson. Draper is concerned with the consistency of the dramatist in presenting certain philosophic, political, and religious points of view. These he discusses separately rather than as their meanings accumulate in the audience's mind through the sequence of events on the stage. Then, in a chapter on The Plot of *Hamlet,* with running comment similar in method to Mark Van Doren's, he ties his numerous discussions together. In this series of analyses he demonstrates the artistic greatness of *Hamlet* according to modern aesthetic criteria. Of any drama he writes, "the theme constitutes the major significance of the play, the regards in which it reflects some fundamental principles of life; and the greater the play, the more of these principles are reflected in their complex interactions and the deeper and more serene the insight that they portray; for a supreme artist must 'see life steadily and see it whole.' " [28]

One theme in *Hamlet,* and perhaps the one which most Elizabethans were principally aware of, was a very fundamental problem in Renaissance life, regicide. This was not mere murder, but murder affecting a whole nation, and involving of necessity the whole web of Elizabethan values, such as succession to the throne, Divine Right, and Papal authority.[29] "But the theme of *Hamlet*," writes Draper, from modern perspective, "is more deeply grounded in human nature than the theory of regicide. In illustrating his timely political point, Shakespeare depicts a perennial social struggle, the *one* against the *many,* the individual in revolt against a society that has, unwittingly or not, compromised with evil until it cannot, or should not, stand."[30]

The most fundamental aspect of *Hamlet,* and one which would provide a critical theme to which every other element of the play is related, is the growth of Hamlet's ability to cope with his environment and achieve certain purposes which he sets up for himself from time to time. Draper like Barzun in his article "Hamlet's Politics,"[31] makes this explicit in his discussion of Prince Hamlet: "Hamlet, . . . during the tragedy, grows from a courtier in mere outward form of etiquette and charming manners to a manipulator of the weapons of intrigue."[32] By the last scene "he has run the entire gamut of emotion"[33] and, we infer, the self which unchallenged would have known no growth, rises to its highest Renaissance potentialities. He achieved his purpose, but with it a dynasty ends and a now mature individual dies too soon to put into practice consciously any of his emergent ideals. Draper draws a final lesson from this tragic resolution of conflicts. "The individualist . . . must learn to use, rather than merely to combat, the social organization of the age."[34]

These examples of modern aesthetic criticism by Knight, Wilson, and Draper are all moving in the same direction. In varying degrees they involve the explication of how the form of the consciously designed play leads the reader to perceive certain human values. Their direction is consistent with that of modern ideas of aesthetic experience which we have seen in modern psychology, anthropology, and spokesmanship for the modern Humanities. The World Literature staff at Colorado State College of Education has taken this scholarly support for a modern idea of aesthetic experience as its base in the critical study of five epochs. But the staff has sought an extension of this base to point out more specifically the kind of synthesis that the teacher of literature can make. The following pages represent an exemplification of one possible synthesis which has been made by approximately six hundred students in the past three years.

We turn now to critical aspects of Elizabethan culture which provide part of the re-created intellectual climate which modern readers must bring to their sympathetic imaginative projection into Shakespeare's creative process.

Elizabethan Culture and Attitudes

For the world-view of Englishmen near the end of Elizabeth's reign, we may well revert almost a hundred years to the sailing of Columbus and Cabot, and to the publication of Castiglione's *Courtier*. From such different sources came the traits of Elizabethan society. The successors to Columbus and Cabot were Drake and Hawkins, whose work laid the germs of empire; out of the *Courtier,* translated into English by Thomas Hoby in 1561, came the code for individual cultivation and refined and intellectual intercourse among men. Here was the making of the Renaissance mind that saw wide horizons and yet disciplined itself to the realization of its greatest potentialities. This world-view was part of a growing nationalism, fostered perhaps by Elizabeth's excommunication in 1570 and the defeat of the Spanish Armada in 1588, both of which accented England's break with medieval Catholic influence. With growing nationalism, great value was placed on England's symbol of unity, the royal personage. This in its turn involved the valuation of succession to the throne and the perpetuation of the integrity of the symbol. For eighteen years England had been a tomb for Mary Stuart before her execution in 1587, the best years of her life cut off by jealousy and intrigue. Elizabeth was obviously to bear no children. In 1601, aged sixty-eight, she executed her favorite, the Earl of Essex. In Scotland was James VI, nearest of kin to the throne. What was he like, a foreign Scotsman with a still more foreign wife, Anne of Denmark? These were the circumstances that made the succession to the throne a paramount question to every Englishman.

Also in the atmosphere of the 1590's, according to Ethel Seaton's *Literary Relations of England and Scandinavia in the Seventeenth Century* (1935), was a growing awareness of Scandinavian countries. Gustav of Sweden had sued on several occasions for Elizabeth's hand, and his emissaries had created a flurry in the English court and among the citizenry. English shipping to Norway and Sweden had reached such proportions that one traveler reported three hundred colliers in an English harbor consigned to Scandinavian ports. English ships bound for Russia were forced to pay tribute in the Sound of Denmark. "Sound tribute," as it was called, was a recognized institution until 1628. The animosity which it aroused toward Denmark did not, however, keep James VI of Scotland from marrying Anne of Denmark, or many wealthy merchants from finding Danish wives. Nor, indeed, did the animosity keep English players from the Danish court, for two of Shakespeare's fellow actors played there in 1596. To this multiple interest in Denmark, from Queen Anne to itinerant players, the coronation of Christian IV of Denmark in 1596 [35] turned a sharper focus upon the still unnamed heir to Elizabeth's throne.

The problem could not well be discussed on the Elizabethan stage, for, according to E. K. Chambers' *The Elizabethan Stage* (1923), a statute remained on the books that state and church affairs should not be dramatized—"this beinge a thing very unfitte, offensive and contrary to such direccion as have bin heretofore taken that no plays should be openly showed but such as were first perused and allowed and that might minister no occasion of offense or scandall. . . ." [36]

Pressing as were these immediate cultural concerns, the depth of Renaissance meaning is to be reached only in an understanding of 16th century man's "pessimistic humour," as Don Cameron Allen terms it in "The Degeneration of Man and Renaissance Pessimism" in *Studies in Philology*.[37] Sampling English and continental philosophic tracts dealing with "the dignity and fortunes of man" Allen concludes that the conflict between medieval absolutism and the idea of the eternity of the world, and Renaissance empiricism and hypotheses of the decline of the universe and the plurality of worlds gave rise to a "continual repetition of the formula . . . that man is an altogether calamitous thing."[38] Degeneration of macrocosm and microcosm went hand in hand. While the world was becoming increasingly senile as it approached the end of its allotted 6000 years, 5544 of which, according to Richard Harvey, had already passed, man's original perfection of physique, reason and knowledge was being dissipated through the ages.[39]

This pessimistic hypothesis, according to Allen, was generally received. But the Renaissance humanist's "confidence in the intrinsic worth of life, his glories in the values of this world,"[40] led to numerous harmonizations of the paradox in both philosophy and philosophic literature. Unlike the man of the Middle Ages, who retreated from the confusion of earth to contemplation of the glories of Heaven, the humanist, "to whom the classics had given new values of the world, considered the discomforts of this life to ask 'Why?' or to seek an answer to 'What shall man do?' "[41] Some philosophers, Eugubinus and Alstedius, for instance, sought the answer in philosophical reconciliation of ancient authorities and new knowledge.[42] In the empirical spirit others, Lipsius and Hakewill particularly, drew attention to the rhythms of nature to show that corruption and generation were complementary phenomena.[43]

Allen brings to light this same conflict of values in the leading English philosophical poets of the 16th century, Spenser, Dekker, and Shakespeare. Their affirmations of the human values of this life are nowhere more explicit, as we shall see, than in Hamlet's struggle for self-realization.

If, now, we bring together the Elizabethan's concern for the succession to the throne, the contemporary interest in Denmark, the enforced abandonment of contemporary figures on the stage, and the conflicts of Renaissance philosophy, we can feel much of the Elizabethan's interest in the symbolic Hamlet whose original, "Amleth," was then current in an English translation of Saxo, and perhaps in a lost play of Thomas Kyd. All the trappings of court life, Elizabethan language, and superstition go to create the verisimilitude necessary for effectiveness with the audience. These things which the Elizabethan called to mind during the progress of the play, we may also recall in the running comment which nearest resembles the sequence of impressions that watching the play produces. And we must remember above all that the Elizabethan entered the theatre with doubts and uncertainty for the meaning of his life and the future of the throne of England. The play is an effort to resolve some of these doubts, or at least put some of the questions clearly. We must know what it seeks to resolve.

Now, following a pattern suggested by Dover Wilson, Draper, and Van Doren, which sophomore students at Colorado State College of Education have sharpened through two years of experimentation, we reconstruct Shakespeare's aesthetic experience and sense of self and that of his audience from the symbols of this play—remembering that the play was presented without act divisions, such as are here inserted in the printed versions, but rather as a cinema-like succession of scenes.

Hamlet [44]

Scene one: We are plunged into the gloom of night—a gloom not lightened by the nervous apprehension of Bernardo and Francisco, who pace the castle walls. In three lines we know that "Long live the King" is a password which dispels suspicion and fear. In thirteen short lines we know that it is the time of walking spirits, midnight, that Francisco is not only cold, but "sick at heart," and that a "quiet guard" is not always certain. There is an air of uneasiness, even among these lowly, lonely guards, although their thoughts tie us to the nation at large with "Long live the King." Within the next thirty lines, all the apprehension centers in the third appearance of an armed ghost—the ghost of the former King. To Bernardo he is first "the king that's dead," then to Bernardo and Marcellus simply "the king," and to Horatio "the majesty of buried Denmark" (1.1.47). A first scene so sharply focused on loyalties to the throne must tell us the center from which the action of the play will radiate. Who, we wonder, is the king-in-name who lives, guarded only by common soldiers still spiritually loyal to the former king? Who indeed, when the

> ... portentous figure
> Comes arméd through our watch so like the king
> That was and is the question of these wars (1.1.109).

Where, too, is the prince who has been announced as the titular hero of this play? While we wait for him, Horatio's analogy to Roman ghosts, "a little ere the mightiest Julius fell" (1.1.114), bodes ill for Denmark and the tyranny which sits upon its throne.

Scene two: The new king's first council since his coronation is not unlike the frequent Privy Council meetings that Elizabeth holds, despite its setting in Denmark. Beyond the fringe of light, glitter, and color of the royal pair is a solitary figure in black— young but not juvenile, pale—a sombre tie with the midnight scene we have just left. Why, we ask, knowing the depth of tradition for succession to the throne, is the student-prince in the shadow of another's splendor? We learn that Claudius has succeeded his brother on the throne, married his brother's wife, won the council to approve his succession, and promised Hamlet the throne when he is through. Not only has the King thus violated the traditions of state and the laws of the church; he has done so with "mirth in funeral, and with dirge in marriage" (1.2.12).

He turns to another young man, Laertes, and honeys over his name four times in nine lines, no ordinary way for a king to address one so far inferior in station. To his nephew-stepson, he turns finally with, "But now my cousin Hamlet, and my son . . ." (1.2.64). The "but" accents the irreparable breach of sympathies between uncle and nephew, and the values for which they stand.[45] It gives added meaning to the contrast of royal purple and gold and sombre black.

Claudius' sentence is incomplete. In his pausing he turns attention to Hamlet and waits to see what position Hamlet will assume. The precision of "A little more than kin, and less than kind"[46] (1.2.65), tells Claudius that Hamlet has not yet lost his sense of himself, nor of his identification with the deceased king, his father. This is a shrewd Hamlet who simultaneously takes his bearings from the past and present; as we presently see, he can also affront the King by ignoring him and addressing himself to Gertrude. "Good mother," he calls her, as though imploring that she too should "have that within which passes show" (1.2.85), but when he discovers that Gertrude is wholly and insensibly with Claudius, his appealing "good mother" changes to an austere "I shall in all my best obey you, madam" (1.2.120).

There follow the most "wild and whirling" words that Hamlet utters, springing not from craft but from near-distraction:

> O, that this too too sullied[47] flesh would melt,
> Thaw and resolve itself into a dew (1.2.129).

The rest of the soliloquy accents the long-pent feelings that have almost robbed him of his sanity. So also does Hamlet's welcome to his college friend from Wittenberg: "Horatio—or I do forget myself!" (1.2.162). We feel emphatically the confusion of self that appeared in the soliloquy—and, very important, the fact that Hamlet is still sufficiently master of himself to recognize the insecurity of his mental state.

His conversation with Horatio leads in fifteen lines to consideration again of his father's funeral, his mother's wedding, and Claudius' usurpation of the throne. Gertrude and Hamlet are after all inseparable, for Gertrude, as Queen, is the "imperial jointress" that links Hamlet to his dead father, his living uncle, and his own rights to the throne in the future. Hamlet's references, however, have all been in comparison of the two kings—with no indication yet that he feels a responsibility to his people to carry on as the rightful king. It will take many educative jolts to bring him to this realization. An auspicious beginning is made by Horatio, who now speaks of "the king your father" and brings the word "father" into the conversation six times in thirty-five lines.

When the scene closes, Hamlet declares his utter loneliness, in an alien-spirited court. Is Hamlet asking support that Claudius will later fear, when his soldier friends leave him with "Our duty to your honour," and Hamlet replies: "Your loves, as mine to you. Farewell" (1.2.254).

Scene three: Hamlet will need these loves, we find. Glib Laertes primes Ophelia for suspicion of Hamlet's intentions. Ophelia is not too credulous—she, like Hamlet, knows that men may not suit their actions to their words, and chides her brother on this account. She would be aligned with Hamlet, but her enforced dependence upon brother and father makes her incapable of any kind of independent action. Before Polonius she wavers, protests, then submits to his instructions. Intuitively, she is as fine as Hamlet—she knows him to be fine—but she cannot survive as her *self* in a villainous circle in the corrupt court. Can he?

Significant in Laertes' advice is his reference to Hamlet's intentions, "for on his choice depends the sanity and health of this whole state" (1.3.20). So far Claudius' coronation has not really registered in the thinking of the court. Hamlet has been the center of focus for thirty years, and people still consider him the next king, which, indeed, he is, though one lifetime has interposed itself between his election—that of Claudius.

Polonius enters. How alike this father and son are—in speech, in bearing, in values held, and in attitude toward Ophelia. He admonishes Laertes to remain true "to thine own self" (1.3.78)— the word "self" is in the air. Our imagination flies to descriptions of King Hamlet. What might Prince Hamlet have been had he resembled his noble father as closely as Laertes does Polonius? An evil day for Denmark that his accession was thwarted.

Before the Ghost appears in the fourth scene to focus Hamlet's attention on the "foul deeds" of Claudius, we have met nine clearly distinguishable personalities and one ghost, each with a different relationship to Hamlet. While the varied scenes and the characters of Gertrude and Claudius, Polonius, Ophelia and Laertes, Horatio, Marcellus, Bernardo and Francisco, and Fortinbras and the Ghost are still fresh in mind, we have a feeling that Hamlet is the point of convergence for eleven radial figures in the culture of Denmark—or England. What will happen if Hamlet moves, or does not?

Scene four: Once more we are back in "a nipping and an eager air" (1.4.2) on the castle walls, waiting for the ghost of King Hamlet. Depressed by Claudius' carousal—the custom "more honor'd in the breach than the observance" (1.4.17)—Hamlet philosophizes on "the vicious mole of nature" (1.4.24), the "stamp of one defect" (1.4.31), that leads each man "to his own scandal" (1.4.38).

But Hamlet's spirit is not entirely crushed. When the Ghost appears, Hamlet identifies it first with himself, finally with the Danish nation. "I'll call thee Hamlet, King, father, royal Dane" (1.4.44). And the resolved patience for foul deeds to rise, has changed to

> O, answer me!
> Let me not burst in ignorance, but tell
> Why thy canonized bones hearsèd in death
> Have burst their cerements? (1.4.45)

Disturbance and curiosity is the first step to action; and when Hamlet twice says, "I'll follow thee . . ." (1.4.80), "my fate cries out . . ." (1.4.83), we think of that one blemish of "revenge" that the ghost of a previous generation is about to plant in Hamlet, and with kindred-spirited Marcellus we sense that "something is rotten in the state of Denmark" (1.4.90).

Scene five: This Ghost is from the fires of Purgatory; its intentions are good. But speaking out of the past generation like a Greek chorus echoing the folk mind, it cries three times (on its third visit) for "revenge," and drives its message home with "O, horrible! O, horrible! most horrible! . . ." (1.5.80), "Adieu, adieu, adieu" (1.5.91), and three admonitions from the cellarage to "swear." There can be no mistaking its message nor its sincerity—and its quick movements in the cellarage suggest its invisible watchfulness over the remaining action of the play.

At the end of the first act, Hamlet is still the constant center for the life of Denmark. He is beginning to plan his actions. With lightning resolve, "So be it," he begins the wild and whirling words of his "antic disposition," and then forces the oaths from his friends Horatio, Bernardo, and Marcellus never to reveal what they have seen, or heard—or will see. He is already planning for the future; and from "revenge his foul . . . unnatural murder" (1.5.25), we know he is turning toward Claudius who "may smile, and smile, and be a villain" (1.5.108).

The first act ends on a note of brooding, despite the revelation of plans that have been made.

> The time is out of joint, O cursèd spite,
> That ever I was born to set it right! (1.5.188)

Act II, Scene one: With that note in mind, even after the rest-pause of Reynaldo's conversation with Polonius, we hear from Ophelia that Lord Hamlet has stood before her

> with his doublet all unbraced,
> No hat upon his head, his stocking fouled,
> Ungart'red, and down-gyvèd to his ankle,
> Pale as his shirt, his knees knocking each other,
> And with a look so piteous in purport
> As if he had been loosèd out of hell
> To speak of horrors . . . (2.1.74).

Five previous references—"sanity and health" (1.3.20), "breaking down the pales and forts of reason" (1.4.28), "madness" (1.4.74), waxing "desperate with imagination" (1.4.87), and "taint not thy mind" (1.5.85), on the one hand, and on the other his stated intention to put an "antic disposition on," have prepared us for such an appearance. Has Hamlet really cracked under the strain of responsibility and contamination? We do not know. We can only guess from Polonius' extreme simplification of the problem that there is more to it than meets the eye.

We see next that Rosencrantz and Guildenstern have been summoned at the instigation of both the King and Gertrude to sound

Hamlet's intentions. Polonius whets the King's appetite for knowledge of the "very cause of Hamlet's lunacy" (2.2.49). Claudius confides to Gertrude that "the head and source of all your son's distemper" (2.2.55) is about to be disclosed. Gertrude does not question her son's madness, but with a hint of regret she says,

> I doubt it is no other but the main,
> His father's death and our o'erhasty marriage (2.2.56).

While this suggestion lies fallow, as it were, we hear for the second time of restless young Fortinbras. Bribed from war on Denmark, he must nevertheless be marching on to Poland, and, if it please Claudius, through the Danish territory. While the little microcosm of the court continues its machinations, we are never quite unmindful of the opportunism of this foreign prince.

The messengers from Norway withdrawn, Polonius discloses his deduction of love-sickness for Hamlet, as well as a plan for decoying him into exposure. Hamlet appears in an aperture in the hangings just as Polonius says, "I'll loose my daughter to him" (2.2.162). We are still uncertain of his state of mind. When, in his second sentence to Polonius, Hamlet calls him a fishmonger, or "so honest a man," the epithet so fits his so-called "loosing" of Ophelia that we have a faint suspicion that Hamlet is quite sane. We are surer, when, free of Polonius, we hear his contemptuous "These tedious old fools!" (2.2.222). The expostulation carries at once a suggestion of triumph and disgust, and prepares us for the immediate appearance of the young fools, Rosencrantz and Guildenstern, whose stupid references to "ambition" so reflect Claudius' promptings that Hamlet concludes a sarcastic remark with, "I know the good king and queen have sent for you" (2.2.284). The line tells us two things—"the good king and queen," thus punctuated, are now as one person in Hamlet's mind, and for him to have used the adjective *good* is at once an evidence of self-control and an ability to match methods with anyone, for so simple a reference could easily allay the suspicions of Rosencrantz and Guildenstern. It is an admirable time, after two successful encounters with ignorant fops, to eulogize *man*. As though contrasts had set his imagination afire, he says,

What a piece of work is a man, how noble in reason, how infinite in faculties, in form and moving, how express and admirable in action, how like an angel in apprehension, how like a god (2.2.307).

Despite his dejected conclusion on "this quintessence of dust," this is the utterance of a mind no longer seeing the world as an "unweeded garden" but beginning ironically to recognize the extent of human potentialities. He is, in effect, creating a working hypothesis for his own life to demonstrate. Framing the hypothesis is the first part of the process.

Circumstances play into Hamlet's hands. Without seeking a means to achieve his end, he is nevertheless ready to adapt any tool that presents itself. The player group arrives. Instantly Hamlet sees a design in the types of actors who will comprise the company. In seven lines, he symbolizes all that has already happened, much that will happen in the play. "He that plays the King shall be welcome, his majesty shall have tribute on me, the adventurous Knight shall use his foil and target, the Lover shall not sigh gratis, the Humorous Man shall end his part in peace, the Clown shall make those laugh whose lungs are tickle o'th'sere, and the Lady shall say her mind freely . . . or the blank verse shall halt for't" (2.2.323). He still keeps us in doubt of the meaning he attaches to these forecasts.

It is significant that he concludes with "the Lady shall say her mind freely . . . or the blank verse shall halt for't" (2.2.328). We revert imaginatively to Ophelia's inability to carry her intuitive point and to Gertrude's having sought delay in marriage—and we are presently to hear of the "mobled queen" (2.2.507)—the changeable, muffled, inarticulate shrouded queen. What brings these thoughts to Hamlet? Does he feel the essential fineness of Ophelia and Gertrude, which has been overridden by officious Polonius and lustful Claudius? Again we do not know, and Hamlet appears not quite to know himself the significance of his symbols; only 250 lines later does he explicitly frame the ideas that seem to have been maturing, when he says,

> About, my brains; hum, I have heard
> That guilty creatures . . . (2.2.592).

Thus far in the second act, we have been allowed to forget the issue of succession to the throne. It is out of Hamlet's mind—though repetition of "ambition" from Claudius via Rosencrantz and Guildenstern suggests that it is still in the background. Now Hamlet brings us back to it as he generalizes on the success of the children's companies in London theatres.

It is not very strange, for my uncle is king of Denmark, and those that would make mows at him while my father lived, give twenty, forty, fifty, a hundred ducats apiece for his picture in little. 'Sblood, there is something in this more than natural, if philosophy could find it out (2.2.366).

Hamlet seems increasingly able to find it out. Where once his "prophetic soul" had suggested his uncle's crime but his intuition had remained inarticulate until confirmed by the Ghost, now Hamlet can say as he sees Polonius coming, "I will prophesy, he comes to tell me of the players, mark it" (2.2.390). It is another significant step in his growth. It is also important when, on top of the accurate prophecy, Hamlet's analogy of Polonius and Jephtha demonstrates an intimate insight into the character of another person. He has yet to clarify his own position analogously as well as he has that of Polonius.

It is not only from biblical drama that he can draw analogies. He knows long passages from the tale of Aeneas and Dido. But what is more significant, the lines he chooses to recite symbolize so perfectly his own state and the state of Denmark, that he impresses upon us the necessity for turning to symbolized values in this drama rather than to the succession of incidents or catalogues of kinds, which is the extent of Polonius' knowledge. Ironically and symbolically, he is so engrossed in his expression that he does not see the true import of

> . . . blood of fathers, mothers, daughters, sons,
> Baked and impasted with the parching streets,
> That lend a tyrannous and damnéd light
> To their lord's murder (2.2.462).

The player finishes the speech which completes the analogy to Hamlet's own state of indecision. But Hamlet is not yet conscious of his indecision and hence does not say these lines himself.

> So as a painted tyrant Pyrrhus stood,
> And like a neutral to his will and matter,
> Did nothing (2.2.484).

During the momentary silence that follows there is more happening to Hamlet than his perception of the starting tears in the player's eyes. He had not himself phrased the conditions which produced his indecision. The player's words "did nothing" now drive home the needed message. In explicit comparison with Pyrrhus and the demonstrated emotion of the player, he has taken the next step beyond a silent thought or witty action toward self-knowledge. But there is much yet to learn. And that he upbraids himself for using only words, suggests that he will be an apt scholar to his own necessity. "About, my brains"; he commands, telling us that this is the first conscious effort that he is making to fulfill the ghostly admonition to revenge.

> About, my brains; hum, I have heard
> That guilty creatures sitting at a play
> Have by the very cunning of the scene
> Been struck so to the soul, that presently
> They have proclaimed their malefactions (2.2.592).

Hamlet's first action (decided upon as the second act closes) will befit his Renaissance background—his constant search for knowledge in philosophy;

> ... I'll have grounds
> More relative than this—the play's the thing
> Wherein I'll catch the conscience of the king (2.2.607).

Act III, Scene one: Polonius, busy "loosing" Ophelia to Hamlet, unwittingly softens the king's receptivity to Hamlet's coming lines, by instructing Ophelia that

> 'Tis too much proved, that with devotion's visage
> And pious action we do sugar o'er
> The devil himself (3.1.47).

To himself Claudius says, "How smart a lash that speech doth give my conscience" (3.1.50). Then the King's conscience is active—because of fear of Hamlet's new strength? As Hamlet searches his own soul in his soliloquy (3.1.56): "To be or not to be, that is the question ... shuffled off this mortal coil ... quietus ... bare bodkin ... Conscience does make cowards of us all," we realize that a searching conscience has also been determining his actions. He must have been serious, then, in the former scene with Polonius when he said:

You cannot, sir, take from me any thing that I will more willingly part withal: except my life, except my life, except my life (2.2.218).

We know by this time that words repeated three times in this play are repeated to a purpose. They are more than idiosyncrasies of speech. These repetitions tell us of certain feelings and ideas in Hamlet that persist through all uncertainties.

By now we know that Hamlet rises to meet each occasion as it presents itself. He has great, though latent, power and ability. We know too that each challenge successfully met has been adding to his moral stature. How will he meet the new plot of Polonius and Claudius in which Ophelia as decoy introduces conflicting emotions of loyalty to self, loyalty to his father, love of Ophelia—and choices of ultimate values? A master of inflection and emphasis, he disavows his previous gifts to Ophelia with

> no, not I,
> I never gave you aught.

And when Ophelia fails to catch the implied change that has taken place in both of them, he tries a second indirection to point directions out. In tones more earnest than angry, he pleads: "Get thee to a nunnery, why wouldst thou be a breeder of sinners?" (3.1.121). If Ophelia's mind has not been too heavily poisoned, she will see a sincere appeal to take the veil—but if her thinking has taken its direction from Laertes and Polonius, she will interpret "nunnery" with the bawdy connotation of Polonius and Claudius. Ophelia does not rise to the intimations of the touching speech in which Hamlet also is preserving himself for future action with a show of lunacy— although his thoughts are not on self-preservation, of course. Describing himself in terms clearly audible to the King, he says, "I am very proud, revengeful, ambitious, with more offences at my back, than I have thoughts to put them in, imagination to give them shape, or time to act them in . . ." (3.1.125). Only an increased self-confidence permits Hamlet to describe himself as something other than "poor" (which he has done explicitly three times in Act I, and once in Act II). Added to it, "I say we will have no mo marriages—those that are married already, all but one, shall live . . ." (3.1.150), is a flung gauntlet—not quite an overt slap to Claudius— concluded with a fourth desperate admonition: "to a nunnery, go" (3.1.152).

Keener than either Polonius or Ophelia, Claudius sniffs at the diagnosis of love-madness:

> Love! his affections do not that way tend,
> Nor what he spake, though it lacked form a little,
> Was not like madness—there's something in his soul,
> O'er which his melancholy sits on brood
> And I do doubt the hatch and the disclose
> Will be some danger; which for to prevent
> I have in quick determination
> Thus set it down: he shall with speed to England . . . (3.1.165).

Claudius now realizes that he is dealing with a dangerous adversary, while Hamlet seems to think that he alone is concerned with his still subtle machinations. Claudius' metaphorical "sits on brood" looks into the future and to consequences, for "madness in great ones must not unwatched go" (3.1.192). He is the man of action—Hamlet presumably a man of contemplation. Together they present those Renaissance virtues that must be blended if man is to attain his "more human" stature.

This minor clash of Claudius and Hamlet, carried on when neither one sees nor speaks directly to the other, is a powerful prologue to the play of the murder of Gonzago, where, seated opposite to Claudius, with Ophelia and the players and Gertrude to talk to, Hamlet will have three points of vantage from which to prick the conscience of the king.

Scene two: There is no break now between scenes, no new complicating evidence to be introduced. The rhythm of the play is picking up. Both King and Queen will see the play. "Bid the players make haste," says Hamlet. To Horatio, whom he calls hither to observe the King's actions, he reveals his attainment of selfhood though he appears to be speaking of Horatio rather than himself:

> Since my dear soul was mistress of her choice,
> And could of men distinguish her election
> Sh'hath sealed thee for herself, for thou hast been
> As one in suff'ring all that suffers nothing,
> A man that Fortune's buffets and rewards
> Hast ta'en with equal thanks; and blest are those
> Whose blood and judgment are so well co-medled,
> That they are not a pipe for Fortune's finger
> To sound what stop she please: give me that man
> That is not passion's slave, and I will wear him
> In my heart's core, ay in my heart of heart,
> As I do thee (3.2.61).

This is notable self-criticism, a moment of near-maturity before the great antagonists meet at the play. We see now that Hamlet no longer waits to adjust himself to a changing situation, as he has done before. He forecasts his means and says: "They are coming to the play. I must be idle. Get you a place" (3.2.88).

The players' play brings us to the middle of *Hamlet;* all the characters but Laertes are present, drawn close before they are once more scattered by the explosive revelations of the scene. Within five lines, Claudius is on the defensive: "These words are not mine," he replies to Hamlet's subtle metaphor of latent power: "I eat the air, promise-crammed—you cannot feed capons so" (3.2.92). On the tenth line, as Hamlet prods the sensitiveness of each of his adversaries toward the relevance of "plays" to life, Polonius says, "I did enact Julius Caesar. I was killed i' th' Capitol, Brutus killed me" (3.2.100). There are then acknowledged precedents for regicide, as Horatio had once recalled in Caesar's case.

With the intuitive feeling that both Polonius and Claudius are sufficiently engaged, Hamlet turns to Ophelia, and in his actions and words diverts the attention of the King, Queen, and Counsellor to their own whisperings while the dumb-show proceeds. The dumb-show, of course, was no device of Hamlet's. It threatened to undermine his plot, to let Claudius steel himself to the words which will follow—but Claudius' thoughts are elsewhere. For us, the dumb-show is a brief pattern of what we are about to see unfold in the play-within-a-play. Elizabethans know this Will Shakespeare is a clever playwright. The plot is apt to prove a little complicated if we are not used to such devices, but Ophelia clears it all with her naive "Belike this show imports the argument of the play" (3.2.136). While Gonzago and Baptista play "some dozen or sixteen lines" of Hamlet's devising, we need not divert our attention too far from the analogous figures of the main play.

Like King Hamlet and Gertrude, the player King and Queen have been married thirty years when the action of the play begins. The King, feeling a premonition of his death in coming action, and foreseeing his wife's second marriage, wishes her well. But the Queen, in seeming sincerity, replies:

> Such love must needs be treason in my breast,
> In second husband let me be accurst,
> None wed the second, but who killed the first (3.2.177).

With the emphasis that rhymed couplets afford, we hear the Queen a second time affirm:

> A second time I kill my husband dead,
> When second husband kisses me in bed (3.2.184).

And the King, concluding a long speech emphasizing the transitory nature of human loyalties:

> So think thou wilt no second husband wed,
> But die thy thoughts when thy first lord is dead (3.2.213).

And the Queen again:

> Both here and hence pursue me lasting strife,
> If once a widow, ever I be wife! (3.2.221)

Seemingly engrossed in the play as Hamlet is, his "If she should break it now!" is innocent enough, but giving his pointing of the lines time to sink in he turns abruptly to Gertrude with: "Madam, how like you this play?" And when Gertrude, apparently unperturbed, notes only that "the lady doth protest too much . . ." Hamlet again thrusts home by way of emphasis—"O, but she'll keep her word." Suspicious, yet thrown off his guard by the indirection of Hamlet's attack upon his central crime, Claudius invites the next thrust to be directed to himself.

"Have you heard the argument? Is there no offence in't?" It is Hamlet's cue to summarize and interpolate and to become as Ophelia reminds us, "as good as a chorus." As the play proceeds Hamlet creates Lucianus as "nephew to the king" (3.2.243). Simultaneously, then, the pattern of action resembles—without being exactly like—what has occurred and what the future holds if Hamlet "sits on brood." It is a more palpable hit than "we will have no mo marriage" (3.1.150), and "you cannot feed capons so" (3.2.92)—on promises.

As Hamlet, following the Ghost's message, brings the interpretation to a focus in "A' poisons him i'th'garden for's estate, . . . you shall see anon how the murderer gets the love of Gonzago's wife" (3.2.263), the king rises: "Give me some light—away!" (3.2.269).

"Lights, lights, lights!" (3.2.270) cries Polonius.

Hamlet now has moved from a "Horrible, horrible, horrible" hell, through a physical ". . . life . . . life . . . life" to the possession of light—upon the honesty of the Ghost, upon self, upon the next direction which his vengeance must take. It is symbolic of Polonius' too deeply-rutted mind that in his blindness he should call for light— and justly ironic that, failing to see, he should be the first to perish in subsequent action.

As though the call for lights were also to symbolize a return to good spirits, Hamlet is jubilant and playful—as he had been after the Ghost had confirmed the suspicions of his prophetic soul. He culls out the metaphor of Damon and Pythias for the strengthening ties between himself and Horatio. To Rosencrantz and Guildenstern he can be light and frivolous, and then as suddenly deathly serious as he had been in the cellarage scene. We have the suspicion, however, that he is carried away with delight in his own ingenuity. All his next actions suggest the preoccupation with the intricacies of his own design. The rhythm of the play slows again. Hamlet debates with Polonius, he watches Claudius pray, and postpones vengeance until, spiritually, it can be more nearly commensurate with King Hamlet's death.

Scene four: It is the same sort of delay that brings the Ghost to the Queen's bedroom to "whet thy almost blunted purpose . . ." (3.4.111).

The bedroom scene opens with Hamlet's "Mother, mother, mother!" (3.4.6). With accentuation upon this basic family relationship he opens his interview. But from there, since his indirections have apparently passed over her less keen consciousness, he proceeds to

. . . set you up a glass
Where you may see the inmost part of you (3.4.20).

It is a fairly mature man who turns now to the instruction of his mother's consciousness. Gertrude, thinking that in his madness he means to murder her, calls for help. Polonius repeats the cry, Help! help! help! But Polonius has meddled too long. This third time that he fools Hamlet to the top of his bent, he dies as Hamlet thrusts his rapier at the voice behind the curtains.

> O what a rash and bloody deed is this!

cries Gertrude, as Polonius' body is revealed; and Hamlet, following up three hints at his knowledge of crime, says openly this time,

> A bloody deed—almost as bad, good mother,
> As kill a king, and marry with his brother.
>
> *Queen:* As kill a king! (3.4.26)

And while Hamlet turns nonchalantly to Polonius, the awful implications of those four words go through Gertrude's mind. Imaginatively, we too sense the chaos of surmise and retrospect and planning that typifies both minds upon the stage—surging visions of Claudius, of the first Hamlet, hopes for the future of young Hamlet, and of the intrusions and suspicions and fate of Polonius.

It is fitting that we should bring all these elements of the play together into the small tense scene. The home, the state, the church are here met in the integrity of one woman—loyalty to her first husband, loyalty to him as King, loyalty to her "self" in marrying outside the rules of the church. Here is the core of rottenness in the state of Denmark. Here in her bedroom is the "capitol" in which Polonius had unwittingly foreshadowed his own death. Now we hear Hamlet say that such action as hers

> . . . makes marriage vows
> As false as dicers' oaths, O such a deed
> As from the body of contraction plucks
> The very soul, and sweet religion makes
> A rhapsody of words (3.4.44).

The play-within-the-play and the bedroom scene are great climactic moments in *Hamlet*. We know that still others are to follow, for while Hamlet is temporarily triumphant over his enemies, his triumph has not issued in an action expressive of his complete resolved self. This is not a play of "falling action" in the second half.

Act IV: Act IV is one of confusion and reorientation among the characters. The fragments scattered by the play-scene, the realignment required in Polonius' death and Gertrude's chastening—all demand that the characters take their bearings from one another again. The first scenes of the act acquaint Claudius with the death of Polonius and show us Gertrude's fidelity to Hamlet. Scene three finds Hamlet again face to face with the King. He is confident in his knowledge of the King's guilt—confident to the point of insult. "Your worm is your only emperor for diet" (4.3.21), he says by way of comment on Polonius' death.

Claudius is powerless to punish Hamlet, largely, we presume, because, as Claudius tells us, Hamlet is "loved of the distracted multitude" (4.3.4). Here is a shift of fortunes, due apparently to the desire of the people for a continuing symbol on the throne. Why doesn't Hamlet capitalize upon this altered allegiance? Is it that the responsibilities of royalty sit lightly on him, or that in his sensitiveness to interrelationships he knows that an overt act of violence toward Claudius will bring suspicion on Gertrude? Or does the throne also have some symbolic value to him that makes it inviolate, no matter who its occupant? This seems unlikely in the face of Hamlet's corrective, parting words:

My mother—father and mother is man and wife, man and wife is one flesh, and so my mother: come, for England! (4.3.50)

As Hamlet seems thus lightly leaving the responsibilities that he has sworn to assume, the third appearance of Fortinbras carries a deeper significance for us. We remember that he rattled his sabre when King Hamlet died. He started his march through Denmark at the very time when Hamlet's lunacy seemed deepest. Now as Hamlet is shipped to England, this young man of action takes on a sinister aspect for the future of internally torn Denmark. His presence on the borders provides an undertone of insecurity in Denmark's succession. We are apprehensive, for this play is *The Tragicall Historie of Hamlet, Prince of Denmark*.

Scene five. Following hard upon Polonius' death, Hamlet's departure, and Fortinbras' arrival, comes Ophelia's madness. The small world she has known is confused in her mind, and in fact. Hamlet gone, the people call: "Choose we, Laertes shall be king!" (4.5.106) But the courage of Gertrude and the guile of Claudius lull Laertes and the people to quiescence again. A stabilization of realigned forces seems accomplished.

Scene six throws it out of alignment again, for by some strange circumstance Hamlet is back in Denmark, subtly contemptuous in his salutation to Claudius: "High and mighty, you shall know I am set naked on your kingdom" (4.7.44). We wonder what Hamlet means by "naked," but Claudius reveals its meaning for him: " 'Tis Hamlet's character . . . 'Naked'—" (4.7.51). While Laertes takes "character" only in the sense of handwriting, we know that it is a subtle recognition by Claudius of a direct challenge from Hamlet. Hamlet says that he will see Claudius "alone." There will be no more shouted threats, insinuations, and insults. Hamlet is for his man—openly now. Claudius and Laertes surpass each other in contrivances insuring Hamlet's death—unbated foil, poisoned tip, and poison draught.

The queen interrupts the villainous plotting, weeping for the death of Ophelia—her hopes and those of Denmark dashed, for we remember how to Ophelia she had said,

> . . . I do wish
> That your good beauties be the happy cause
> Of Hamlet's wildness, so shall I hope your virtues
> Will bring him to his wonted way again,
> To both your honours (3.1.38).

Act V opens with the interlude of the grave diggers, whose comic insensitiveness is plain in their speech clipped to the rhythm of the foot's pressure on a spade in hard earth. We feel the tragedy of an innocent creature's embroilment in the machinations of revenge and the irony of Hamlet's realization that even revenge is fruitless. This again is the contemplative Hamlet, not the man roused to meet challenging circumstances. It is a long scene—longer even than the bedroom scene between Hamlet and his mother. Like that scene, it draws into mind a network of emotions that key us more intensely to the conflicts we have witnessed serially. "Cain's jaw-bone" jowled to the ground by the clown carries us back to Claudius'

> O, my offence is rank, it smells to heaven,
> It hath the primal eldest curse upon't,
> A brother's murder! (3.3.36)

and back to Hamlet's prophetic

> . . . foul deeds will rise,
> Though all the earth o'erwhelm them, to men's eyes (1.2.258).

It carries us back to the "emperor" worm, to Imperious Caesar, to Hamlet's departure for England—and, as the funeral procession approaches, to the disunity in the royal pair—"here comes the king, the queen, the courtiers" (5.1.211). There is nothing "conjunctive" between them now—even the courtiers have no allegiances; they march alone.

As the burial proceeds, the summation becomes heavier and heavier.

> Lay her i' th' earth,
> And from her fair and unpolluted flesh
> May violets spring! (5.1.233)

Violets—Ophelia's symbol of faithfulness, we remember, had "withered all, when my father died" (4.5.185). Finally, as Hamlet leaps into the grave with Laertes, he cries: "This is I, Hamlet the Dane" (5.1.251). These are the *essential* words of his address to the Ghost: "I'll call thee *Hamlet,* King, father, royal *Dane*" (1.4.44). The lessons of the graveyard have eliminated all but the individual personality come to nearly full development as a member of his nation— "*Hamlet* the *Dane.*"

Scene one ends on the ominous note of Claudius:

> An hour of quiet shortly shall we see,
> Till then, in patience our proceeding be (5.1.292).

Scene two. Hamlet seems to be *instructing* Horatio in the circumstances of his escape from death—at the instigation of Claudius —not merely relating the sequence of events. We will remember this in the final scene. But at the moment the events themselves take precedence over the manner or cause of their impartation to Horatio. Hamlet has proved himself not only equal to any situation that presents itself, but capable of forestalling evil by his own planning for the future. For one supreme moment on board ship he has been as much a man of action as of contemplation; he has revealed that he can be a force for good as well as an island of virtue which lets evil currents circulate around him.

"Why, what a king is this!" (5.2.63) says Horatio in admiration when he realizes the active intelligence of the Prince he is speaking to. Hamlet, ignoring the tribute from his friend, summarizes in two phrases the regicide and incest of Claudius:

> He that hath killed my king, and whored my mother (5.2.65),

and takes two full sentences to convey what now seems infinitely more significant, Hamlet's future,

> Popped in between th'election and my hopes,
> Thrown out his angle for my proper life,
> And with such cozenage— (5.2.66)

Claudius' crimes are manifold now—he has usurped a throne, threatened the life of the next generation, and that through sneaking intrigue. Refusal of one's responsibilities to eliminate such an evil from the world is equivalent to perpetuating the evil itself. To do nothing is actually to condone evil,—

HAMLET AS EXAMPLE

> an is't not to be damned,
> To let this canker of our nature come
> In further evil? (5.2.68)

It is indeed

> ... perfect conscience
> To quit him with this arm? (5.2.66)

for, to use Claudius' own phrasing of a philosophy of action,

> Diseases desperate grown
> By desperate appliance are relieved,
> Or not at all (4.3.9).

But Hamlet's righteous indignation and philosophic resolve, which he entertains only in the form of questions, are softened as his self grows to include Laertes too.

> But I am very sorry, good Horatio,
> That to Laertes I forgot myself;
> For by the image of my cause I see
> The portraiture of his (5.2.75).

This speech engenders a hope for the future of Denmark. There are regenerative, coöperative forces to be mustered for good ends. Polonius is gone, with his sham excellence. His lesser counterparts, Rosencrantz and Guildenstern are also gone. Claudius is about to be cut off from power—when suddenly Osric emerges, a still more diminutive and far more vapid courtier—bearing the foreboding challenge to Hamlet to duel with Laertes. Thrown off his guard by the Queen's entreaty that he "use some gentle entertainment to Laertes"—and his own humane inclination toward the young man—confident in his skill, he ignores his once "prophetic soul" and overrides his intuitive premonition with "It is but foolery, but it is such a kind of gaingiving as would trouble a woman." He makes his most mature philosophical statement when, not permitting Horatio to forestall the danger, he says:

Not a whit, we defy augury. There is special providence in the fall of a sparrow. If it be now, 'tis not to come—if it be not to come, it will be now—if it be not now, yet it will come—the readiness is all. Since no man, of aught he leaves, knows what is't to leave betimes, let be (5.2.217).

Before they fall to play, Hamlet apologizes to Laertes for his actions at Ophelia's funeral. Then, confident in his new philosophy of defensive "readiness," he even passes lightly over what must have been a faint suspicion with a perfunctory "These foils have all a length?" With Osric's thoughtless "Yes, my lord," the duel begins.

Hamlet's confidence in himself is well founded. Realizing that Laertes' unbated foil may fail, Claudius invites Hamlet to drink. But Hamlet, either as good sportsman or as suspicious nephew, says, "I'll play this bout first, set it by a while" (5.2.283). Gertrude takes up the poisoned cup, ignoring Hamlet's restrained "Good madam" and Claudius' "Gertrude, do not drink." As she dies, we realize that she is the fourth innocent pawn sacrificed while Claudius and Hamlet play for the high stake of kingship. At Gertrude's death, only Hamlet exclaims, "O villainy! ho! let the door be locked—Treachery! seek it out" (5.2.310). But when Hamlet stabs the King, his own death already assured by the prick of the poisoned foil, the whole court cries "Treason! treason!" for every legitimate successor to the throne is gone.

Horatio, like an "antique Roman," would join his friend in death, but Hamlet, finally realizing the responsibilities of kingship, commands Horatio to live and tell the story. His final act is in the capacity of forward-looking king—naming his successor.

> . . . I do prophecy th'election lights
> On Fortinbras, he has my dying voice (5.2.354).

In his fullest realization of self in thought and action, he now knows that his life has meaning for himself and his society. The loss of it means something. Horatio and Fortinbras must carry on as "vessels" of this self so tardily realized. For us they are symbols of the unity of philosophy and action—the more so when the new king, young Fortinbras, recognizes the nobility to which Hamlet has risen:

> Let four captains
> Bear Hamlet like a soldier to the stage,
> For he was likely, had he been put on,
> To have proved most royal (5.2.394).

Measuring the dimensions to which Hamlet has grown, one representative student, at Colorado State College of Education, concludes her critical running commentary on the play by a comparison with symbols of cultures antedating *Hamlet,* and a questing forward vision:

> With his dying words he provides for the state of Denmark: "I do prophecy the election lights on Fortinbras." Even though Hamlet has developed a feeling of social responsibility, though he can project himself through sympathetic imagination into the viewpoint of other people, and though he has steeled his will to act, he has acquired these phases of his Renaissance self just before his death. And what is more important he has acquired them through the destructive methods and intentions of vengeance. He has not had the vision to see a course of action which would accomplish the commandment of the ghost and free the people of Denmark from an unjust king without entailing destruction for Ophelia, his mother, Polonius, Rosencrantz, Guildenstern, and finally himself. In this one respect he has been no "more human" in his actions than Iphigenia and Orestes, who followed a course of personal vengeance. In the consciousness of his method, however, he is far advanced over the Greeks. And the Hamlet who acts now in the present on earth has come a long way from the medieval Dante's ideas of rewards and punishments. But in terms of a modern "world development" of man's individuality he has a long way to go.
> Shakespeare, whose play is an "abstract and brief chronicle of the time," leaves us today with the imaginative ideal that in the gradual development of the comman man whose 'toe—comes so near the heel of the courtier,' who cries 'choose we; Laertes shall be king!' and perhaps in the ideally harmonized Horatio who finally says 'I shall have also cause to speak,' lies the future advancement of man. Hamlet symbolizes a little step ahead. Many great strides are yet to be taken.

CONCLUSIONS

IN THE COURSE of this study we have witnessed growing concern among natural scientists, social scientists, critical scholars, educators, synthesizing philosophers, and creative artists for the value of aesthetic experience. Increasingly leaders in modern thought are turning, like Alfred North Whitehead in *Science and the Modern World,* to literature as the medium in which "the concrete outlook of humanity receives its expression . . . [and to which] we must look, particularly in its most concrete forms in poetry and drama, if we hope to discover the inmost thoughts of a generation."[1] And the fact that responsible people are recognizing the totality of the present World War—not only in every phase of American life but in deep-lying global patterns as well—is intensifying concern for the breadth and focus of studies in the humanities and world literature.

Our evidence shows that the modern emphasis on aesthetic experience in the study of the humanities and world literature is not a sudden or chance development. In brief review of key figures in the streams of idealistic and empirical philosophies, whose ideas are current in the thinking of modern writers on aesthetic experience, we have found a persistent concern with the values of art—now individual, now social, now both—reaching focus in our time in such books as Dewey's *Art as Experience,* where aesthetic experience in art is seen as the creative-critical process through which self-realization is achieved by artist and observer alike. Similarly, in key writers in traditional English literary criticism, we found increasingly pointed emphasis, from Sidney to Arnold, on the function of literature in the individual's recognition of his own dignity through increased critical awareness of his cultural heritage.

These ideas, until the last half century the subject chiefly of speculative development, have been materially extended in the findings of the various schools of psychological inquiry. Among the many treatments of aesthetic experience in the revived "faculty" psychology, and in behaviorism, psychoanalysis, dynamic psychology, social psychology, and Gestalt psychology, we have found a common concern with the development of self. In recent syntheses of philosophical values with specialized research in psychology and anthropology, as in Rusu and Müller-Freienfels, we have found a biological base for the formative impulse central to aesthetic creation. Here the self, maturing to spirituality in critical interaction with the culture, is shown to involve the will and the "more human" qualities of intelligence, intuition, imagination, and sympathy vital to sustained democratic living.

Our investigation of anthropological ideas of aesthetic experience has shown increasing emphasis on the idea that language is the fundamental symbolic process. It is the medium for self-realization; and literature is a symbol of the degree of self-realization reached within the culture from which it springs.

Various of these ideas from philosophy, psychology, and anthropology we have found current in the writing of spokesmen for the humanities and aesthetic experience, who are translating them into educational theory and practice with specific reference to the critical study of values through world literature. Among these spokesmen we discovered two contemporary educational philosophies showing antithetical treatments of language and literature. One of these schools of thought advocates return to the established authority of medieval-classical metaphysics. The other moves in an empirical belief in a changing world in which individuals, seeking unity in ever-more-inclusive syntheses of emerging values, are able to maintain great diversity and individuality, and in which the development of individual persons is the ultimate responsibility of society. Modern humanists of the latter group, to whom human history appears as a constant redefinition of values, find it important that teachers of literature distinguish carefully between similar terminologies of "return to the classics," "great books," and "grammar-rhetoric-logic," where one philosophy takes over these ancient terms in their ancient meaning, and the other redefines them in the light of modern psychological-anthropological knowledge.

In the growing number of Humanities and World Literature courses also we have seen modern psychological-anthropological concern for the relationship of the individual to his community. While neither the nationally-known spokesmen for the modern humanities nor the courses which they and many other teachers offer show such a clean-cut single approach to the teaching of the "great books" as do the advocates of the medieval liberal arts, it is evident that there are important unifying elements in the merging of philosophical aesthetics and classical literary criticism with the newer psychological-anthropological aesthetic.

Following the lines which spokesmen and teachers of the humanities have marked out, we have looked critically at one major culture epoch in Western civilization and at *Hamlet* as one of the most memorable symbols of that epoch. Here also we found scholarly concern with the work of art as harmonization of individual-cultural values—further proof of the pervasiveness of the newer ideas of aesthetic experience. Extending the trends which modern scholars have established, we have sought to exemplify in our analytical synthesis of *Hamlet* the teacher's aesthetic approach to human values presented in the play.

What conclusions may we draw from this evidence? We may look for increasingly conscious concern for the unity which aesthetic values are providing in the teaching of Humanities and World Literature courses—first a clear unity for all the arts as symbols of culture expressing through the several media contemporaneous attitudes toward life, and second an increasingly clear focus upon the individually-experienced human values and, in further research and philosophically-planned experimentation, relativistic critical disciplines for developing them. It seems likely that in the next few years many courses will call for critical value judgments of a few selected works of art entire in their quest for the artist's resolution of the cultural concerns of his epoch. This development seems to offer one practical alternative to the four-year "Great Books" program, without loss of emphasis on human values. The trend may continue through the next decade, until a representative number of teachers will have carried its perspectives, though not necessarily its subject matter, into lower grades. The trend may be augmented by the speed-up in education to meet war-time needs, and the growing demands for "work-experience" in the community—where largeness of view available through the unity of specific works in the short time between work periods will be essential.

The concern for relative breadth of world perspectives central to the World Literature concept is present also in the expanding ideas about regionalism in this country. From the rising interest in regionalism, the government-sponsored American Guide Series and the series called *Rivers of America*—which Carl Van Doren notes in *The American Novel* (1940) "was to reinterpret American history and culture by fixing attention on natural and not arbitrary divisions of the map"[2] and to recapture what John Crowe Ransom calls the "esthetic quality"[3] of regional economy—and from the several schools already devoting time to American culture in World Literature courses—we may expect more and more attention to ecological-sociological-aesthetic formulations of world views in figures comparable to Tom Joad in *The Grapes of Wrath*.

The rapidly unfolding concern for aesthetic experience in the movies, indicated in such books as Sergei Eisenstein's *The Film Sense* (1942),[4] will expand, particularly under the impetus of audio-visual teaching in the armed forces. It is conceivable that some World Literature programs will include a large proportion of motion picture and radio appreciation for all students, and particularly for those of limited experience and intellectual ability. This use of radio and movies as integral subject-matter rather than merely as "teaching aids" will draw attention to methods of criticism appropriate to these composite, coöperative arts, so that the conscious attention to art as the integrating agent for the values of science, society, and religion—in Disney's *Fantasia,* to cite one instance—will be advanced without undue culture lag between leaders and followers.[5]

In addition, these newer ideas of aesthetic experience will probably bring a revaluation of sequences of "period" and "types" courses in American and English literature. But this must be the subject of additional research as scholars and teachers explore more fully the concept of the *genre* in relation to national literatures within the comprehensive designs of World Literature.

In addition to probable developments in World Literature courses, certain of the values they consistently emphasize are coming into clearer focus in society with the increased understanding of aesthetic experience. Paramount seems to be the recognition of the human personality as the most plastic of all materials which, in the laborious process of formation, has evolved consciousness of self as the supreme value in human living—and a political organization (where politics is the art of living together peaceably) whose primary function, as Mumford tells us in *Faith for Living*,[6] is the "creation of persons."

In so far as the development of self for millions today seems to some scholars to be influenced by the world view achieved by their nation's most significant literary figure, whether Dante, Hamlet, Faust, Ishmael, Ahab, or Levin in *Anna Karenina,* modern humanists would have us know the varying modes of self with which we will live in a new world united in a new polar geography by air transport and communication, as Roderick Peattie tells us in *Geography in Human Destiny* (1940).

From widespread concern with aesthetic experience, we will find stronger emphasis upon self as the fundamental value in a democracy—the one about which there must be no uncertainty, no question. It is the only absolute. But in another sense, as we know in re-experiencing the emergence of conscious selfhood in the aesthetic formulations of successive culture epochs in the Western world, and as we look critically about us today, this *self* value is a relative value. It is relative to concern with theocentric or anthropocentric values; it is relative in the inclusiveness and intensity of its disciplined identification with other selves; and from the cultural side, it is relative to the opportunities which society provides for its development in all people, and to the degree in which "rugged" individualistic or communal actions are the accepted means of expression and development. Because society is an aggregate of individual selves of varying degrees of maturity, the extent to which each balances his group responsibility with his personal privilege will determine the degree to which a high measure of selfhood will be possible for mounting numbers of people.

But the idea of democracy cannot be limited to one people, for, paraphrasing John Donne, no nation is an island unto itself. There are those who, with Louis Adamic, would carry the idea of democracy to foreign lands that other peoples may participate in aesthetically-exciting global designs for coöperative living. There are many too who hold with W. T. Stace in *The Destiny of Western Man* (1942) and I. A. Richards in *How to Read a Page* (1942) and George R. Stewart in *Storm* (1941) that the degree to which every individual on every continent reaches conscious recognition and control of self will be the degree to which man will control the intellectual, social, and economic climate in which he lives, and the degree to which he will substitute rational processes for war as a method of settling his differences. A primary responsibility for making clear these values pertaining to human dignity must rest upon teachers of literature and the arts. They no less than the armed forces must be recognized as one front in militant democracy or militant humanism—to use Thomas Mann's terms—of world proportions. With this pervasive emphasis in our schools, more and more people, as Maxwell Anderson suggests in *The Bases of Artistic Creation* (1942),[7] will be able to enter creatively into the evolutionary processes of democracy through their own critical value judgments of ways of living together, presented in the theatres and broadcasting studios of the world, as well as in print.

NOTES

INTRODUCTION

1. Sir James Jeans, *The Stars in Their Courses,* Preface.
2. Albert Einstein, "Notes on the Origin of the General Theory of Relativity," in *The World As I See It,* pp. 20-21.
3. John Steinbeck and E. F. Ricketts, *The Sea of Cortez,* p. 1.
4. Another symbolic pointer is the concern of the American Association for the Advancement of Science for ethical direction to scientific advancement. In the annual meeting in Philadelphia in 1940, the Association formulated this "scientific expression" of the Golden Rule: "The probability of survival of a relationship between humans or groups of humans increases with the extent to which the relationship remains mutually satisfying." From Chauncey D. Leake, "Science Implies Freedom," p. 314, in *Studies in the History of Culture.*
5. John Dewey, "Humanism and Naturalism," in *A Cyclopedia of Education,* Vol. III, p. 338. Speaking for the humanistic point of view, Dewey writes: "Humanism may be defined as the conviction that spiritual and ideal values are of supreme rank in the make-up of reality, and that these values are most adequately expressed in the great or classic achievements of humanity in literature and art —especially literature."
6. Patricia Beesley, *The Revival of the Humanities in American Education,* pp. 7-24.
7. Edna Hays, *College Entrance Requirements in English,* p. 1.
8. A critical history of Comparative Literature in American Colleges and Universities has been brought together by Dr. Edna Hays of the English Department, Teachers College, Columbia University, titled "Comparative Literature and the Modern Humanities, A Study in History and Methods." Dr. Hays' unpublished manuscript will complement and extend the work of Paul Van Tieghem in France.
9. Lennox Grey, in "The Revival of the Humanities in American Education," p. 8, states: "This aesthetic experience pervades all life, but art and literature have made it their object of special quest to record it in moving and enduring form. It is the response of the

scientist when his vision extends through the neat array of test tubes and beakers in the "objective" laboratory to the role of science in the whole panorama of life, or when he speaks of a "beautiful experiment" or a "beautiful operation," or hears the music [that Pythagorean name for physics again] of the spheres." It is our response to a beautifully balanced and moving system of philosophical values, ethical values, or moral values. It includes deep and far reaching religious visions. It includes (sometimes alas!) the profound or passionate response to a political ideology, or to concepts of epic destiny. For all these responses, art and literature remain the enduring record, our readiest key to them, and so by common agreement it is in art and literature we study them most comprehensively."

10. *A Correlated Curriculum*, A Report of the Committee on Correlation of the National Council of Teachers of English, Ruth Mary Weeks, Editor, p. 3.
11. Committee of Twenty-Four, "Aims of the Teaching of Literature," *English Journal*, College Section, April, 1939, p. 261.
12. Louise Rosenblatt, *Literature as Exploration*, p. 3.
13. Theodore Meyer Greene, *The Arts and the Art of Criticism*, p. 3.
14. Irwin Edman, *Arts and the Man*, p. 151.
15. Jacques Barzun, *Of Human Freedom*, p. 8.
16. I. A. Richards, *Principles of Literary Criticism*, p. 62.
17. St. John's College, Catalogue, July, 1938, p. 28.

PART I

1. Ideas From Philosophical Aesthetics and the Tradition of Literary Criticism: A Brief Review

1. This broad classification is apparent in such college texts as T. V. Smith, *Philosophers Speak for Themselves*; Arthur Kenyon Rogers, *Student's History of Philosophy*; and Joseph H. Burgess, *Introduction to the History of Philosophy*.
2. An extended discussion of these value theories is presented in W. P. Montague, *The Ways of Things*, pp. 558-59, and in John Dewey, *The Quest for Certainty*, p. 256.
3. For discussion of this aspect of experience, see *The Dialogues of Plato*, translated into English by B. Jowett (New York, Random House, 1937, I, 484. (In other editions of Plato the selection may be found by following the Stephanus numbers in the margin of

the text: *Phaedo* 100. In subsequent notes both page numbers will be given in respective order, the Stephanus numbers in parenthesis.)
4. Plato, *Epistle* VII, 342a; 344d.
5. Plato discusses the philosopher's experience in the passage on pleasure and pain; *Republic*, Jowett trans., Vol. I, pp. 840-4 (581-82); *Philebus* 65a; also the latter part of Book X of the *Republic*, Vol. I, pp. 864-65; (606-7).
6. *Ibid.*, Vol. I, pp. 852-66 (595-608).
7. *Ibid.*, Vol. I, pp. 744-800 (484-540). Plato here discusses the qualities of the philosophic nature and the method of training the philosopher. For the differences between the Platonic and Aristotelian concepts of perfection see *Republic*, Vol. I, pp. 621-82 (357-418) and *Poetics* in *The Basic Works of Aristotle*, edited by Richard McKeon, particularly pp. 1457-58 (1448b), where Aristotle discusses basic human instincts. For numerous other criticisms see "Plato" in the index of this edition.
8. *The Basic Works of Aristotle*, pp. 1457-58 (1448b).
9. *Ibid.*, pp. 1463-64 (1451b).
10. *Ibid.*, pp. 1458-59 (1449a).
11. *Ibid.*, pp. 1483-84 (1460b).
12. *Ibid.*, pp. 1479-80, 1483-84 (1459a, 1460b).
13. *Ibid.*, pp. 1459-69 (1449b, 1450b, 1453b); *Rhetoric*, pp. 1388-92 1382-83).
14. *Ethics*, p. 950 (1102a).
15. The fullest discussions of the aesthetics of St. Thomas Aquinas are presented in Jacques Maritain, *Art and Scholasticism,* and an essay by Gerald B. Phelan, "The Concept of Beauty in St. Thomas Aquinas," in *Aspects of the New Scholastic Philosophy*, Charles A. Hart, editor, pp. 121-46.
16. St. Thomas Aquinas, *Summa Theologica*, literally translated by Fathers of the English Dominican Province, I, 26, 2; I, 26, 3, where St. Thomas discusses the concept of "Beatitude."
17. *Ibid.*, I, 44, 3; I, 85, 7. Maritain extends St. Thomas' discussion of the artist's perception in modern scholastic idiom in *Art and Scholasticism*, pp. 25-29.
18. In his discussion of the relationship of art and prudence in *Art and Scholasticism*, p. 85, Maritain lays the base for much of Adler's later presentation of the art-prudence relationship in *Art and Prudence*.
19. See, for example, the careful distinction of sign, word, part of

speech, term, and "voice sound" made by Thomas of Erfurt, *On the Modes of Signifying: a Speculative Grammar,* trans. for the Classics of the St. John's Program by Charles Glenn Wallis, Chap. vi, p. 5. For a discussion of the place of the various language arts in medieval education, see Abelson, *The Seven Liberal Arts.*
20. Maritain, *Art and Scholasticism,* note 116b, p. 192. For the function of words as instruments, cf. Gerald B. Phelan, *St. Thomas and Analogy,* esp. p. 8.
21. Benedict de Spinoza, *Ethic,* translated W. Hale White, p. 113; Part 2, Prop. 3.
22. *Ibid.,* pp. 43-44; Part 1, Appendix.
23. Spinoza, *Improvement of the Understanding,* p. 30.
24. Spinoza, *Ethic,* p. 243; Part 4, Appendix.
25. *Ibid.,* pp. 207-12; Part 4, Prop. 37.
26. *Ibid.,* p. 264; Part 5, Prop. 15; Page 274; Part 5, Prop. 32.
27. Immanuel Kant, Critique of Aesthetic Judgment, translated by James Creed Meredith. Part III of the Introduction extends the discussion of the "moral imperative"; also Part I, Book II, p. 155.
28. For extension of the idea of "moral good," see Ibid., Part I, Book I, No. 5, pp. 48-50.
29. Kant, *Introduction to Logic,* Chapter V.
30. G. W. F. Hegel, *The Philosophy of Fine Art,* translated by F. P. B. Osmaston, I, 180.
31. *Ibid.,* I, 112-13; 181-83.
32. *Ibid.,* pp. 114-15.
33. *Ibid.,* p. 121.
34. Schopenhauer discusses the synonymousness of man's "will" and "will to live," in *The World as Will and Idea,* translated by R. B. Haldane and J. Kemp, I, Book III, 233-34.
35. *Ibid.,* I, Book IV, 354.
36. *Ibid.,* I, Book IV, 458; also I, Book I, 72.
37. George Santayana, *Reason in Art,* p. 222.
38. Santayana points to the necessity for leisure to develop the arts in *The Sense of Beauty,* p. 220. For exemplification of Santayana's critical method, generally, see *Three Philosophical Poets.*
39. Santayana, *Reason in Art,* p. 218; also *The Sense of Beauty,* pp. 197-98.
40. Santayana, *The Sense of Beauty,* pp. 168-69.
41. *Ibid.,* p. 265.
42. *The Philosophy of John Dewey,* Paul Arthur Schilpp, editor, p. 98.

43. *The Life and Works of Mencius,* translated by James Legge, provides an original source for these significant ideas. See also I. A. Richards, *Mencius on the Mind,* which indicates most clearly the semantic concerns that Richards has found stimulating in Mencius.
44. David Hume, *A Treatise of Human Nature,* Book I, Sec. IV, "Of Personal Identity."
45. *Ibid.,* Book III, pp. 484-501; Hume discusses the cultural-moral origins of justice and property.
46. John Stuart Mill, *A System of Logic,* Ratiocinative and Inductive, Vol. I, p. 376.
47. *Ibid.,* p. 17.
48. J. S. Mill, *Dissertations and Discussions,* pp. 54-64.
49. *Ibid.,* pp. 69-70.
50. For discussion of intuitional knowledge in contrast to experiential knowledge, see J. S. Mill, *A System of Logic,* Vol. I, p. 7. For Mill's ideas on the discovery of cause-effect relationships essential to ordering society, see *Ibid.,* Vol. I, pp. 359-85.
51. Nietzsche, in *The Birth of Tragedy,* from *The Complete Works of Friedrich Nietzsche,* O. Levy, Editor, treats the Apollonian and the Dionysian on every page, but the Dionysian idea of unorganized activity vs. the Apollonian discipline of "shaping" is clearest on pages 21, 94, 118.
52. *Ibid.,* pp. 78-79.
53. *Ibid.,* p. 192.
54. *Ibid.,* pp. 158-67.
55. *Ibid.,* p. 192.
56. Nietzsche points up the individual life as a work of art in: *Ibid.,* pp. 26, 182. In *The Will to Power,* A. M. Ludovici, Trans., aphorisms 518, 705, 714, 811, 852, 1032 emphasize related points on the power of art in shaping human life.
57. *The Birth of Tragedy,* p. 50.
58. Benedetto Croce, *The Essence of Aesthetic,* Douglas Ainslie, trans., pp. 43-45.
59. *Ibid.,* p. 73 and following.
60. William James, *Principles of Psychology,* Vol. II, p. 356.
61. *Ibid.,* p. 359.
62. James, *Pragmatism,* pp. 136-145; for empirical vs. idealistic concept see: pp. 49-51.
63. James, *Essays in Radical Empiricism,* pp. 42-48. See also: *A Pluralistic Universe,* p. 280. See also: *The Will to Believe,* p. 278.

64. Philip Sidney, "An Apology for Poetry," from *English Belles-Lettres, from A. D. 901-1844*, edited by Oliver H. G. Leigh, p. 125.
65. *Ibid.*, p. 122.
66. Ben Jonson, "Timber; or Discoveries made upon Men and Matter." *The Works of Ben Jonson*, edited by William Gifford, p. 764.
67. *Ibid.*, p. 759.
68. *Ibid.*, p. 759.
69. John Dryden, "An Essay of Dramatic Poesy," from *Dryden, Essays on the Drama*, edited by William Strunk, Jr., pp. 16-17.
70. *Ibid.*, p. 87.
71. *Ibid.*, pp. 57-58.
72. Alexander Pope, "An Essay on Criticism," from *The Works of Alexander Pope*, Vol. I, line 121.
73. *Ibid.*, line 151.
74. *Ibid.*, lines 233-34.
75. *Ibid.*, line 139.
76. *Ibid.*, lines 87-88.
77. Samuel Johnson, "The Rambler" No. 158, from *The Works of Samuel Johnson*, Vol. VI. See also "The Rambler" No. 168.
78. Samuel Taylor Coleridge, *Biographia Literaria*, prepared for publication in part by Henry N. Coleridge, Vol. I, Chap. XIII, p. 371.
79. *Ibid.*, p. 378.
80. *Ibid.*, Chap. XIV, p. 451.
81. *Ibid.*, p. 449.
82. *Ibid.*, Chap. XVIII, p. 503.
83. Thomas Carlyle, *Heroes and Hero Worship*, p. 117.
84. *Ibid.*, p. 121.
85. Thomas Carlyle, "Critical and Miscellaneous Essays," from *Complete Works of Thomas Carlyle*, p. 12. Cf. also *Heroes and Hero Worship*, p. 124.
86. Thomas Carlyle, *Heroes and Hero Worship*, p. 192.
87. Matthew Arnold, "Literature and Science," in *Discourses in America*, p. 107.
88. Matthew Arnold, "The Function of Criticism at the Present Time," in *Essays in Criticism*, pp. 5-6.
89. *Ibid.*, p. 4.

2. Ideas from Modern Psychology: Aesthetic Experience and the Individual

1. Volumes I and II of Müller-Freienfels' *Psychologie der Kunst*, pub-

lished in 1912 before Jennings' most significant works appeared, acknowledge biological bases in the work of William James. Volume III appeared in 1933.
2. Mortimer J. Adler, *What Man Has Made of Man*, Introduction, p. xi.
3. Adler, *How to Read a Book*, p. 38.
4. Adler, *Art and Prudence*, p. 47.
5. *Ibid.*, pp. 218-19.
6. *Ibid.*, p. 48.
7. *Ibid.*, p. 46.
8. *Ibid.*, p. 46.
9. J. B. Watson, *Psychology from the Standpoint of the Behaviorist*, p. 285.
10. *Ibid.*, p. 10.
11. *Ibid.*, p. 379.
12. *Ibid.*, p. 298.
13. Sigmund Freud, *Introductory Lectures on Psychoanalysis*, p. 293.
14. *Ibid.*, p. 314.
15. Freud, *A General Introduction to Psychoanalysis*, p. 327.
16. Freud, *Collected Papers*, Vol. IV, Chap. IX, "The Relation of the Poet to Day-Dreaming," p. 183.
17. *Ibid.*, Vol. IV, Chap. I, "Formulations Regarding the Two Principles in Mental Functioning," 1911, p. 19.
18. Freud, *A General Introduction to Psychoanalysis*, p. 327.
19. Freud, *Collected Papers*, Vol. IV, Chap. XVIII, "Some Character-Types Met with in Psycho-Analytic Work," pp. 318-41.
20. Freud skirted still another aspect of psychological-aesthetics in 1926 when in his *Beyond the Pleasure Principle* he characterized life as constituting the accumulation and release of tensions, as the social psychologist, H. G. Lasswell notes in *Psychopathology and Politics*, p. 74.
21. Kenneth Burke, *The Philosophy of Literary Form*, p. 266.
22. For extended comment on this issue, the reader may consult Jacques Barzun's *Of Human Freedom*, pp. 135-37.
23. Charles Baudouin, *Psychoanalysis and Aesthetics*, passim.
24. Ludwig Lewisohn, *Expression in America*, Preface, p. vii.
25. Burke, *op. cit.*, p. 261.
26. Otto Rank, *Art and Artist*, p. 374.
27. *Ibid.*, p. 368.
28. *Ibid.*
29. *Ibid.*

30. *Ibid.*, p. 384.
31. *Ibid.*, p. 379.
32. *Ibid.*, p. 387.
33. Carl Jung, *Contributions to Analytical Psychology*, p. 33.
34. *Ibid.*, p. 246.
35. *Ibid.*, p. 157.
36. *Ibid.*, p. 152.
37. *Ibid.*, p. 82.
38. *Ibid.*, p. 36.
39. *Ibid.*, p. 228.
40. *Ibid.*, p. 248.
41. *Ibid.*, p. 238.
42. *Ibid.*, p. 235.
43. *Ibid.*, p. 241.
44. *Ibid.*, p. 235.
45. *Ibid.*, p. 248.
46. *Ibid.*, p. 241.
47. John Dewey, *Art as Experience*, p. 101.
48. Richard Müller-Freienfels, *Psychologie der Kunst*, II, 88.
49. Hugo Münsterberg, *Psychology and Life*, p. 155.
50. Münsterberg, *The Principles of Art Education*. Quoted from Melvin M. Rader, *A Modern Book of Aesthetics*, p. 368. See also Ethel Puffer, *The Psychology of Beauty*, passim.
51. Edward Bullough, "Psychical Distance," *British Journal of Psychology*, V, (1912), 87-118.
52. Vernon Lee, *The Beautiful, An Introduction to Psychological Aesthetics*, p. 33.
53. *Ibid.*, p. 121.
54. *Ibid.*, pp. 30-31, 133.
55. Robert Sessions Woodworth, *Dynamic Psychology*, p. 137.
56. *Ibid.*, p. 133.
57. William McDougall, *An Introduction to Social Psychology*, pp. 48-91.
58. Gordon W. Allport, *Personality, A psychological interpretation*, p. 61.
59. *Ibid.*, Chapter XIII; also Muzafer Sherif, *The Psychology of Social Norms*, passim; also H. D. Lasswell, *World Politics and Personal Insecurity*, pp. 1-26; also James S. Plant, *Personality and the Culture Pattern*, chapters I and II.
60. John Dollard, *Criteria for a Life History*, passim; also Karen Horney, *The Neurotic Personality of Our Time*, passim; also H. D.

Lasswell, *Psychopathology and Politics*, Chap. XI; also J. R. Kantor, "The Current Situation in Social Psychology," *Psychological Bulletin*, Vol. 36, No. 5 (May, 1939), pp. 307-60.
61. Joseph K. Folsom, *Social Psychology*, pp. 502-3.
62. Kimball Young, *Personality and Problems of Adjustment*, Preface, p. viii.
63. *Ibid.*, Chaps. IX and X.
64. *Ibid.*, p. 191.
65. *Ibid.*, p. 794.
66. *Ibid.*
67. *Ibid.*, p. 797.
68. Dollard, *op. cit.*, Chap. 11.
69. Dollard, et al, *Frustration and Aggression*, pp. 183-84.
70. H. D. Lasswell, *World Politics and Personal Insecurity*, p. 73.
71. Allport, *op. cit.*, p. 48.
72. *Ibid.*, p. 50.
73. *Ibid.*, p. 214.
74. *Ibid.*, pp. 350-51.
75. *Ibid.*, p. 492.
76. Kurt Koffka, *Principles of Gestalt Psychology*, p. 19.
77. Kurt Lewin, *A Dynamic Theory of Personality, passim.*
78. Koffka, *op. cit.*, p. 110.
79. Herbert S. Langfeld, *The Aesthetic Attitude*, pp. 166-68.
80. Burke, *op. cit.;* see Burke's Index for references throughout the book.
81. Müller-Freienfels, *Psychologie der Kunst*, II, 89.
82. Koffka, *op. cit.*, p. 69.
83. Norman R. F. Maier and H. Willard Reninger, *A Psychological Approach to Literary Criticism*, p. 39.
84. *Ibid.*, p. 67.
85. *Ibid.*, p. 46.
86. R. M. Ogden, *The Psychology of Art*, p. 22.
87. *Ibid.*, p. 26.
88. *Ibid.*, p. 87.
89. Kate Hevner, "The Aesthetic Experience: a Psychological Description," *Psychological Review*, XLIV, 256.
90. Viktor Löwenfeld, *The Nature of Creative Activity, passim.*
91. P. C. Daniels, "Discrimination of Compositional Balance at the Pre-School Level," *Psychological Monograph*, XLV, No. 1, 1-11.
92. V. B. Grippen, "Creative Artistic Imagination in Children," *Psychological Monograph*, XLV, No. 1, *Studies in Psychology of Art*,

Norman C. Meier, Editor. For extended discussion of these ideas, see Meier's *Art in Human Affairs; an Introduction to the Psychology of Art.*

93. George D. Birkhoff, *Aesthetic Measure, passim.*
94. Birkhoff, "The Present Status of Aesthetic Measure," *Scientific Monthly*, XLVI (April, 1938), 351-57.
95. J. F. Dashiell, "Some Rapprochements in Contemporary Psychology," p. 20. Following the lead of Jennings and other biologists, Dashiell asks psychologists to "cease invoking the concepts of 'heredity' and 'environment' in an absolutist manner, and, bending our efforts to the mapping of *development*, to inquire in each particular case: Just how much of this observed change can we trace to extrinsic factors operating recently or now; just how much to intrinsic ones?" (p. 7) See also: *Proceedings of the American Philosophical Society*, A Symposium on Recent Advances in Psychology, Philadelphia, April 25, 1941.
96. Liviu Rusu, *Essai sur la création artistique comme révélation du sense de l'existence*, pp. 30-35.
97. *Ibid.*, pp. 52-57. Specifically Rusu says: "La création artistique a donc son origine dans *un conflict avec la nature primitive.* Elle n'est pas un simple prolongement du fond biologique, elle le dépasse par l'attitude *opposée à ce fond,*" p. 56.
98. Müller-Freienfels, *op. cit.*, II, 156.
99. Rusu, *op. cit.*, pp. 82-83.
100. *Ibid.*, p. 59. Italicizing for emphasis, Rusu states: *"La création artistique est une attitude générale, totalitaire de l'âme envers un déséquilibre qui ne peut être résolu que par un effort créature."*
101. *Ibid.*, p. 61.
102. *Ibid.*, p. 89. These four phases include the principles of the three stages suggested by Henri Delacroix in *Psychologie de l'art; essai sur l'activité artistique,* and by Müller-Freienfels in his *Psychologie der Kunst:* (1) the background for creation; (2) the preparation and assembling of materials; (3) the creative process of organization and expression.
103. Rusu points up this attention to anthropological background by a comparative listing of Dante's medieval political embroilment, Leonardo da Vinci's, Michelangelo's, Cellini's, and Shakespeare's characteristically-many Renaissance preoccupations, and Goethe's comprehension of all the cultural roots and social life of contemporaneous Germany.
104. Rusu, *op. cit.*, pp. 92-103.

105. *Ibid.*, p. 123.
106. *Ibid.*, p. 127.
107. *Ibid.*, pp. 124-33.
108. *Ibid.*, p. 165.
109. *Ibid.*, pp. 167-68.
110. *Ibid.*, p. 218.
111. Müller-Freienfels, *op. cit.*, I, 218-19. See also Rusu, p. 199.
112. Rusu, *op. cit.*, p. 200.
113. Stefan Zweig: *Jeremiah*, Preface to the American edition.
114. Rusu, *op. cit.*, p. 200.
115. *Ibid.*, p. 173.
116. *Ibid.*, pp. 223-27.
117. *Ibid.*, p. 208.
118. *Ibid.*, p. 208.
119. *Ibid.*, pp. 202-5.
120. Müller-Freienfels, *op. cit.*, I, 223-24.
121. *Ibid.*, I, 220-21.
122. *Ibid.*, I, 226; and Rusu, *op. cit.*, pp. 281-82.
123. Rusu, *op. cit.*, p. 290.
124. *Ibid.*, p. 279.
125. *Ibid.*, pp. 124-33.
126. Müller-Freienfels, *op. cit.*, I, 224.
127. Rusu, *op. cit.*, p. 347.
128. *Ibid.*, pp. 346-47.
129. *Ibid.*, p. 338.
130. Müller-Freienfels, *op. cit.*, II, 94.
131. *Ibid.*, II, 86-89.
132. Burke, *op. cit.*, pp. 12-18.
133. Müller-Freienfels, *op. cit.*, II, 84. Müller-Freienfels finds this especially important because it seems to be valid even for languages which are not interdependent. Otto Jespersen makes this same point in his article "Language" in the *Encyclopaedia Britannica*, 14th Edition, XIII, 701.
134. Müller-Freienfels, *op. cit.*, II, 90.
135. *Ibid.*, II, 94.
136. *Ibid.*, II, 154.
137. *Ibid.*, III, 242.
138. *Ibid.*, III, 256. In extension, Müller-Freienfels says: "In primitive and early levels the "I" of the lyric is very general—usually just "we." Where it is "I" the "I" is not thought of as individual but

includes the tribal group, for all early lyrics are group lyrics and not individual expressions."
139. *Ibid.*, III, 251.
140. *Ibid.*, III, 260-67. Of this growth of the drama as a symbol of urban culture, Lewis Mumford says: ". . . the collective sharing of experience, and the powerful stimulus of rational criticism, turn the rites of the village festival into the more powerful imaginative forms of the tragic drama; experience is deepened, as well as more widely circulated through this process." (*The Culture of Cities*, p. 5.) For discussion of the aesthetics of composition, stage technique, and acting, see Koffka, "The Art of the Actor as a Psychological Problem," *American Scholar*, XI (Summer, 1942), 318-26.

3. Ideas from Anthropology: Aesthetic Experience and the Culture

1. Anthropological studies concerned strictly with aesthetic processes are not abundant, as Ralph Linton, George Herzog, and Gladys A. Reichard stated in discussions with the present writer.
2. Max Lerner and Edwin Mims, Jr., "Literature," *Encyclopaedia of Social Sciences*, X, 523.
3. Edward Sapir, "The Contribution of Psychiatry to an Understanding of Behavior in Society," *American Journal of Sociology*, XL, (May, 1937), 870.
4. Charles W. Morris, "Foundations of the Theory of Signs," *International Encyclopedia of Unified Science*, I, No. 2, p. 2. See also: Thomas Clark Pollock, *The Nature of Literature*, Its Relation to Science, Language and Human Experience, Chap. V, VI.
5. Ralph Linton, "The Present Status of Anthropology," *Science*, March 18, 1938, p. 243.
6. Yrjo Hirn, *The Origins of Art*, p. 242.
7. Melvin M. Rader, *A Modern Book of Aesthetics*, p. 3.
8. *Ibid.*, p. 52 f.
9. Linton, *The Study of Man*, p. 90.
10. Herbert Read, *Art and Society*, pp. 70-71. Read writes of art as *hedonistic*, where it is a matter of purely sensational pleasure, tending toward abstract, that is, geometric, design; as *purposive*, where it has a ritualistic, pedagogic and essentially symbolic character; as *expressive*, where it has an emotive and primarily representative quality.
11. W. I. Thomas, "The Comparative Study of Cultures," *American Journal of Sociology*, XLII, (Sept., 1936) 184. "Theories of differ-

ence in degrees of mental endowment among races and populations and of inborn racial 'psyches' have not been sustained." See also Linton, *op. cit.*, p. 68; also Progressive Education Association, *When Peoples Meet*, Alain Locke and Bernhard J. Stern, Editors. 1942, pp. 420-64.
12. Frederick Osborn, "To What Extent Is a Science of Man Possible?" *Scientific Monthly*, Nov., 1939, pp. 456-57.
13. Franz Boas, "Anthropology," *Encyclopaedia of Social Sciences*, II, 108-9.
14. Herbert Read, *op. cit.*, pp. xii-xiii.
15. Bronislaw Malinowski, "Culture," *Encyclopaedia of Social Sciences*, IV, 621-23. These wide concerns are dealt with in archeology and ethnology. For detailed discussion of the purpose of archeology as the reconstruction of human history through "the authenticated presentation of a series of human events," see A. L. Kroeber, "Archeology," *Encyclopaedia of Social Sciences*, II, 163. See also Robert H. Lowie on the correlation of stratigraphic findings and geological and paleontological data in "Cultural Anthropology: A Science," *American Journal of Sociology*, XLII (November, 1936), 315. For Lowie's discussion of ethnology as an objective discipline for coordinating data, investigating the causes of cultural change, and bringing to conscious recognition the functional relationships upon which the continuation of an integrated culture depends, see *Ibid.*, p. 320.
16. Malinowski, *op. cit.*, p. 623.
17. *Ibid.*, p. 624.
18. Boas, "The Methods of Anthropology," *The American Anthropologist*, XXII (1920), 311.
19. Malinowski, *op. cit.*, p. 624.
20. Boas, *op. cit.*, p. 312.
21. Boas, *Race, Language and Culture*, p. 269. Much of Boas' earlier work exhibits the diffusionist point of view. But in concluding the chapter on "Methods of Cultural Anthropology" (1940) he writes: "An error of modern anthropology, as I see it, lies in the overemphasis on historical reconstruction, the importance of which should not be minimized, as against a penetrating study of the individual under the stress of the culture in which he lives."
22. Malinowski, *op. cit.*, p. 625.
23. George Herzog, *Jabo Proverbs from Liberia*. For the material on anthropological method, the author is considerably indebted to Professor George Herzog, of Columbia University. Professor Herzog

also generously provided detailed oral description of many of his studies in native languages and music. See also: Sapir, "Time Perspective in Aboriginal American Culture, A Study in Method," and for a related process, Kurt Lewin, "Field Theory and Experiment in Social Psychology: Concepts and Methods," *The American Journal of Sociology*, XLIV (May, 1939), 868-95.
24. *Ibid.*, (Reprint of the Introduction) p. 2.
25. *Ibid.*, p. 12.
26. *Ibid.*, pp. 14-15.
27. Edward Sapir, "Language," *Encyclopaedia of Social Sciences*, IX, 160.
28. Sapir, *Language*, pp. 14-15.
29. George Herbert Mead, *Mind Self and Society*, p. 146.
30. *Ibid.*, p. 147.
31. I. A. Richards, *Interpretation in Teaching*, p. 4.
32. *Ibid.*, p. 4.
33. Mead, *op. cit.*, p. 50.
34. Sapir, "Language," *Encyclopaedia of Social Sciences*, IX, 159. Sapir's elaboration on this point is significant:

. . . while speech as a finished organization is a distinctly human achievement, its roots probably lie in the power of the higher apes to solve specific problems by abstracting general forms or schemata from the details of given situations; that the habit of interpreting certain selected elements in a situation as signs of a desired total one gradually led in early man to a dim feeling for symbolism; and that in the long run and for reasons which can hardly be guessed at the elements of experience which were most often interpreted in a symbolic sense came to be the largely useless or supplementary vocal behavior that must have often attended significant action. According to this point of view language is not so much directly developed out of vocal expression as it is an actualization in terms of vocal expression of the tendency to master reality, not by direct and ad hoc handling of its elements but by the reduction of experience to familiar forms.

35. Linton, *op. cit.*, pp. 80-84.
36. E. E. Eubank, *The Concepts of Sociology*, pp. 27-28.
37. William James, *Psychology; Briefer Course*, p. 312.
38. Sapir, *Language*, p. 11.
39. Sapir, "Time Perspective in Aboriginal American Culture; a Study in Method," pp. 41-52.

40. Sapir, whose most striking work was in the field of language, starts from a physiological base. For his discussion of the "psychological-tone" of certain uses of language, see *Language*, p. 80. See also: Franz Boas, *Primitive Art*, p. 326, and *Anthropology and Modern Life*, pp. 168-201.
41. Linton, *op. cit.*, p. 143.
42. Boas, "Language and Culture," *Studies in the History of Culture*, p. 183.
43. Boas, "Anthropology," *Encyclopaedia of Social Sciences*, II, 93.
44. *Ibid.*, p. 93.
45. *Ibid.*, p. 92.
46. C. G. Seligman, "Anthropological Perspective and Psychological Theory," publication of Royal Anthropological Institute of Great Britain and Ireland, LXII (July-December, 1932), 193-228.
47. R. S. Rattray, *Religion and Art in Ashanti*, pp. 122-43.
48. Boas, "Stylistic Aspects of Primitive Literature," *Journal of American Folk-lore Society*, XXXVIII (1923), 331.
49. Boas, *Primitive Art*, p. 335.
50. Gladys A. Reichard, "Form and Interpretation in American Art," Reprinted from Proceedings of the Twenty-Third International Congress of Americanists, September, 1928, pp. 459-62.
51. Hutcheson Macaulay Posnett, *Comparative Literature*, p. 71.
52. The significance of "types of literature" has been a subject of considerable dispute among scholars and critics since Posnett's day. A dissertation in progress by Irvin Ehrenpreis on "The Types Approach to Literature" at Teachers College, Columbia University, discusses the issues in detail.
53. H. Munro Chadwick and N. Kershaw Chadwick, *The Growth of Literature*, I, pp. 64-65.
54. *Ibid.*, I, 422.
55. *Ibid.*, II, 307.
56. Lerner and Mims, *op. cit.*, p. 524.
57. *Ibid.*, p. 529.
58. *Ibid.*
59. Karl Vossler, *The Spirit of Language in Civilization*, p. 8.
60. J. B. S. Haldane, "Science and Theology as Art Forms." From *Possible Worlds*, 1928. Quoted from *The New Criticism*, E. B. Burgum, editor, pp. 165-78.
61. W. P. Montague, *The Ways of Things*, Chapter I.
62. Irwin Edman, *Arts and the Man*, *passim*.

NOTES TO PAGES 68–70

63. Lewis Mumford, *Technics and Civilization, passim.*
64. George Sarton, *Introduction to the History of Science,* Vol. I, Introduction.
65. The implications of these theories of cultural evolution for the teaching of world literature are the subject of a dissertation-in-progress by Elbert Lenrow, Chairman of the Department of English, Fieldston School, and Lecturer at The New School for Social Research, New York City.
66. Sidney Ratner, "Patterns of Culture in History," *Philosophy of Science,* VI, No. 1 (January, 1939), 90.
67. *Ibid.,* p. 91.
68. *Ibid.,* p. 92.
69. *Ibid.,* p. 94.
70. *Ibid.*
71. Sapir, *Language,* p. 235. "It goes without saying, that the mere content of language is intimately related to culture. A society that has no knowledge of theosophy need have no name for it; aborigines that have never seen or heard of a horse were compelled to invent or borrow a word for the animal when they made his acquaintance. In the sense that the vocabulary of a language more or less faithfully reflects the culture whose purposes it serves it is perfectly true that the history of language and the history of culture move along parallel lines" (p. 234).
72. Mumford, *The Culture of Cities,* p. 5.
73. Malinowski, "The Group and the Individual in Functional Analysis," *American Journal of Sociology,* XLIV (May, 1939), 955-56.
74. Mead, *op. cit.,* p. 119.
75. Ruth Benedict, *Patterns of Culture,* p. 253.
76. Malinowski, *op. cit.,* p. 964.
77. Linton, *The Study of Man,* p. 363.
78. A course entitled "Anthropology and Education," taught by Professor Lyman Bryson, has been a regular curricular offering at Teachers College, Columbia University, since 1934. As the catalogue description states, it deals with the "genetics of society."
79. Max Carl Otto, *The Human Enterprise,* p. 212.
80. Malinowski, *op. cit.,* p. 964.
81. John Dewey, *Art as Experience,* p. 338. In his chapter entitled "Art and Civilization," Dewey writes:

"From one point of view the problem of recovering an organic place for art in civilization is like the problem of reorganizing our heritage from the past and the insights of present knowledge into a coherent and integrated imaginative union.

"The problem is so acute and so widely influential that any solution that can be proposed is an anticipation that can at best be realized only by the course of events. Scientific method as now practiced is too new to be naturalized in experience. It will be a long time before it so sinks into the subsoil of mind as to become an integral part of corporate belief and attitude. Till that happens, both method and conclusions will remain the possession of specialized experts, and will exercise their general influence only by way of external and more or less disintegrating impact upon beliefs, and by equally external practical application."

82. Dewey, *Freedom and Culture*, p. 176. "At the end as at the beginning the democratic method is as fundamentally simple and as immensely difficult as is the energetic, unflagging, unceasing creation of an ever-present new road upon which we can walk together."

83. Jacques Barzun, *Of Human Freedom*, p. 276. "If the desire to accept rather than exclude, the love of variety rather than of sameness, should combine with an actively pragmatic attitude in a democracy like ours, even the private, static absolutes in philosophy and religion could find a place."

84. Louise Rosenblatt, *Literature as Exploration*, p. 326:

"Literary experiences may help to fasten . . . [the student's emotion] upon new and happier types of relationships or upon images of new and more socially valuable satisfactions to be derived from life. Thus, he may acquire the sympathy and insight, the critical attitudes, and the sense of human values needed for his creation of new ideals and new personal and social goals. The organic nature of literary experience provides some assurance that such new understandings will be assimilated emotionally as well as intellectually. There will already be at work in him impulses toward the kind of active behavior needed to create a new way of life."

85. Mumford, *Men Must Act*, p. 171. Emphasizing the necessity for inclusive new patterns of action, Mumford writes: ". . . unless the active will-to-create be present, we shall achieve neither security nor a society that is worth the effort to safeguard it."

86. Mumford, *Faith for Living*, pp. 283, 299. Mumford demands a "transvaluation" of existing economic and political values in the

interest of balance of more human values—since "the creation of persons is the first and last task of a democracy,"—saying: "Here is why religion and the expressive arts have a particular message for our generation; for they have never abandoned the cultivation of the self; and they have done this by methods that are generally valid, not those which promote mental unbalance and corruption. Plainly, a great part of the work that must be done during the next century, by way of either salvage or construction, is of a formative nature: old routines will provide no guide for it."

87. Robert Sherwood, *There Shall Be No Night*, Preface.
88. Norman Corwin, *We Hold These Truths*, a dramatic celebration of Bill of Rights Day, 1941.
89. Richards, "What is Belief?" *The Nation*, CXXXIX (July 18, 1934), 71-72.
90. Richards, "Our Lost Leaders," *Saturday Review of Literature*, IX, 510.
91. *Ibid.*, p. 510.
92. Eubank, *op. cit.*, pp. 13-15.
93. R. R. Marett, "Anthropology," *Encyclopaedia Britannica*, 14th edition, II, 44.
94. Ratner, *op. cit.*, p. 92.
95. Patricia Beesley, *op. cit.*, pp. 10-23.

PART II

National Council of Teachers of English

1. *An Experience Curriculum in English,* English Monograph No. 4, National Council of Teachers of English, edited by W. Wilbur Hatfield, p. x.
2. It was at the University of Michigan that Charles Mills Gayley, pioneer in Comparative Literature, introduced his first courses in that field in 1887-1889, and that O. J. Campbell, Howard Mumford Jones, Charles Carpenter Fries, and others carried on in comparable spirit. O. J. Campbell is now Professor of English and Comparative Literature at Columbia University where George Edward Woodberry, Jefferson Butler Fletcher, and Joel E. Spingarn have also fostered the comparative method.
3. *The Teaching of College English,* English Monograph No. 3, National Council of Teachers of English, edited by O. J. Campbell, p. 7.

4. *Ibid.*, pp. 4, 6.
5. *Ibid.*, p. 7.
6. *Ibid.*, p. 4.
7. *Ibid.*, pp. 8-9.
8. *Ibid.*, p. 10.
9. *Ibid.*, pp. 10-11.
10. *Ibid.*, p. 11.
11. *Ibid.*
12. *Ibid.*
13. *Ibid.*
14. *Ibid.*, p. 12; see Richards' *Principles of Literary Criticism*, p. 59.
15. *An Experience Curriculum in English*, p. 9.
16. *Ibid.*, p. 124.
17. *Ibid.*, p. 22.
18. *Ibid.*, p. 124.
19. *Ibid.*, p. 17.
20. *Ibid.*, p. 73.
21. *Ibid.*, p. 77.
22. *Ibid.*, p. 3.
23. *Ibid.*, p. 4.
24. *Ibid.*, p. 6.
25. *Ibid.*, p. 135.
26. *Ibid.*, pp. 125-27.
27. *Ibid.*, p. 20.
28. *Ibid.*, p. 44.
29. *Ibid.*, p. 47.
30. *Ibid.*, p. 50.
31. *Ibid.*, p. 52.
32. *Ibid.*, p. 60.
33. *Ibid.*, p. 62.
34. *Ibid.*, pp. 64, 67.
35. *Ibid.*, p. 3.
36. *A Correlated Curriculum,* English Monograph No. 5, National Council of Teachers of English, edited by Ruth Mary Weeks, p. 3.
37. *Ibid.*, p. 4.
38. *Ibid.*, p. 80.
39. *Ibid.*, p. 7.
40. *Ibid.*, p. 129.
41. *Ibid.*, p. 130.
42. *Ibid.*, p. 132.
43. *Ibid.*, pp. 147-54. Part One sweeps over literature of China, Japan,

India, Arabia, Persia, Egypt, and Palestine, with notation on the prevailing emotional attitude toward life observable in each group of selections. A similar concern with attitude toward life is noted for Greek literature, which is considered in more detail with respect to *types*. The section concludes with *kinds* of writing representative of Roman Culture. As though implying the preponderant value to students of European backgrounds, oriental literatures are not considered in subsequent sections of the course. Part Two opens on the upswing of another rhythm of cultural advance, moving from the Dark Ages through Dante and Chaucer. Parts Three, Four, and Five treat respectively the Reformation, the period of individual and political revolution in Europe, and the Age of Democracy (all with strong English literature weighting). Part Six in itself represents a composite approach, implying perhaps that no one approach seems adequate to our day—we find concern for a prevailing theme for *types* of literature, and also for the less inclusive division into *kinds*. Teaching method accents the rhythmic progression of this vast sweep of human culture. One piece of literature in each period is read in detail. Others are reviewed rapidly as a kind of supporting context.

44. *Ibid.*, p. 156.
45. *Ibid.*
46. *Ibid.*
47. *Ibid.*, p. 159.
48. *Ibid.*
49. *Ibid.*, pp. 163-76.
50. *Ibid.*, p. 197.
51. *Ibid.*, p. 229.
52. *Ibid.*, p. 301.
53. *Ibid.*, p. 293.

The Progressive Education Association
John Dewey: Social Philosopher

1. "The Contribution of Education to Democracy," Progressive Education Association Booklet No. 3, p. 25.
2. *Ibid.*, p. 6.
3. "Democratic Education," A Report from the Board of Directors to the Members of the Progressive Education Association, September, 1940, pp. 14-15.
4. John Dewey, *Reconstruction in Philosophy*, p. 209.

NOTES TO PAGES 85–88   255

5. "The Contribution of Education to Democracy," Progressive Education Association Booklet No. 3, p. 8.
6. John L. Childs and William H. Kilpatrick, *John Dewey as Educator*, Progressive Education Association Pamphlet, 1942.
7. Dewey, *Art as Experience*, p. 274.
8. The Progressive Education Association through its Commission on Secondary School Curriculum (which had worked informally with I. A. Richards) published two additional books: *Language in General Education*, (1940), edited by Louis Zahner and others, and *Readers Guide to Prose Fiction* (1940), by Elbert Lenrow. The Committee on Workshops has sponsored a third volume explicitly devoted to anthropological ideas in education: *When Peoples Meet: a Study in Race and Culture Contacts* (1942), edited by Alain Locke and Bernhard J. Stern.
9. Dewey, *Art as Experience*, pp. 139-40.
10. *Ibid.*, p. 55.
11. *Ibid.*, p. 13.
12. *Ibid.*, p. 25.
13. *Ibid.*, pp. 13-14.
14. *Ibid.*, p. 14.
15. *Ibid.*, p. 15.
16. *Ibid.*, p. 23.
17. *Ibid.*, p. 281.
18. *Ibid.*, p. 263.
19. *Ibid.*, p. 264.
20. *Ibid.*, pp. 71, 89.
21. *Ibid.*, p. 264.
22. *Ibid.*, p. 263.
23. *Ibid.*, pp. 59, 281.
24. *Ibid.*, p. 277.
25. *Ibid.*, p. 118.
26. *Ibid.*, p. 346. In describing the act of expression, Dewey refers only to its origin in "impulsions" set up by some need. Later, however, he refers to the necessity of the critic's reëxperiencing to some extent the state of mind of the artist—and the "sense of possibilities that are unrealized . . . put in contrast with actual conditions."
27. *Ibid.*, p. 65.
28. *Ibid.*, p. 266; see also p. 67.
29. *Ibid.*, p. 65.
30. *Ibid.*
31. *Ibid.*, pp. 67, 192.

32. *Ibid.*, p. 191.
33. *Ibid.*, p. 75.
34. *Ibid.*
35. *Ibid.*, p. 266.
36. *Ibid.*
37. *Ibid.*, p. 243.
38. *Ibid.*, p. 154.
39. *Ibid.*, p. 150.
40. *Ibid.*, Chap. VIII.
41. *Ibid.*, pp. 147-48.
42. *Ibid.*, p. 137.
43. Nowhere in *Art as Experience* does Dewey make this idea of *type* explicit. He does, however, deplore the narrowing effects of classification of literature according to externally recognizable *kinds* (p. 217) and explicitly refers in the context of one sentence to "the epic, lyric, the dramatic" in a way to imply this manner of classification. Elsewhere (p. 151) we find implicit recognition of types as expressive forms for various stages of culture—the drama as characteristic of urban society, the lyric as embodying the spirit of personal spontaneity.
44. *Ibid.*, p. 137.
45. *Ibid.*, p. 106.
46. *Ibid.*, p. 108.
47. *Ibid.*, pp. 98-99.
48. *Ibid.*, p. 299.
49. *Ibid.*, pp. 304-5.
50. *Ibid.*, p. 309.
51. *Ibid.*, p. 109.
52. *Ibid.*, p. 299.
53. *Ibid.*, p. 325. Although *Art as Experience* is not explicitly concerned with teaching method in its relation to critical method, we may infer from these passages of Dewey's the necessity for students themselves to draw together many of the background materials which would contribute to an understanding of the form and substance of the work of art. We may also infer that these should be set down as part of the active process of recreating the author's experience during creation.
54. *Ibid.*, p. 324.
55. *Ibid.*, p. 314.
56. *Ibid.*
57. *Ibid.*, p. 277.

58. *Ibid.*, p. 195.
59. *Ibid.*
60. *Ibid.*, p. 339.
61. *Ibid.*, p. 339.
62. *Ibid.*, p. 274. Dewey's most explicit statement is this: ". . . while the theory of esthetics put forth by a philosopher is incidentally a test of the capacity of its author to have the experience that is the subject-matter of his analysis, it is also much more than that. It is a test of the capacity of the system he puts forth to grasp the nature of experience itself. There is no test that so surely reveals the one-sidedness of a philosophy as its treatment of art and esthetic experience."
63. *Ibid.*, p. 297.
64. *Ibid.*, p. 139.
65. *Ibid.*, p. 290.

Progressive Education Association
Louise Rosenblatt: Liberal Arts Progressive

1. Louise Rosenblatt, *Literature as Exploration*, p. 3.
2. *Ibid.*, p. 196.
3. *Ibid.*, p. 155.
4. *Ibid.*, p. 124.
5. *Ibid.*, p. 5.
6. *Ibid.*, p. 192.
7. *Ibid.*, p. 154.
8. *Ibid.*, p. 162.
9. The three major sections of *Life and Growth* show this continuing interaction of the individual and his society: I. Human Life and Social Progress; II. The Individual and the Way He Grows; III. New Life and Social Change.
10. Rosenblatt, *op. cit.*, pp. 188, 223.
11. *Ibid.*, p. 182.
12. *Ibid.*, p. 267.
13. *Ibid.*, p. 231.
14. *Ibid.*, pp. 161, 164.
15. *Ibid.*, p. 231.
16. *Ibid.*, p. 267.
17. *Ibid.*, p. 319.
18. *Ibid.*, p. 320.
19. In her chapter on "Broadening the Framework" Professor Rosen-

blatt indicates the desirability of using other subject-matters than literature to clarify the judgments made on values presented in literary syntheses of cultural materials. On p. 142 she writes: "This spontaneous turning to the other disciplines for information was illustrated by a group of freshmen in a woman's college who had read Ibsen's *Doll's House.*" Disciplines as here used might mean simply areas of inquiry, but with the feeling for the unity of materials, values, and methods that Professor Rosenblatt shows throughout her book, we may infer a concern for all of these as she speaks of disciplines. The implication in "other disciplines" is, of course, the existence of specific internal disciplines for literature and language. As her treatment of the critical process shows, these may be interpreted after the functional meanings of I. A. Richards.

20. *Ibid.,* p. 301.
21. *Ibid.,* p. 195.
22. *Ibid.,* p. 196.
23. *Ibid.,* p. 198.
24. John Dewey, *Art as Experience,* p. 346.
25. Rosenblatt, *op. cit.,* pp. 42-43.
26. *Ibid.,* pp. 49-50.
27. *Ibid.,* p. 53. It is significant to note that in a more recent publication of the Progressive Education Association, *Reader's Guide to Prose Fiction,* by Elbert Lenrow, the same stress upon internal logic occurs. On page 14 of the introduction he writes: "Thus in truly great created works we look for and ordinarily find a balance and inner logic that leaves us with a sense of completeness of underlying organic patterns and relationships, and hence of the communication of something 'of philosophic and grave import.' "
28. *Ibid.,* p. 59.
29. *Ibid.,* pp. 56-57.
30. *Ibid.,* p. 40; See also, Dewey, *Art as Experience,* p. 192.
31. Rosenblatt, *op. cit.,* p. 40.
32. *Ibid.,* p. 48.
33. *Ibid.,* p. 49.
34. *Ibid.,* p. 50.
35. *Ibid.,* p. 238.
36. *Ibid.,* p. 245.
37. *Ibid.*
38. *Ibid.,* p. 238.
39. *Ibid.,* p. 239.
40. *Ibid.,* pp. 88-89; this is very similar to Richards' idea that the value

of a work of art is the "readiness for this or that kind of behavior" which it establishes.
41. *Ibid.*, p. 134.
42. *Ibid.*, p. 135.
43. *Literature as Exploration* is definitely concerned with the manner in which the student gives himself evidence of his mastery of this sense of life. Considerable emphasis is placed upon class discussion and the exchange of student opinion—all products of "the setting for spontaneity." (Chapter 3.) Value is also indicated in the kind of critical statement which is exemplified in I. A. Richards' *Practical Criticism* (p. 77). In addition, an appreciation of the author's problems in shaping ideas is to be discovered by students in their own attempts at creative writing. "In this way they will themselves be involved in wrestling with the materials offered them by life or by their reaction to it" (*Literature as Exploration*, p. 59). In none of these experiences is there explicit necessity for using written language to recreate the creative process by which a specific work of art came into being (p. 133).
44. *Ibid.*, p. 254.
45. *Ibid.*, p. 262. See Lenrow in *Reader's Guide to Prose Fiction*. "There is . . . no need to set up a dilemma of alternative choices between the 'old' and the 'contemporary'. Both kinds of material can and need to be selected and related, on the basis of underlying ideas" (p. 10).
46. *Ibid.*, p. 263.
47. Professor Rosenblatt is not explicitly concerned with the expressive character of literary forms themselves. More frequently than from any other form she draws her illustrations from the novel and drama. In one of three references to moving pictures she cites them as extensions of dramatic literature. Other Progressive Education Association spokesmanship recognizes more explicitly the importance of forms. Lenrow's *Reader's Guide to Prose Fiction* speaks thus of the novel: "Today the novel is preëminently the literary form of our time, and in its innumerable manifestations it embodies virtually every human and social aspect of modern civilization" (p. 16). The preparation of a library of films for school use by the Commission on Human Relations under the direction of Alice Keliher should be cited as evidence of awareness of the possibilities of a new art form, although they have not been prepared for the purpose of studying art form particularly.

Committee of Twenty-Four

1. The meeting of this group of twenty-four teachers of English was sponsored by the Joint Committee on Trends in Education (representing both the Association and the National Council of Teachers of English). "The Aims of the Teaching of English" was discussed by the since-named Committee of Twenty-Four. Revisions were entertained, and the original formulators delegated to revise the statement and publish it over the signatures of the Committee of Twenty-Four. The statement appeared in the PMLA Supplement, Vol. LIII, 1938, pp. 1367-71, and in the *English Journal,* College Edition, for April, 1939.

   The Committee of Twenty-Four was composed of the following members: Allan Abbott, Teachers College, Columbia University; W. F. Bryan, Northwestern University; Oscar James Campbell, Columbia University; Stanley P. Chase, Bowdoin College; Earl Daniels, Colgate University; Lennox Grey, Teachers College, Columbia University; Robert M. Gay, Simmons College; Frederick Hard, Tulane University; Wilbur W. Hatfield, Chicago Teachers College; Hoyt H. Hudson, Princeton University; Burgess Johnson, Union College; Howard Mumford Jones, Harvard University; J. F. Mack, Oberlin College; Maynard Mack, Yale University; G. B. Parks, Washington University, St. Louis; George F. Reynolds, University of Colorado; Warner G. Rice, University of Michigan; Louise M. Rosenblatt, Brooklyn College; Reed Smith, University of South Carolina; Theodore Spencer, Harvard University; Robert E. Spiller, Swarthmore College; Clarence O. Thorpe, University of Michigan; H. A. Watt, New York University; Louis B. Wright, Huntington Library.
2. This phase of the statement was opened for reëxamination at the Modern Language Association meeting in New Orleans, 1940. (See *English Journal,* College Edition, March, 1940, pp. 545-47.)
3. "The Aims of the Teaching of Literature," *English Journal,* College Edition, April, 1939, p. 262.
4. *Ibid.,* p. 263.
5. *Ibid.*
6. *Ibid.,* p. 266.
7. *Ibid.*
8. *Ibid.*
9. *Ibid.*

10. Ibid.
11. Ibid., p. 267.
12. Ibid., p. 266.
13. Ibid., p. 263.
14. Ibid., p. 265.
15. Ibid., p. 264.
16. Ibid.
17. Ibid.
18. Ibid.
19. Ibid., p. 265.
20. Rosenblatt, op. cit., p. 245; supra, p. 109.
21. Ibid., p. 238.
22. Ibid., p. 242.
23. Ibid., p. 243.
24. "The Aims of the Teaching of Literature," p. 265.
25. Ibid., p. 265.
26. Ibid., p. 266.
27. Ibid.
28. Ibid., p. 265.
29. Ibid., p. 267.
30. Ibid., p. 264.

Theodore Meyer Greene: Philosophical Spokesman for the Disciplines

1. Theodore Meyer Greene, editor, *The Meaning of the Humanities*. Five Essays by Ralph Barton Perry, August Charles Krey, Erwin Panofsky, Robert Lowry Calhoun, Gilbert Chinard, with an introduction by the editor.
2. Ibid., p. xiii.
3. Ibid., pp. xiv-xv.
4. Ibid., p. xviii.
5. Ibid., p. xix.
6. Ibid., p. xx.
7. Ibid., p. xxi.
8. Ibid.
9. Ibid.
10. Ibid., p. xxii.
11. Ibid., p. xxiii.
12. Ibid.
13. Ibid., p. xxv.

14. *Ibid.*
15. *Ibid.,* p. xxvi.
16. *Ibid.*
17. *Ibid.,* p. xxvii.
18. *Ibid.,* p. xxviii.
19. *Ibid.*
20. *Ibid.,* pp. xxviii-xxix.
21. *Ibid.,* p. xxxi.
22. *Ibid.,* p. xxxii.
23. *Ibid.,* p. xxxiii.
24. *Ibid.*
25. *Ibid.*
26. *Ibid.,* p. xxxv.
27. *Ibid.,* p. xxxvi.
28. In Ralph Barton Perry's "A definition of the Humanities," the values "peculiarly concerned with man" (p. 11) are made most explicit. He posits first the condition of freedom, which, as he qualifies the word, means the ability to make "enlightened choice," to pursue "action in which habit, reflex or suggestion are suspended by an individual's fundamental judgments of good and evil; the action whose premises are explicit; the action which proceeds from personal reflection and integration" (p. 4). The peculiarly human values which conduce to this freedom are *learning,* which extends man's range of alternative actions (p. 6); *imagination,* which "enables the mind to entertain new possibilities of truth" (p. 8); and *sympathy,* which surrounds factual and imaginative conceptions with an emotional aura of value. These values lend themselves to the singularly human quality of dignity or consciousness of self which is present only in the self-critical, self-directive individual (pp. 11-12). Even beyond the possession of self-feeling is the value of manners in which *civility* is expressive of all the visible manifestations of inner spiritual freedom.

To all of these values, Perry indicates literature's contribution from the viewpoint of critical reading only. Literature "presents life concretely, presenting models for admiration or condemnation —for imitation or rejection. It enlarges the range of immediate experience, and communicates it feelingly; it stimulates the imagination and breaks the moulds of habit; it expresses the diverse visions and aspirations of great men; it integrates the different cultural elements of a society or an epoch; it embodies beauty and commends it as an object of disinterested pleasure; at its best, it brings a sense of moral elevation" (p. 39). We pause particularly on Perry's statement showing art to be a cultural symbol synthesizing the various elements of a society or epoch, for in this respect it approaches philosophy which proceeds "to the completest possible integration of experience" (p. 40).

While August Charles Krey's "History and the Humanities" is not specifically concerned with literature and the other arts, one of his concluding statements is significant for our inquiry into the values inherent in the psychological-anthropological idea of aesthetic experience. Historians, he tells us, "have learned . . . that, however much men may have in common and however important these common characteristics may be, the dynamic quality of society is derived from the individual who sets the mass in motion or determines its direction, and is therefore distinctive" (p. 85).

We find a closer concern with the nature of aesthetic experience in Erwin Panofsky's "The History of Art as a Humanistic Discipline." His theory is based on a fundamental dichotomy of manmade as distinct from natural objects, and, among man-made objects, the artistic as distinct from practical ones. The principal distinction in this latter classification is that artistic objects demand to be experienced aesthetically, i.e., in respect to the proportioned emphasis on *idea* and *form* as these contribute to a revelation of *content*. Artistic objects demand to be aesthetically experienced because the artist has embodied certain communicable "intentions" in the mutually expressive qualities of idea and form. These "intentions," while they may never be definitely known because of incomplete biographical data, may be approximated, for they are "conditioned by the standards of their period and environment" (p. 104). An intention within any work of art may be "the basic attitude of a nation, a period, a class, a religious or philosophical persuasion—all this unconsciously qualified by one personality, and condensed into one work" (p. 105). The work of art, while executed by an individual artist, is influenced by the "cosmos of culture" from which it springs. Hence to experience the work aesthetically, the observer must "re-enact the actions and re-create the creations" in an "organic situation" in which intuitive aesthetic reconstruction combines with archeological data to form an appreciative synthesis (p. 107). The critical method implicit here is dependent upon historical data. But evaluation, as Panofsky makes clear, is dependent upon a natural sensitiveness to the medium of a given art, a professional training in the techniques of that art, and the cultural-anthropological knowledge that alone could orient a specific work of art in its school and tradition. Definitely this approximates the modern psychological-anthropological approach to aesthetic experience with which we are concerned.

Robert Lowry Calhoun, in "Theology and the Humanities," draws upon modern biology, psychology, and anthropology to show the singularly human attributes which distinguish men from other animals. One of these is the need for self-respect, a feeling of personal unity. Accompanying and contributory to this search for self is the persistent quest for some comparable integration in his environment. "This craving for order appears to be one of our basic wants, quite possibly the most distinctly human of all" (pp. 123-24). While Calhoun does not use the term "aesthetic experience," this craving for order and design seems to be one with the aesthetic impulse as we have come to know it, and to lead to comparable personal and social values.

As an individual attempts to bring various factors of his environment into relationship he frequently meets with temporary stoppages or frustrations which induce a heightened emotional tension. The individual may fulminate against these obstructions to his formative impulse, seek outside aid, or resolve them through deliberate, purposive methods. When he finds a satisfying solution in a new pattern of behavior or values, he is "saved," i.e., he is momentarily "set free, made whole, or put in the way of meaningful, profoundly satisfying life. . ." (pp. 142-43). Such rational activity proceeds on faith that it will lead to satisfaction, and "provides for religious faith the crucial evidence that God is good" (p. 143).

There are in human experience configurations of events that refuse to yield over a long period of time to an individual's best efforts. Then suddenly a satisfying design is seen: "The barrier itself against which he has to struggle becomes itself a source of meaning, through which he comes to be what he neither foresaw nor desired in any specific way: a self matured and realized" (p. 145). This self is matured in an understanding of its potentialities and also of its limitations, an understanding of the existence of a force which as yet eludes human control.

The religious insight either of salvation or of God so perceived is similar to the aesthetic experience in its feeling of self-reliance and spiritual amplification. It is similar also, in so far as religious tradition shows historical periods in which individuals found orientation in their worlds through religious ceremony. Theology from this point of view may be seen as an art form itself. (Note: For a discussion of this concept one should see J. B. S. Haldane's "Science and Theology as Art Forms.") The attitude which pervades modern theology is similar to that of the art critic working from a psychological-anthropological idea of aesthetic experience; theology proceeds on faith and the critic proceeds on the assumption of some measure of value which a work of art may communicate. While modern theology may proceed on faith in a power higher than man, it does not remove from man the responsibility for planning and executing his own affairs in realms of humanly measurable and humanly directable activity.

Gilbert Chinard treats of "Literature and the Humanities." Within his lecture we find implicit indications of the cultural origins of art (p. 162), and of the intellectual climate of a generation, its dreams, moods and aspirations reflected in literature (p. 163). Chinard's concern is primarily with the values which the reader gains from literature. He writes of the "intellectual pleasure of the highest order" (p. 158) which accompanies the analysis and comprehension of an author's style, the form which enables the reader "to gain an insight into the mind of another human being" (p. 158). Another value for the reader is the excitation of a variety of emotions and feelings and the quickening to sensitiveness of ideas of the past and present (p. 160). These feelings and aspirations are communicated to the reader through the artist's arrangement of words. The critical method implicit here involves an exposition of the expressiveness of words in their contexts, for "through word-order the degrees of emphasis, passion and moods of writers are expressed . . ." (p. 158). Chinard finds considerable value in the history-of-ideas approach to literature (p. 165), suggesting a study of Greek and Latin to find our intellectual origins (p. 170). Whether we should interpret this to mean that our present ideas stem from similar ones in ancient civilization, or whether we should infer that Greece represents the beginnings of a Western civilization which has gone through several changes of attitudes toward life does not become explicit.

29. Theodore Meyer Greene, *The Arts and the Art of Criticism*, p. 6.
30. *Ibid.*, pp. 7-8. From this we may infer a relativistic analogical logic which admits of no absolute organizations, no tight categories of kinds recognizable through external form.
31. *Ibid.*, p. 232.

32. *Ibid.*
33. *Ibid.*
34. *Ibid.*, p. 239.
35. *Ibid.*, p. 253.
36. *Ibid.*, p. 477.
37. *Ibid.*, p. 231.
38. *Ibid.*, p. 426. Greene acknowledges Croce here. The similarity to the theories of Rusu and Müller-Freienfels should not be overlooked.
39. *Ibid.*, p. 103.
40. *Ibid.*, p. 105.
41. *Ibid.*, p. 112.
42. *Ibid.*, p. 232.
43. *Ibid.*, p. 181.
44. *Ibid.*, p. 182.
45. *Ibid.*, p. 183.
46. *Ibid.*
47. *Ibid.*, p. 184.
48. *Ibid.*, p. 9.
49. *Ibid.*, p. 23.
50. *Ibid.*, p. 9.
51. Erwin Panofsky, "The History of Art as a Humanistic Discipline." In Greene, *The Meaning of the Humanities,* p. 107.
52. Greene, *op. cit.*, pp. 476-77.
53. *Ibid.*, p. 21.
54. *Ibid.*, p. 476.
55. *Ibid.*, pp. 487-506.
56. *Ibid.*, p. 391.
57. *Ibid.*, pp. 450-51.
58. *Ibid.*, p. 458.
59. *Ibid.*, pp. 467-68.
60. *Ibid.*, p. 468.
61. *Ibid.*, pp. 468, 472.
62. *Ibid.*, p. 24.

Irwin Edman: Poet Philosopher

1. Irwin Edman, *Fountainheads of Freedom,* p. 9.
2. Edman, "Man's Humanities to Man," *Saturday Review of Literature,* XX (September 2, 1939), 3.
3. *Ibid.*, p. 4.

4. Edman, "Culture in a Democracy," *Saturday Review of Literature*, XII (June 29, 1935), 4.
5. *Ibid.*, p. 16.
6. Edman, "Man's Humanities to Man," *Saturday Review of Literature*, XX (September 2, 1939), p. 4.
7. Edman, "Culture in a Democracy," *Saturday Review of Literature*, XII (June 29, 1935), p. 4.
8. Edman, *Arts and the Man*, p. 153.
9. *Ibid.*, p. 148. "Ideas, themes, intuitions occur to the artist as they occur to the man in the street or to the man in the laboratory. But these ideas in existence or in art must be realized by understanding, by discipline, and by control."
10. *Ibid.*, pp. 17-18.
11. *Ibid.*, p. 118.
12. *Ibid.*, p. 121.
13. *Ibid.*, p. 14.
14. *Ibid.*, p. 12.
15. *Ibid.*, p. 15.
16. *Ibid.*, p. 19. While this phrasing seems to imply a dichotomy that modern science does not admit, the total context of *Arts and the Man* implies the unity of the psychophysical organism. He later implies the inadvisability of a separation of "Spirit as over against the Flesh" (p. 123).
17. *Ibid.*, p. 12.
18. *Ibid.*, p. 31.
19. *Ibid.*, pp. 37-38.
20. *Ibid.*, p. 53.
21. *Ibid.*, p. 78.
22. *Ibid.*
23. *Ibid.*, p. 66.
24. *Ibid.*, p. 151.
25. *Ibid.*, p. 82.
26. *Ibid.*, p. 60.
27. *Ibid.*, p. 61.
28. *Ibid.*, p. 69.
29. *Ibid.*, p. 65.
30. *Ibid.*, p. 75.
31. *Ibid.*, p. 67.
32. *Ibid.*, p. 62.
33. *Ibid.*, p. 63.
34. *Ibid.*, p. 64.

35. *Ibid.*, p. 115.
36. *Ibid.*, p. 84.
37. *Ibid.*, pp. 17-18.
38. *Ibid.*, p. 21.
39. *Ibid.*, p. 19.
40. *Ibid.*, p. 135.
41. *Ibid.*, p. 136.
42. *Ibid.*, p. 149.
43. *Ibid.*, p. 148.
44. *Ibid.*, p. 147.
45. *Ibid.*, p. 143.
46. *Ibid.*, p. 131.
47. *Ibid.*, p. 121.
48. Edman, "After a Mozart Quartet," *Nation*, CXXXII (February 25, 1931), 217.
49. Edman, *Arts and the Man*, p. 122.
50. *Ibid.*, p. 134. See also "No Blackout for the Arts," *New York Times Magazine*, April 19, 1942.

Jacques Barzun: Humanistic Historian

1. Jacques Barzun, *Of Human Freedom*, p. 3.
2. *Ibid.*, p. 277.
3. *Ibid.*, p. 116.
4. *Ibid.*, p. 8.
5. *Ibid.*
6. *Ibid.*, pp. 94-95.
7. *Ibid.*, p. 33.
8. *Ibid.*, p. 230.
9. *Ibid.*, p. 235.
10. *Ibid.*, pp. 11, 235, 277.
11. *Ibid.*, p. 107 and following, in the chapter entitled "The Arts, the Snobs, and the Democrat."
12. *Ibid.*, p. 107.
13. Theodore Meyer Greene, *The Arts and the Art of Criticism*, cf. p. 107 *supra.*
14. Barzun, *op. cit.*, p. 127.
15. *Ibid.*, p. 127.
16. *Ibid.*, p. 57.
17. *Ibid.*, p. 111.

18. *Ibid.*, p. 135.
19. *Ibid.*, p. 42.
20. *Ibid.*, p. 42.
21. *Ibid.*, p. 234.
22. *Ibid.*, p. 22. Barzun writes: "Many men, many minds, is the basis of democracy."
23. *Ibid.*, p. 204.
24. *Ibid.*, p. 195.
25. *Ibid.*, p. 118. This might be compared to Greene's statement that reading is not in the first place a creative, but a receptive activity.
26. *Ibid.*, p. 118.
27. *Ibid.*, p. 104.
28. *Ibid.*, p. 142.
29. *Ibid.*, p. 115.
30. *Ibid.*, p. 120. As Edman has already shown, the moralistic and legislative critics act from a feeling of responsibility to society. Barzun implies that good intentions are not enough—that art can set its own standards, and that only those critics who are competent to handle artistic disciplines should assume responsibility of criticism. "A democracy where the individual can freely choose his cultural sustenance can safely leave to human genius the making of an art adequate to its greatness. . . . Granting freedom to the artist means relieving him from the necessity of justifying himself, showing a greater appetite for a variety of styles and individual manners, stifling critical suspiciousness and doctrinaire expectations, and taking what is offered for what it is worth instead of trying to make it fit into the set categories of what is American, or modern, or classical, or proletarian."
31. *Ibid.*, pp. 104-5.
32. Barzun, "The American as Critic," *Saturday Review of Literature*, XXVIII (December 7, 1940), 32.
33. Barzun, *Of Human Freedom*, pp. 186-187. He states: ". . . every study, while giving up claims to impartiality and certitude, shall embody an idea or a hypothesis, frankly stated and loyally worked out." The critical analysis itself is a second artistic product; like Greene's "re-creation," it is "an organization, a scale of values and tenable conclusions, the whole to be welded into a work of art by a combination of faithful scholarship and straight thinking."
34. *Ibid.*, p. 32.
35. *Ibid.*, p. 116.

36. *Ibid.*, p. 116. Barzun exemplifies this critical method briefly in "Hamlet's Politics," *Saturday Review of Literature*, XXI (April 13, 1940), 6-7, in which he moves sequentially through the events of *Hamlet* as they have bearing upon the attempts of Hamlet to achieve personal security.
37. Barzun, "Scientific Humanism," *Nation*, CXLVIII (April 29, 1939), 502-3.
38. Barzun, *Of Human Freedom*, p. 7.
39. *Ibid.*, pp. 220-24.
40. *Ibid.*, p. 219.
41. Miss Rosenblatt and Barzun look upon the origins and values of a work of art from the same psychological-anthropological base. Each notes the value of an individual's acquiring facility with some expressive medium; each recognizes individual differences and would make provision for them in materials for study; each distrusts any absolute list of Best Books. Their points of view seem to lie very close together, diverging perhaps, on the students' initial acquaintance with various pieces of literature. While Miss Rosenblatt would prefer to start with contemporary works of art which would meet each reader on his own level and attempt to raise the standard of complexity and increase the historical range, she nevertheless recognizes the economy of group study and the possibility that a partial interpretation on a student's part may flower for him later. Barzun, if we may judge from his spokesmanship for the Humanities course in Columbia College ("The Humanities—Proper Study of Mankind") would prefer to expose students to a historical sequence of masterpieces, testing for facts and discussing for human meanings.
42. Barzun, *Of Human Freedom*, p. 211.
43. *Ibid.*, p. 232.
44. *Ibid.*, pp. 228-29.
45. *Ibid.*, p. 233.
46. *Ibid.*, p. 42.
47. *Ibid.*, p. 234.
48. *Ibid.*, p. 230.
49. *Ibid.*, p. 218.
50. *Ibid.*, p. 217. See also Barzun, "The Humanities—Proper Study of Mankind," *The English Journal*, College Edition, October, 1938, pp. 637-48.
51. *Ibid.*, p. 218.
52. Barzun, *Darwin, Marx, Wagner, Critique of a Heritage*, p. 4.

I. A. Richards: International Psychologist-Semanticist

1. It is significant of leanings toward pragmatic thought in this country that while periodicals already carried a sizeable bibliography for Richards before 1929, he received most attention here when *Practical Criticism* appeared as a teacher's statement of teaching method in literary criticism in Cambridge University. *Practical Criticism* was followed by *Mencius on the Mind* and other semantic inquiries in periodicals, such as "What is Belief?" in the *Nation* in 1934. From this time on, his influence in American education seems to have been felt as much through word of mouth as through actual publication. In preparing for the General Education Board a "Statement on the Application of Theory of Interpretation to General Education," he drew together much of *Interpretation in Teaching,* which was originally to have been called "The Humanities in General Education." Paralleling in point of time his association with the General Education Board was his similarly informal association with members of the Commission on Human Relations and the Commission on Secondary School Curriculum of the Progressive Education Association, and with members of the staff of Teachers College, Columbia University, and other university groups. His influence in these groups has been acknowledged by Louise Rosenblatt in *Literature as Exploration* and by the Commission on Secondary School Curriculum in the preface to *Language in General Education,* first prepared on mimeographed form and distributed to the thirteen Progressive Education Association Workshops in the summer of 1938. In revised form it was published in the fall of 1940. These informal associations have been followed by affiliation with the Orthological Institute at Harvard University.
2. I. A. Richards, *Interpretation in Teaching,* p. 3.
3. Richards, "Science and Poetry," *The Atlantic Monthly,* CXXXVI (October, 1925), 482.
4. Richards, *Principles of Literary Criticism,* p. 83. It is appropriate to note again the detailed study which William A. Dollard is carrying on as another member of the Coöperative Research Group in the Humanities at Teachers College, Columbia University. The forthcoming study is entitled: "The Grammar-Logic-Rhetoric of I. A. Richards: A Study in Progression from the Traditional Discipline of the English Humanities Tripos Toward a Modern Psychological 'Practical Criticism.'"

5. Richards, C. F. Ogden, and James Woods, *Foundations of Aesthetics*, p. 80.
6. Richards, "Science and Poetry," *Atlantic Monthly*, CXXXVI (October, 1925), 483.
7. Richards' relationship with anthropological method as well as psychological data is apparent in *The Meaning of Meaning*, to which Bronislaw Malinowski contributed a forty-page supplement on "The Problem of Meaning in Primitive Languages." (*The Meaning of Meaning*, pp. 296-336.
8. Richards, "Science and Poetry," *op. cit.*, p. 483.
9. Richards, *Coleridge on Imagination*, p. xii.
10. See William McDougall, *An Introduction to Social Psychology*, pp. 48-91.
11. Richards, *Principles of Literary Criticism*, p. 83.
12. *Ibid.*, p. 83.
13. *Ibid.*, p. 82. Richards, like Dewey, uses "mind" in the sense of psychophysical activity.
14. *Ibid.*, p. 50. Cf. also *Practical Criticism*, p. 285.
15. Richards, "Science and Poetry," *op. cit.*, p. 490.
16. Richards, *Principles of Literary Criticism*, p. 106.
17. These ideas are implicit in such statements as the following: The first is concerned with a psychological theory of value. "It may very well be the case that a person's own interests are such that, *if he understood them,* were well organized in other words, he would be a useful and charming member of his community . . ." (*Principles of Literary Criticism*, p. 54). "It is certain, however, that the chief difference lies in the fact that the obtuse person has not learned to *interpret* the changes in his general bodily consciousness in any systematic fashion. The changes may occur and occur systematically, but they mean nothing definite to him" (*Ibid.*, p. 100). The increment which Richards explicitly adds to previous spokesmanship is this consciousness of contributing factors to one's own development, although Dewey's reference to consciousness of the creative process is closely related to it.
18. Richards, *Principles of Literary Criticism*, pp. 95-102.
19. *Ibid.*, p. 183.
20. Richards, "Science and Poetry," *op. cit.*, p. 490.
21. *Ibid.*, p. 490.
22. Richards, *Principles of Literary Criticism*, p. 55.
23. Richards, "Science and Poetry," *op. cit.*, p. 491.
24. Richards, *The Meaning of Meaning*, p. 149.

25. Richards, "What is Belief?" *The Nation*, CXXXIX (July 18, 1934), 71-74.
26. Richards, *The Meaning of Meaning*, p. 150.
27. Although these may be very difficult to isolate as entities, Richards gives us a testing block for their existence when, writing of Materialism and Idealism, he makes this generalization: "Like all terms used in the vain attempt (vain because the question is non-sensical) to say what things are, instead of to say how they behave, they state nothing" (*Principles of Literary Criticism*, p. 84).
28. Richards, *Principles of Literary Criticism*, p. 137.
29. Richards, *The Meaning of Meaning*, pp. 239-40. Also *Principles of Literary Criticism*, p. 145.
30. Among the modes open to his choice are three: "statement, full and explicit, or condensed (by abstraction, ambiguity or implication, the hint, the aposiopesis); (or) statement literal or direct, and indirect (by metaphor, simile, comparison, parallel, etc.); (or) suasion, open (from appeal to cajolery) or concealed (either as mere statement or as mere ornament) and so on" (*Interpretation in Teaching*, pp. 14-15).
31. Richards, *Principles of Literary Criticism*, p. 137. Here again we note similarity to Dewey and Greene.
32. Richards, *Interpretation in Teaching*, p. 16.
33. *Ibid.*, p. 16. Lest we think of the "ethics of thinking" as a catch-phrase, to use Richards' term, we should consider pragmatically (i.e., in its broadest human consequences) the ethics of certain modes of expression current in our time. In *The American Cause*, pp. 16-17, Archibald MacLeish draws attention to the technique of confusion and defamation which the enemies of democracy have developed with success abroad and are now using in this country. We find similar awareness of this in the responsible observations of Thomas Mann in *The Magic Mountain* and in *The Beloved Returns*. Whatever implications may be present, we are witnessing similar techniques, perhaps unconsciously employed, in the writing of some of the advocates of a return to the teaching of formal logic.
34. *Ibid.*, p. 18.
35. Richards, "The Interactions of Words," *The Language of Poetry*, edited by Allen Tate, p. 71.
36. Part of the definition of *vigilance* which we glean from context is: "The range, delicacy, and the freedom of the connections he is able to make between different elements of his experience" (*Principles of Literary Criticism*, pp. 181-85).

37. Richards, *Principles of Literary Criticism*, p. 181.
38. *Ibid.*, p. 59.
39. *Ibid.*, p. 61.
40. Richards, "Science and Poetry," *op. cit.*, p. 485.
41. Richards, *Principles of Literary Criticism*, pp. 118-19.
42. Richards, "Science and Poetry," *op. cit.*, p. 487.
43. Richards uses *catharsis* only in connection with tragedy, though it is implicit that the experience with other literary types varies only in degree. He is aware of the various senses in which catharsis has been translated previously, and is careful to include his own translation to supplant the confusions resulting from purgation, etc. "Tragedy is an imitation of an action—effecting through Pity and Terror the correction and refinement (Κάθαρςις) of such passions" (*Principles of Literary Criticism*, Footnote, p. 113).
44. *Ibid.*, pp. 245-46. If a harmonization of conflicts is not achieved through a balanced expression or more particularly, if the tensions are suppressed, the results to the individual, as Dewey has also remarked, are psychologically harmful. See Dewey, *Art as Experience*, p. 65.
45. Richards, *Practical Criticism*, p. 348.
46. *Ibid.*, p. 305.
47. Richards, *Principles of Literary Criticism*, p. 236.
48. Samuel Taylor Coleridge, *Biographia Literaria, op. cit.*, Chap. XIV, p. 449. In *The Principles of Literary Criticism*, Richards himself writes, "To read a poem for the sake of the pleasure which will ensue if it is successfully read is to approach it in an inadequate attitude" (pp. 96-97).
49. Richards, *Principles of Literary Criticism*, p. 234.
50. Richards, *Practical Criticism*, p. 276. See also *Principles of Literary Criticism*, p. 132.
51. Richards, *Principles of Literary Criticism*, p. 132.
52. *Ibid.*, p. 66.
53. *Ibid.*, p. 61.
54. *Ibid.*, p. 234.

Advocates of a Return to the Medieval Liberal Arts

1. Gerald B. Phelan, *Saint Thomas and Analogy*, pp. 2-3.
2. Scott Buchanan, "A Crisis in Liberal Education," Reprinted from the Amherst Graduates' Quarterly, February, 1938.
3. *Ibid.*, p. 13. The unity of this group of spokesmen is explicit also

in Adler's *How To Read a Book*, which contains eight references to St. John's College. See particularly pp. 102, 325, 328.
4. Robert Maynard Hutchins, *The Higher Learning in America*, p. 105-107.
5. *Ibid.*, p. 59.
6. It is significant to note, in comparison with the rationale in which Theodore Meyer Greene provides for the interpretative synthesis of specialized inquiry, that Hutchins leaves us without explicit indication of how the intellectual pursuits on the University level might be translated into the life of the common man.
7. Hutchins, *op. cit.*, p. 73.
8. See pp. 26-27 *supra*.
9. Hutchins, *op. cit.*, p. 66.
10. *Ibid.*, p. 67.
11. *Ibid.*, p. 78. The content is not exclusively drawn from these epochs. The emphasis we infer lies there. "What are the permanent studies?" he asks. "They are in the first place those books which have through the centuries attained to the dimensions of classics. Many such books, I am afraid, are in the ancient and medieval period."
12. *Ibid.*, p. 82.
13. *Ibid.*, p. 83.
14. *Ibid.*, p. 84. This is a purely syllogistic logic, opposed to Dewey's logic as a theory of inquiry and to Richards' analogical logic as clarification of experience. But the neo-scholastic group on the authority of St. Thomas also takes up an "analogical logic" position, if we are to judge by Gerald B. Phelan's Aquinas Lecture for 1941, *St. Thomas and Analogy*. Recognizing the modern senses of "analogy," but discrediting them as superficial, Phelan develops the Thomistic idea of analogy as the base of metaphysical analysis and hence the true form of analogy. In this concept whatever object appears to the senses is but an analogy of its true nature to which the intellect can penetrate in the "pure light of metaphysical contemplation" (p. 6). Analogy then is an established relationship between a material object and its Form, rather than a process of discovering and clarifying new relationships. This seems to be so much the case that when Phelan refers to all *being* as analogical, he also states that "those who have attempted to express it in clear distinct ideas have sinned against intelligence; for, clear and distinct ideas banish mystery and bring death to metaphysics" (p. 8).
15. *Ibid.*, p. 103.

16. *Ibid.*, p. 98.
17. *Ibid.*, p. 63.
18. To some it has appeared that when Hutchins and Adler accuse the more completely aesthetic critics of being "anti-intellectual" and "anti-rationalistic," Hutchins and Adler are in turn "anti-aesthetic." Hutchins' writings are seldom concerned, for instance, with the novels which for most modern readers are the most comprehensive expression of our total feelings and intuitions about life —potentially as significant for modern Americans as the *Odyssey* was for ancient Greeks.
19. Mortimer J. Adler, *Art and Prudence*, pp. 448-49.
20. *Ibid.*, pp. 449-50. In his prudent or political capacity, the statesman has "three potential alternatives with respect to art: (1) extirpation or total exclusion, (2) various forms of regulation and control, (3) inaction, or granting the arts their freedom" (p. 449).
Exclusion or extirpation of an art on purely political grounds is to be preferred to the prudent man's exceeding his own boundaries of knowledge. As Adler metaphorically phrases it (and perhaps the violence of censorship as we know it in the world today justifies his figure): "It is better to kill an art than to choke or mangle it" p. 449). It seems preferable for the "prudent man to supervise the ways in which works of art reach their audience, to say, not what shall be made, but what shall be received and by whom and under what conditions. . . . Here the difficulties of the prudent man are of another order. He does not go out of his proper sphere in imposing a censorship which rejects a work of art as unfit to be received" (p. 450). It seems that the practical effects of this regulation, i.e., the incompleteness of the artist's aesthetic experience for lack of a public, are similar to overt censorship.

If, as may occur, the prudent man finds the question of judgment "genuinely insoluble," the final critical authority will fall upon divine insight. "Wisdom," says Adler, [and Wisdom in Thomistic vocabulary is the possession of only the Contemplator or Philosopher] "being endowed with the outlook of God and ranging over Action and Making alike, alone can completely reconcile Art and Prudence" (pp. 90-91). See also Maritain, *Art and Scholasticism*, p. 86.
21. *Ibid.*, p. 90. This emphasis upon prudence (or the knowledge of right action) and politics should not be passed over without reference to other indications of Adler's central concern with rhetoric. In addressing the American Catholic Philosophical Association, he

writes of "a few ultimate principles of speculative rhetoric which bear on the problem of profitable communication." Also in the St. John's Catalogue for 1938-39, we find this: "It seems that we in our *political preoccupation,* and economic energy, coupled with experimental science, are primarily concerned with rhetoric and music . . ." (p. 28). (Italics not in the original.)

22. *Ibid.*, Preface ix-x. For further comment on the relationship of these men, see W. C. Barrett, "Reading and the Liberal Arts," *Kenyon Review* (winter, 1942), or the reference to this article in *College English,* March, 1941, pp. 609-10.
23. *Ibid.,* p. 436.
24. *Ibid.*
25. Action for Adler is "political behavior," i.e., behavior which has to do with the actions and reactions of men and the morals which regulate their society. Action so defined lies within the sphere of the prudent man and is subject to his censorship.
26. Adler, "Tradition and Communication," Reprinted from the Proceedings of the American Catholic Philosophical Association, Thirteenth Annual Meeting, December 29 and 30, 1937, p. 106.
27. *Ibid.,* p. 106.
28. *Ibid.,* p. 107.
29. *Ibid.,* p. 106.
30. *Ibid.*
31. *Ibid.,* p. 107.
32. *Ibid.,* p. 106, Footnote #9.
33. *Ibid.,* p. 107. *How to Read a Book* is less explicit in delineating the trivium as St. Thomas saw it. Grammar, we infer, is a basic discipline in which words are recognized and understood. Grammar permits of two widely different uses, one poetical, the other logical. But because logic is always concerned with "unambiguous explicitness" (p. 302), which the syllogism affords, it plays little part in a work of art. The factor which provides unity for a work of art is "a temporal scheme, a progress from a beginning through the middle to its end" (p. 308). The Aristotelian echo here is familiar. Logic remains as Hutchins indicated, "a statement in technical form."
34. *Ibid.,* p. 105.
35. Hutchins, *op. cit.,* p. 87. With administrative concern for the adoption of his system for disciplining the intellectual virtues, Hutchins calls "for the establishment of a new college or for an evangelistic movement in some old ones which shall have for its

object the conversion of individuals and finally of the teaching profession to a true conception of general education."
36. Adler, *How to Read a Book*, pp. 48, 102, 238-39.
37. Adler, *St. Thomas and the Gentiles*, pp. 18-19. Delivering the Aquinas Lecture for 1938 before the Aristotelian Society of Marquette University, Adler names (as he does also in "Tradition and Communication") those whom St. Thomas designated as gentiles, Jews, and heretics. Adler then raises the question of modern discipleship to St. Thomas in relation to these groups. "The burden of proof was upon us, and we have failed so far. Until every effort has been made, until every device has been strenuously tried and patiently exhausted, it is no defense to say that those who will not see cannot be shown. In this case I do not think we can say with Maritain, when we undertake to explain to our contemporaries the necessity of taking St. Thomas for a teacher, that we are there "only to tell them so, not to persuade them in spite of themselves. . . . I am not counseling the patience of Job because, in a sense, no man deserves that much at our hands."
38. Adler, *Art and Prudence*, p. 49.
39. *Ibid.*, p. 49.
40. *Ibid.*, p. 49. See also, *How to Read a Book*, p. 38.
41. Adler, *Art and Prudence*, p. 49.
42. M. Alain is the pseudonym of Jacques-Emile Chartier, whom the International Who's Who (1936) calls "French philosopher and essayist." Adler acknowledges indebtedness to "Alain's" *Système des beaux arts* (1926) and *Vingt Leçons sur les beaux-arts* (1921) in *Art and Prudence*, p. 45.
43. *Ibid.*, p. 48.
44. *Ibid.*
45. Adler, *How to Read a Book*, p. 300.
46. *Ibid.*, p. 102.
47. *Ibid.*, p. 116.
48. *Ibid.*, p. 124 in the Chapter "From Many Rules to One Habit," and pp. 266-67 in "And Still More Rules."
49. Adler, *Art and Prudence*, p. 490.
50. *Ibid.*, p. 490.
51. Adler, *How to Read a Book*, p. 307. See also *Art and Prudence*, p. 492.
52. Adler, *Art and Prudence*, p. 503.
53. Adler, *How to Read a Book*, p. 351.

54. *Ibid.*, p. 350.
55. *Ibid.*, p. 313.
56. *Ibid.*, p. 124.
57. *Ibid.*, p. 315.
58. *Ibid.*
59. *Ibid.*, p. 313.
60. St. John's College, Catalogue, 1937-38, p. 17.
61. *Ibid.*, p. 28.
62. Adler, *How to Read a Book*, pp. 254-56.
63. St. John's College, Catalogue, 1939-40, p. 19.
64. *Ibid.*, p. 31.
65. *Ibid.*, p. 25.
66. *Ibid.*, p. 31.
67. *Ibid.*, p. 32.
68. *Ibid.*, p. 33.
69. *Ibid.*
70. St. John's College, Catalogue, 1941-42, p. 28.
71. St. John's College, Catalogue, 1939-40, p. 34.
72. *Ibid.*, p. 35.
73. Adler, "Tradition and Communication," *op. cit.*, p. 105.

PART III

1. Louise Dudley and Austin Faricy, *The Humanities*, Applied Aesthetics, p. v.
2. *Ibid.*, p. 3.
3. *Ibid.*
4. *Ibid.*, p. 4.
5. *Ibid.*
6. *Ibid.*, p. 3.
7. *Ibid.*, p. 6.
8. This point of view is explicit in the section on Art and Life. "Art, as we are considering it from the point of view of the critic who recreates rather than the artist who creates, belongs to the contemplative phase; the quiet storing up of feelings that influence behavior in the more active phases" (*Ibid.*, p. 567).
9. *Ibid.*, p. 534.
10. *Ibid.*, p. 548.
11. *Ibid.*, p. 551. The text continues with its hierarchy of classification:

"Some emotions are admittedly of a nobler kind than others. Love is higher than hate; forgiveness is higher than revenge. The positive emotions are higher than the negative; the constructive are higher than the destructive. Within the constructive positive emotions some are higher than others. Love of one's wife is higher than love of pleasure, and love of truth is higher than either."

12. *Ibid.*, p. 564.
13. H. S. Cayley, Professor of English, New Jersey State Teachers College, Montclair, New Jersey, personal letter, June 1, 1940.
14. John F. Fitchen III, "A Challenge," *Journal of Higher Education,* VIII (March, 1937), 120.
15. Fitchen, "A Challenge," p. 121.
16. *Ibid.*, p. 122.
17. *Ibid.*
18. *Ibid.*, VIII (April, 1937), 200.
19. Professor Raymond S. Stites, who offers this course, uses his *The Arts and Man* (1940) as a text. See p. 17 for objectives.
20. Antioch College, Aesthetics 103-104 and Creative Aesthetics: Syllabus, 1937-38, p. 1 (mimeographed).
21. Raymond S. Stites, *The Arts and Man*, p. 761.
22. *Ibid.*, p. 318. In his letter of March 9, 1942, Professor Stites notes the introduction of an additional course, "Philosophies of Art" at Antioch, which deals specifically with these points of view.
23. *Ibid.*, p. 16.
24. Antioch College, Syllabus, *op. cit.*, p. 3.
25. *Ibid.*, p. 3. It is indicative of trends that Professor Stites writes in his letter of March 9, 1942, "The reason I have been able to 'stick to my guns' with the program and philosophy stated in the Conclusion (p. 832) [of *The Arts and Man*] is that most of the members of our Administration and my colleagues in Music, Psychology, Education and Literature subscribe to the same view. We are all looking toward the future and we are trying to use those elements of the past which will help us to face the future courageously."
26. University of Florida, Comprehensive Course in the Humanities: Syllabus, 1937.
27. Boston University, Bulletin, 1941-42, p. 143.
28. Reed College, General Literature 11 and History of Civilization 11: Syllabi, 1936-37.
29. Reed College, Bulletin, January, 1941, p. 51.
30. *Ibid.*, pp. 43-44.
31. Frederic C. Lane, "Why Begin at the Beginning?" Reprinted from

Proceedings of the Middle States Association of History and Social Science Teachers, XXXV (1937), 73.
32. *Ibid.,* p. 76.
33. Robert P. Griffing, Jr., letter, June 19, 1940.
34. Missouri Valley College, Catalogue, 1939-40, p. 40.
35. Claude L. Fichthorn, Dean of Music, Missouri Valley College, letter, May 24, 1940.
36. Bucknell University Bulletin, Catalogue Issue, 1940-41, p. 114.
37. *Ibid.,* p. 100.
38. *Ibid.,* p. 130.
39. Talladega College, Catalogue, 1940, p. 35.
40. Northwest Missouri State Teachers College, General Catalogue, 1940-41, p. 39.
41. Lorraine Peter, Professor of History, Alabama College for Women, letter, March 12, 1942.
42. Alabama College for Women, History of Civilization: Syllabus and Reading Lists, 1938-39. In the very comprehensive examination for History 101, January, 1939, individual sections were devoted to Government and History, Geography and Economic Life, General Culture, Art, and Religion, Law, Science, and Literature. Questions like these occurred: "Draw and label a picture of the Doric Order of Architecture. Include: Capital, Shaft, Triglyph, Fluting, Pediment, Metope, Stylobate, Cornice, Architrave, Frieze" (p. 7). "Name three principles of music that make it a finished art" (p. 7). In a battery of matching questions, *Iliad* seemed the best answer for "A great conflict occurred at a city near straits which are strategically located today" (p. 12).
43. Eureka College, Humanities 107: Syllabus, Term II, 1939-40.
44. College of St. Scholastica, Bulletin, 1939-40, p. 67.
45. Dominican College of San Rafael, Catalogue, 1938-39, p. 66.
46. Patricia Beesley, *The Revival of the Humanities in American Education,* p. 12.
47. Julian L. Ross, "What Should the Freshman Read?" *English Journal,* College Edition, XXV (November, 1936), 749-52.
48. Wilfred Payne, Professor of Philosophy and Chairman of Humanities, University of Omaha; personal letter, March 4, 1942.
49. Municipal University of Omaha, Humanities 101-102: Syllabus, First and Second Semester, 1936-37, p. 1.
50. *Ibid.,* p. 2.
51. *Ibid.,* p. 1.
52. St. Cloud State Teachers College, Catalogue, 1940, p. 54.

53. *Ibid.*, p. 54.
54. Florida State College for Women, Supplementary material, Humanities 103, Second Semester, 1939-40.
55. Queens College, English 1: Syllabus, 1940, p. 1.
56. Queens College, Music Appreciation, "Program Music: The Symphonic Poem:" Syllabus, p. 2.
57. *Ibid.*, p. 2.
58. Queens College, Music Appreciation, "Music and the Romantic Movement:" Syllabus, p. 5.
59. Pasadena Junior College, "Humanities Survey:" Syllabus, p. 1.
60. *Ibid.*
61. University of Minnesota, Report on Problems and Progress of the General College, June, 1938, p. 70. See also Bulletin of the College of Education, 1940-41.
62. *Ibid.*, p. 7.
63. University of Minnesota, "An Effective General College Curriculum as Revealed by Examination," a Report of the Committee on Educational Research, p. 173.
64. E. C. Hassold, "The Louisville Survey of the Humanities," a statement prepared for Miss Beesley by Professor Hassold, December, 1939.
65. *Ibid.*
66. University of Louisville, Survey of the Humanities: Syllabus, p. 1.
67. Hassold, letter, May 16, 1940.
68. Hassold, "Survey of the Humanities, 1932-42," p. 3.
69. Hassold, letter, March 6, 1942.
70. George Williams College, Bulletin, 1940, p. 22.
71. Dorothy S. Bucks, letter, March 10, 1942.
72. University of Georgia, Bulletin, 1938, p. 114.
73. Georgia School of Technology, Bulletin, 1941-42, p. 124.
74. A. J. Walker, Georgia School of Technology, letter, March 9, 1942.
75. Menlo Junior College, Catalogue, 1939-40, p. 42.
76. *Ibid.*, p. 42.
77. Jacques Barzun, "The Two-Year Course in the Humanities: The First Year;" in Columbia College Education, The Plan of the First Two Years, p. 27.
78. Columbia College, Catalogue, 1940-41, p. 87.
79. Barzun, *op. cit.*, pp. 27-28.
80. *Ibid.*, p. 28.
81. *Ibid.*, p. 31.
82. Douglas Moore, "The Two Year Course in the Humanities: The

Second Year;" in Columbia College Education, The Plan of the First Two Years, p. 34.
83. F. E. Ward, E. H. Booth, and Grace J. L. May, *Earning our Heritage,* an Introduction to the Humanities and the Language Arts, Vol. I, Introduction, p. iii. In 1937 the central materials of the Macalester College course were published, under the direction of Professor Ward, in the form of this text.
84. *Ibid.,* p. iii.
85. *Ibid.*
86. Norman F. Coleman, Macalester College, letter, March 7, 1942.
87. Robert W. Talley, University of Houston, letter, March 17, 1942.
88. Frank H. Fowler, Melvin T. Solve, Mathew M. R. Schneck, University of Arizona, General Course in the Humanities: Syllabus, 1937, p. 17.
89. *Ibid.*
90. Melvin T. Solve, University of Arizona, letter, March 14, 1942.
91. Don A. Keister, University of Akron, letter, March 6, 1942.
92. Princeton University, Catalogue, 1941-42, p. 170.
93. *Ibid.,* p. 173.
94. *Ibid.,* p. 148.
95. Rollins College, Catalogue, 1940-41, p. 70.
96. University of Pittsburg, Bulletin, 1940-41, p. 54.
97. University of Wisconsin, Bulletin, 1940-42, p. 67.
98. Adelphi College, Catalogue, 1940-41, p. 84.
99. Scripps College, Catalogue, 1938, pp. 28-29.
100. *Ibid.,* p. 27.
101. University of Chicago, "Introductory General Course in the Humanities:" Syllabus, 7th edition, 1937, p. ix.
102. *Ibid.,* p. viii.
103. *Ibid.,* p. x.
104. *Ibid.,* 9th edition, 1939, p. xiv.
105. *Ibid.*
106. *Ibid.,* p. xv.
107. *Ibid.,* p. xvi.
108. B. Lamar Johnson, *What About Survey Courses?* pp. 301-10.
109. Colorado State College of Education, Report to the Committee on Evaluation, Spring, 1941, p. 2.
110. Colorado State College of Education, Catalogue, 1942-43, p. 86.
111. Illinois Wesleyan University, Catalogue, 1942-43, p. 56.
112. Ralph E. Browns, Chairman of Humanities Survey, letter, March 6, 1942.

113. Chicago City Junior Colleges, "Definitions and Objectives in the Humanities Course," p. 1. We should note at this point a similarity of point of view with the Humanities General Course at the University of Chicago, and the fact that numerous lecturers in the Chicago Junior College courses have been from the staff of the University of Chicago.
114. Chicago City Junior Colleges, "Humanities Survey": Syllabus, September, 1938, p. 8.
115. Dorothy Weil, Director of Humanities, Woodrow Wilson Junior College, personal letter, June 7, 1940.
116. Chicago City Junior Colleges, Comprehensive Examination, Humanities 201-202, June, 1937, and June, 1938.
117. These critical approaches are instanced by such comments as these: Concerning *Paradise Regained*—"The poem, however, holds our interest because of its revelation of the poet himself and the changes it shows in his spirit." (Syllabus, p. 60); concerning *Faust*—It is the "autobiography of Goethe's mind and soul" (p. 86); concerning *Moby Dick*—This novel is one "of the greatest adventure stories of all times" (p. 110); "Accused of being an out-and-out romancer, Melville decided to deserve this charge, and published *Mardi* (1849); *White Jacket* (1850) is another autobiographical narrative" (p. 109).
118. Chicago City Junior Colleges, "Humanities Survey," Syllabus, 1938, p. 111.
119. Dorothy Weil, Woodrow Wilson Junior College, Chicago, letter, March 16, 1942.
120. Hendrix College, Catalogue, 1940-41, p. 29.
121. Robert Campbell, Hendrix College, letter, March 20, 1942.
122. Stanford University, "History of Western Civilization": Syllabus, Winter Quarter, 1938-39, p. 10.
123. Stanford University, "History of Western Civilization": Syllabus, Spring Quarter, 1938-39, p. 34.
124. Max Savelle, Stanford University, letter, April 18, 1942.
125. Stanford University, "Stanford Goes Humanist," *Time,* March 23, 1942, p. 60.
126. Stanford University, "The School of Humanities," by Lewis Mumford, p. 11.
127. *Ibid.,* p. 11.
128. *Ibid.,* p. 11.
129. *Ibid.,* p. 12.

NOTES TO PAGES 187–96 285

130. Oklahoma Agricultural and Mechanical College, Humanities 214, Western Culture, Outline, First Semester, 1939-40, pp. 1-3.
131. Oklahoma Agricultural and Mechanical College, Humanities 214, 224, and English 221; Final Examination, May 29, 1940.
132. M. D. Clubb, Professor of English, Oklahoma Agricultural and Mechanical College, letter, May 13, 1940.
133. University of West Virginia, Humanities General Course, Syllabus, Second Edition, 1938, pp. 102-3.
134. Claude C. Spiker, University of West Virginia, letter, March 31, 1942.
135. Judson College, Catalogue, 1941-42, p. 40.
136. Elsie F. Brickett, Judson College, letter, April 10, 1942.
137. University of Minnesota, College of Science, Literature and The Arts, Bulletin, 1940-41, pp. 18-19.
138. University of Newark, College of Arts and Sciences, Bulletin, 1941-42, pp. 38-39.
139. Cooper Union for the Advancement of Science and Art, Day and Night courses, 1941-42, pp. 80-82.
140. Knox College, Catalogue, 1942-43, p. 80.

PART IV

1. Colorado State College of Education, Report to the Committee on Evaluation, Spring, 1941, p. 2. (*Storm* was added in 1942.)
2. Critical analyses of symbols of other culture epochs comprise a sequel volume, dealing with the cultural origins of contemporary world views.
3. G. Wilson Knight, *The Shakespearean Tempest*, p. 11.
4. *Ibid.*, p. 1.
5. *Ibid.*, p. 11.
6. *Ibid.*
7. *Ibid.*, pp. 15-16.
8. *Ibid.*, p. 16.
9. Knight, *The Imperial Theme*, p. 29.
10. Knight, *The Wheel of Fire*, p. 34.
11. Knight, *The Imperial Theme*, p. 104.
12. *Ibid.*, p. 122.
13. *Ibid.*, p. 29.
14. Knight, *The Shakespearean Tempest*, p. 179.
15. *Ibid.*, p. 178.

16. *Ibid.*, p. 179.
17. John Dover Wilson, *What Happens in Hamlet*, p. 26.
18. Wilson, *Hamlet, Introduction*, p. xlvii.
19. Wilson, *What Happens in Hamlet*, p. 43.
20. *Ibid.*, p. 44.
21. *Ibid.*, p. 202.
22. London *Times*, Literary Supplement, October 10, 1935, p. 617, quoted from *The Book Review Digest*.
23. Mark Van Doren, "What Happens in Shakespeare," *The Nation*, cxli (November 27, 1935), 627-28.
24. Wilson, *What Happens in Hamlet*, p. 290.
25. John W. Draper, *The Hamlet of Shakespeare's Audience*, p. 11.
26. *Ibid.*, p. 232.
27. *Ibid.*, p. 229.
28. *Ibid.*, p. 228.
29. *Ibid.*, p. 237.
30. *Ibid.*, p. 240.
31. Barzun, "Hamlet's Politics," *Saturday Review of Literature*, xxi (April 13, 1940), 6-7.
32. *Ibid.*, p. 200.
33. *Ibid.*, p. 205.
34. *Ibid.*, p. 243.
35. Ethel Seaton, *Literary Relations of England and Scandinavia in the Seventeenth Century*, p. 51.
36. E. K. Chambers, *The Elizabethan Stage*, IV, 332.
37. Don Cameron Allen, "The Degeneration of Man and Renaissance Pessimism." *Studies in Philology* University of North Carolina Press, XXXV, No. 2 (April, 1938), p. 211.
38. *Ibid.*, p. 203.
39. *Ibid.*, p. 213.
40. *Ibid.*, p. 212.
41. *Ibid.*, p. 205.
42. *Ibid.*, p. 208.
43. *Ibid.*, pp. 225-26.
44. The text used in the following commentary is: *Hamlet*, Edited for the Syndics of the Cambridge University Press by John Dover Wilson, Cambridge University Press, Second Edition, 1936.
45. Wilson suggests the assurance of conflict between Claudius and Hamlet in this word. *Ibid.*, p. 3.
46. *Ibid.*, note 65, p. 150.
47. Dover Wilson's reading. Most editions give "solid." It is signifi-

cant to note that the collotype facsimile copy of the Devonshire edition of the second quarto, edited by O. J. Campbell in 1938, shows the spelling "sallied."

CONCLUSION

1. Alfred North Whitehead, *Science and the Modern World*, p. 110.
2. Carl Van Doren, *The American Novel, 1789-1939*, p. 357.
3. John Crowe Ranson, "The Esthetics of Regionalism," in *Literary Opinion in America*, edited by Morton D. Zabel, p. 107.
4. Sergei Eisenstein, *The Film Sense, passim*.
5. Robert D. Feild, *The Art of Walt Disney*, pp. 281-84.
6. Lewis Mumford, *Faith for Living*, p. 283.
7. Maxwell Anderson, Rhys Carpenter, and Roy Harris, *The Bases of Artistic Creation*, pp. 17-18.

BIBLIOGRAPHY

Abercrombie, Lascelles. The Theory of Poetry. New York, Harcourt, Brace, 1926.
Adamic, Louis. Two Way Passage. New York, Harper, 1941.
Adelphi College. Catalogue, 1940-41.
Adler, Mortimer J. Dialectic. New York, Harcourt, Brace, 1937.
—— Art and Prudence. New York, Longmans, Green, 1937.
—— "Tradition and Communication". Reprinted from the Proceedings of the American Catholic Philosophical Association, Thirteenth Annual Meeting, December 29 and 30, 1937.
—— What Man has Made of Man. A Study of the Consequences of Platonism and Positivism in Psychology; with an introduction by Dr. Franz Alexander. New York, Longmans, Green, 1937.
—— St. Thomas and the Gentiles. Aquinas Lecture for 1938 before the Aristotelian Society of Marquette University.
—— "The Crisis in Contemporary Education," *Social Frontier*, Vol. V, No. 42, February, 1939.
—— How to Read a Book. New York, Simon and Schuster, 1940.
Aeuer, J. A. C. F. Humanism States Its Case. Boston, Beacon Press, 1933.
Akron, University of. Don A. Keister, letter, March 6, 1942.
Alabama College for Women. History of Civilization: Syllabus and Reading Lists, 1938-39. History 101, Comprehensive Examination, January, 1939. Mimeographed.
—— Lorraine Peter, letters, May 15, 1940, and March 12, 1942.
Alden, Raymond Macdonald. Shakespeare. New York, Duffield, 1922.
Alexander, Franz. "Psychoanalysis and Social Disorganization," *American Journal of Sociology*, XLII (May, 1937), 781-813.
Alexander, Samuel, Beauty and Other Forms of Value. London, Macmillan, 1933.
Allegheny College. Julian L. Ross, "What Should the Freshman Read?" *English Journal*, College Edition, XXV (November, 1936), 749-52.
Allen, Don Cameron. "The Degeneration of Man and Renaissance Pessimism," *Studies in Philology*, University of North Carolina Press, Vol. XXXV, No. 2, April, 1938.
Allport, Gordon W. Personality: a Psychological Interpretation. New York, Henry Holt, 1937.

American Council on Education. Youth and the Future; a General Report of the American Youth Commission. American Council on Education, Washington, D. C., 1942.
—— Youth Work Programs. Prepared for The American Youth Commission by Lewis L. Lorwin, American Council on Education, Washington, D. C., 1941.
American Philosophical Society. Symposium on Recent Advances in Psychology. Philadelphia, 1941.
Ames, Van Meter. Aesthetics of the Novel. Chicago, University of Chicago Press, 1928.
Anderson, Maxwell, Rhys Carpenter, and Roy Harris. The Bases of Artistic Creation. New Brunswick, N. J., Rutgers University Press, 1942.
Anshen, Ruth. Science and Man, 24 original essays, with an introduction and conclusion by Ruth Nanda Anshen. New York, Harcourt, Brace, 1942.
Antioch College, Aesthetics 103-104 and Creative Aesthetics: Syllabus, 1937-38. Mimeographed.
—— Raymond S. Stites, *The Arts and Man,* New York, McGraw-Hill, 1940.
—— Raymond S. Stites, letter, March 9, 1942.
Aquinas, Thomas. "Summa Theologica." Part I. Literally translated by Fathers of the English Dominican Province. First Number (Q. Q. 1.-XXVI) London, R. and T. Washbourne, 1911.
Aristotle. The Basic Works of Aristotle. Edited and with an Introduction by Richard McKeon. New York, Random House, 1941.
Arizona, University of. General Course in the Humanities: Syllabus, edited by F. H. Fowler, M. T. Solve, and M. M. R. Schneck. Fifth Edition. Ann Arbor, Edwards Brothers, 1937. Photolithographed.
—— Melvin T. Solve, letter, March 14, 1942.
Arnold, Matthew. Discourses in America. New York, Macmillan, 1902.
—— Essays in Criticism. New York, Macmillan, 1902.

Babbitt, Irving. The New Laokoon. New York, Houghton Mifflin, 1910.
—— Rousseau and Romanticism. New York, Houghton Mifflin, 1930.
—— "Genius and Taste," In *Criticism in America—Its Function and Status.* New York, Harcourt, Brace, 1924.
—— "English and the Discipline of Ideas," *English Journal,* IX (February, 1920), 61-70.
Baldwin, Charles Sears. Renaissance Literary Theory and Practice.

Edited with Introduction by Donald Lemen Clark. New York, Columbia University Press, 1939.

Barzun, Jacques. "The Humanities—Proper Study of Mankind," *English Journal,* College Edition, October, 1938, pp. 637-48.

—— Of Human Freedom. Boston, Little, Brown, 1939.

—— "Scientific Humanism," *Nation,* CXLVIII, (April 29, 1939), 502-3.

—— "Hamlet's Politics," *Saturday Review of Literature,* XXI, (April 13, 1940), 6-7.

—— "The American as Critic," *Saturday Review of Literature,* XXVIII, (December 7, 1940), 30.

—— Darwin, Marx, Wagner, Critique of a Heritage. Boston, Little, Brown, 1941.

—— "The Nature of Race Thinking," excerpts from *Race: a Study in Modern Superstition*; in *When Peoples Meet* (1942) edited by Alain Locke and Bernhard Stern for The Progressive Education Association.

Barrett, W. C. "Reading and the Liberal Arts," *Kenyon Review,* Winter 1941.

Baudouin, Charles. Psychoanalysis and Aesthetics. Tr. from the French by Eden and Cedar Paul. London, Allen, 1924.

Beesley, Patricia. The Revival of the Humanities in American Education. New York, Columbia University Press, 1940.

Bell, Clive. Art. New York, Stokes, 1913.

Benedict, Ruth. "Myth," *Encyclopaedia of Social Sciences,* Vol. XI, 1933.

—— "Anthropology and the Abnormal," *Journal of General Psychology,* X (January, 1934), 59-82.

—— Patterns of Culture. Boston, Houghton Mifflin, 1934.

—— "Anthropology and Cultural Change," *American Scholar,* XI (Spring, 1942), 243-48.

—— "Some Comparative Data on Culture and Personality with Reference to the Promotion of Mental Health," *Mental Health,* American Association for the Advancement of Science, Publication No. 9, pp. 245-49.

Beneš, Eduard. Democracy Today and Tomorrow. New York, Macmillan, 1939.

Bergson, Henri. Creative Evolution. New York, Henry Holt, 1911.

—— Laughter; an Essay on the Meaning of the Comic. Authorized Translation by Cloudesley Brereton and Fred Rothwell. New York, Macmillan, 1914.

Bews, J. W. Human Ecology. London, Oxford University Press, Humphrey Milford, 1935.

Birkhoff, George D. Aesthetic Measure. Cambridge, Mass., Harvard University Press, 1933.
—— "The Present Status of Aesthetic Measure," *Scientific Monthly,* XLVI (April, 1938), 351-57.
Blackmur, Richard P. The Double Agent; Essays in Craft and Elucidation. New York, Arrow Editions, 1935.
Blinkenberg, Chr. The Thunderweapon in Religion and Folklore; a Study in Comparative Archeology. Cambridge, Cambridge University Press, 1911.
Boas, Franz. "Introduction to Handbook of American Indian Languages," Smithsonian Institute, Bureau of American Ethnology, Bulletin 40, Two Volumes. Washington, D. C., 1911-12.
—— "The Methods of Anthropology," *American Anthropologist,* XXII, (1920) 311-21.
—— "Stylistic Aspects of Primitive Literature," *Journal of American Folk-Lore Society,* XXXVIII (1923), 329-40.
—— Primitive Art. Oslo, Norway, 1927.
—— Anthropology and Modern Life. New York, Norton, 1928.
—— "Anthropology," *Encyclopaedia of Social Sciences,* II, 90.
—— The Mind of Primitive Man. New York, Macmillan, 1938.
—— General Anthropology. Boston, Heath, 1938.
—— Race, Language and Culture. New York, Macmillan, 1940.
—— "Language and Culture," Studies in the History of Culture, Published for the Conference of Secretaries of the American Council of Learned Societies. Menasha, Wis., 1942.
Boas, George. A Primer for Critics. Baltimore, Johns Hopkins Press, 1937.
—— "Habit, Fact, and Value," *Journal of Philosophy,* XXXVI, No. 19 (September 14, 1939), 526-30.
Bosanquet, Bernard. A History of Aesthetics. New York, Macmillan, 1910.
Boston University. Bulletin, 1941-42.
Bovet, Ernest. Lyrisme, épopée, drame, une loi de l'histoire littéraire expliquée par l'évolution générale. Paris, Libraire Armand Colin, 1911.
Bowman, James C. Contemporary American Criticism. New York, Henry Holt, 1926.
Boynton, Percy H. The Challenge of Modern Criticism. Chicago, Rockwell, 1931.
Bradley, Andrew Cecil. Oxford Lectures on Poetry. London, Macmillan, 1911.

―― Poetry for Poetry's Sake. Oxford, Clarendon Press, 1901.
―― Shakespearean Tragedy. Lectures on Hamlet, Othello, King Lear, Macbeth. London, Macmillan, 1932.
Bridges, Robert. The Testament of Beauty. New York, Oxford University Press, 1930.
Brooks, Van Wyck. "The Critics and Young America," In *Criticism in America—Its Function and Status*. New York, Harcourt, Brace, 1924.
Bryson, Lyman. Adult Education. New York, American Book Company, 1936.
―― "Readable Books for the People," *Publishers Weekly*, CXXXV (February 18, 1939), 778-79.
―― editor. Science, Philosophy and Religion. New York, Conference on Science, Philosophy and Religion, 1942.
Buchanan, Scott. "A Crisis in Liberal Education." Reprinted from *Amherst Graduates' Quarterly*, February, 1938.
Buck, Philo M. Literary Criticism; a Study of Values in Literature. New York, Harper, 1930.
―― "Science, Literature, and the Hunting of the Snark," *English Journal*, XXXI (October, 1942), 579-86.
Bucknell University, Bulletin, Catalogue Issue, 1940-41.
―― William H. Coleman, letter, March 20, 1942.
Bullough, Edward. "Psychical Distance," *British Journal of Psychology*, V, (1912), 87-118.
―― "The Relation of Aesthetics to Psychology," *British Journal of Psychology*, X (1919-20), 580-91.
Burdell, Edwin Sharp. "Scientific Humanism," *School and Society*, XLVIII (November, 1938), 611-20.
Burgum, Edwin Berry. The New Criticism. New York, Prentice-Hall, 1930.
Burgess, J. H., Introduction to the History of Philosophy. McGraw-Hill, 1937.
Burke, Kenneth. Permanence and Change; an Anatomy of Purpose. New York, New Republic, 1936.
―― The Philosophy of Literary Form; Studies in Symbolic Action. Baton Rouge, La., Louisiana State University Press, 1941.
―― "Freud—and the Analysis of Poetry," *American Journal of Sociology*, XLV (November, 1939), 391-417.
Bush, W. T. "Concerning the Concept of Pattern," *Journal of Philosophy*, XXXVII, No. 5 (February 29, 1940), 113-34.

Callahan, Leonard. A Theory of Esthetic According to the Principles of St. Thomas Aquinas. Washington, D. C., Catholic University of America, 1927.

Campbell, Oscar James, Editor. Shakespeare's Hamlet, The Second Quarto, 1604. Reproduced in facsimile from the copy in the Huntington Library, San Marino, California, 1938.

—— Louise Rosenblatt and Howard Mumford Jones. "The Aims of the Teaching of Literature" Committee of Twenty-Four. *English Journal, College Edition,* April, 1939.

Canby, Henry Seidel. Definitions; Essays in Contemporary Criticism. New York, Harcourt, Brace, 1922.

Carlyle, Thomas. Critical and Miscellaneous Essays. In *The Complete Works of Thomas Carlyle,* Vol. III. Boston, Colonial Press, 1869.

—— Heroes and Hero-Worship. Chicago, McClurg, 1891.

Carr, Harvey A. Psychology; a Study of Mental Activity. New York, Longmans, Green, 1925.

Carritt, E. F. The Theory of Beauty. 2d edition. London, Methuen, 1923.

—— What is Beauty? A First Introduction to the Subject and to Modern Theories. Oxford, Clarendon Press, 1932.

Cazamion, Louis. Aims and Methods of Higher Literary Criticism. Rice Institute Pamphlet, XVI (January, 1929), 1-45.

—— Criticism in the Making. New York, Macmillan, 1929.

Chadwick, H. Munro and N. Kershaw Chadwick. The Growth of Literature. Vols. I, II, III. New York, Macmillan, 1932-40.

Chambers, E. K. The Elizabethan Stage. Oxford, Clarendon Press, 1923.

Chandler, Albert R. Beauty and Human Nature; Elements of Psychological Aesthetics. New York, Appleton-Century, 1934.

Chesterton, G. K. St. Thomas Aquinas. London, Hodder, and Stoughton, 1933.

Chicago City Junior Colleges. Humanities Survey 201-202: Syllabus, edited by Dorothy Weil and others. Chicago, 1938.

—— Dorothy Weil, letters, June 7, 1940, and March 16, 1942.

—— Humanities 201-202: Comprehensive Examination. June, 1937; June, 1938.

Chicago, University of. Introductory General Course in the Humanities: Syllabus, edited by Hayward Keniston, Ferdinand Schevill, and Arthur P. Scott. Seventh Edition, 1937; Ninth Edition, September, 1939. Photolithographed.

—— Arthur P. Scott, letters, May 15, 1940, and July 12, 1940.

Clark, Cumberland. Shakespeare and the Supernatural. London, Williams and Norgate, 1931.
Clark, J. A. "Confusion Among the Critics," *Sewanee Review,* XXXIX (January, 1931), 1-12.
Closs, Hannah P. Art and Life. Oxford, B. Blackwell, 1936.
Coghill, G. E. Anatomy and the Problem of Behavior. New York, Macmillan, 1929.
Cohen, Joseph W. "Aspects of the Relations between Philosophy and Literature." In University of Colorado Studies, Series B, Studies in the Humanities, I, No. 2, 117-68. Boulder, Colorado, June, 1940.
Cohen, Morris R. Reason and Nature; an Essay on the Meaning of Scientific Method. New York, Harcourt, Brace, 1931.
―― and Ernest Nagel. An Introduction to Logic and Scientific Method. New York, Harcourt, Brace, 1934.
Coleman, W. H. "Background of the Humanities," *English Journal,* College Edition, Vol. XXV, May, 1936.
Coleridge, Samuel Taylor. Biographia Literaria, or Biographical Sketches of My Literary Life and Opinions. Prepared for publication in part by the late Henry Nelson Coleridge, completed and published by his widow. Vol. I. New York, American Book Exchange, 1881.
Colgate University. John F. Fitchen III, "A Challenge," *Journal of Higher Education,* VIII (March, 1937), 117-22; VIII (April, 1937), 194-200.
―― John F. Fitchen III, letters, May 13, 1940, and March 12, 1942.
Colorado State College of Education, Catalogue, 1942-43.
―― Report to the Committee on Evaluation, Spring, 1941.
Columbia College, Columbia University. Catalogue, 1940-41.
―― Jacques Barzun, "The Two-Year Course in the Humanities: The First Year" in Columbia College Education, The Plan of the First Two Years.
―― Douglas Moore, "The Two-Year Course in the Humanities: The Second Year" in Columbia College Education, The Plan of the First Two Years.
Committee of Twenty-Four, "Aims of the Teaching of Literature," *English Journal,* College Edition, April, 1939, pp. 261-67.
Cook, Albert S. The Art of Poetry; the Poetical Treatises of Horace, Vida, and Boileau. New York, Stechert, 1926.
Cooper Union for the Advancement of Science and Art, Day and Night Courses, 1941-42.
Corwin, Norman. We Hold These Truths; a Dramatic Celebration of the American Bill of Rights. New York, Howell, Soskin, 1942.

—— Thirteen Radio Dramas, with a Preface by Carl Van Doren. New York, Henry Holt, 1942.
—— Samson, a complete radio drama. *Theatre Arts*, September, 1942, pp. 547-64.
Craig, Hardin. The Enchanted Glass. New York, Oxford University Press, 1936.
Crane, Ronald S. "History or Criticism in the University Study of Literature," *English Journal*, College Edition, XXIV (1935), 645-67.
Croce, Benedetto, The Essence of Aesthetic. Tr. Douglas Ainslie. London, William Heinemann, 1921.
Cross, E. A. World Literature. New York, American Book Company, 1935.
Curtis, Winterton. "The Spirit of the Humanities and the Spirit of Science." In *Washington University Studies*, XII (April, 1925), 153-69.

Daniels, P. C. "Discrimination of Compositional Balance at the Pre-School Level." In *Studies in Psychology of Art*, Norman Meier, editor. *Psychological Monograph*, XLV, No. 1, 1-11.
Dashiell, John Frederick. "Some Rapprochements in Contemporary Psychology," Presidential address delivered before the *American Psychological Association*, Columbus, Ohio, September 9, 1938. *Psychological Bulletin*, XXXVI (January, 1939), 1-24.
Delacroix, Henri. Psychologie de l'art; essai sur l'activité artistique. Paris, Libraire Felix Alcan, 1927.
DeMille, George E. Literary Criticism in America. Toronto, Longmans, Green, 1931.
Deonna, W. L'Archéologie, son valeur, ses methods. Vol. I, Paris. Libraire Renouard, 1912. H. Laurens, éditeur.
—— L'Archéologie, son domaine, son but. Ernest Flammarion, éditeur. Paris, 1922.
Dewey, John. Reconstruction in Philosophy. New York, Henry Holt, 1920.
—— The Quest for Certainty: a Study of the Relation of Knowledge and Action. Gifford Lectures, 1929. New York, Minton, Balch, 1929.
—— "What Humanism Means to Me," *Thinker*, XI (June, 1930), 9-12.
—— Human Nature and Conduct; an Introduction to Social Psychology. New York, Modern Library, 1930.
—— Construction and Criticism. The First Davies Memorial Lecture, delivered February 25, 1930 for the Institute of Arts and Sciences. New York, Columbia University Press, 1930.

—— Philosophy and Civilization. New York, Minton, Balch, 1931.
—— "A Humanist Manifesto," *New Humanist,* Vol. VI, No. 3, May-June, 1933.
—— "Humanism and Naturalism," *A Cyclopedia of Education,* Vol. III.
—— A Common Faith. New Haven, Yale University Press, 1934.
—— Art as Experience. New York, Minton, Balch, 1934.
—— Logic, the Theory of Inquiry. New York, Henry Holt, 1938.
—— Freedom and Culture. New York, Putnam, 1939.
—— Intelligence in the Modern World, John Dewey's Philosophy. Edited, and with Introduction by Joseph Ratner. New York, Modern Library, 1939.
—— The Philosophy of John Dewey. The Library of Living Philosophers, Vol. I, Paul Arthur Schilpp, editor. Chicago, Northwestern University, 1939.
Dodsley, Robert. Old English Plays, Vol. I. W. Carew Hazlitt, editor. 4th edition. London, Reeves and Turner, 1874.
Dollard, John. Criteria for the Life History, with Analyses of Six Notable Documents. The Institute of Human Relations. New Haven, Yale University Press, 1935.
—— et al. Frustration and Aggression. Institute of Human Relations, New Haven, Yale University Press, 1939.
Dominican College of San Rafael. Catalogue, 1938-39.
—— Sister Catherine Marie, letter, June 15, 1940.
Donnelly, Francis P. Art Principles in Literature. New York, Macmillan, 1925.
Downey, June. Creative Imagination. New York, Harcourt, Brace, 1929.
Draper, John W. The Hamlet of Shakespeare's Audience. Durham, N. C. Duke University Press, 1938.
Dryden, John. Dryden, Essays on the Drama, edited with an introduction and notes by William Strunk, Jr. New York, Henry Holt, 1898.

Eastman, Max. Art and the Life of Action, with other essays. New York, Knopf, 1934.
—— The Enjoyment of Poetry. New York, Scribner, 1913.
Edman, Irwin. "After a Mozart Quartet," a sonnet, *Nation,* CXXXII (February 25, 1931), 217.
—— "Culture in a Democracy," *Saturday Review of Literature,* XII (June 29, 1935), 3-4.

—— "Man's Humanities to Man," *Saturday Review of Literature,* XX (September 2, 1939), 3-4.

—— Arts and the Man; a Short Introduction to Aesthetics. New York, Norton, 1939.

—— Fountainheads of Freedom; the Growth of the Democratic Idea. With the collaboration of Herbert W. Schneider. New York, Reynal and Hitchcock, 1941.

—— "No Blackout for the Arts," *New York Times Magazine,* April 19, 1942, pp. 12-13.

Einstein, Albert. The World as I See It. New York, Covici, Friede, 1934.

Eisenstein, Sergei. The Film Sense. New York, Harcourt, Brace, 1942.

Eshleman, Lloyd W. Moulders of Destiny, Renaissance Lives and Times. New York, Covici, Friede, 1938.

Eubank, E. E. The Concepts of Sociology. New York, Heath, 1932.

Eureka College. Humanities 107: Syllabus, Term II, 1939-40. Mimeographed.

—— Thomas E. Wiggins, letter, March 3, 1942.

Feild, Robert D. The Art of Walt Disney. New York, Macmillan, 1942.

Fletcher, Jefferson Butler. Literature of the Italian Renaissance. New York, Macmillan, 1934.

—— Dante. New York, Henry Holt, 1916.

Flexner, Abraham. The Burden of Humanism. Oxford, Clarendon Press, 1928.

Florida State College for Women. Humanities 103: Supplementary Material, Second Semester, 1939-40. Mimeographed.

Florida, University of. Comprehensive Course C-5, The Humanities: Syllabus, Second Preliminary Edition, August, 1937. Photolithographed.

—— James D. Glunt, letter, March 12, 1942.

Foerster, N. "Literary Scholarship and Criticism," *English Journal,* College Edition, XXV (March, 1936), 224-32.

Folsom, Joseph K. Social Psychology. New York, Harper, 1931.

Frank Lawrence K. "Society as Patient," *American Journal of Sociology,* XLII (November, 1936), 335-44.

Freis, Jacob. Shakespeare and Montaigne. London, Kegan Paul, 1884.

Freud, Sigmund. Introductory Lectures on Psycho-Analysis. Tr. by Joan Riviere, with a Preface by Ernest Jones. London, George Allen & Unwin, 1922.

―― Collected Papers. Published by Leonard and Virginia Woolf and the Institute of Psycho-Analysis. London, Hogarth Press, 1925.

―― A General Introduction to Psychoanalysis. Tr. by G. Stanley Hall. New York, Boni and Liveright, 1920.

―― Civilization and Its Discontents. Tr. by Joan Riviere. Published by Leonard and Virginia Woolf and the Institute of Psycho-Analysis. London, Hogarth Press, 1930.

―― New Introductory Lectures on Psychoanalysis. Tr. by W. J. H. Sprott. Published by Leonard and Virginia Woolf and the Institute of Psycho-Analysis. London, Hogarth Press, 1933.

―― Totem and Taboo: Resemblances between the Psychic Lives of Savages and Neurotics. Tr. with an introduction by A. A. Brill. New York, New Republic, 1927.

Fry, Roger. "The Artist and Psycho-Analysis." *Hogarth Essays,* 1924.

―― Transformations; Critical and Speculative Essays on Art. New York, Brentano, 1927.

―― Vision and Design. London, Chatto, 1929.

Funck-Brentano, Frantz. The Renaissance. London, Geoffrey Blex, Centenary Press, 1936.

Gardiner, Alan H. The Theory of Speech and Language. Oxford, Oxford University Press, 1932.

Gayley, Charles Mills and Fred Newton Scott. An Introduction to the Methods and Materials of Literary Criticism; the Bases in Aesthetics and Poetics. Boston, Ginn, 1899.

―― and Benjamin Putnam Kurtz. Methods and Materials of Literary Criticism; Lyric, Epic, and Allied Forms of Poetry. Boston, Ginn, 1920.

George Williams College. Bulletin, 1940.

―― Dorothy S. Bucks, letter, March 10, 1942.

Georgia, University of. Catalogue, 1940-41.

―― A. J. Walker, Georgia School of Technology, letter, March 9, 1942.

―― Institute of Technology. Catalogue, 1941-42.

Gideonse, Harry D. The Higher Learning in a Democracy. New York, Farrar & Rinehart, 1937.

Goldenweiser, Alexander A. "Spirit, Mana, and the Religious Thrill," *Journal of Philosophy, Psychology and Scientific Method,* XII (November 11, 1915), 632-40.

―― "Culture and Environment," *American Journal of Sociology,* XXI (March, 1916), 628-33.

―― Early Civilization; an Introduction to Anthropology. New York, Knopf, 1922.
―― History, Psychology and Culture. New York, Knopf, 1933.
Goldsmith, Elizabeth E. Life Symbols. New York, Putnam, 1928.
Greene, Theodore Meyer, editor. The Meaning of the Humanities. Five Essays by Ralph Barton Perry, August Charles Krey, Erwin Panofsky, Robert Lowry Calhoun, Gilbert Chinard. Princeton, Princeton University Press, 1938.
―― The Arts and the Art of Criticism. Princeton, Princeton University Press, 1940.
―― "In Praise of Reflective Commitment," *American Scholar*, XI (Winter, 1941-42), 59-68.
Grey, Lennox. "The English Teacher Faces the Humanities," *Teachers College Record*, XXIX (October, 1937), 31-50.
―― "Critical Methods in the Humanities," *Advanced School Digest*, Teachers College, Columbia University, March, 1940, pp. 77-80.
―― "The Revival of the Humanities in American Education," from a paper delivered in Cleveland, Ohio, March, 1939. Mimeographed.
Grippen, V. B. "Creative Artistic Imagination in Children." In *Studies in Psychology of Art*, Norman Meier, Editor. *Psychological Monograph*, XLV, No. 1.

Haldane, J. B. S. The Philosophy of Humanism and of Other Subjects. London, Murray, 1922.
―― "Science and Theology as Art Forms," In *Possible Worlds*, New York, Harper, 1928. Quoted from *The New Criticism*, E. B. Burgum, editor.
Hankins, F. H. An Introduction to the Study of Society. New York, Macmillan, 1935.
Hardman, David. What about Shakespeare? London, Nelson, 1938.
Harrison, Jane Ellen. Ancient Art and Ritual. New York, Henry Holt, 1913.
Hartmann, George W. "Value as the Unifying Concept of the Social Sciences," *Journal of Social Psychology*, X (November, 1939), 563-76.
Hays, Edna. College Entrance Requirements in English. New York, Bureau of Publications, Teachers College, Columbia University, 1936.
―― Comparative Literature and the Modern Humanities; a Study in History and Methods. Unpublished manuscript.
Hegel, G. W. F. The Introduction to Hegel's Philosophy of Fine Art. Translated by Bernard Bosanquet. London, Kegan Paul, 1905.

BIBLIOGRAPHY

——— The Philosophy of Fine Art. 4 vols. F. P. B. Osmaston. London, Bell, 1920.

Heidbreder, Edna. Seven Psychologies. New York, Century, 1933.

Hendrix College. Catalogue, 1940-41.

——— Robert Campbell, letter, March 20, 1942.

Herzog, George. Jabo Proverbs from Liberia. (Reprint of Introduction.) Published for the International Institute of African Languages and Cultures. London, Oxford University Press, Humphrey Milford, 1936.

Hevner, Kate. "The Aesthetic Experience; a Psychological Description," *Psychological Review*, XLIV (1937), 245-63.

——— "Expression in Music; a Discussion of Experimental Studies and Theories," *Psychological Review*, XLVII (1935), 186-204.

Hirn, Yrjo. The Origins of Art. New York, Macmillan, 1900.

Hocking, William E. The Lasting Elements of Individualism. New Haven, Yale University Press, 1937.

——— Living Religions and a World Faith. New York, Macmillan, 1940.

——— "What Man Can Make of Man," *Fortune*, February, 1942.

Hogben, Launcelot. Retreat from Reason, with notes by Isabel S. Sterns. New York, Random House, 1937.

——— "The Creed of the Scientific Humanist," *Nation*, CXLVII (November 12, 1938), 506-9.

Hollingworth, H. L. The Psychology of Thought. New York, Appleton, 1927.

Horner, Harry. "Designing for the Screen," *Theatre Arts*, XXV (November, 1941), 794-98.

Horney, Karen. The Neurotic Personality of Our Time. New York, Norton, 1937.

Houston, University of. Catalogue, 1940-41.

——— Robert W. Talley, letter, March 17, 1942.

——— W. W. Kemmerer, letter, March 9, 1942.

Hume, David. *A Treatise of Human Nature*. Oxford, Clarendon Press, 1838.

Hutchins, Robert Maynard. The Higher Learning in America. New Haven, Yale University Press, 1936.

——— No Friendly Voice. Chicago, University of Chicago Press, 1936.

Illinois Wesleyan University. Catalogue, 1942-43.

——— Ralph E. Browns, letter, March 6, 1942.

Jaegar, Werner. Paideia, The Ideals of Greek Culture. Translated from the second German edition by Gilbert Highet. New York, Oxford University Press, 1939.

James, William. Varieties of Religious Experience. New York, Longmans, Green, 1903.

——— A Pluralistic Universe. New York, Longmans, Green, 1912.

——— The Will to Believe. New York, Longmans, Green, 1915.

——— The Principles of Psychology. New York, Henry Holt, 1918.

——— Pragmatism. New York, Longmans, Green, 1922.

——— Psychology; Briefer Course. New York, Henry Holt, 1928.

——— Essays in Radical Empiricism. New impression. New York, Longmans, Green, 1938.

Jeans, Sir James. The Stars in Their Courses. New York, Macmillan, 1931.

Jeffery, Violet M. John Lyly and the Italian Renaissance. Paris, Libraire Ancien Honoré Champion, 1928.

Jennings, H. S. Behavior of the Lower Organisms. New York, Columbia University Press, 1906.

——— Prometheus. New York, Dutton, 1925.

——— The Biological Basis of Human Nature. New York, Norton, 1930.

Jespersen, Otto. Language; Its Nature, Development and Origin. London, G. Allen & Unwin, 1925.

——— Mankind, Nation, and Individual from a Linguistic Point of View. Cambridge, Mass., Harvard University Press, 1925.

——— "Language," *Encyclopaedia Britannica,* 14th edition, XIII, 696-703.

Joachim, H. H. "'Absolute' and 'Relative' Truth," *Mind,* Vol. XIV, No. 53, January, 1905.

Johns Hopkins University. Frederic C. Lane, "Why Begin at the Beginning?" Reprinted from Proceedings of the Middle States Association of History and Social Science Teachers, Vol. XXXV, 1937.

——— Robert P. Griffing, Jr., letter, June 19, 1940.

Johnson, B. Lamar. What about Survey Courses? New York, Henry Holt, 1937.

Johnson, Samuel. The Works of Samuel Johnson. A New Edition in Twelve Volumes, with an Essay on His Life and Genius by Arthur Murphy, Esq. Vol. VI. New York, William Durell, 1811.

Jones, Howard Mumford. "Humanities in General Education," *English Leaflet,* June, 1938.

Jones, Llewellyn. How to Criticize Books. New York, Norton, 1928.

Jonson, Ben. The Works of Ben Jonson, with a Biographical Memoir

by William Gifford. A new edition. London, Routledge, 1838.
Judson College. Catalogue, 1941-42.
—— Elsie F. Brickett, letter, April 10, 1942.
Jung, Carl Gustav. Contributions to Analytical Psychology. Translated by H. G. and Cary F. Baynes. New York, Harcourt, Brace, 1928.
—— The Integration of the Personality. Translated by Stanley Dell. New York, Farrar and Rinehart, 1939.

Kallen, Horace M., William James, and Henri Bergson; a Study in Contrasting Theories of Life. Chicago, University of Chicago Press, 1914.
Kant, Immanuel. Critique of Aesthetic Judgment. Translated by James Creed Meredith. Oxford, Clarendon Press 1911.
—— Critique of Practical Reason. Translated by T. K. Abbott. 6th edition. London, Longmans, Green, 1927.
—— Introduction to Logic, and His Essay on the Mistaken Subtlety of the Four Figures. Translated by Thomas Kingsmill Abbott. London, Longmans, Green, 1885.
—— "The Current Situation in Social Psychology," *Psychological Bulletin*, XXXVI, No. 5 (May, 1939), 307-60.
Kantor, J. R. "An Analysis of Psychological Language Data," *Psychological Review*, XXIX (1922), 267-309.
Kaulfers, Walter V. "Our Creative Role as Teachers of the Language Arts," *Modern Language Journal*, XXV (February, 1941), 368-74.
—— Modern Language for Modern Schools. New York, McGraw-Hill, 1942.
—— and Holland D. Roberts. A Cultural Basis for the Language Arts; an Approach to a Unified Program in the English and Foreign Language Curriculum. Stanford University, Calif., Stanford University Press, 1937.
Keith, Sir Arthur. The Place of Prejudice in Modern Civilization. New York, John Day, 1931.
Keyser, Cassius Jackson. Humanism and Science. New York, Columbia University Press, 1931.
Kirkwood, Kenneth P. Renaissance in Japan; a Cultural Survey of the Seventeenth Century. Tokyo, Meiji Press, 1938.
Kitto, H. D. F. Greek Tragedy; a Literary Study. London, Methuen, 1939.
Knight, E. H. "Some Aesthetic Theories of Mr. Richards," *Mind*, 1927, pp. 69-70.

Knight, G. Wilson, The Wheel of Fire. London, Oxford University Press, 1930.
—— The Imperial Theme. London, Oxford University Press, 1931.
—— The Shakespearean Tempest. London, Oxford University Press, 1932.
—— The Principles of Shakespearean Production, with especial reference to the Tragedies. London, Faber and Faber, 1936.
Knox College. Bulletin, 1942-43.
Koffka, Kurt. The Growth of the Mind. Translated by Robert Morris Ogden. London, Kegan Paul, 1924.
—— Principles of Gestalt Psychology. New York, Harcourt, Brace, 1935.
—— "The Art of the Actor as a Psychological Problem," *American Scholar*, XI (Summer, 1942), 318-26.
Kohler, Wolfgang. The Place of Value in a World of Facts. New York, Liveright Publishing Corporation, 1938.
—— The Mentality of Apes. Translated by E. Winter. New York, Harcourt, Brace, 1925.
—— "The Intelligence of Apes," *Journal of Genetic Psychology*, XXXII (1925), 674-90.
Kroeber, A. L. "Archeology," *Encyclopaedia of Social Sciences*, Vol. II.
Krutch, Joseph Wood. The Modern Temper. New York, Harcourt, Brace, 1929.
—— Experience and Art. New York, Smith and Haas, 1932.

Langfield, Herbert S. The Aesthetic Attitude. New York, Harcourt, Brace, 1920.
Lashley, K. S. "Mass Action in Cerebral Function," *Science*, LXXIII (1921), 245-54.
Lasswell, H. D. Psychopathology and Politics. Chicago, University of Chicago Press, 1930.
—— World Politics and Personal Insecurity. New York. Whittlesey House, McGraw-Hill, 1935.
—— "The Contribution of Freud's Insight Interview to the Social Sciences," American Journal of Sociology, XLV (November, 1939), 375-90.
Leake, Chauncey D. "Science Implies Freedom." In *Studies in the History of Culture*. Published for the Secretaries of the American Council of Learned Societies. Menasha, Wis., George Banta Publishing Company, 1942.

Lee, Otis. "Instrumentalism and Action," *Journal of Philosophy,* XXXVII, No. 3 (February 1, 1940), 57-75.
Lee, Vernon. The Beautiful; an Introduction to Psychological Aesthetics. Cambridge, Cambridge University Press, 1913.
Legge, James, tr. The Life and Works of Mencius. Philadelphia, Lippincott, 1875.
Lepley, Ray. "The Transposability of Facts and Values," *Journal of Philosophy,* XXXVI, No. 11 (May 25, 1939), 281-90.
Lerner, Max, and Edwin Mims, Jr. "Literature," *Encyclopaedia of Social Sciences,* X, 523-41.
Letourneau, Charles. L'Évolution littéraire dans les diverses races humaines. Paris, Vigot Frères, éditeurs, 1894.
Lewin, Kurt. A Dynamic Theory of Personality. Translated by Donald K. Adams and Karl E. Zener. New York, McGraw-Hill, 1935.
—— "Field Theory and Experiment in Social Psychology: Concepts and Methods," *American Journal of Sociology,* XLIV (May, 1939), 868-95.
Lewisohn, Ludwig. A Modern Book of Criticism. New York, Modern Library, 1919.
—— The Drama and the Stage. New York, Harcourt, Brace, 1922.
—— Expression in America. New York, Harper, 1932.
—— Modern Drama. New York, Huebsch, 1915.
Linton, Ralph. The Study of Man. New York, Appleton-Century, 1936.
—— "The Present Status of Anthropology," *Science,* March 18, 1938, pp. 241-48.
Lipps, Theodor. Psychological Studies. Psychology Classics, Vol. II. Translated by Herbert C. Sanborn. Baltimore, Williams & Wilkins, 1926.
Longinus, Cassius. Longinus, on the Sublime. The Greek text edited after the Paris manuscript, with introduction, translation, facsimiles, and appendices, by W. Rhys Roberts. Cambridge, Cambridge University Press, 1899.
Louisville, University of. "Survey of the Humanities." Syllabus.
—— "The Louisville Survey of the Humanities," a statement prepared for Patricia Beesley by E. C. Hassold, December, 1939.
—— "Survey of the Humanities, 1932-42." Prepared by E. C. Hassold.
—— E. C. Hassold, letters, May 16, 1940, and March 6, 1942.
Löwenfeld, Viktor. The Nature of Creative Activity. New York, Harcourt, Brace, 1939.
Lowes, John Livingston. Convention and Revolt in Poetry. Boston, Houghton Mifflin, 1931.

Lowie, Robert H. Primitive Religion. New York, Boni and Liveright, 1924.
—— An Introduction to Cultural Anthropology. New York, Farrar and Rinehart, 1934.
—— Cultural Anthropology: A Science, *American Journal of Sociology,* XLII (November, 1936), 301-20.
Ludovici, Anthony M. The Secret of Laughter. New York, Viking Press, 1933.
Lynd, Robert. "Biographical Element in Criticism," *London Mercury,* VII (February, 1923), 399-408.

Macalester College. F. E. Ward, E. H. Booth, and Grace J. L. May. *Earning Our Heritage,* Two vols. Harcourt, Brace, New York, 1937.
—— Norman F. Coleman, letter, March 7, 1942.
McDougall, William. An Introduction to Social Psychology. Boston, Luce, 1918.
Macintosh, Douglas C. "Responsibility, Freedom, and Causality," *Journal of Philosophy,* XXXVII, No. 2 (January 18, 1940), 42-51.
Mackenzie, A. S. Evolution of Literature. New York, Crowell, 1911.
Maier, Norman R. F., and H. Willard Reninger. A Psychological Approach to Literary Criticism. New York, Appleton, 1933.
Malinowski, Bronislaw. "Culture," *Encyclopaedia of Social Sciences,* IV, 621-45.
—— "The Group and the Individual in Functional Analysis," *American Journal of Sociology,* XLIV (May, 1939), 938-64.
Mann, Thomas. "Coming Humanism," *The Nation,* CXLVII, 617-19.
Marett, R. R. Anthropology and the Classics. Oxford, Clarendon Press, 1908.
—— Psychology and Folklore. London, Methuen, 1920.
—— "Anthropology," *Encyclopaedia Britannica,* 14th edition, II, 44-45.
Maritain, Jacques. Art and Scholasticism. New York, Scribner, 1930.
—— "Christian Humanism; a Catholic Interpretation of a Well-Equipped, Rational Society, with a Heroic Philosophy and Divine Inspiration," *Fortune,* XXV (April, 1942), 106 ff.
Markey, John F. The Symbolic Process and Its Integration in Children. London, Kegan Paul, 1928.
Marshall, Henry Rutgers. Pain, Pleasure and Aesthetics; an Essay Concerning the Psychology of Pain and Pleasure, with Special Reference to Aesthetics. London, Macmillan, 1894.
—— "The Relation of Aesthetics to Psychology and Philosophy," *Philosophical Review,* XIV (1905), 1-20.

Mead, George H. Mind, Self and Society. Edited, with Introduction, by Charles W. Morris. Chicago, University of Chicago Press, 1934.
—— The Philosophy of the Act. Edited, with Introduction by Charles W. Morris, in collaboration with John M. Brewster, Albert M. Dunham, and David L. Miller. Chicago, University of Chicago Press, 1938.
Mead, Margaret. Coming of Age in Samoa. New York, Morrow, 1928.
—— "The Comparative Study of Culture and the Purposive Cultivation of Democratic Values." In *Science, Philosophy and Religion*. Second Symposium. Conference on Science, Philosophy and Religion. New York, 1942.
Meier, Norman C. "Studies in the Psychology of Art," *Psychological Monograph*, Vol. XLV, No. 1.
—— Art in Human Affairs; an Introduction to the Psychology of Art. New York, Whittlesey House, McGraw-Hill, 1942.
Mencken, H. L. "Criticism of Criticism of Criticism." In *Criticism in America—Its Function and Status*. New York, Harcourt, Brace, 1924.
—— The American Language. New York, Knopf, 1937.
Menlo Junior College. Catalogue, 1939-40.
Mercier, Louis. The Challenge of Humanism. New York, Oxford University Press, 1933.
Mill, John Stuart. Dissertations and Discussions. New York, Dutton, 1905.
—— A System of Logic, Ratiocinative and Inductive. 8th edition. 2 vols. London, Longmans, Green, 1872.
Minnesota, University of. Report on the Problems and Progress of the General College. Prepared by the Staff of the General College, Minneapolis, Minnesota, June, 1938. Mimeographed.
—— "An Effective General College Curriculum as Revealed by Examination," a report of the Committee on Educational Research of the University of Minnesota. Mimeographed.
—— College of Science, Literature, and the Arts. Bulletin, 1940-41.
Missouri Valley College. Catalogue, 1939-40.
—— Claude L. Fichthorn, letter, May 24, 1940.
Montague, W. P. The Ways of Things. New York, Prentice-Hall, 1940.
—— "Philosophy in a World at War," *Fortune*, Vol. XXV, No. 3, March, 1942.
Morgan, C. Lloyd. Emergent Evolution. London, Williams and Norgate, 1923.
Morris, Charles W. Foundations of the Theory of Signs. *International*

Encyclopedia of Unified Science, Vol. I, No. 2. Chicago, University of Chicago Press, 1938.

Mullet, Hendrik Clemens. Lectures on the Science of Literature. Haarlem, V. Loojes, 1904.

Muller, H. J. "Pathways in Recent Criticism," *Southern Review,* Vol. I, 1938.

Müller-Freinfels, Richard. Psychologie der Kunst; eine Darstellung der Grundzüge. Vol. I, II. Leipzig, Teubner, 1912.

—— Psychologie der Kunst, Vol. III. Munchen, Ernst Reinhardt, 1933.

Mumford, Lewis. Aesthetics, a Dialogue. Troutbeck Leaflets, No. 3, Amenia, N. Y., privately printed at the Troutbeck Press, 1925.

—— Herman Melville. New York, Harcourt, Brace, 1929.

—— Technics and Civilization. New York, Harcourt, Brace, 1934.

—— The Culture of Cities. New York, Harcourt, Brace, 1938.

—— Men Must Act. New York, Harcourt, Brace, 1939.

—— Faith for Living. New York, Harcourt, Brace, 1940.

Münsterberg, Hugo. Psychology and Life. New York, Riverside Press, 1899.

—— The Principles of Art Education. New York, Prang Educational Co., 1905.

Murchison, Carl A. Social Psychology; the Psychology of Political Domination. Worcester, Mass., Clark University Press, 1929.

—— editor. Psychologies of 1930. By Alfred Adler, Madison Bentley, Edwin G. Boring, and others. Worcester, Mass., Clark University Press, 1930.

Mursell, J. L. The Psychology of Music. New York, Norton, 1937.

National Council of Teachers of English. The Teaching of College English. Oscar James Campbell, editor. English Monograph No. 3. New York, Appleton-Century, 1934.

—— An Experience Curriculum in English. W. Wilbur Hatfield, editor. English Monograph No. 4. New York, Appleton-Century, 1935.

—— A Correlated Curriculum. Ruth Mary Weeks, editor. English Monograph No. 5. New York, Appleton-Century, 1936.

New Jersey State Teachers College at Montclair. H. G. Gayley, letter, June 1, 1940.

Nicoll, Allardyce. The Theory of Drama. London, Harrap, 1931.

—— Masks, Mimes and Miracles. London, Harrap, 1931.

Nietzsche, Friedrich. The Birth of Tragedy; or Hellenism and Pessimism. Translated by William A. Haussmann. In *The Complete*

Works of Friedrich Nietzsche, Ed. Oscar Levy. Vol. III. Edinburgh. T. N. Foulis, 1910.
—— The Will to Power; an Attempted Transvaluation of all Values. Translated by Anthony M. Ludovici. Vols. I and II. London, George Allen and Unwin, 1924.
Nitchie, Elizabeth. The Criticism of Literature. New York, Macmillan, 1928.
Nobbs, Perry E. Design. London, Oxford University Press, 1937.
Northwest Missouri State Teachers College. General Catalogue, 1940-41.
—— Blanche H. Dow, letter, April 9, 1942.

Odum, Howard W., and Harry Estill Moore. American Regionalism: A Cultural-Historical Approach to National Integration. New York, Henry Holt, 1938.
Ogden, Robert M. The Psychology of Art. New York, Scribner, 1938.
Oklahoma Agricultural and Mechanical College. Humanities 214, Western Culture, Outline, First Semester, 1939-40.
—— Humanities 214-224, and English 221: Final Examination. May, 1940.
—— M. D. Clubb, letters, May 13, 1940, and March 5, 1942.
—— Hans H. Andersen, letter, March 5, 1942.
Omaha, Municipal University of. Humanities 101-102: Syllabus, First and Second Semester, 1936-37. Mimeographed.
—— Wilfred Payne, letter, March 4, 1942.
Osborn, Frederick. "To What Extent is a Science of Man Possible?" *Scientific Monthly,* November, 1939, pp. 452-59.
Osgood, Charles Grosvenor. The Voice of England. New York, Harper, 1935.
Osler, Sir William. The Old Humanities and the New Science. London, Murray, 1919.
Otto, Max Carl. The Human Enterprise. New York, Crofts, 1940.
Overstreet, H. A. Our Free Minds. New York, Norton, 1941.

Parker, De Witt Henry. The Principles of Aesthetics. Boston, Silver, Burdett, 1920.
—— The Analysis of Art. New Haven, Yale University Press, 1926.
Parkhurst, Helen Huss. Beauty. New York, Harcourt, Brace, 1930.
Pasadena Junior College. Introduction to the Humanities. Syllabus. Mimeographed.
Perry, Ralph Barton. A General Theory of Value. New York, Longmans, Green, 1926.

Phelan, Gerald B. "The Concept of Beauty in St. Thomas Aquinas." In *Aspects of the New Scholastic Philosophy*. Charles A. Hart, editor. New York, Benziger Brothers, 1932, pp. 121-46.

—— Saint Thomas and Analogy. The Aquinas Lecture, 1941, under the auspices of the Aristotelian Society of Marquette University. Milwaukee, Marquette University Press, 1941.

Picard, Maurice. "Intrinsic Value and Intrinsic Good." *Journal of Philosophy*, XXXVI, No. 10 (May 11, 1939), 253-63.

Pinto, V. De Sola. The English Renaissance, 1510-1688. New York, McBride, 1938.

Pittsburgh, University of. Bulletin, 1940.

Prince, Morton. Problems of Personality; Studies Presented to Dr. Morton Prince, Pioneer in American Psychopathology. Board of Editors: C. MacFie Campbell, H. S. Langfeld, Wm. McDougall, A. A. Roback, E. W. Taylor. New York, Harcourt, Brace, 1925.

Princeton University. Catalogue. 1941-42.

Plant, James S. Personality and the Cultural Pattern. New York, Commonwealth Fund, 1937.

Plato. The Dialogues of Plato. Translated into English by B. Jowett. New York, Random House, 1937.

—— Dialogues, with an English Translation by R. G. Bury. Vol. VII. London, Heinemann, 1929.

Pollock, Thomas Clark. The Nature of Literature, Its Relation to Science, Language, and Human Experience. Princeton, Princeton University Press, 1942.

Pope, Alexander. The Works of Alexander Pope, Esq. In six volumes complete. With his last corrections and additions and improvements; together with all his notes, as they were delivered to the editor a little before his Death: Printed verbatim from the Octavo Edition of Mr. Warburton. London, 1788.

Posnett, Hutcheson Macaulay. Comparative Literature. International Scientific Series. New York. Appleton, 1886.

Potter, C. F. Humanism, a New Religion. New York, Simon and Schuster, 1930.

Prall, David W. Aesthetic Judgment. New York, Crowell, 1929.

Progressive Education Association. Life and Growth, by Alice Keliher. Progressive Education Association, Commission on Human Relations. New York, Appleton-Century, 1938.

—— Literature as Exploration, by Louise Rosenblatt. Progressive Education Association, Commission on Human Relations. New York, Appleton-Century, 1938.

—— Reader's Guide to Prose Fiction, by Elbert Lenrow. Progressive Education Association, Commission on Secondary School Curriculum. New York, Appleton-Century, 1940.

—— "Democratic Education," Suggestions for Education and National Defense by the Progressive Education Association. Washington, D. C., American Council on Public Affairs, 1940.

—— Language in General Education. A Report of the Committee on the Function of English in General Education for the Commission on Secondary School Curriculum. Louis Zahner, editor. New York, Appleton-Century, 1940.

—— When Peoples Meet; a Study in Race and Culture Contacts. Alain Locke and Bernhard J. Stern, editors. Committee on Workshops. New York, 1942.

—— "The Contribution of Education to Democracy." Progressive Education Association Booklet No. 3.

—— "John Dewey as Educator." Progressive Education Association Pamphlet containing two essays: "The Educational Philosophy of John Dewey," by John L. Childs, and "Dewey's Influence on Education," by William H. Kilpatrick. New York, 1942.

Pound, Louise. Poetic Origins and the Ballad: The Ballad and the Dance. Publication of Modern Language Association, September, 1919.

Powicke, F. M. The Christian Life in the Middle Ages. Oxford, Clarendon Press, 1935.

Puffer, Ethel D. The Psychology of Beauty. New York, Houghton Mifflin, 1905.

Queens College. English I: Syllabus. 1940. Typewritten.

—— Music Appreciation: "Music and the Romantic Movement": Syllabus. Mimeographed.

—— Music Appreciation, "Program Music: The Symphonic Poem": Syllabus. Mimeographed.

—— Edwin J. Stringham, letter, March 26, 1942.

—— Emory Holloway, letters, May 15, 1940, and March 6, 1942.

Rader, Melvin M. A Modern Book of Aesthetics. New York, Henry Holt, 1935.

Randall, J. H. Religion and the Modern World. New York, Stokes, 1929.

—— The Making of the Modern Mind; a Survey of the Intellectual Background of the Present Age. Boston, Houghton Mifflin, 1940.

Rank, Otto. Art and Artist; Creative Urge and Personality Development. New York, Knopf, 1932.
Ransom, John Crowe, "The Esthetics of Regionalism." In Literary Opinion in America. Morton D. Zabel, editor.
Ratner, Sidney. "Patterns of Culture in History," *Philosophy of Science*, Vol. VI (January, 1939).
―― "The Historian's Approach to Psychology," *Journal of the History of Ideas*, Vol. II, No. 1 (January, 1941).
Rattray, R. S. Religion and Art in Ashanti. Oxford, Clarendon Press, 1930.
Read, Herbert. The Meaning of Art. London, Faber and Faber, 1931.
―― Surrealism. London, Faber and Faber, 1936.
―― Art and Society. New York, Macmillan, 1937.
Reed College. Bulletin, January, 1941.
―― General Literature 11, and History of Civilization 11: Syllabi, 1936-37. Mimeographed.
Reichard, Gladys A. "Form and Interpretation in American Art." Reprinted from Proceedings of the Twenty-third International Congress of Americanists. September, 1928.
―― "The Style of Coeur D'Alêne Mythology." Sonderabdruck aus den Verhandlungen des XXIV Internationalen Amerikanisten-Kongresses Hamburg. 7 bis 13. September, 1930. (Reprint).
Reid, John R. A Theory of Value. New York, Scribner, 1938.
Reiser, Oliver L. Philosophy and the Concepts of Modern Science. New York, Macmillan, 1935.
Richards, I. A., C. K. Ogden, and James Woods. Foundations of Aesthetics. London, G. Allen & Unwin, 1922.
Richards, I. A. "Science and Poetry," *Atlantic Monthly*, Vol. CXXXVI, (October, 1925).
―― Practical Criticism; a Study of Literary Judgment. New York, Harcourt, Brace, 1929.
―― Mencius on the Mind; Experiments in Multiple Definition. International Library of Psychology, Philosophy, and Scientific Method. New York, Harcourt, Brace, 1932.
―― Coleridge on Imagination. London, Kegan Paul, 1934.
―― Principles of Literary Criticism. New York, Harcourt, Brace, 1934.
―― "What is Belief?" *Nation*, CXXXIX (July 18, 1934), 71-74.
―― "Our Lost Leaders," *Saturday Review of Literature*, IX (April 1, 1933), 510.

——— and C. K. Ogden. The Meaning of Meaning. New York, Harcourt, Brace, 1936.
——— Interpretation in Teaching. New York, Harcourt, Brace, 1938.
——— "The Interactions of Words." In *The Language of Poetry*, by Philip Wheelwright, Cleanth Brooks, I. A. Richards, and Wallace Stevens. Edited by Allen Tate. Princeton, Princeton University Press, 1942.
——— How To Read a Page. New York, Norton, 1942.
Ridley, M. R. Shakespeare's Plays; a Commentary. London, Dent, 1937.
Rogers, A. K. A Student's History of Philosophy. New York, Macmillan, 1907.
Rollins College. Catalogue, 1940-41.
Rusu, Liviu. Essai sur la création artistique comme révélation du sense de l'existence. Paris, Libraire Felix Alcan, 1935.

St. Cloud State Teachers College. Catalogue, 1940.
St. John's College. Catalogues, 1937-38, 1938-39, 1939-40.
St. Scholastica, College of. Bulletin, 1939-40.
Saintsbury, George. The Earlier Renaissance. New York, Scribner, 1901.
——— A History of Criticism. London, Blackwood, 1900-1904.
——— A History of English Criticism. London, Blackwood, 1911.
——— (Ed.) Loci Critici. Boston, Ginn, 1903.
Santayana, George. Character and Opinion in the United States. New York, Scribner, 1920.
——— The Life of Reason: Reason in Art. New York, Scribner, 1905.
——— The Sense of Beauty. New York, Scribner, 1896.
Sapir, Edward. "History and Varieties of Human Speech," *Popular Science Monthly*, LXXIX (1911), 45-67.
——— "Language and Environment," *American Anthropologist*, XIV (1912), 226-42.
——— "Time Perspective in Aboriginal American Culture; a Study in Method," Canada Department of Mines, Geological Survey, Memoir 90, No. 13, Anthropological Series. Ottawa, Government Printing Bureau, 1916.
——— Language. New York, Harcourt, Brace, 1921.
——— "Sound Patterns in Language," *Language*. I (1925), 37-51.
——— "Language as a Form of Human Behavior," *English Journal*, XVI (1927), 421-33.
——— "A Study in Phonetic Symbolism," *Journal of Experimental Psychology*, XII (1929), 225-39.

―― "Language," *Encyclopaedia of the Social Sciences,* IX, 155-68.
―― "The Contribution of Psychiatry to an Understanding of Behavior in Society," *American Journal of Sociology,* XLII (May, 1937), 862-70.
Sarton, George. Introduction to the History of Science. Published for the Carnegie Institution of Washington. Baltimore, Williams and Wilkins, 1927.
―― The History of Science and the New Humanism. Cambridge, Mass., Harvard University Press, 1937.
Schilder, Paul. Mind: Perception and Thought in Their Constructive Aspects. New York, Columbia University Press, 1942.
―― "The Sociological Implications of Neuroses," *Journal of Social Psychology,* XV (February, 1942), 3-21.
Schiller, F. C. S. Our Human Truths. New York, Columbia University Press, 1939.
Schilpp, Paul Arthur, editor. The Philosophy of John Dewey. Evanston and Chicago, Northwestern University, 1939.
Schneider, Elizabeth. Aesthetic Motive. New York, Macmillan, 1939.
Schneider, Herbert W. "A Note on Dewey's Theory of Valuation," *Journal of Philosophy,* XXXVI, No. 18 (August 31, 1939), 490-95.
Schopenhauer, Arthur. The World as Will and Idea. 3 vols. 7th edition. Translated by R. B. Haldane, and J. Kemp. Kegan Paul, London, 1907-09.
―― The Art of Controversy. Translated by T. B. Saunders. London, George Allen and Unwin, 1896.
―― The Art of Literature. Translated by T. B. Saunders, London, George Allen and Unwin, 1896.
Schütze, Martin. Academic Illusions. Chicago, University of Chicago Press, 1933.
―― "Toward a Modern Humanism." In *Publications of Modern Language Association,* LI (March, 1936), 284-99.
Scripps College. Catalogue, 1938.
Sears, Paul B. Deserts on the March. Norman, Okla., University of Oklahoma Press, 1935.
Seaton, Ethel. Literary Relations of England and Scandinavia in the Seventeenth Century. London, Oxford University Press, 1935.
Seligman, C. G. "Anthropological Perspective and Psychological Theory," *Publication of Royal Anthropological Institute of Great Britain and Ireland,* LXII (July-December, 1932), 193-228.
Shattuck, Marquis E. "Fundamentals in the Language Arts." In *Proceedings of National Education Association,* LXXIX (1941), 127-28.

BIBLIOGRAPHY

Sherif, Muzafer. The Psychology of Social Norms. New York, Harper, 1936.
Sherwood, Robert. There Shall Be No Night. New York, Scribner, 1940.
Shipley, Joseph Twadell. The Quest for Literature. New York, R. R. Smith, 1931.
Sidney, Philip. "An Apology for Poetry." In *English Belles-Lettres from A.D. 901 to 1834,* with special introduction and biographical notes by Oliver H. G. Leigh. London, M. Walter Dunne, 1901.
Smith, Bernard. Forces in American Criticism. New York, Harcourt, Brace, 1939.
Smith, Dora V. Instruction in English. Washington, U. S. Government Printing Office, 1933.
Smith, James H. The Great Critics; an Anthology of Literary Criticism. New York, Norton, 1932.
Smith, Thomas Vernon. Philosophers Speak for Themselves. Chicago, University of Chicago Press, 1934.
Spengler, Oswald. The Decline of the West. New York, Knopf, 1939.
Spingarn, J. E. A History of Literary Criticism in the Renaissance. New York, Columbia University Press, 1908.
—— Creative Criticism and Other Essays. New York, Harcourt, Brace, 1931.
Spinoza, Benedict de. Ethic. Translated by W. Hale White. London, Oxford University Press, 1927.
—— Improvement of the Understanding. Translated by R. M. H. Elwes. London, Dunne, 1901.
Stace, W. T. The Destiny of Western Man. New York, Reynal and Hitchcock, 1942.
Stanford University. History of Western Civilization: Syllabus. Stanford University Press, Autumn Quarter, 1935-36, 1938-39.
—— Max Savelle, letter, April 18, 1942.
—— "Stanford Goes Humanist," Lewis Mumford's address at the dedication of The Division of Humanities at Stanford. *Time,* March 23, 1942, p. 60.
—— "The School of Humanities," by Lewis Mumford, 1942.
Steinbeck, John, and Edward F. Ricketts. Sea of Cortez. New York, Viking, 1941.
Stephens College. Louise Dudley and Austin Faricy, *The Humanities.* McGraw-Hill, New York, 1940.
—— Louise Dudley, letter, March 10, 1942.

Stevens Institute of Technology. Catalogue, 1942.
Stoll, Elmer Edgar. Shakespeare Studies, Historical and Comparative in Method. New York, Macmillan, 1927.
Stone, Calvin P., Chester W. Darrow, Carney Landis, and Lena L. Heath. Studies in the Dynamics of Behavior. Edited by Karl S. Lashley. Chicago, University of Chicago Press, 1932.
Symons, Arthur. The Symbolist Movement in Literature. London, William Heinemann, 1899.

Taine, H. The Philosophy of Art. Translated and revised by John Durand. 2nd Edition. New York, Holt and Williams, 1873.
—— Lectures on Art, Translated by John Durand. New York, Henry Holt, 1875.
Talledega College. Catalogue, 1940.
Teeter, L. "Literary History and the Aesthetic Experience," *English Journal,* College Edition, XXV (November, 1936), 737-49.
Thomas, Charles Swain. "Amid the Carnage," *English Leaflet,* October, 1939.
Thomas, W. I. "The Comparative Study of Cultures," *American Journal of Sociology,* XLII, September, 1936.
Thomas of Erfurt. On the Modes of Signifying; a Speculative Grammar. Translated as one of the Classics for the St. John's Program by Charles Glenn Wallis. Ann Arbor, Edwards Brothers, 1938.
Thorburn, John M. Art and the Unconscious. London, Kegan Paul, 1925.
Thorndike, E. L. Your City. New York, Harcourt, Brace, 1939.
Tolman, Edward Chace. "Motivation, Learning and Adjustment," *Proceedings of the American Philosophical Society,* LXXXIV (June 30, 1941); 543-63.
Tolstoy, Leo. What is Art? Translated from the Russian by Charles Johnston. Philadelphia, H. Altemus, 1898.
Torossian, Aram. A Guide to Aesthetics. Stanford University, Calif., Stanford University Press, 1937.
Tracy, Henry Chester. Towards the Open; a Preface to Scientific Humanism . . . with an Introduction by Julian Huxley. New York, Dutton, 1927.

Urban, W. M. Fundamentals of Ethics. New York, Henry Holt, 1930.

Van Doren, Carl. The American Novel, 1789-1939. New York, Macmillan, 1940.

BIBLIOGRAPHY

Van Doren, Mark. "What Happens in Shakespeare?" *Nation*, CXLI (November 28, 1935), 627-28.
—— Shakespeare. New York, Henry Holt, 1939.
Van Tieghem, Paul. La Littérature comparée. Paris, Libraire Armand Colin, 1931.
Veblen, Thorstein. The Theory of the Leisure Class. New York, Viking Press, 1924.
Véron, Eugène. Aesthetics. Translated from the French by W. H. Armstrong. London, Chapman and Hall, 1879.
Vossler, Karl. The Spirit of Language in Civilization. London, Kegan Paul, 1929.

Warden, Carl J. The Emergence of Human Culture. New York, Macmillan, 1936.
Watson, J. B. Behaviorism. New York, Norton, 1930.
—— Psychology from the Standpoint of the Behaviorist. Third Revision. Philadelphia, Lippincott, 1929.
Wells, H. G. The Outline of History. New York, Macmillan, 1921.
—— The Science of Life. With Julian S. Huxley and G. P. Wells. Garden City, N. Y., Doubleday, Doran, 1931.
West Virginia, University of. Humanities General Course: Syllabus, Second Edition, 1938.
—— Claude C. Spiker, letter, March 31, 1942.
Wheeler, W. M. Emergent Evolution and the Development of Societies. New York, Norton, 1928.
Wheelwright, Philip. A Critical Introduction to Ethics. New York, Doubleday, Doran, 1935.
Whitehead, Alfred North. Science and the Modern World. Lowell Lectures, 1925.
—— Symbolism, Its Meaning and Effect. The Barbour-Page Lectures, University of Virginia, 1927. New York, Macmillan, 1927.
—— Adventures of Ideas. New York, Macmillan, 1933.
Woodberry, G. E. Heart of Man; a New Defense of Poetry; Two Phases of Literary Criticism, Historical and Aesthetic. New York, Macmillan, 1901.
—— "Journal of Comparative Literature," January-March, 1903, pp. 3-9.
—— "Two Phases of Criticism." In *Criticism in America—Its Function and Status*. New York, Harcourt, Brace, 1924.
Woodworth, Robert Sessions. Dynamic Psychology. New York, Columbia University Press, 1918.

Wilson, Edmund. Axel's Castle. New York, Scribner, 1931.
Wilson, John Dover. What Happens in Hamlet. New York, Macmillan, 1935.
—— London *Times,* Literary Supplement, October 10, 1935. Review of *What Happens in Hamlet.* Quoted from Book Review Digest.
—— Hamlet. Second Edition. Cambridge, Cambridge University Press, 1936.
Wisconsin, University of. Catalogue, 1940-42.
Wundt, Wilhelm. Lectures on Human and Animal Psychology. Translated from the second German edition by J. E. Creighton and E. B. Titchener. London, Swan Sonnenschein and Company, 1894.
—— The Facts of the Moral Life. Translated by Julia Gulliver and E. B. Titchener. London, Swan Sonnenschein and Company, 1897.

Young, Karl. The Drama of the Medieval Church. 2 vols. Oxford, Clarendon Press, 1933.
Young, Kimball. Personality and Problems of Adjustment. New York, Crofts, 1941.

Zabel, Morton D. Literary Opinion in America. New York, Harper, 1937.
Zilboorg, Gregory. "Changing Cultural Values." Round Table No. 9. *Free World,* August, 1942, pp. 236-51.
Zinsser, Hans. "What is a Liberal Education?" *School and Society,* XLV (June, 1937), 801-7.
Zweig, Stefan. Jeremiah; a Drama in Nine Scenes. New York, Viking Press, 1939.

INDEX

Acquired, phase of the unconscious, 48
Action, need for new patterns of, 251; Adler's concept of, 277
Adamic, Louis, 233
Adams, Henry, 68
Adelphi College, course in the Humanities, 179 f.
Adler, Mortimer J., 6, 9, 12, 123, 128, 130; reconciliation of faculty and clinical psychologies, 25, 27, 142; words as absolutes, 112; mixed background, 138; favors return to medieval liberal arts, 142-149, 150; aesthetics, 142 f.; concern with political and religious statesmanship, 142; functions of grammar, rhetoric, and logic, 144 f., 153, 276; three levels of reading, 147-49; primary concern with technique and structure, 148; unity of ideas with Hutchins, 149; anti-aesthetic, 276; emphasis on prudence, 276; concept of action, 277
——Works: *Art and Prudence*, 28, 142, 145, 147, 148; *Dialectic*, 150; *How to Read a Book*, 26, 27, 142, 145, 147-49, 150, 277; *St. Thomas and the Gentiles*, 145, 278; "Tradition and Communication," 144, 145
Aeschylus, use of Electra symbol, 193
Aesthetic Attitude, The (Langfield), experiments in perception, 42 f.
Aesthetic experience, through the arts, 3, 4, 7, 8, 13, 14, 18, 27 f., 35, 37, 38, 43-45, 47 ff., 69, 82 f., 86, 91, 93 f., 113, 114, 115, 121, 122, 125, 137, 156 ff., 235, 263; in modern Humanities, 3, 4, 6, 8, 11-73, 74 ff., 83 f., 228, 230; in literature, 3, 4, 7 f., 9, 11 ff., 19 ff., 43, 46, 74 ff., 81, 95, 155 ff., 192 ff., 228, 230, 235; in World Literature, 3, 7, 11-73, 81, 155 ff., 192 ff., 228, 230; in science, 3, 4, 91, 122; of the 1890's, 4, 7; modern ideas, 7; ideas from modern psychology, 7, 12, 24-56, 72, 74, 117, 118, 200, 263, 264, 265; and anthropology, 7, 12, 24, 32, 36, 45, 46, 56-73, 74, 117, 118, 200, 229, 263, 264, 265; view of spokesmen for the Humanities, 7-9, 74-154; The National Council of Teachers of English, 7, 74-84; Progressive Education Association, 8, 84-98; Committee of Twenty-four, 8, 98-104; individual writers on various aspects of the Humanities, 8, 104-37; T. M. Greene, 8, 104 ff.; Irwin Edman, 8, 105, 116-23; Jacques Barzun, 8, 123-29; I. A. Richards, 8, 129-37; advocates of return to medieval liberal arts, 9, 137-54; Hutchins, 9, 139-42; Adler, 9, 142-49; St. John's College, 9, 149-53; in critical process, 11, 19-24, 53-56, 90 f., 121; ideas from philosophy, 11-24, 72, 92, 122 f., 257; Dewey's position on, 11, 13, 19, 23, 86-92, 257; enlarging ideas of, in teachers of literature, 11, 74 ff.; value of, 13, 94, 95-97, 228; in perception of beauty, 14, 131; two primary sources of Western, 14; in language, 14, 15, 16, 17, 18, 20, 153; Müller-Freienfels' concept of, 26, 46, 47, 50, 51, 52, 53, 54, 55, 56; natural bases of creation, 47 f.; the creative process, 48-53; and culture, 56-73, 110; in other channels than art, 69; in self-realization, 69, 71, 72, 91; therapeutic quality, 77, 101; unifying force of ideas, 81-84, 230; in achievement of form, 89; similar to religious experience, 91, 122 f., 264; and philosophy of experience, 92; character-forming effect, 101; two broad complementary consequences, 101; a cumulative process, 104; five levels of experience, 105-10; of the reader, 113 f., 127, 135 f.; in Edman's poetic resolution, 117; and the formative impulse, 119, 120, 132, 264; relationship to philosophy, science, religion, and civilization, 122 f.; con-

Aesthetic experience (*Continued*) cern with political considerations, 137, 142; medieval-classical idea of, 142; spectacle as, 146; place of emotions, 146; degrees of emphasis on, in college courses, 155-91; *Hamlet* as example of approach to World Literature, 192-227, 230; in movies, 231
"Aesthetic Experience . . ., The" (Hevner), 44
Aesthetic Measure (Birkhoff), 45
Africa, function of proverbs in, 62
"Aims of the Teaching of Literature, The," analysis of, 98 ff.; Social Studies and Humanities evaluated, 98 f.; *Literature as Document*, 99 f.; *Literature as Delight*, 99, 100; *Literature as Imaginative Experience*, 99, 101
Akron, University of, Course in the Humanities, 177
Alabama College for Women, course in the Humanities, 165 f.; 281
Alain, M., 146; pseudonym of Jacques-Emile Chartier, 278
Alexander, Franz, on Adler, 27
Allegheny College, course in the Humanities, 167
Allen, Don Cameron, 202, 203
Allport, Gordon W., 40 f.
Alstedius, Renaissance humanist philosopher, 203
American Association for the Advancement of Science, concern for ethical direction to scientific advancement, 235
American Association of Teachers Colleges, represented in Curriculum Commission, 75
American Cause, The (MacLeish), 273
American Guide Series, 231
American Journal of Sociology, 56, 59
American literature, revaluation of sequences of "period" and "types" courses, 232
American Novel, The (Van Doren), 231
American University, Washington, D. C., 166
Analogy, Thomistic idea of, 275
Anderson, Maxwell, 233
Animals, similarity and difference between man and, 101
Anne of Denmark, 202

Anthropology, modern ideas of aesthetic experience, 7, 12, 24, 32, 36, 45, 46, 56-73, 74, 117, 118, 200, 229, 263, 264, 265; and language, 43, 57, 61-64, 76; perpetuation of the race, 46; physical anthropology, 57-60; symbolic role of words, 57; cultural anthropology, 60-73; individual as medium of all society, 61; and symbols of culture, 64-68; and values, 68-71; Nazi Germany legislates own, 70; overemphasis on historical reconstruction, 247
Anthropology and the Classics (Marett), 57
Antioch College, course in the Humanities, 159 f., 172
Antisocial emotions, redirection of, 96
Apollonian impulse in art, 18
Apology for Poetry, An (Sidney), 19
Appreciation, four levels of literary, 90
Archeology, purpose of, 247
Aristotle, 11, 12, 13, 20, 26, 27, 113, 143; development of the self, 14 f.; aesthetic, 20, 21; Aristotelian catharsis, 77, 96, 101, 145, 146; classification of, 128; reconciliation of values of, with Christianity, 138; *Politics*, 141; classical disciplines of, 141; Aristotelian criticism, 147; *Ethics*, 148; *Poetics*, 182; concept of perfection, 237
Arizona, University of, course in the Humanities, 176 f.
Arnold, Matthew, aesthetic criticism, 19, 23 f., 228; "Literature and Science," 23
Art, aesthetic experience through, 3, 4, 7, 8, 13, 14, 18, 27 f., 35, 37, 38, 43-45, 47 ff., 69, 82 f., 86, 91, 93 f., 113, 114, 115, 121, 122, 125, 137, 156 ff., 235, 263; fine arts, 4, 82 f.; philosophy and, 8, 92, 105, 109, 115, 118, 170 f., 263; harmonizing function, 8; Aristotelian and Platonic views, 14; Dionysian and Apollonian impulses, 18; modern ideas of, in psychology, 24-56, 125, 270; faculty psychology as a basis for, 25, 26-28; concept of, in dynamic psychology, 26, 37; concept in social psychology, 26, 38-41; in Gestalt and organismic psychology, 26, 41-46; in newer syntheses, 26, 46-56; theories of identification, detachment, and em-

pathy, 26, 35-37; Freudian concept, 29-35, 38; and culture, 36, 93 f., 99, 103, 112, 119, 124, 126, 135, 148, 230, 263, 265; natural bases of creation, 47 f.; the creative process, 48-53, 88; the critical process, 53-56, 115, 122; artist-reader relationship, 53, 114, 126 f., 147; ideas from anthropology, 56-73, 125, 270; physical anthropology, 57-60; origins of, 58, 111, 270; ideas from cultural anthropology, 60-73; values, 69, 156, 258, 259, 270; place in society, 71, 136, 171 ff., 250; self-realization of artist, 89, 112, 132, 133, 135, 228, 229; rhythms of activity, 89; achievement of form, 89; and philosophy of experience, 92; historico-philosophical synthesis, 105, 109, 115; artist's interaction with environment, 111, 119; as self-expression, 112; five levels of critical appraisal, 115; a symbol of civilization, 119, 250; artist's interpretations of experience, 119; as escape, 121; Edman's concept of criticism, 122; approaches realm of religion, 122; and democracy, 124, 269; Barzun's concept, 125 ff.; desire for organization and order, 125; artist challenged by inharmonious situation, 133; fits individual for greater responsibility in society, 136; medieval emphasis upon persuasion, 137; prudence in, 143, 144, 237; centrifugal force of, 143; creative artist a remote image of the divine, 143; as illusion rather than experience, 149; Humanities courses based on society and, 171-76; hedonistic, purposive, and expressive, 246; intention within work of, 263; sets its own standards, 269; statesman's concern with, 276; factor providing unity, 277; as part of the contemplative phase, 279
Art and Artist (Rank), 32
Art and Prudence (Adler), 28; statement on aesthetics, 142; political censorship of art, 145; classical-medieval idea of catharsis, 145; epic narrative, 147; the novel, 148
Art and Scholasticism (Maritain), 143
Art and Society (Read), 59
Art as Experience (Dewey), 8, 12, 70, 78, 91, 94, 228; analysis of, 86 ff.; stages of the creative process, 88; place of art in civilization, 250; process of recreating author's experience, 256; narrowing effects of literary types, 256; harmonization of conflicts, 274
Arts and Man, The (Stites), objectives in Antioch aesthetics course, 159 f.
Arts and the Art of Criticism, The (Greene), 8, 105, 127; relativistic organic creative-critical process, 110; supplementary essay on Beethoven's Third Symphony, 115
Arts and the Man (Edman), 8, 117 f.; concern with poetry, 120; unity of the psychophysical organism, 267
Astronomy, poetical science, 3
Athens, literature and culture, 67; concern for trivial values, 70
Atlantic Monthly, article on "Science and Poetry," 131
Atomistic awareness, experience level, 105
Author, delineation of character, 40
Authoritarianism, dictatorships and anthropology, 69; causes of, 72

Babbitt, Irving, New Humanist movement, 5
Bacon, Sir Francis, 20
Bailey, Temple, 126
Balance, natural preference for, 45
Barr, Stringfellow, 6, 9, 139, 150
Barzun, Jacques, 70, 131; hazards of amateur psychiatry, 104; humanistic historian, 123-29; naturalistic point of view, 123; concern with aesthetic experience, 124 ff.; concept of art, 124, 269, 270; relation of the arts to democratic culture, 124; communication between artist and reader, 126 f.; on American education, 128 f.; on Columbia Humanities course, 174 f.; pragmatic attitude in democracy, 251; on critical analysis, 269; origins and values of art, 270
——Works: *Darwin, Marx, Wagner*, 129; "Hamlet's Politics," 200, 270; "The Humanities—Proper Study of Mankind," 129; *Of Human Freedom*, 8, 31, 104, 123, 124 ff., 127-29, 251, 269

Bases of Artistic Creation, The (Anderson), 233
Baudouin, Charles, 31
Beard, Charles Austin, 57
Beautiful, The (Lee), 37
Beauty, highest perception of, 14; various senses of, 131; *see also* Aesthetic experience
Beesley, Patricia, 4, 154
Beethoven, Ludwig van, Third Symphony, 115
Behaviorism, 41; effect on ideas of aesthetic experience, 25, 28 f.
Being, five levels of, 105-10
Benedict, Ruth, 69
Beowulf, 66
Biographia Literaria (Coleridge), 22
Biological Basis of Human Nature, The (Jennings), 46
Biology, approach to aesthetics, 46; and creative abilities, 57-60; influences Dewey's philosophy, 86
Birkhoff, George D., 45
Birth of Tragedy, The (Nietzsche), 18
Birth trauma, prototype for creative activity, 31
Bishop, Merrill, Fine Arts course, 83
Boas, Franz, *Primitive Art*, 57, 66; *Race, Language, and Culture*, 57; language as symbol of culture, 65; "Stylistic Aspects of Primitive Literature," 66; anthropology's overemphasis on historical reconstruction, 247
Body, duality of mind and, 26
Boileau—Despreaux, Nicolas, 21
Books, *see* Great Books program
Boston University, course in the Humanities, 161
Bovet, Ernest, 113
Bradley, A. C., 44
British Journal of Psychology, article on "Psychical Distance," 36
Brooks, Van Wyck, 24
Buchanan, Scott, revival of the Humanities, 6, 9, 138, 139, 150
Bucknell University, course in the Humanities, 164
Bucks, Dorothy, 173
Bullough, Edward, 36
Burke, Kenneth, 11, 31, 39, 43, 54

Cabot, John, 201
Calhoun, Robert Lowry, 264 f.
Campbell, O. J., 78, 146, 194; edits *The Teaching of College English*, 75, 76, 77; "The Aims of the Teaching of Literature," 98; comparative method, 252
Campbell, Robert, on Humanities course at Hendrix College, 185
Carlyle, Thomas, aesthetic criticism, 19, 23
Castiglione, Baldassare, Count, 201
Catharsis, therapeutic function of literature, 77, 96, 102, 104; Aristotelian, 77, 96, 101, 145, 146; of reader's emotional tensions, 136; classical-medieval idea of, 145; purgation in art, 145, 146; Adler's concept, 146; Richards' concept, 274
Catholicism, Humanities courses in Catholic colleges, 166; England's break with, 201
Catholic Philosophical Association, Proceedings of the American, Adler's statement on nature of liberal arts, 144
Cayley, H. S., on the Humanities course at New Jersey State Teachers College, 157 f.
Censorship, Adler's view of, 145, 276
Cervantes Saavedra, Miguel de, 151
Chadwick, H. M. and N. K., *The Growth of Literature*, 57, 66
"Challenge, A" (Fitchen), Humanities course at Colgate, 158 f.
Chambers, E. K., 202
Chartier, Jacques-Emile, *see* Alain, M.
Chicago, University of, 192; Humanities General Course, 83, 84, 181, 284; Plan, 138, 140
Chicago City Junior Colleges, course in the Humanities, 184, 284
Chinard, Gilbert, 265
Christian IV, king of Denmark, 202
Christianity, reconciliation of Aristotelian values and, 138
Chronology, college Humanities courses which emphasize, 161-65
Civility, concept of, 262
Civilization, ethical and aesthetic bases of conduct, 82; relationship of aesthetic experience to, 122 f.; place of art, 250
Classics, widespread break with classi-

INDEX

cal education, 11; Hutchins, view of, 128, 141; and problems of modern society, 129
Coleman, Norman F., on Humanities course at Macalester College, 176
Coleridge, Samuel Taylor, 43; aesthetic criticism, 19, 22; *Biographia Literaria*, 22; influence on Richards' poetic theories, 136
Coleridge on Imagination (Richards), 131
Colgate University, course in the Humanities, 158 f.
College English, Teaching of, 75, 76-78, 96
Colleges and universities, Humanities courses, 4, 6, 9, 11 ff., 56, 57, 71, 73, 83, 155-91, 230; based on formal aesthetic principles, 156-61; emphasizing chronology, 161-66; emphasizing types of literature, 166-71; based on relationships of art and society, 171-76; based on intellectual history, 176-80, accenting social backgrounds and cultural epochs, 180-89; values, 189; unifying concepts, 189 f.; subject matter, 190 f.; imbalance of curricular offerings in past, 116; *see also names of institutions:* Chicago, University of; Columbia College, etc.
Colorado State College of Education, course in the Humanities, 182 f., 192 f., 201, 204, 227
Columbia College, Honors Course, 6; Colloquium, 116, 123; Humanities course, 128, 174 f., 178, 192, 270
Columbus, Christopher, 201
Commission on Human Relations, 271; preparation of film library for school use, 259
Commission on Secondary School Curriculum, 271
Committee of Tewnty-four, spokesmanship for Humanities, 8, 98-104; on theory of empathy, 37; recognizes therapeutic quality of aesthetic experience, 78; "The Aims of the Teaching of Literature," 98 ff.; use of "purged," 101, 102; doctrine of empathy, 102; use of "disciplined," 102; members and organization, 260
Comparative literature, 5, 7, 67; courses in, 252

Comparative Literature (Posnett), 66
Conceptual quality of words, 111
Conduct, ethical and aesthetic bases of, 82
Consciousness, attainment of, 87; level of conscious being, 106; not an aggregate of unrelated mental states, 110
Content, in art, 263
Contributions to Analytical Psychology (Jung), 33
Cooper Union, Humanities program, 188
Correlated Curriculum, A, 5, 8; analysis of, 75, 80-84; contents, 254
Correlation Theory of, 80
Corwin, Norman, 71
Courtier (Castiglione), 201
Creative process, 48-53, 88; Rank's concept, 31-33; phase of the unconscious, 48 f.; phase of inspiration, 49-51; of elaboration, 51 f.; image in, 51, 54, 88; phase of execution, 52 f.; and culture, 65; in *An Experience Curriculum*, 78; understanding the creative impulse, 82; creative values of literature, 102f.; creative and critical specialization, 108, 109, 110; self-fulfilling values of the, 127
Criticism, of arts and letters, 7; tradition of literary, 7, 11, 19-24; break with tradition of philosophical, 11; two primary sources of Western, 14; ideas from modern psychology, 24; psychoanalytic, 31; critical process, 53-56; finest type of, 90 f.; unifying strand for, 91; involves vicarious projection, 97; creative and critical specialization, 108, 109, 110; establishing *rapport* with the work of art, 114; five levels, 115; aesthetic experience of critic, 115; Edman's concept of, 122; philosophy a criticism of, 123; Barzun's concept of, 127; aesthetic, 149; critical-judgment level of reading, 149; recent trends in *Hamlet* scholarship, 194-201; need for reëxperiencing artist's state of mind, 255; theology similar to, 265; moralistic and legislative critics, 269
Critique of Aesthetic Judgment, The (Kant), development of self, 16
Croce, Benedetto, 11, 13, 52; *The Essence of Aesthetic*, 18; development of the self, 19; insight into creative process, 111

Cross, E. A., *World Literature*, 57, 182
Cultural naturalism, development of the self, 13
Culture, and art, 36, 93 f., 99, 103, 112, 119, 124, 126, 135, 148, 230, 263, 265; cycles of, 55, 100; symbols of, 56, 57, 64, 67, 94, 246; and aesthetic experience, 56-73, 110; and physical anthropology, 57-60; cultural anthropology, 60-73; connection with anthropology and language, 61-64, 72, 250; anthropology and symbols, of, 64-68; Greek civilization, 66, 67; literary types as symbols of, 67, 256; figures largely in creative expression, 78; values attained in completion of symbol of, 94; historico-philosophical synthesis, 105, 109, 115; constituents of culture pattern, 107; delight in color and line in primitive, 119; college Humanities courses emphasizing culture epochs and social backgrounds, 180-89; *Hamlet* a symbol of Elizabethan, 196 ff.; Elizabethan, 201-4; drama as symbol of urban, 246
Curiosity, role in creative process, 88
Curriculum, *A Correlated Curriculum*, 5, 8, 75, 80-84, 254; *An Experience Curriculum*, 5, 75, 78-80; *The Teaching of College English*, 75, 76-78, 96, 101; place of language in well-organized, 80; imbalance of curricular offerings in past, 116; Commission on Secondary School Curriculum, 271
Curriculum Commission, National Council of Teachers of English, 74-84

Dante Alighieri, 23, 137, 148, 149, 150, 151; 193
Darwin, Charles Robert, 60; art origins, 58
Darwin, Marx, Wagner (Barzun), 129
Dashiell, John Frederick, 46; concepts of heredity and environment, 244
Dekker, Thomas, conflict of values, 203
Delacroix, Henri, 26, 46, 244
Democracy, aesthetics of, 71; Progressive Education Association's view, 85; need for stressing enduring values, 98; sympathetic understanding of other people, 101; and the individual, 116; relation of the arts to, 124, 269; emphasis upon self, 232; cannot be limited to one people, 233; militant, 233; democratic method, 251; first and last task, 252; basis of, 269; techniques employed by enemies of, 273
"Democratic Education," Progressive Education Association pamphlet, 85
Denmark, relations with Elizabethan England, 202, 203
Descartes, René, 151
Descriptive literary treatment, 113
Destiny of Western Man, The (Stace), 233
Detachment, psychological theory of, 26, 35, 36
Dewey, John, 93, 131, 136; aesthetic, 11, 13, 19, 23, 257; social philosopher, 85, 86-92, 104; stages of the creative process, 88; idea of literary form, 89; art as self-expression, 112; influence on Edman, 116, 117, 121, 122; pragmatism of, 124; man and environment, 132; definition of humanism, 235; place of art in civilization, 250; on democratic method, 251; act of expression, 255; narrowing effect of literary types, 256; on philosophy and aesthetics, 257; use of term, "mind," 272; creative process, 272; harmonization of conflicts, 274; logic, 275
——Works: *Art as Experience*, 8, 12, 70, 78, 86 ff., 91, 94, 228, 250, 256, 274; *Freedom and Culture*, 70, 251; *Logic, A Theory of Inquiry*, 91
Dialectic, discipline acquired at St. John's College, 152
Dialectic (Adler), 150
Dictatorships and anthropology, 69
Diffusionist approach to anthropology, 60
Dionysian impulse in art, 18
"Disciplined," Committee of Twenty-four's use of, 102
Disciplines, of literature, 103, 258; Greene as spokesman for, 104-15; of language, 120; concept of relativistic, 130
Divine Comedy, The (Dante), 148, 149, 150, 193
Dollard, John, *Frustration and Aggression*, 39
Dollard, William A., study of Richards' contributions, 271

INDEX

Donne, John, 233
Drake, Sir Francis, 201
Drama, 113; evaluation of, 54, 55; in Greek literature, 66, 67; catharsis in tragedy, 77, 96, 101; compared with motion picture, 148; characteristic of urban society, 246, 256
Draper, John W., critical approach to Shakespeare, 194, 199 f., 204
Dryden, John, 11; aesthetic criticism, 19, 21
Duchesne College, 166
Dudley, Louise, Humanities course, 83; and Austin Faricy, *The Humanities*, 156-57, 185
Dynamic psychology, 26, 37
Dynamic Psychology (Woodworth), 37

Earning Our Heritage, 176
Economy of Effort, Law of, 42
Edman, Irwin, 68, 105, 116-23, 131; poetic resolution, 117; synthesis of art and philosophy, 118; arts as escapes, 121; aesthetic experience' relationship to philosophy, science, religion, and civilization, 122 f.; concept of criticism, 122; unity of the psychophysical organism, 267
——Works: "After a Mozart Quartet," 122; *Arts and the Man*, 8, 117 f., 120, 267; "Culture in a Democracy," 116; *Fountainheads of Freedom*, 116; "Man's Humanities to Man," 116
Education, Humanities courses, 4, 6, 9, 11 ff., 56, 57, 71, 73, 83, 155-91, 230; break with classical, 11; development of faith in scientific method, 93; historico-philosophical synthesis, 115; individual values emphasized, 116; relation of arts to democratic culture, 124; transmission of cultural ideas through critical teachers, 127; Barzun's attitude toward progressive, 128; province is to facilitate use of language, 130; advocates of a return to medieval liberal arts, 137-54; Hutchins, 139-42; Adler, 142-49; St. John's College, 149-53; colleges giving courses in World Literature and the Humanities, 155 ff.; function of learning, 262; *see also organizations*: National Council of Teachers of English; Progressive Education Association, etc.
Effort, Law of Economy of, 42
Ego, Jung's concept, 33; *see also* Self
Einfühlung, psychological theory, 26, 35
Einstein, Albert, aesthetic drive, 3; Eisenstein, Sergei, 231
Elaboration, phase in creative process, 51 f.
Electra, symbol of attitude toward life, 193
Elizabeth, queen of England, excommunication of, 201; Privy Council meetings, 205
Elizabethan culture, 201-4; *Hamlet* a symbol of, 196 ff.
Elizabethan Stage, The (Chambers), 202
Emotions, redirection and release of, 96; 104; controlled through meter, 134; concept of, in modern aesthetics, 146 f.; hierarchy of, 280
Emotive-conative quality of words, 112
Emotive function of language, 133
Empathy, theories of, 26, 35, 37, 102
Empirical philosophers, 17-19
Encyclopedia Britannica, The, article on anthropology, 57
Encyclopedia of Social Sciences, The, articles dealing with individual-social relationships, 56; cultural anthropology, 60; article on language, 63, 248; article on anthropology, 65
Energy, conservation of human, 132, 135
England, Elizabethan, 196 ff., 201-4; break with Roman Catholicism, 201; relations with Scandinavian countries, 202
English, Teaching of College, 75, 76-78, 96
English Journal, 125
English language, *see* Language
English literature, scope of, 5; aesthetic criticism, 11, 19-24; revaluation of sequences of "period" and "types" courses, 232
Environment, interaction of living organism with its, 87, 89; artist's interaction with his, 111; absolutist concept of, 244
Epic, evaluation of, 54 f.; in Greek literature, 66, 67; similar to history, 147

Epicurus, association with hedonism, 13
Erskine, John, Columbia Honors Course, 6, 138
Escape, value of, in aesthetic experience, 95; from reality, 103; arts as, 121
Essai sur la création artistique . . . (Rusu), aesthetic theory, 47-56; natural bases of artistic creation, 47 f.; creative process, 48 ff.
Essay of Dramatic Poesy, An (Dryden), 21
Essay on Criticism, An (Pope), 21
Essence of Aesthetic, The (Croce), 18
Essex, Carl of, 202
Ethic (Spinoza), 15
Ethics of thinking, 273
Ethnology, as an objective discipline, 247
Eubank, E. E., 71; development of human understanding, 64
Euclid, speculative rhetoric, 144; *Elements*, 152
Eugubinus, Renaissance, humanist philosopher, 203
Eureka College, Course in the Humanities, 166
Euripides, use of Electra symbol, 193
Evolutionary anthropology, 60
Execution, phase in creative process, 52 f.
Experience, in Dewey's social philosophy, 86 ff.; leading to work of art, 88; Greene's five levels, 105-10; intrinsic value, 118; artist's interpretation of, 119; man's awareness of, 132; conservation of energy applied to, 135; art as illusion rather than, 149; and intuitive knowledge, 156; nature of literary, 251
Experience Curriculum, An, 5; analysis of, 75, 78-80
Experimental Junior College, Fine Arts course, 83
Expression, act of, 255
Expression in America (Lewisohn), 24, 31
Expressive art, concept of, 246

Faculty psychology, as a basis for art, 25, 26-28, 29, 38, 142
Faith for Living (Mumford), 71, 232; importance of human values, 252
Faricy, Austin, *see* Dudley, Louise
Faust (Goethe), 40, 149, 193, 284; Goethe finds salvation for, 40

Fear, Aristotelian catharsis of, 101
Fechner, Gustav Theodor, measurement of sensation, 45
Fichthorn, Claude L., on Humanities course at Missouri Valley College, 163
Field, concept in Gestalt psychology, 43
Films, *see* Motion picture
Film Sense, The (Eisenstein), 231
Fine arts, aesthetic drive in, 4, 82 f.
Fitchen, John F., III, on the Humanities course at Colgate, 158 f.; "A Challenge," 158 f.
Fletcher, Jefferson Butler, comparative method, 252
Florida, University of, course in the Humanities, 160 f.
Florida State College for Women, course in the Humanities, 169
Folsom, Joseph K., 38
Form, and culture, 66; Dewey's definition of, 89; understanding subtleties of expressive, 100; Richards' concept of, 134; in art, 263
Formal aesthetic principles, in college courses in the Humanities, 156-61
Formative impulse, 119, 120, 132, 264
Foundations of Aesthetics (Richards), 131
"Foundations of the Theory of Signs" (Morris), 57
Fountainheads of Freedom (Edman), 116
Freedom, meaning of, 262
Freedom and Culture (Dewey), 70, 251
Freud, Sigmund, 27, 143; clinical psychology, 25, 29-35, 38, 39; *A General Introduction to Psychoanalysis*, 29; Freudian catharsis, 77; idea of sublimation, 145, 146; life as accumulation and release of tensions, 241
Friedel, Egon, 68
Fries, Charles Carpenter, comparative method, 252
Frustration and Aggression (Dollard), imbalances in personality, 39
Functional anthropology, 60, 64, 68

Gayley, Charles Mills, courses in Comparative Literature, 252
General College, *see under* Minnesota, University of
General education, concept of, 140

INDEX

General Education Board, Richard's association with, 271
General Introduction to Psychoanalysis, A (Freud), 29
Genius, concept of, in dynamic psychology, 37; in creative process, 51
Geography in Human Destiny (Peattie), 232
George Williams College, course in the Humanities, 173
Georgia, University of, course in the Humanities, 173 f.
Georgia School of Technology, course in the Humanities, 174
Germany, the epic in Germanic culture, 55; Legislates own anthropology, 70
Gestalt psychology, 26, 38, 41-46, 51, 54, 130, 131; effect upon teaching, 24; compared with dynamic psychology, 37; three basic concepts, 41; in field of literature, 43 f.
Glunt, James D., 161
God, as First Cause, 143
Goethe, Johann Wolfgang von, 23, 137; *Faust*, 40, 149, 193, 284; on inspiration, 50
Golden Rule, scientific expression of, 235
Good, supreme human, 14
Grammar, 145; intellectual discipline associated with literature, 103; Richards' concept, 134; Hutchins' concept, 141; has to do with physical word, 144; art of instruction, 153; Adler's view of, 277
Grapes of Wrath, The (Steinbeck), 231
Graves, Mary, course in the history of the arts, 83
Great Books program, 6, 137, 138, 150, 231
Greatness, artistic, 115
Greece, literature and culture, 55, 56, 66, 67; metaphysics, 139; tragedy, 146; view of life, 193
Greek Tragedy (Kitto), 67
Greene, Theodore Meyer, philosophical spokesman for the disciplines, 104-15, 116, 117, 121, 125, 132; *Arts and the Art of Criticism*, 8, 105, 110, 115, 127; edits *The Meaning of the Humanities*, 8, 105, 110, 111; five experience levels, 105 ff.; historico-philosophical synthesis of culture, 105, 109, 115; relativistic organic creative-critical process, 110; art as self-expression, 112; literary genres, 113; rationale, 140, 275; on Humanities course at Princeton, 178; "re-creation," 269
Grey, Lennox, on aesthetic experience in art and literature, 235
Griffing, Robert P., Jr., on Humanities course at Johns Hopkins, 163
Groos, Karl, play as origin of art, 58
Growth of Literature, The (Chadwick), 57, 66
Gustav, king of Sweden, sues for Elizabeth's hand, 202

Hakewill, Renaissance humanist philosopher, 203
Haldane, J. B. S., 3, 68
Hamlet, 89; example of aesthetic approach to World Literature, 192-227, 230; struggle for self-realization, 193, 197, 198, 200, 203, 204; theme, 193, 195, 196, 199 f.; recent trends in scholarship, 194-201; symbols of music and tempests, 194, 195 f.; a symbol of Elizabethan culture, 196 ff., 201-4; a microcosm of the Renaissance, 199; analysis of, 204 ff.; original "Amleth," 204; state of indecision, 213; man of contemplation, 216, 223, 224
"Hamlet's Politics" (Barzun), 200, 270
Happiness, supreme human good, 14
Hardman, David, 194
Harvard University, Orthological Institute, 271
Harvey, Richard, 203
Hassold, Ernest, on Humanities course at University of Louisville, 171 f.
Hatfield, W. Wilbur, 75
Hawkins, Sir John, 201
Hays, Edna, 235
Hedonism, values in aesthetic experience, 13; hedonistic art, 246
Hegel, Georg Wilhelm Friedrich, 11; *The Philosophy of Fine Art*, 16; attainment of the self, 16
Hellenic culture and literature, *see* Greece
Hendrix College, course in the Humanities, 184 f.
Herder, Johann Gottfried, von, 23
Heredity, concept of, 244

Heroes and Hero Worship (Carlyle), 19; 23
Heroic poetry, emergence of, 66
Herzl City College, Chicago, 184
Herzog, George, 61 f., 64
Hevner, Kate, 44
Higher Learning in America, The (Hutchins), 138; medieval trivium of Aquinas, 141; problem of aesthetics, 141; call for evangelistic movement, 145
Hirn, Yrjo, *The Origin of Art*, 58
History, intellectual discipline associated with literature, 103; historico-philosophical synthesis of culture, 105, 109, 115; emphasis in St. John's College, 150
"History and the Humanities" (Krey), 263
"History of Art as a Humanistic Discipline, The" (Panofsky), 114, 263
Hitler, Adolf, perversion of aesthetic drive, 3
Hoby, Thomas, 201
Hogben, Launcelot, 127
Homer, the epic form, 55; *Iliad*, 66, 148, 149, 181; *Odyssey*, 149
Horace, 20
Housman, A. E., 89
Houston, University of, course in the Humanities, 176
How to Read a Book (Adler), 26, 27, 145; statement on aesthetics, 142; three levels of reading, 147-49; the novel, play, and lyric, 148; definition of dialectic, 150; the trivium, 277
How to Read a Page (Richards), 233
Hrdlicka, Ales, 84
Human beings, individuality as supreme quality of, 70; knowledge of self, 87; compared with other animals, 101; five experience levels, 105-10; Richard's concept of man, 131; tendency toward order in experience, 132; Hutchins' concept of human nature, 140 f.; *see also* Individual; Self
Human Enterprise, The (Otto), 70
Humanism, Dewey's definition, 235
Humanities, the, aesthetic drive of, 3, 4, 6, 8, 11-73, 74 ff., 83 f., 155 ff., 228, 230; revival of, 4, 73, 117, 128 f., 155 ff.; courses, 4, 6, 9 11 ff., 56, 57, 71, 73, 83, 155-91, 230; New Humanist movement, 5; external frame and internal method, 6; spokesmanship for the modern, 7-9, 43, 56, 74-154. National Council of Teachers of English, 7, 74-84; Progressive Education Association, 8, 84, 98; Committee of Twenty-four, 8, 98-104; individual writers on various aspects of, 8, 104-37; T. M. Greene, 8, 104 ff.; Irwin Edman, 8, 105, 116-23; Jacques Barzun, 8, 123-29; I. A. Richards, 8, 129-37; advocates of a return to medieval liberal arts, 9, 137-54; Hutchins, 9, 139-42; Adler, 9, 142-49; St. John's College, 9, 149-53; ideas from modern psychology, 24-56; modern revival of classical-medieval psychology, 25, 26-28; Behaviorism, 25, 28 f.; psychoanalysis, 26, 29-35; theories of identification, detachment, and empathy, 26, 35-37; dynamic psychology, 26, 37; social psychology, 26, 38-41; Gestalt and organismic psychology, 26, 41-46; newer syntheses, 26, 46-56; ideas from anthropology, 56-73; from physical anthropology, 57-60; cultural anthropology, 60-73; differences between Social Studies and, 98 f.; historico-philosophical synthesis, 105, 109, 115; significance for human survival, 123; definition of, 156, 262; *Hamlet* as example of aesthetic approach to World Literature, 192-227, 230; aesthetic experience provides unity in teaching of, 230
Humanities, The (Dudley and Faricy), 156 f., 185
"Humanities—Proper Study of Mankind, The" (Barzun), 129
Human Relations, Commission on, 259, 271
Hume, David, 19, 22; *Treaties of Human Nature*, 17; concept of self, 17, 18
Hutchins, Robert Maynard, 6, 9, 12, 130; words as absolutes, 112; favors a return to medieval liberal arts, 128, 139-42, 150; legalistic mind, 138; *No Friendly Voice*, 138; *The Higher Learning in America*, 138, 141, 145; urges general education, 140; use of "common human nature," 140 f.; on truth, 141, 145; problem of aesthetics, 141; con-

INDEX

cern with political and religious statesmanship, 142; practical intellect includes art and prudence, 144; call for evangelistic movement, 145, 277; unity of ideas with Adler, 149; comparison with Greene's rationale, 275; anti-aesthetic, 276

Ibsen, Henrik, Freud's analysis of works, 31
Idealistic philosophers, 14-17
Ideas, doctrine of, 14, 15; Idea of God, 143; in art, 263; history-of-ideas approach to literature, 265
Identification, psychological theory of, 26, 35
Iliad, 66, 148, 149, 181
Illinois Wesleyan University, course in the Humanities, 183
Illusion, art as, 149
Image, in creative process, 51, 54, 88; imagistic quality of words, 111
Imagination, place in idealistic philosophies, 15; role in creative process, 88; values of, 99; in level of conscious being, 106, 111; function, 262
Imperial Theme, The (Knight), 195
Improvement of the Understanding (Spinoza), 16
Impulse, redirection of, 96; formative, 119, 120, 132, 264
Individual, aesthetic experience and the, 24-56; concept of, in dynamic psychology, 37; preservation of, 46; and society, 61, 69; individuality as supreme quality of human nature, 70; Progressive Education Association's view, 85; attainment of consciousness, 87; relation to his environment, 89; literature important in development of, 99, 103, 104; human beings compared with other animals, 101; five experience levels, 105-10; and democracy, 116; recognition of worth leads to revival of Humanities, 117; Richards' concept of man, 131; tendency toward order in experience, 132; Hutchins' concept of human nature, 140 f.; *see also* Self
Innate, phase of the unconscious, 48
Insight, artistic, 115
Inspiration, phase in creative process, 49-51, 88

Instincts, theory of, 38
Institution, role in social convention, 107
Instrumentalism, development of the self, 13
Integrity, artistic, 115
Intellect, Hutchins' concept of human, 141; intellectual virtues, 142; practical includes art and prudence, 144
Intellectual disciplines, *see* Disciplines
Intellectual history, college Humanities courses based on, 176-80
Interest, role in creative process, 88
Interpretation, two modes of, 109; level of reading, 148
Interpretation in Teaching (Richards), 131, 271; province of education, 130
Intuition, intuitive inspiration, 50; in creative process, 88; intuitive knowledge, 156

Jabo Proverbs from Liberia (Herzog), 61 f., 64
Jaeger, Werner, *Paideia* . . ., 67
James VI, king of Scotland, 202
James, William, 11, 46, 64, 118; aesthetic, 13, 19; "tough-mindedness" of empiricists, 17; pragmatism, 123, 124
Jeans, Sir James, 3
Jennings, Herbert, influence, 25, 26, 46, 47, 244;
Jeremiah (Zweig), inspiration for, 50
Johns Hopkins University, course in the Humanities, 162 f.
Johnson, Lamar, 182
Johnson, Samuel, 11; aesthetic criticism, 19, 22
Jones, Howard Mumford, "The Aims of the Teaching of Literature," 98; comparative method, 252
Jonson, Ben, 11; aesthetic criticism, 19, 20, 21; "Timber; or Discoveries," 20
Judson College, course in the Humanities, 187 f.
Jugoslavian literature, 66
Jung, Carl, psychoanalytical art theory, 31, 33-35

Kant, Immanuel, 11, 13, 26; *The Critique of Aesthetic Judgment*, 16; development of the self, 16; emphasis upon genius, 37

Keats, John, 89
Keliher, Alice, 93; preparation of film library for school use, 259
Kilpatrick, William H., individual-cultural pattern, 85
Kirk, Hanna E., World Literature course, 82
Kitto, H. D. F., 67
Knight, G. Wilson, critical approach to Shakespeare, 194-96, 200
Knox College, Humanities program, 189
Koffka, Kurt, Gestalt psychology, 41
Köhler, Wolfgang, concept of dynamic interaction, 41
Krey, August Charles, 263
Krutch, Joseph Wood, 24
Kunstler (Rank), 32
Kyd, Thomas, original of Hamlet, in play of, 204

Lalo, M. Charles, 26, 46
Lane, Frederic C., Humanities course at Johns Hopkins, 162 f.
Lange, Konrad, play as origin of art, 58
Langfield, Herbert S., 64; *The Aesthetic Attitude*, 42 f.; psychological aesthetic, 135
Language, reservoir of human experience, 7; in doctrine of Ideas, 14; and the aesthetic, 14, 15, 16, 17, 18, 20, 153; functions and qualities, 15, 133-35; psychological aspects of, 17, 39, 40, 43, 76; and anthropology, 43, 57, 61-64, 76; intercommunication between artist and reader, 53 f.; symbolic nature of, 56, 57, 68, 72, 89, 112, 120, 133, 229; article in *Encyclopedia of Social Sciences*, 63, 248; and culture, 64, 65, 72, 250; makes us "heirs to all the ages," 71; and self-realization, 79, 80; place in well-organized curriculum, 80; disciplines of, 94, 95, 120, 134, 135, 258; Greene's definition, 107; three types of verbal meaning, 111; metaphorical values of, 112, 120; physical properties of sound, 112; of prose and poetry, 119 f.; education's province to facilitate, 130; origins of, 248
Language (Sapir), 63
Language in General Education, 271
Language of Poetry, The (Richards), 134

Lasswell, H. D., 39
Learning, function of, 262
Lee, Vernon, psychological theory of empathy, 35, 37, 102
Lenrow, Elbert, 258, 259
Leonardo da Vinci, Freud's analysis of works, 31
Lerner, Max, on functionalist standpoint as developed in anthropology, 56; literature as the formulation of cultural values, 67
Lewin, Kurt, dynamic theory of personality, 41
Lewisohn, Ludwig, 24, 31
Liberal arts, advocates of a return to medieval, 128, 130, 137-54; Hutchins, 139-42; Adler, 142-49; St. John's College, 145, 149-53; nature of the, 144; of the trivium, 145, 150, 151
Liberia, Jabo proverbs, 61 f.
Libido, sexual drives of the, 30, 33
Liddell, Anna, 169
Life, as accumulation and release of tensions, 241
Life and Growth (Rosenblatt), 93; interaction of individual and society, 257
Linton, Ralph, 57, 58, 69, 70; symbolic character of language, 64, 65
Lipps, Theodore, theory of *Einfühlung*, 35, 102
Lipsius, Renaissance, humanist philosopher, 203
Literary Relations of England and Scandinavia . . . (Seaton), 202
Literature, aesthetic experience in, 3, 4, 7 f., 9, 11 ff., 19 ff., 43, 46, 95, 235; world, 3, 5, 6, 7, 11-73, 81, 83, 136, 155-91, 192 ff., 228, 230, 231, 232; comparative, 5, 7, 67, 252; English, 5, 11, 19-24, 232; spokesmen for the Humanities, 7-9, 43, 56, 74-154; The National Council of Teachers of English, 7, 74-84; Progressive Education Association, 8, 84-98; Committee of Twenty-four, 8, 98-104; individual writers on various aspects of the Humanities, 8, 104-37; T. M. Greene, 8, 104 ff.; Irwin Edman, 8, 105, 116-23; Jacques Barzun, 8, 123-29; I. A. Richards, 8, 129-37; harmonizing function, 8; advocates of a return to medieval liberal arts, 9, 137-

INDEX

54; Hutchins, 9, 139-42; Adler, 9, 142-49; St. John's College, 9, 149-53; break with classical education and philosophical tradition, 11; literary genres, 20, 54 f., 57, 66, 67, 80, 89, 113, 120, 148, 166 ff., 232, 249, 256, 259; poetry, 20, 54, 55, 66, 67, 113, 119 f., 136, 148, 245, 256; convergence of philosophy and, 20; impact of modern psychology, 24-56, 80, 89; psychoanalysis as a means of evaluating, 31; Gestalt concept of aesthetic experience, 43; importance of language, 53 f., 94, 133, 143; the drama, 54, 55, 66, 67, 77, 96, 101, 113, 148, 246, 256; the epic, 54 f., 66, 67, 147; critical process, 53-56; value of sensory impressions, 54; and culture, 57, 67, 72, 256; effect of restrictions on, 72; teachers of, 74 ff., 90, 92, 97, 98 ff., 103, 104, 233; repository of human values, 76, 102 f., 262, 265; therapeutic function of, 77, 96, 102; psychological-anthropological concepts of types, 80, 89; four levels of appreciation, 90; intellectual disciplines, 94, 103, 258; materials to be used in study of, 97; aims in the teaching of, 98 ff.; part of living tissue of society, 99; important in development of individual, 99, 103, 104; expressive medium of literary artist, 111 f.; three types of verbal meaning, 111; the novel, 120, 148, 259; values approach, 131; the "unassailables," 136; three reading levels, 147-49; College courses in the Humanities emphasizing types of, 166-71; American, 232; nature of literary experience, 251; importance of forms, 259; history-of-ideas approach to, 265
"Literature, Aims of the Teaching of," 98 ff.
"Literature and Science" (Arnold), 23
"Literature and the Humanities" (Chinard), 265
Literature as Exploration (Rosenblatt), 8, 46, 57, 86, 92 ff., 101, 271; analysis of, 92 ff.; an extension of Dewey's philosophy, 92; concern with critical function of reader, 93, 94 f.; materials to be used in study of literature, 97; use of "purged," 101, 102; on literary experiences, 251; emphasis upon class discussion and exchange of student opinion, 259
Logic, intellectual discipline associated with literature, 103; Richards' concept, 134; Hutchins' concept, 141; function, 144, 153; relativistic analogical, 265; plays little part in work of art, 277
Logic, A Theory of Inquiry (Dewey), 91
Louisville, University of, course in the Humanities, 172 f.
Löwenfeld, Viktor, 45
Lyric, evaluation of, 54, 55; in Greek culture, 66, 67; lyrical tone of literature, 113; in poetry and music, 120; compared with the novel and play, 148; primitive and early levels, 245; spirit of personal spontaneity, 256

Macalester College, course in the Humanities, 176, 283
McDougall, William, 131; theory of instincts, 38
McKeon, Richard, 138, 139
MacLeish, Archibald, 273
Maier, Norman, R. F., 43, 44
Malinowski, Brownislaw, 69, 70, 272; on cultural anthropology, 60
Man, individuality supreme quality of, 70; knowledge of self, 87; compared with other animals, 101; five experience levels, 105-10; Richards' concept of, 131; tendency toward order in experience, 132; Hutchins' concept of human nature, 140 f.; *see also* Individual; Self
Mann, Thomas, 71, 126, 233; *The Magic Mountain*, 89, 273; *The Beloved Returns*, 273
Manners, value of, 262
Marett, R. R., 57, 67; on culture as communicable intelligence, 71
Maritain, Jacques, 15, 143, 278; relationship between art and prudence, 237
Mary Stuart, imprisonment, 201
Mathematics, in Hutchins' scheme of education, 141
Matter, Richards' concept of, 134
Mead, George Herbert, 63, 64, 68

INDEX

Meaning of Meaning, The (Richards), 131; relationship with anthropological method, 272
Meaning of the Humanities, The (Greene, ed.), 8, 105, 110, 111
Medievalism, *see* Middle Ages
Meier, Norman C., experimental approaches to aesthetics, 45
Melville, Herman, 193, 284
Memory, role in creative process, 88; in level of conscious being, 106, 111
Mencius, Chinese sage, 17
Mencius on the Mind (Richards), 271
Menlo Junior College, course in the Humanities, 174
Men Must Act (Mumford), 71; need for new patterns of action, 251
Metaphor, metaphorical values of language, 112, 120; sorting of meaning in, 134
Metaphysics, Greek, 139; Hutchins' metaphysical aesthetic, 142
Middle Ages, advocates of a return to medieval liberal arts, 137-54; theocentric unity of, disintegrates, 139; medieval view of life, 193; retreat from confusion of earth, 203
Mill, John Stuart, 11; hedonism, 13; development of the self, 18; *A System of Logic*, 18
Millikan, Robert, contribution to *A Correlated Curriculum*, 84
Milton, John, *Paradise Regained*, 284
Mims, Edwin, 67
Mind, duality of and body, 26; Jung's view of, 33; and the realization of self, 87; attributes of, 132
Mind, Self, and Society (Mead), 63, 64
Minnesota, University of: College of Science, Literature and the Arts, course in the Humanities, 188; General College, course in the Humanities, 171 f.
Missouri Valley College, course in the Humanities, 163
Moby Dick (Melville), 193, 284
Modern Book of Aesthetics, A (Rader), 58
Modern Language Association, represented in Committee of Twenty-four, 98
Mohr, E. E., 182

Montague, W. P., 68
Moore, Douglas, on Columbia Humanities course, 175
More, Paul Elmer, New Humanist movement, 5
Morris, Charles W., 57
Motion picture, compared with drama, 148; an art form, 149; concern for aesthetic experience, 231; as extension of dramatic literature, 259
Müller-Freienfels, Richard, 67, 86, 229; aesthetic theory, 26, 46, 47, 50, 51, 52, 53, 54, 55, 56; on theory of *Einfühlung* 35; language and physical properties of sound, 112; *Psychologie der Kunst*, 244; primitive and early levels of the lyric, 245
Mumford, Lewis, 46, 57, 68; *Faith for Living*, 71, 232, 252; *Men Must Act*, 71, 251; language greatest of human inventions, 72; drama as symbol of urban culture, 246; need for new patterns of action, 251
Municipal University of Omaha, course in the Humanities, 167 f.
Münsterberg, Hugo, theory of detachment, 36
Music, history and appreciation, 170; symbol in Shakespeare, 195, 196

Narrative, as symbol of primitive culture, 65
Nation strength depends upon aesthetic discrimination, 82
Nation (periodical), 125, 133, 271; on Wilson's Shakespearean criticism, 198
National Association of Journalism Advisers, represented in Curriculum Commission, 75
National Association of Teachers of Speech, represented in Curriculum Commission, 75
National Council of Teachers of English, spokesmanship for the Humanities, 5, 6, 7, 74-84; *A Correlated Curriculum*, 5, 8, 80-84, 254; *An Experience Curriculum*, 5, 75, 78-80; Curriculum Commission, 74 ff.; *The Teaching of College English*, 75, 76-78, 96, 101; represented in Committee of Twenty-four, 98

National Education Association, represented in Curriculum Commission, 75
Naturalism, cultural, 13
Nazism, legislates own anthropology, 70
Neo-scholastics, spokesman for modern Humanities, 9, 137-54; advocates of a return to medieval liberal arts, 9, 137 ff.; Hutchins, 9, 139-42; Adler, 9, 142-49; St. John's College, 9, 149-53; concern with politics, 137, 142; "analogical logic" position, 275
Neurosis, preconditions of, 34, 39
Newark, University of, Humanities program, 188
New Humanist movement, 5
New Jersey State Teachers College, Montclair, course in the Humanities, 157 f.
Nibelungenlied, the epic form, 55
Nietzsche, Friedrich, 11, 13, 30, 113; development of the self, 18; *The Birth of Tragedy*, 18
No Friendly Voice (Hutchins), 138
North Carolina, University of, course in the history of the arts, 83
North Central Association of Colleges and Secondary Schools, represented in Curriculum Commission, 75
Northwest Missouri State Teachers College, course in the Humanities, 165
Norway, relations with Elizabethan England, 202
Novel, most forceful literary art form, 120, 259; comparison with lyric, 148

Odyssey (Homer), 149
Of Human Freedom (Barzun), 8, 31, 123; hazards of amateur psychiatry, 104; concern with aesthetic experience, 124 ff.; on American education, 127-29; revival of the Humanities, 128 f.; pragmatic attitude in democracy, 251; on critical analysis, 269
Ogden, R. M., 44
Oklahoma Agricultural and Mechanical College, course in the Humanities, 186 f.
Omaha, Municipal University of, 167 f.
Ordeal of Mark Twain (Brooks), 24
Order, artist's deep desire for, 125, 264; mind's tendency toward increased, 132

Organismic psychology, 26, 41-46; effect upon teaching, 24, 25
Organization and order, artist's desire for, 125
Origins of Art, The (Hirn), 58
Orthological Institute at Harvard University, 271
Osborn, Frederick, on racial characteristics, 59
Otto, Max Carl, *The Human Enterprise*, 70

Paideia . . . (Jaeger), 67
Panofsky, Erwin, 114, 263
Paradise Regained, 284
Pasadena Junior College, course in the Humanities, 171
Patterns of Culture (Benedict), 69
Payne, Wilfred, on Humanities course at Omaha University, 167 f.
Peattie, Roderick, 232
Peirce, C. S., on logic, 134
People's Institute, passing of, 138
Perception, theory of the Span of, 42
Perfection, Platonic and Aristotelian concepts, 237
Perry, Ralph Barton, 112, 262
Personality, social consequences of imbalances, 39; role of words in development of, 56; growth of, 93, 95; evolves consciousness of self, 232
Personality, a Psychological Interpretation (Allport), 40 f.
Personality and Problems of Adjustment (Young), art theory, 39
Peter, Lorraine, 165
Phelan, Gerald B., 138, 275
Philosophy, convergence between the arts and, 8, 92, 118, 170 f., 263; poetic qualities of, 8, 117; neo-scholastics, 9, 137 ff.; relationship between aesthetic experience and, 11-24, 72, 122 f., 257; idealistic philosophers, 14-17; empirical philosophers, 17-19; convergence of literature and, 20; psychology once a branch of, 25; primary concern of philosophers, 57; of experience, 92; historico-philosophical synthesis of culture, 105, 109, 115; a criticism of criticism, 123; Renaissance, 202 f., 204; *see also individual philosophers:* Dewey; Edman, Greene, etc.

Philosophy of Fine Art, The (Hegel), 16
Philosophy of Literary Form, The (Burke), 31, 43, 54
Philosophy of Science, "Patterns of Culture in History," 68
Physical anthropology, 57-60
Pittsburgh, University of, course in the Humanities, 179
Pity, Aristotelian catharsis of, 101
Plato, 11, 12, 13, 20, 26, 27, 28, 117; concept of perfection, 14, 15, 237; and the neo-scholastics, 137; speculative rhetoric, 144; *Dialogues*, 152
Play, *see* Drama
Play, instinct, as origin of art, 58
Pleasure, concept of, 126
Poe, Edgar Allan (Krutch), 24
Poetics (Aristotle), Univ. of Chicago Syllabus commentary on, 182
Poetry, astronomy most poetical of the sciences, 3; compared with philosophy, 20; the lyric, 54, 55, 66, 67, 113, 120, 148, 245, 256; literary forms, 66, 67; as language medium, 119 f.; Richards' poetic theories, 136
Politics, Neo-scholastics' concern with, 137, 142; political censorship of art, 145; primary function, 232; statesman's concern with, 276; *see also* Democracy
Pope, Alexander, 11; aesthetic criticism, 19, 21; *An Essay on Criticism*, 21
Populations, differences of mental endowment among, 247
Posnett, Hutcheson Macaulay, 66; literary types, 113
Power, Freudian view of, 30
Practical Criticism (Richards), 131, 259, 271
Pragmatism, development of the self, 13
Prägnanz, Law of, 41, 42, 43, 64, 132
Primitive Art (Boas), 57, 66
Princeton University, Spencer Trask Series, 105; course in the Humanities, 177 f., 179
Principles of Art Education, The (Münsterberg), 36
Principles of Literary Criticism (Richards), 8; concern for ways of thinking, 130, 131; definition of vigilance, 273; concept of catharsis, 274; how to read poetry, 274

Progressive education, Barzun's attitude toward, 128
Progressive Education Association, 271; spokesmanship for Humanities, 8, 84-98; John Dewey, 8, 86-92; Louise Rosenblatt, 8, 86, 92-98; emphasis on psychological and social needs, 85; "Democratic Education," 85; represented in Committee of Twenty-four, 98; stress upon internal logic, 258; importance of literary forms, 259
Prometheus (Jennings), 46
Prose, as language medium, 119 f.
Proverbs, use of, by Jabo people, 61 f.
Prudence, in art, 143, 144; Adler's emphasis on, 276
Psychiatry, hazards of amateur, 104
"Psychical Distance" (Bullough), 36
Psychoanalysis, effect upon literature, 24; affinity with faculty psychology, 26, 29; and aesthetic experience, 26, 29-35
Psychoanalysis and Aesthetics (Baudouin), 31
Psychological Approach to Literary Criticism, A (Maier and Reninger), 43, 44
Psychological Review, The, article on the aesthetic experience, 44
Psychologie de l'art . . . (Delacroix), 244
Psychologie der Kunst (Müller-Freienfels), 244
Psychology, modern ideas of aesthetic experience, 7, 12, 24-56, 72, 74, 117, 118, 200, 263, 264, 265; and language, 17, 39, 40, 43, 76; Gestalt school, 24, 26, 37, 38, 41-46, 51, 54, 130, 131; break with philosophy, 25; modern revival of classical-medieval, 25, 26-28; Behaviorism, 25, 28 f.; psychoanalysis, 26, 29-35; theories of identification, detachment, and empathy, 26, 35-37; dynamic, 26, 37; social, 26, 38-41; newer syntheses, 26, 46-56; individual as medium of all society, 61; teachers required background in, 104; theory of value, 272
Psychology and Life (Münsterberg), 36
Psychology from the Standpoint of the Behaviorist (Watson), 28
Psychology of Art, The (Ogden), 44
Psychology of Social Norms, The (Sherif), 40

Ptolemy, astronomy, 148
Purgation, literature as an emotional, 77; in art, 145, 146; *see also* Catharsis
"Purged," Committee of Twenty-four's use of, 102
Purposive art, concept of, 246

Quadrivium, liberal arts of, 150, 151, 152
Quality or perfection, artistic, 115
Queens College, course in the Humanities, 169-71, 178

Race, Language, and Culture (Boas), 57
Races, biologic urge to perpetuate, 46; equivalent capacities, 59; Hutchins' concept of, 140; differences of mental endowment, 247
Rader, Melvin, 58
Radical empiricism, development of the self, 13
Radio, use of, in World Literature program, 231
Rank, Otto, psychoanalytical art theory, 31-33
Ransom, John Crowe, 11, 231
Rationalism, approach to values in aesthetic experience, 13
Ratner, Sidney, 68, 72
Rattray, R. S., 39, 65, 77, 102
Read, Herbert, 59; concept of art, 246
Reader's Guide to Prose Fiction (Lenrow), stress upon internal logic, 258; the old and the contemporary, 259; the novel, 259
Reading, intercommunication between artist and reader, 53, 114, 126 f., 147; concern with literary form, 89; levels of appreciation, 90, 100, 147-49; critical function of, 93, 94 f., 97; therapeutic value of literature, 96, 102, 104; aesthetic experience, 113 f., 127, 135 f.; achieving *rapport* with work of art, 114; values gained by, 265; a receptive activity, 269
Reason, place in idealistic philosophies, 15; in level of conscious being, 106, 111
Reason in Art (Santayana), 17
Reed College, course in the Humanities, 161 f.
Reflective inspiration, 50
Reflective tone of literature, 113

Regicide, theme in *Hamlet*, 200
Regionalism, rising interest in, 231
Reichard, Gladys A., 66
Relativity, theory of, 3
Religion, aesthetic experience' similarity to, 91, 264; art approaches realm of, 122
Religion and Art in Ashanti (Rattray), 102
Renaissance, English literary criticism, 20; theocentric unity of Middle Ages disintegrates, 139; world view, 193; *Hamlet* a microcosm of state and society, 199; making of mind, 201; conflicts of philosophy, 202 f., 204
Reninger, H. Willard, 43, 44
Revival of the Humanities in American Education, The (Beesley), 4, 154
Rhetoric, intellectual discipline associated with literature, 103; Richards' concept, 134; Hutchins' concept, 141; two kinds, 144; function, 153; Adler's concern with, 276
Rhythm, in the work of art, 89; importance of, 120; evokes distinguishable attitudes, 134
Richards, I. A., 71, 77, 141; spokesmanship for the Humanities, 8, 17, 129 ff.; functions and qualities of language, 56, 63, 94, 95, 112, 133-35; international psychologist-semanticist, 129-37; influence, 130, 271; concept of relativistic disciplines, 130; concept of man, 131; idea of aesthetic experience, 131, 135 f.; poetic theories, 136, 274; role of the emotions, 147; value of work of art, 258; functional meanings, 258; relationship with anthropological method, 272; use of term, "mind," 272; definition of vigilance, 273; concept of catharsis, 274; analogical logic, 275
——Works: *Coleridge on Imagination*, 131; *Foundations of Aesthetics*, 131; *How to Read a Page*, 233; *Interpretation in Teaching*, 130, 131, 271; *The Language of Poetry*, 134; *The Meaning of Meaning*, 131, 272; *Mencius on the Mind*, 271; *Practical Criticism*, 131, 259, 271; *Principles of Literary Criticism*, 8, 130, 131, 273, 274; "Science and Poetry," 131, 133; "What is Belief?" 271
Ridley, M. R., 194

336 INDEX

Rivers of America, 231
Rollins College, course in the Humanities, 178, 179
Roman Catholic Church, *see* Catholicism
Rosenblatt, Louise, liberal arts progressive, 71, 86, 92-98, 112, 116, 121, 146; influenced by Dewey, 92; concern with critical function of reader, 93, 94 f.; materials to be used in study of literature, 97; use of "purged," 101, 102; pragmatism, 128; on literary experiences, 251; disciplines for literature and language, 258; not concerned with literary forms, 259; origins and values of art, 270
——Works: "The Aims of the Teaching of Literature," 98; *Life and Growth*, 257; *Literature as Exploration*, 8, 46, 57, 86, 92 ff., 101, 102, 251, 259, 271
Ross, Julian, on Allegheny College Humanities course, 167
Rusu, Liviu, 26, 41, 47, 64, 86, 229; *Essai sur la création artistique*, 47-56 attention to anthropological background, 244

Sagas, in Hellenic and Teutonic literatures, 66
St. Cloud State Teachers College, course in the Humanities, 168 f.
St. John's College, Humanities program, 6, 9, 128, 131, 139, 149-53; neo-scholastics' concern with political considerations, 137, 145; return to medieval liberal arts, 149-53; catalogues, 149 ff.; subject-matter of curriculum, 151; teaching techniques, 152; concern with rhetoric, 277
St. Scholastica, College of, course in the Humanities, 166
St. Thomas and Analogy (Phelan), appeal of moral-religious values, 138; "analogical logic" position, 275
St. Thomas and the Gentiles (Adler), 145, 278
San Antonio, Texas, Junior High School, Fine Arts course, 83
San Raphael, College of, 166
Santayana, George, 11, 13; achievement of self-realization, 17; *Reason in Art*, 17

Sapir, Edward, research in language, 56, 63, 64, 248
Sarton, George, 68
Saturday Review of Literature, 125; "Man's Humanities to Man," 116; *Culture in a Democracy*, 116
Savelle, Max, 186
Saxo, English translation of, 204
Scandinavia, relations with England, 202
Schiller, Friedrich, on inspiration, 50; origin of art, 58
Schools, *see* Colleges and universities
Schopenhauer, Arthur, 11, 13, 26, 117; attainment of selfhood, 16, 18; *The World as Will and Idea*, 16; "will-to-live," 37; concept of will, 238
Science, aesthetic drive of, 3, 4, 122; development of the self, 13; influences empiricism, 17; primary values pursued by, 91; ethical direction to scientific advancement, 235
Science, article on present status of anthropology, 57
Science and the Modern World (Whitehead), 228
"Science and Theology as Art Forms" (Haldane), 3, 68
Scientific Humanism, new programs of, 4
Scientific Humanism (Hogben), 127
Scientific Monthly, excerpt, 59
Scripps College, course in the Humanities, 180
Sea of Cortez, The (Steinbeck), 3
Seaton, Ethel, 202
Secondary School Curriculum, Commission on, 271
Self, development and realization of, 13 ff., 40, 87, 262, 264; concepts of idealistic philosophers, 14-17; of empirical philosophers, 17-19; in English literary criticism, 19-24; Behaviorist concept of, 29; point of convergence among schools of psychology, 46; artistic expression arises from disequilibrium of, 47; in the creative process, 48-53; self-realization by reader or observer, 53, 136, 228; self-fulfilling values of the critical process, 53; aesthetic experience in self-realization, 69, 71, 72, 91; self-realization by means of language, 79, 80, 120 f.; self-

INDEX

realization of artist, 89, 132, 133, 135, 228, 229; self-realization by means of literature, 99, 103, 104; on level of atomistic awareness, 106; art as self-expression, 112; self-realization of characters, 122; self-fulfilling values of the creative process, 127; Hamlet's struggle for self-realization, 193, 197, 198, 200, 203, 204, 207, 213, 216, 221, 226; various concepts of, revealed in national literatures, 232; democracy's emphasis upon, 232; *see also* Individual
Seligman, C. G., 65
Sensation, measurement of, 45; literary value of sensory impressions, 54
Sex, Freudian view of, 30, 33; as origin of art, 58
Shakespeare, William, 23, 137; Freud's analysis of works, 31; *Hamlet* as example of aesthetic approach to World Literature, 192-227, 230; recent trends in *Hamlet* scholarship, 194-201; symbol of the tempest, 194; influenced by Elizabethan culture and attitude, 201-4; conflict of values, 203
Shakespeare (Van Doren), 115, 198, 199, 204
Shakespearean Tempest, The (Knight), 194, 195
Sherif, Muzafer, 40
Sherwood, Robert E., *There Shall Be No Night*, 71
Sidney, Sir Philip, 11; aesthetic criticism, 19, 228; *An Apology for Poetry*, 19
Sign, concept of, 57
Social backgrounds and culture epochs, college Humanities courses emphasizing, 180-89
Social convention, level of, 107
Social psychology, approach to aesthetic experience, 26, 38-41
Social Psychology (Folsom), view of art, 38
Social Studies, aesthetic drive of, 3; differences between Humanities and, 98 f.
Society, individual as medium of all, 61; aesthetic implications, 69-71; place of art, 71; redirection of anti-social emotions, 96; living tissue of, 99; social convention, 107; control of tendencies toward chaos, 143

Solve, Melvin T., on Humanities course at University of Arizona, 177
Sophocles, use of Electra symbol, 193
Sorokin, P. A., 57
Sounds, physical properties of, 112; evoke distinguishable attitudes, 134; psychophysical effects of, 135
Southern Association of Colleges and Secondary Schools, represented in Curriculum Commission, 75
Spanish Armada, defeat of, 201
Specialization, creative and critical, 108, 109, 110; disintegrating tendency of, 140
Species, perfection of, 14, 15; preservation of the, 46
Spectacle, as aesthetic experience, 146
Speech, origins of, 248
Spencer, Herbert, art origins, 58
Spencer Trask Series, Princeton University, 105
Spengler, Oswald, 68
Spenser, Edmund, conflict of values, 203
Spiker, Claude C., 187
Spiller, Robert, on meaning of correlation, 80
Spingarn, Joel E., comparative method, 252
Spinoza, Benedict 11; concept of self-realization, 15; *Ethic*, 15; *Improvement of the Understanding*, 16
Spirit of Language in Civilization, The (Vossler), 67
Spurgeon, Caroline, 194
Stace, W. T., 233
Stanford University, course in the Humanities, 185 f., 192
Stars in Their Courses, The (Jeans), 3
Statesman, concern with art, 276
Steinbeck, John, aesthetic drive, 3; *The Sea of Cortez*, 3; *The Grapes of Wrath*, 231
Stephens College, Humanities course, 83, 156 f., 167
Stewart, George R., *Storm*, 233
Stites, Raymond S., 159 f., 280
Stoll, E. E., 194
Storm (Stewart), 233
Structural level of reading, 147 f.
Study of Man, The (Linton), 58
Style, one of criticism's five levels, 115
Subconscious, point of convergence among schools of psychology, 46

Sublimation, literature a means of, 96; Freudian idea of, 145
Sublime, Kant's concept of, 16
Summa Theologica (Thomas Aquinas), 15, 148, 150, 151
Survival, concept of, 60
Swarthmore High School, World Literature course, 82, 83
Sweden, relations with Elizabethan England, 202
Symbols, symbolic function of language, 56, 57, 68, 72, 89, 112, 120, 133, 229; of culture, 56, 57, 64 ff., 94, 246
Sympathy, role in creative process, 88; values of, 99, 262
Synaesthesia, concept of, 131, 136
System of Logic, A (Mill), development of the self, 18

Taine, H., 36, 68
Tale, as symbol of primitive culture, 65
Taliaferro, Catesby, 139
Talladega College, course in the Humanities, 164 f.
Talley, Robert W., on Humanities course at University of Houston, 176
Teachers, enlarging ideas of aesthetic experience, 11, 74 ff.; break with classical education, 11; use of psychology, 24, 104; anthropological ways of thinking, 57; critical evaluation by, 90; stress on human meaning, 92; materials to be used in study of literature, 97; "The Aims of the Teaching of Literature," 98 ff.; to provide guidance, 103, 104; function of critical, 127; Richards' popularity, 130; teaching technique in St. John's College, 152; one front in militant democracy, 233; *see also teacher organizations:* National Council of Teachers of English; Progressive Education Association, etc.
Teaching of College English, The, 96, 101; analysis of, 75, 76-78; concern with language, 76
Teaching of Literature, Aims of the," analysis of, 98 ff.
Tempest, symbol that pervades Shakespeare, 194, 195
Teutonic literature, 66

Theology, return to unity of Middle Ages, 139; as an art form, 265
"Theology and the Humanities" (Calhoun), 264 f.
Therapeutic function of literature, 77, 96, 102, 104
There Shall Be No Night (Sherwood), 71
Thomas, W. I., 59
Thomas Aquinas, Saint, 6, 11, 13, 20, 27, 44, 52; chief authority for neo-scholastics, 12, 138, 141, 142, 278; *Summa Theologica*, 15, 148, 150, 151; faculty psychology, 25, 26, 27; theory of art, 27; hierarchy of, 128; synthesizing effect of philosophy, 138, 193; reconciliation of Aristotelian and Christian values, 138; speculative rhetoric, 144; aesthetics of, 237; idea of analogy, 275; the trivium, 277
Thorndike, E. L., work in faculty psychology, 26
Thought, process of, 63; ethics of, 273
Throne, succession to, in Elizabethan England, 200, 202, 203, 204, 205, 212, 221
"Timber; or Discoveries" (Jonson), 20
Times, London, comment on Wilson's Shakespearean criticism, 198
Tolstoy, Leo, *War and Peace*, 148
Toynbee, Paget, 57, 68
Tradition, role in social convention, 107
"Tradition and Communication" (Adler), 144, 145; primary importance of rhetoric, 144
Tragedy, catharsis resulting from experience of, 77, 96, 101; Greek, 146
Trask, Spencer, *see* Spencer Trask series
Treaties of Human Nature (Hume), concept of self, 17
Trivium, revival of the, 128, 130, 134, 141, 145, 277; use in St. John's College, 150, 151, 152
Truth artistic, 115; everywhere the same, 141, 145
Twenty-four, Committee of *see* Committee of Twenty-four

Unconscious, phase in creative process, 48 f.
Universities, *see* Colleges and universities

Values, of aesthetic experience, 13, 94, 95-97, 228; evaluation of, 54; language a source of, 63; contemporaneous expressions of, 68; and anthropology, 68-71; of work of art, 69, 258, 259, 270; basis of, 69; literature a repository of human, 76, 131, 265; need for stressing enduring, 98; differentiation of, in Humanities and Social Studies, 98 f.; of imagination and sympathy, 99; through understanding subtleties of expressive form, 100; timeless world, 129; approach to literature, 131; appeal of certain moral-religious, 138; self-consciousness supreme, 232; concern with, peculiar to man, 262; psychological theory of, 272
Van Doren, Carl, 231
Van Doren, Mark, 194; *Shakespeare*, 115, 198, 199, 204; on Wilson's Shakespearean criticism, 198
Vigilance, definition of, 273
Virtues, intellectual, 142
Vocabulary of a language, 250
Vossler, Karl, 67
Vowels, feeling value, 54

Walker, A. J., on University of Georgia's Humanities course, 174
Wallis, Charles, 139
War and Peace (Tolstoy), 148
Watson, J. B., 28, 41
Weeks, Ruth Mary, 75; Fine Arts course, 83
Weil, Dorothy, on Humanities course in Chicago City Junior Colleges, 184
Welch, Roy Dickinson, 115
Wertheimer, Gestalt psychologist, 41
Western civilization, culture of, 56, 192; major epochs, 114
West Virginia, University of, course in the Humanities, 187
What about Survey Courses? (Johnson), 182
What Happens in Hamlet (Wilson), 196 ff.; reviews, 198
Wheel of Fire, The (Knight), 195
Whitehead, Alfred North, 228
Will, in Gestalt psychology, 41; Schopenhauer's concept of, 238

Wilson, John Dover, critical approach to Shakespeare, 194, 196-99, 200, 204; *Hamlet*, 196 ff.
Winnberg, Thelma, Fine Arts course, 83
Wisconsin, Univ. of, course in the Humanities, 179
Women, Freudian view of, 30, 31
Woodbery, George Edward, comparative method, 252
Woodrow Wilson Junior College, Chicago, 184
Woods, George B., 166
Woodworth, Robert Session, 26, 37
Words, symbolic role of, 56, 57; conceptual quality of, 111; three types of verbal meaning, 112; as absolutes, 112; *see also* Language
Wordsworth, William, 89
World as I See It, The (Einstein), 3
World as Will and Idea, The (Schopenhauer), 16
World Literature, ideas of aesthetic experience in, 3, 7, 11-73, 81, 155 ff., 192 ff., 228, 230; increased reading of, 3, 6, 24; courses, 5, 12, 56, 57, 67, 71, 83, 155-91, 230; ideas from modern psychology, 24-56; ideas from anthropology, 56-73; physical anthropology, 57-60; cultural anthropology, 60-73; chief purposes, 81; the "unassailables," 136; *Hamlet* as example of aesthetic approach to, 192-227, 230; aesthetic experience provides unity in teaching of, 230; world perspectives, 231; to include motion picture and radio appreciation, 231; future developments, 232
World Literature (Cross), 57, 182
World Politics and Personal Insecurity (Lasswell), 39
Wright Junior College, Chicago, 184
Writer, Freudian attitude toward, 30
Wundt, Wilhelm, establishment of experimental laboratory, 25, 41

Young, Kimball, 39, 40

Zweig, Stefan, *Jeremiah*, 50

801.93
Sh73a